Defending a
Free Society

Defending a Free Society

Edited by
Robert W. Poole, Jr.
The Reason Foundation

A Reason Foundation Book

LexingtonBooks
D.C. Heath and Company
Lexington, Massachusetts
Toronto

Library of Congress Cataloging in Publication Data
Main entry under title:

Defending a free society.

   "A Reason Foundation book."
   Includes index.
   1. United States—Defenses—Addresses, essays,
lectures.   2. United States–Military policy–Addresses,
essays, lectures.   3. United States–Armed Forces–Addresses, essays, lectures.   I. Poole, Robert W.,
1944–   .
UA23.D416 1984   355′.033073   83–48627
ISBN 0–669–07240–0

Published simultaneously in Canada

Printed in the United States of America

International Standard Book Number: 0–669–07240–0

Library of Congress Catalog Card Number: 83–48627

Contents

Preface and Acknowledgments

This book was several years in gestation. As editor of *Reason* magazine, I am under continual pressure to select articles and write editorials dealing with national defense. Yet I have long been frustrated by the ad hoc nature of most of what passes for debate on defense issues. So naturally I was intrigued when Joseph P. Martino, a former air force researcher (and the technological forecasting editor of *The Futurist*) invited me to a 1981 Liberty Fund colloquium in Dayton, Ohio, whose theme was Defending a Free Society while Preserving Individual Freedom. For three exhilarating days a diverse group of people discussed and debated defense issues *from first principles*. This, I decided, was how the matter needed to be addressed.

Inspired both by the level of those discussions and by the caliber of the participants, I set about recruiting a project team for what was projected to be year-long Reason Foundation policy research project (which ended up taking eighteen months). The final team of nine people included five of those who had taken part in the Dayton gathering. By design, the team included a political philosopher as well as a quantitatively oriented political scientist, a nuclear physicist as well as a military/diplomatic historian, economists, and sociologists, as well as full-time defense analysts.

Each participant wrote an initial draft of his chapter on his own, responding to a general outline from the editor. After some revisions, drafts of all the chapters were circulated to the entire project team, who assembled in Santa Barbara in December 1982 for three days of intensive discussion. Their different backgrounds and disciplinary frameworks produced numerous clashes, but by the end of the three-day conference, everyone agreed that what had been eleven independent essays could actually come together into a coherent assessment of national defense policy. A final round of redrafting and editing produced the present volume.

The book begins with two chapters laying out the fundamentals from which any defense policy for a free society must be derived. Political philosopher Eric Mack sets forth a moral framework, derived in part from classic theory of a just war as applied to the nuclear age. And political scientist Rudolph Rummel summarizes the principal empirical findings of several decades of research on war and peace, to provide a framework for assessing conflict between nations. Rummel then goes on, in the third chapter, to apply this framework to the present relationship between the United States and its principal threat, the Soviet Union.

Against this theoretical and empirical backdrop, the next four chapters derive the implications for, respectively, strategic defense (physicist Sam Cohen), military alliances (historian Laurence Beilenson), naval forces (defense analyst Michael Dunn), and tactical land and air forces (defense analyst Michael Burns). Three additional applications of the general principles are fleshed out in chapters on military personnel (economist Roger Folsom), military intelligence (sociologist Joseph Ford), and an alternative to CIA-type covert action (historian Laurence Beilenson). Finally, sociologist Jack Douglas returns to the moral issue with a chapter setting forth an overall strategy for foreign policy consistent with the book's defense policy proposals.

The first phase of this project was supported by a grant from the Earhart Foundation. Additional funding was contributed by more than 100 individual donors to the Reason Foundation. Lynn Scarlett, a Ph.D. candidate in political science, was an unusually effective manuscript editor. Besides her painstaking efforts to meld nine different styles into a consistent whole, her substantive suggestions, background research, and fact-checking were especially helpful.

Not all of the authors agree with every word in the other chapters, but each is in agreement with the overall thrust of the book's proposals. The views expressed in these pages do not necessarily represent the views of the trustees, officers, or advisory board of the Reason Foundation. But as the person who conceived and edited this volume, I'm pleased to say that they do represent mine.

—Robert W. Poole, Jr.

Introduction

Defense has become the most important public policy issue of the 1980s. It is also the most confused, and potentially divisive, issue confronting Americans today.

The Reagan administration came into office committed to correcting a widely acknowledged shift in the balance between U.S. and Soviet military might. Yet the administration's four-year $1.5 trillion defense program is helping to produce politically unacceptable deficits. And the basic moral legitimacy of key elements of that program—present and proposed nuclear weapons—has been challenged by the Catholic bishops and a growing peace movement. Further, the Vietnam War has left as its legacy a broadly based opposition to U.S. intervention overseas, which conflicts with the administration's intentions for the Persian Gulf and Central America—intentions with major consequences for the defense program.

Underlying the debates between hawks and doves, between spenders and reformers, between advocates of containment and advocates of nonintervention, are more fundamental questions. What is our government's proper role as defender of the country? What is the overall objective of defense policy? What means are acceptable—and which are unacceptable—for defending a free society?

It makes no sense to debate whether or not we should build an MX missile system or add an aircraft carrier task force or build up a Rapid Deployment Force without addressing and answering these basic questions. Yet this is precisely what the current defense debates have failed to do. It is the purpose of this book to ask and answer such questions.

In doing so, it begins at the beginning: with the nature of government in a free society. The United States was created as a new type of society: one in which government was to be an instrument for the protection of the individual rights of the citizens, as delineated by John Locke. The founding fathers rejected the idea of the state as the organizer and director of society. In their view, government was always a potential danger, capable of turning into a master rather than a servant, and therefore needing to be strictly limited. It must be bound by the chains of the Constitution, by inherent checks and balances, and by a Bill of Rights making clear the sovereignty of the individual rather than the state.

Two centuries of experience have shown us the wisdom of these principles. For all its faults, the United States became the freest and most prosperous country in the world by keeping its government limited and giving full rein to the creative energies of its people.

Yet when it comes to defense and foreign affairs, we seem to have forgotten these principles. Our statesmen talk endlessly about interests rather than rights. They embark on grandiose plans to "make the world safe for democracy" or "bear any burden, pay any price" without stopping to ask whether such lofty objectives are within the scope of the job they've been hired by the citizens to do. While such open-ended claims upon the lives and fortunes of the citizenry might be consistent with a collectivist society—a society seen as an organic unity animated by some sort of transcendent goal (e.g., communism)—they are hardly consistent with the limited government of a society of free and independent individuals.

The purpose of a free society's government is to protect the rights of the citizens. At the micro level, that means operating a system of criminal justice to protect against domestic threats to people's rights. And at the macro level, it means operating military forces sufficient to ensure the nation's survival as a free society. That means the prevention of military attacks on the country, as well as the ability to forestall the loss of our freedoms by the threat of force.

What, then, are the general limits on a free society's government in accomplishing this defense objective? First, as the government of a specific society (specific people and territory), it has *jurisdiction* over only its own territory. It clearly has been given no right to operate within the jurisdiction of other governments, except in retaliation for their acts of aggression against it. While this limitation does not forbid operations in territories beyond national jurisdiction—the oceans and outer space, it clearly proscribes attempts to intervene within other countries, whether the purpose is to prop up a "friendly" government, to protect investments by U.S. citizens, or to destabilize an "unfriendly" government. This limitation does not preclude mutual defense treaties. But both principle and prudence suggest that such treaties must be viewed, and reviewed, very critically, to be sure they are truly *mutual* and truly *defensive*.

A second limitation concerns the *means* of defense. A free society is grounded in the sanctity of individual rights. People are sovereign moral agents; they are ends in themselves, not means to the ends of others. Hence practices that are routinely accepted in collectivist societies must be rejected in the defense of a free society. The intentional killing of civilian populations, though it might serve a military purpose, must be rejected as inconsistent with the very principles we are attempting to defend. Likewise, coercing citizens to join the military is a violation of their basic rights, whose defense is what the military of a free society is all about.

A third limitation is that of cost. As economists never cease to remind us (earning economics the appellation "the dismal science"), resources are limited. We can never do everything we wish to do. Somewhere along the line, trade-offs must be made, to accomplish as much as possible for what we can afford to spend. Naturally, how much we decide we can afford to spend depends on what we perceive the threat to be. There is no more pressing need than to ensure our survival as a free people. But "How much is enough?" is a question which cannot be avoided. It will do us no good to build the world's finest gold-plated military machine if the price turns out to be national bankruptcy and the destruction of all social harmony.

Obviously today's defense policies depart considerably from the principles just outlined. The world has grown accustomed to the United States and the Soviet Union opposing each other as equivalent superpowers, intervening in other countries, threatening each others' populations with mass destruction, and leading a pack of allies and client states around behind them. To change this state of affairs will take time and could pose real risks during the years of transition. But if we are to resolve the horrendous conflicts now besetting the defense debate—and more important, if we are to return to the limited-government principles of our founding fathers—we must begin the process of change. This book lays out an agenda for that kind of change.

Its first major premise is that it is time to acknowledge in our defense policy what is in fact the case in the other spheres of human activity: that we no longer live in a bipolar world. In fact, what used to be called the Free World now includes three roughly co-equal components: the United States, Western Europe, and Japan. Yet our entire defense effort remains stuck in the post–World War II bipolar frame of reference. Yes, there is a large and growing Soviet threat to the Free World. But as long as U.S. taxpayers continue to subsidize their defense, the Europeans and Japanese will continue to cry poverty and threaten self-Finlandization. In a time of $200 billion budget deficits, American patience is understandably wearing thin. But only resolute action to terminate these subsidies will midwife the birth of the new multipolar era.

Given the phase-out of major U.S. overseas commitments, our resources can be focused on restructuring the forces needed for our own defense. Since well over half the current defense budget goes to support the defense of NATO Europe and Japan, there will be considerable scope both for weapons-system improvements *and* for budgetary savings.

In the strategic area, the fundamental change is to break the grip of the philosophy of Mutual Assured Destruction (MAD)—the fundamentally immoral doctrine by which the United States' and the Soviet

Union's principal means of defense is the threat of destroying each other's society. To be sure, present U.S. targeting doctrine does not explicitly aim at wiping out residential areas in the USSR. But our large-yield warheads and the relative inaccuracy of our present submarine-launched missiles (which would probably end up being our principal *available* retaliatory weapons after a Soviet first strike knocked out much of our land-based missile force) mean that even a U.S. attack directed at Soviet military targets would wipe out tens of millions of civilians. Moreover, our arms-control efforts are still guided by the MAD-inspired notion of preserving "stability." Under this doctrine, introducing any realistic effort at *defense* against nuclear missiles is condemned as upsetting the mutual fear of annihilation that allegedly preserves the peace.

Yet if MAD is immoral, then precisely what we need is to replace our large, inaccurate warheads with low-yield, precisely guided warheads. We should also protect American lives and property from attack by (1) removing as many targets as possible from our soil (phasing out fixed-site land-based missiles as the accuracy of other missiles improves), (2) building active defenses against ballistic missiles, both ground-based and space-based, and (3) instituting reasonable civil defense measures to protect as many people as possible from at least the effects of fallout. These measures would make us more secure against the threat of Soviet attack but would also make sure that an accidental Soviet attack or a Third World or terrorist attack would not trigger all-out war, by minimizing its damage.

As a nation devoted to free trade, we will continue to need a strong navy, both to defend our shores and to defend our commerce. But with our allies taking responsibility for their own naval defense (e.g., of oil shipping lanes from the Persian Gulf, on which our allies, not we, depend), the size and composition of our navy will be altered.

With our troops brought home from Europe and Japan, we will no longer need a million-man standing army, except in time of war. So what will be needed is a greatly expanded guard and reserve force, able to mobilize rapidly in time of danger. Its force structure, weapons systems, and training practices must all be designed with the citizen-soldier in mind. Needless to say, these forces—like all the armed forced of a free society—will be recruited by voluntary means, just as we recruit our police forces.

Finally, what about CIA-type forces? Shall they be proscribed as immoral or encouraged as a necessary and cost-effective alternative to war? Clearly, no military defense can operate without an intelligence capability. Just as clearly, when faced with an actual enemy, a threat to the country's survival, then undercover operations are just as legitimate as troops and missiles. Unfortunately, much of the activity by our covert-action forces over the past three decades has not been of this type. Instead, covert action has been one of the principal means by which the U.S. government has intervened in other countries' affairs—sometimes with benign results, sometimes with disastrous results, and always (when uncovered) providing a ready target for left-wing propagandists intent on portraying the United States as (at best) an unprincipled manipulator of others' destinies.

The prudent course would therefore seem to be to proscribe covert-action forces, leaving to intelligence agencies only the task of collecting and analyzing information. In those cases where the government of an *enemy* country might be overthrowable, it would be far less risky to follow the time-honored course of giving aid to that country's own revolutionaries, much as France came to the aid of George Washington's legions.

This major revision of defense policy could not be put in place overnight. And even if it could, it would be risky to do so. The rest of the world will need time to adjust to the emergence of a multipolar defense environment.

Yet the rewards of moving in this direction would be great. By renouncing the threat of mass destruction and shifting to a defensive strategic posture, we would reclaim the moral high ground—in the eyes of our own people as well as the rest of the world. By insisting that our allies stand on their own feet, we will (perhaps grudgingly) earn their respect and bring about a safer multipolar world. By forswearing intervention in other countries, we will undercut Soviet and leftist propaganda about our intentions and demonstrate by our actions that there is a clear moral difference between ourselves and the Soviets. Freed of that propaganda burden, we can once again lift high the lamp of liberty as a beacon and example to the world.

The United States was supposed to be a free society. In many ways we have taken on the trappings of statism, losing sight of our roots in individual liberty. The past decade has brought the beginnings of a return to our roots domestically: witness the tax revolt, deregulation, and disenchantment with big government in general. It is high time we returned to our roots in defense and foreign policy as well. With this book, we hope to point the way to doing so.

1 The Moral Basis of National Defense

Eric Mack

I believe that it is possible for modern war to be waged within the limits set by the laws of morality. [But if] anyone were to declare that modern war is necessarily total, and necessarily involves direct attack on the life of innocent civilians, . . . my reply would be: So much the worse for modern war. If it necessarily includes such means, it is necessarily immoral itself. —John C. Ford[1]

The Political Morality of the Free Society

Central to the idea of a free society is the notion that individuals are, by nature, free and independent. To say that by nature individuals are free and independent is not to say that there is some law of physical nature according to which individuals must be free and independent. This all too obviously is not the case. Rather it is the claim that there is a type of moral equality among persons such that none have a claim of authority or sovereignty over any others. Each individual has a life and set of purposes of his own and there is no ground for subordinating anyone's life to the life or purposes of others. To deny persons this fundamental sovereignty over themselves is to affirm, at least to some degree, that persons are natural servants or slaves of others.

The idea that each person possesses an original moral authority over himself is the distinctive element in our political history. It was expressed by John Locke in terms of individual rights to life, liberty, and property.[2] An individual's specific rights to particular external objects derive from his right to his own labor and from the fact that to deprive that individual of what he consciously labored on would be a form of enslavement.

These Lockean rights to life, liberty, one's own labor, and to property, if coherently interpreted, are all negative rights. They do not impose upon others positive obligations, obligations to provide the

An earlier version of this chapter was written during the tenure of a grant from the Committee on Research, Tulane University.

1

rightholder with goods or services. Negative rights imply only that others are under obligations to leave the rightholder in peaceful enjoyment of his rights. On this Lockean view, persons can and do acquire positive rights against others to goods and services through contractual arrangements. But in the absence of such arrangements no one can claim a right against another to be provided with some good or service.

A free society is one in which these core rights of all persons to their life, liberty, permissibly acquired property, and to the fulfillment of their valid contracts are protected. Such protection provides all individuals, in ways that do not infringe upon others, with a domain within which to pursue their own aims. For the free society there is no politically higher aim such as the aggregate happiness or the prestige of the state. Political and legal institutions have the limited role of securing the rights definitive of the free society and thereby creating the framework within which individuals, families, and other associations may pursue their respective goals either singly or in voluntary cooperation. Since, in the absence of voluntary contractual obligation, no one has a right to a particular standard of living, it cannot be the role of the state to employ its coercive machinery to ensure anybody a particular standard of living. By the same token, no individuals outside our society have any right against individuals of this society to a given standard of living. No failure by us to provide them with a higher standard can be construed as a violation of their rights. Thus any argument that their governments may act forcibly against us to prevent our (further) violation of their positive rights is unconvincing.

While one's rights to life, liberty, and property are negative rights, requiring merely that others forgo trespass upon them, a right to the protection by others of one's rights to life, liberty, and property would be a positive right. On the underlying theory of a free society, such a right can exist only in virtue of its voluntary assumption by the party bound by it. This has two important implications. First, no one within this society is, absent specific explicit and voluntary contract, bound to incur costs or dangers in order to protect the rights of others. Second, no individual or group of individuals outside of this society has any right against members of this society to have their rights protected. We are not morally obligated as individuals or as a group to go to the defense of other parties, no matter how just their cause. There may, of course, be good prudential and moral reasons showing that some individuals *ought* to go to the aid of other individuals or groups. But this moral point must be sharply distinguished from the claim, in political morality, that this or that individual or group has a *right* to assistance. Morally praiseworthy but not obligatory assistance is not the province of a duly limited government—unless that assistance also happens to enhance, all things considered, the rights of those subject to such a government.

Because large-scale defensive activity requires resources and because resources come from people and do not (for the most part) grow on trees, and because individuals are not naturally bound to supply others with these resources, we cannot entirely avoid the question of what mode of manning and financing defensive systems is compatible with our model of the free society. The general answer is that people can be bound to contribute only what they have freely agreed to contribute, as in the manning or financing of any other mutual endeavor. Starting with the assumption that people in fact are bound to contribute to the common defense, Locke and many since him have sought to justify this belief with highly tenuous theories of implicit contract. But such contracts are not worth the paper they aren't written on. It is possible, of course, for individuals freely to become bound to one another, through some institutional mediation, to support in specified ways a common defense. But, in fact, *we* are not so bound. Where, then, does such a claim leave the project of this chapter? It leaves it in need of putting aside for *present* purposes certain of the implications of the principles definitive of the free society.

One implication so direct and manifest that it cannot be put aside is the impermissibility of conscription. Conscription is a form of involuntary servitude and can be acceptable only to those who either reject the ideal of free and independent individuals or who indulge in some fantasy about tacit consent or about some mysterious social indebtedness. In the latter case one gets the argument that since the government bestows protection of rights upon us, all, or at least some, of us are reciprocally bound to pay for this benefit in the form of service in the government's protective endeavors. This indebtedness argument works by suggesting the existence of some transcendent government or society that acts and to which a debt is due.

But whatever protection of rights is provided by the U.S. government is furnished by real individuals who take up the task of protection by voluntarily entering the employ of the government and who are rewarded for doing so. These employees benefit by their own lights, as do the individuals they manage to protect. That, esentially, is the end of the matter. While one may be pleased and even grateful that these beneficial activities are carried out, there is no mysterious social debt left over. Though each of us benefits enormously and in all sorts of ways from many activities, relationships, and institutions in which, as individuals, we play no direct part, this does not make those who directly and freely participate for their own chosen purposes our victims with an enforcible claim, in compensation, upon our lives or fortunes.[3]

It is, then, incoherent to advocate the defense of a free society by means of conscription.

Another implication of our fundamental sovereignty over our own lives is the moral impermissiblity of coercing individuals, through taxation, to pay for a common defense system. A fully free society would finance national-scale defense voluntarily, presumably in large part through the sale of this protection to individuals and associations who would remain legally free not to purchase this service. The special problem with such voluntary financing is that national-scale defense is, in the technical economic sense, a public good. It is a good the enjoyment of which cannot feasibly be withheld from anyone within a given area if it is produced at all. Since particular individuals will not face the certainty of being denied national-scale defense should they decline to purchase it, the normal direct incentive to purchase the good is absent. This may lead to so few people offering to buy the good that it will not be produced even though (nearly) all persons would be better off securing defense at some financial cost to themselves. The public goods problem is not that some will free-ride on the services financed by others, but that these special types of commonly beneficial services will not be financed at all. A complete vindication of the ideal of a free society must address this issue. It must indicate how, by noncoercive means, individuals' incentives can be structured so as to generate sufficient voluntary support for public goods such as national-scale defense. That such mechanisms could be devised is not mere wishful thinking, since work in recent years on market solutions to public goods problems, including that of national defense, has produced some plausible solutions to public goods dilemmas.[4]

Fortunately, however, the problem of financing a defense system in a manner compatible with a free society can be set aside for the purposes of this chapter and book. This is because we can distinguish between the morality of a particular defense system and the morality of its financing mechanisms. No matter what our moral judgment about the financing of military forces, we can independently inquire about the morality of the use of those forces. And the latter is our purpose here with respect to military forces employed by the U.S. government against other governments and peoples. Even if the U.S. government acquired its resources in a perfectly unexceptional way, we would still have to inquire about the character and implications of the moral constraints, if any, on the use of those resources.

We proceed, then, to investigate what people as bearers of individual rights may do or have done for them in the way of forcibly defending their rights in light of other people's possession of the same fundamental rights.

Moral Theories of War

Moral theorizing about war usually focuses on two distinguishable questions. What, if anything, renders a war just? And what constraints, if any, apply to the conduct of a just war? The advocate of the free society, focusing on individual rights, will insist that only wars in defense of these rights can be just. More specifically, the limited government of a given free society will be mandated to prepare for the conduct of wars only for the sake of protecting the rights of its particular citizens. (This mandate is even further qualified in the fourth section of this chapter.) But the question remains, how, if at all, do the rights of all those individuals who may be injured or killed in the course of defending rights constrain what may be done in defense of rights?

This section surveys seven doctrines of moral war. The first six presuppose that the end which, if any, justifies defensive force is the protection of rights. These doctrines diverge on the question of what constraints, if any, there are on the pursuit of this justifying goal. The seventh doctrine is a reminder of the type of goals that cannot, in terms of a free society's principles, vindicate war. These doctrines are presented in terms of their increasing permissiveness toward harmful force. This survey of moral theories of war provides the background for the doctrinal choice arrived at in this chapter's third section.

1. *Principled Pacifism.* Defensive force is just as immoral as the violence against which it is directed. The former violates rights as surely as the "offensive" use of force.

According to this principled pacifism, the prospect of suffering such a rights violation does not absolve one from the obligation not to violate rights. This obligation stands and binds one to pacifist submission (or nonviolent evasion if that is possible). With respect to one's own moral condition, it is better to suffer a wrong (to oneself) than to be the agent of necessarily wrongful violence (even against an aggressor).

2. *Strict Self-defense.* Defensive force may be used against guilty aggressors and only against such guilty aggressors.

A guilty aggressor is one who sets out intentionally or recklessly to perform an action that violates some right of a (nonaggressing) second party. Often the view that defensive force against guilty aggressors, but only against them, is permissible is associated with the view that the guilty aggressor, through his guilt, forfeits his right against harmful force.

3. *Broad Self-defense.* Defensive force may be used against innocent aggressors as well as guilty aggressors.

Innocent aggressors are those whose action or behavior threatens to deprive one of something to which one has a right, but who are not themselves responsible for their threatening action or behavior. Such aggressors are termed "material aggressors" in Catholic moral theory and will also be referred to as "innocent threats." Common examples of innocent threats are psychotic aggressors or children unaware of the dangerous character of their actions. Conscripts in an aggressor's army who themselves are acting under serious duress are also innocent threats. A doctrine of forfeiture of rights cannot be used in the justification of a Broad Self-defense doctrine, since forfeiture is, presumably, a function of blameworthiness.

4. *Just War Defense.* Defensive force may be used against *guilty and innocent* aggressors even if this force (also) inflicts losses on innocent bystanders.[5]

An innocent bystander is a person who is himself no threat to the party under attack but who will be harmed or killed by the use of defensive force against the attacker. Consider, for example, the civilian refugee who happens to be living in the immediate vicinity of an aggressor's artillery. When an attacker makes use of such bystanders in order to inhibit counterattack against his tools of aggression, the bystanders become innocent shields, especially when the attacker forces them into the vicinity of his weapons or locates his weapons among them. (Anyone who is in fact guilty of voluntarily supporting the aggressor, such as the civilian war planner, does not count as a bystander or shield.)

The Just War Defense doctrine does *not* assert that innocent bystanders may be subject to defensive force in the same way that aggressors may be. It allows defensive force directed against threats to proceed even if innocent bystanders will be killed in the process. But the destruction or incapacitation of threats may not, according to the Just War Defense doctrine, proceed by means of the use of force specifically directed against nonthreats. The Just War Defense doctrine would, for example, disallow the World War II Allied (especially British) obliteration bombing of German cities, in which nonthreats were targeted. The idea was to get at the German war production by disrupting civilian life and morale through the destruction of the densely populated, blue-collar sections of German cities and the inhabitants there. The injury and death to these civilians, many of them not involved in war production, were not a by-product of defensive force directed against aggressors or even the machinery of aggression. Instead, the injury and death to these bystanders was the specific goal of the use of force—albeit a goal in virtue of its being thought to be a means of incapacitating genuine threats.[6]

The Just War Defense doctrine is reminiscent of the views set out, especially by Catholic theologians and philosophers, in Just War Theory.[7] There the key and controversial distinction is between the untoward consequences of one's actions that are intended as one's ends or as one's means and untoward consequences of one's actions that are foreseen, but not intended, either as one's ends or one's means. If injury or death suffered by bystanders is a foreseen, but unintended, result of one's defensive force, then one's moral responsibility for such injury or death is at least of a lesser order than if the same injury or death were intended.

Two clarifications are associated with the careful exposition of this view. First, an agent's intention is not understood as a matter of what particular images or feelings he manages to conjure up or banish from his mind at the moment of action. The bombardier on an obliteration mission does not prevent the deaths of bystanders in the conflict from being his intended means, and, hence, an intended result of his action, by focusing his mind at the moment he releases his bombs on something else, for example, the well-being of the people for whom he is fighting. The death of those bystanders is his intended means as long as their prospective death or injury plays an illuminating role in explaining why the bombardier is doing what he is doing—in other words, why he is releasing those bombs at that place and time.

The second clarification is that advocates of Just War Theory have typically claimed that the production of a foreseen but *unintended* evil effect will remain morally impermissible if the evil effect, albeit not intended, is disproportionate to the good intended (or intended and accomplished) by the action. For example, it might be claimed that the evil involved in the death of 100 refugees in whose midst the aggressor's artillery has been placed is so disproportionate to the enhanced security the counterattacking forces will enjoy if that artillery is destroyed by air attack that it would be morally impermissible for that air attack to proceed. Unfortunately, crucial as proposed principles of proportionality are to a full account of a Just War Defense doctrine and to other theories of defense, their final place, if any, within a correct theory of defense cannot be explored within the limits of this chapter.[8] Whatever the final role of proportionality, for a defensive course of action that indirectly kills bystanders to be justified under a Just War Defense, the defender must have chosen that prospectively successful defensive strategy that minimizes bystander injury and death. (The Just War Defense doctrine prohibits going down in a lost cause if this involves harm to bystanders.)

    5. *Necessary Force Defense.* Defensive force may be used in the protection of rights, and it is not worse to direct defensive force against (innocent) bystanders than against (innocent) aggressors.

The Necessary Force Defense doctrine repudiates the proposition, central to a Just War Defense doctrine, that the intentional killing of nonthreats is a special evil that may not be engaged in even in order to protect one's own rightful claims. To see how the Necessary Force doctrine diverges from the Just War doctrine consider this complex example. There are only two ways to eliminate an aggressor's artillery battery. One way is the (counterforce) method of bombing the artillery, with the added consequence that an innocent refugee living in its vicinity is killed. The other way is the (countervalue) method of killing an innocent refugee who is safely distant from the artillery but who is so cherished by the artillery crew that his death will destroy their fighting morale. Doctrines 1, 2, and even 3 would prohibit any defense under both circumstances. The Just War Defense doctrine sharply distinguishes between the two alternatives—allowing the defender the attack upon the artillery (which kills both the nearby refugee and the crew), but prohibiting the attack on the more distant but cherished refugee. In contrast, when only the two refugees are taken into account, doctrine 5, the Necessary Force Defense, is neutral between the two methods. But if any among the crew are innocent threats, the Necessary Force doctrine will endorse the second, morale-destroying, method of defense.

    6. *Limitless Defense.* While there may be some moral limits upon what may be done in self-defense of rights in small-scale or intrasocietal situations, no such moral limits make sense in the case of large-scale conflict.

The Limitless Defense doctrine still requires that any defensive war be fought to protect against the violation of rights. It still limits what counts as a Just War. But it denies that there are any moral constraints on one's conduct within a Just War. The Limitless Defense doctrine may be supported by the claim that once war comes, the only value is winning. In such a context it is nonsense or moral hypocrisy to sermonize about the rights of one's opponent bystanders' rights or even one's own rights to self-defense. Alternatively it may be argued that in modern warfare all distinctions between threats and nonthreats, between combatants and noncombatants, and so on, break down. Everyone under the sway of the aggressor state must be treated as an enemy in a lawless state of nature. The ideology of political collectivism fosters this last line of reasoning by encouraging us to perceive all individuals as functional parts of the state. From this perspective we are not attacked by certain individuals, some of whom are guilty aggressors, others innocent aggressors. Rather, we are attacked by the holistic entity, the state, which encompasses all of the individuals under its sway as parts.

> 7. *National Interest Aggression.* War is an expression of the interests of peoples. A rational war is one that advances the interest of the nation for whom and by whom it is fought.

The shift from a Limitless Defense doctrine to one of National Interest Aggression greatly expands the grounds for morally permissible warfare by substituting interests, indeed, the collective interest, for individual rights. We reach a point at which the use of the term *defensive* is clearly inappropriate. For one may well use force to advance one's interests without that force being defensive. And the notion of the collective interests of a people is vastly less clear than the notion of the interests of an individual. The imprecision of the former is what makes this last doctrine such a flexible and useful tool for those who influence national policy.

Both Limitless Defense and National Interest Aggression can be quickly rejected by proponents of individual rights and the free society. The Limitless Defense doctrine is to be rejected because it turns on the false and dangerous premise that the state and its agents need not abide by the same moral rules that constrain the actions of ordinary individuals and groups. The doctrine of National Interest Aggression is to be rejected because it turns on a shift to vague and overexpandable "interests" and on a collectivist shift to notions like the interest of the nation.

But this leaves us with the question of which position about permissible self-defense among doctrines 1–5 is most plausible. Unless a position at least as permissive as the Just War Defense is adopted, all large-scale defensive measures, in other words, all wars no matter how just their goals, are sure to be morally impermissible. For any large-scale military measures, no matter how purely reactive to violations of rights, are certain to injure and kill innocent bystanders.

Toward Permissible Defense

In seeking to vindicate the forcible defense of rights, it is useful to begin with the case against principled pacifism. If pacifism is rejected, the next question will be, How far do the arguments associated with this rejection carry us toward the conclusion, expressed in the Necessary Force doctrine, that any use of necessary force in the protection of rights is morally acceptable? It is contended here that the most permissive acceptable principle for national-scale defense is the more stringent Just War Defense doctrine, which requires that all defensive force be targeted against aggressive force.

Against Pacifism

In the most forceful recent philosophical critique of pacifism, Jan Narveson focuses on the incoherence of ascribing rights to victims of violence while denying them a right to defend themselves against the violation of those rights.

> What could that right to their own security, which people have, possibly consist in, if not a right at least to defend themselves from whatever violence might be offered them? . . . The prevention of infraction of that right is precisely what one has a right to when one has a right at all. A right just *is* a status justifying preventive action. To say that you have a right to X but that no one has any justification whatever for preventing people from depriving you of it, is self-contradictory. . . . In saying that violence is wrong, one is at the same time saying that people have a right to its prevention, by force if necessary. Whether and to what extend it may be necessary is a question of fact, but, since it is a question of fact only, the *moral* right to use force on some possible occasions is established.[9]

Rights are claims persons can insist others abide by. Such claims are to be contrasted with (mere) measures of moral stature that one person can apply to others, such as their degree of kindliness or degree of integrity. One may judge, quite correctly, that others have acted wrongly on some occasion because they have not displayed kindness or integrity. But in employing such judgments, one does not invoke rights one has against these other individuals. Kindness or integrity is not something one can require of them. More precisely, one can *morally* require or *morally* insist upon kindness or integrity from others by being prepared to judge them harshly for failures to display these traits.

But rights must have more interpersonal force than this. They are the bases for demands one can make upon others, and not merely for advice one can offer them about their lives. The sense in which rights allow the rightholder to require or insist that others act or refrain from action must be more robust than that involved in *morally* requiring or insisting. What could this more robust sense be except that rightholders can require others *in fact* to conform their activity to respect these rights? This can only mean that rightholders may prevent, by injurious force if necessary, infringements upon their rights. The right to resist violations of one's rights, to use injurious force if necessary to preserve one's rights, is then an implication of one's having a *right* against such violence and of this right being a strong moral claim against others for which the rightholder may require respect.

How much force (against those subject to permissible defense) may be used in defense of rights? Narveson's own answer is "enough," by which he means just as much as necessary. The major alternative answer is: no more force than produces injury proportionate to the unjust injury being protected against. This is an alternative because the force that produces a proportionate injury may not be enough to accomplish the defense. The type of argument for permissible forcible defense given by Narveson and myself points to the former, more liberal answer. Endangered individuals need not weigh the loss that threatens them against the loss to those subject to their permissible defensive activity. They may, instead, stand on their right not to submit to a violation of their rights.

Toward Permissible (Counterforce) Defense

The argument against pacifism focuses on the rightholder who is being threatened and not on the party whose actions threaten those rights. It does not rely upon the guilt of the threatening party. So the argument that shows the permissibility of using harmful force when necessary against guilty aggressors also shows its permissibility when necessary against nonguilty (material) aggressors, in other words, against innocent threats. If one has a right to one's life, one cannot be obligated to allow another to be a causal agent in depriving one of that right. When necessary, such a deprivation may be resisted by means of harmful force. When under attack by a conscript one may kill the conscript even though he is attacking only because were he not to do so his rulers would kill him or his family.

What about innocent bystanders? The argument against pacifism seems also to allow necessary defensive killing of them. For it at least seems that the presence of an innocent bystander could not obligate one to submit to the violation of rights that would result if an aggressor's behavior is not thwarted. Although it is the aggressor and not the bystander who is engaged in a process that will violate one's rights unless thwarted, one's right not to submit to a deprivation of life is a right one holds against everyone. No one can demand that one not resist such a deprivation. Nevertheless, one's right to resist violations of rights is not a sanction for engaging in aggressive behavior. And cannot the bystander, who would be killed by one's resistance to the aggressor, insist on one's abstaining from this action in the name of *his* right to life? The difficulty is that a particular course of action in this sort of situation is susceptible to the following two (among other) descriptions: (1) an exercise of one's rightful resistance to the violation of rights; and (2) an aggression against the bystander's right to life. In virtue of description 1, the principle of self-defense applies, and one may proceed with the course of action. In virtue of description 2, one's obligation not to aggress applies, and one may not proceed with the course of action.

Rather than engage in a fruitless attempt to give objective weights to each of these conflicting claims and see which way the scale tips, one can interpret the Just War Defense doctrine as a guide for determining which description and associated principle (self-defense or non-aggression against rights) is the dominant one for the purposes of establishing the permissibility of a given forcible act. That description is dominant that explains the forcible action.

Recall the example discussed previously in comparing the Just War Defense doctrine and the Necessary Force Defense doctrine involving the choice between the defensive counterattack against an artillery battery that foreseeably kills a nearby refugee and the demoralizing counterattack against the distant refugee cherished by the artillery crew. If one were to pursue the first alternative (with weapons designed for precision counterattack), the killing of a nearby refugee would in no way explain the course of one's action. One would have acted exactly in the same manner had the nearby refugee not existed at all. The refugee's death would not at all be a part of one's intention. Thus the dominant description of the counterattack would be in terms of its responsiveness to a threat to rights, and it would be vindicated by the counterattacker's right to defend these rights. In contrast, if one were to pursue the second, antimorale, alternative, one's intermediate purposes would be the killing of the cherished refugee. One's chosen course of action would be contoured by and explicable only by reference to the presence of this refugee. Such a targeting of this bystander would give salience to the description of one's action as an aggression against this refugee. Given this salience and the bystander's right to life, this form of counterattack would be unjustified.

The Just War Defense doctrine incorporates into the overall theory of individual rights moral maxims that are naturally associated with an emphasis on individual autonomy and the separate and equal standing of each person's life and purposes. Specifically it incorporates the idea that it is supremely wrong to employ others as means, against their will and to the detriment of their well-being or freedom, for the sake of one's own goals, no matter how noble or natural those goals may be. Although there is a broad sense in which any action that deprives a person of rightful possessions or conditions treats that person as a means, the use of persons as means is most vividly the case when the untoward result is not merely foreseen but intended. The direct, intentional killing of a bystander as a distinct means to some further end violates this associated maxim about the wrongness of employing persons as means, whereas the indirect, collateral killing of a bystander does not.

There is another line of considerations, indirectly connected with persons not being obligated to forgo resistance, which also suggests that the rejection of pacifism leads to the Just War Defense doctrine, but no further. If pacifism is rejected, the person who escalates from verbal insistence that one surrender some rightful possession to seizing one's rightful possessions forcibly can still be resisted. He does not, by his escalation to forcible seizure, gain a moral advantage. His increased wrongdoing does not confer upon him any immunity. But if either the defensive killing of innocent threats or the defensive collateral killing of shields or bystanders is proscribed, a potential violator of rights will be able to acquire moral immunity in his aggressive pursuits by escalating his wrongdoing. If the defensive killing of innocent threats is proscribed, then guilty aggressors can gain immunity for their projects by organizing their attacks upon others with innocent, coerced, conscripts. If the defensive killing of shields or bystanders is proscribed, guilty aggressors can gain immunity for their projects by forcing bystanders into the vicinity of their weapons or by locating their weapons in the midst of bystanders. Thus, if either the killing of innocent threats or the collateral killing of bystanders is prohibited, the more morally indiscriminate the aggressor, the more moral immunity he will enjoy.

Since the rejection of pacifism, in general, involves a refusal to grant the evil aggressor a moral cloak, one should expect that this rejection would extend to proscriptions on the killing of innocent threats and on collateral killing in the course of defensively necessary action.

In contrast, the Just War Defense doctrine's prohibition on direct killing of bystanders does *not* provide the guilty aggressor with a comparable moral lever. In this case rounding up more and more shields will not increase the aggressor's moral immunity against counterattacks, which remain targeted against the aggressive force.

This conclusion about a person's right to use lethal force against even nonguilty threats or in such a way as to endanger innocent bystanders does not imply that such innocent threats or bystanders must submit to this permissible defensive force. Innocent threats or bystanders may have a right, under the circumstances, to defend themselves against the counterattacker's permissible action. There can be cases in which two innocent parties, thrust into conflict with each other, permissibly battle each other to death.

Still, a Just War Defense may require that we forgo, on moral grounds, a course of defensive action that would be the most (or only) effective one available. Many cases can be constructed that, in virtue of this feature, may raise philosophical doubts about this doctrine. A typical philosophical example would posit the sudden appearance of an assassin who will kill one unless one distracts him by killing his child. A Just War Defense would require that one forgo this act. But to many it will seem that, horrendous as it would be to kill this child (directly), one could not be obligated to submit to the assassination.

Whatever one's sense of this case, however, there are reasons why such a case should not be taken as a basis for a general policy shift to a more permissive doctrine of national-scale defense than the Just War Defense doctrine. As this case is presented, the threat is sudden, immediate, and absolutely certain. There is neither time nor room for the formation of alternative defensive strategies. Furthermore, the threat is removed immediately and with absolute certainty upon killing the aggressor's child. The immediacy of the threat means that the use of the child is less chosen than thrust upon one, and the immediacy of the relief from danger upon the killing of the child blurs the status of that killing as a separate intended consequence of one's action. These immediacies and certainties help explain why killing the child can be (perceived as) something less than thoroughly murderous. National-scale defense should not be modeled on such one-time emergencies. National-scale threats evolve over extended periods of time. We are not required, as in the child case, to react in a given moment to a situation the structure of which is simply presented to us. There are many long-term options. And, because this is so, opting for one that involves the direct targeting of bystanders carries the burden of being a calculated choice of useful aggression against these bystanders. At the very least a system of national defense whose operation would violate the Just War Defense doctrine must be avoided if another system is available that accords with such a doctrine.

Defensive force is to be directed at the actual causal agents of the threatening violation of rights. And mechanisms of defensive force are to be developed and employed in ways that minimize even the collateral killing of innocents. The Just War Defense doctrine is not necessarily satisfied if, at a given moment, the weapons at hand are directed against aggressive forces. For we can ask further questions about whether the development of the weapons at hand was entirely for counterforce purposes and about whether their development embodied a substantial effort to minimize collateral killing. Only if the defending party has, over time, been committed to and constrained in its defensive preparations by a Just War Defense doctrine, and has been known to be so committed and constrained, will the aggressor bear full responsibility for the additional collateral killings that may occur because of his placement of his threatening forces.

The entire discussion to this point might be criticized for systematically relying upon the extreme case in which the potential victim will be *killed* unless aggression is thwarted (and in which defensive acts on the victim's behalf are assumed to be successful). Such a focus may mislead because, especially in the case of international aggression, the alternative facing at least the vast majority of threatened individuals is *not:* Be killed or forcibly thwart the attack. For nonresistance or surrender, either unconditional or negotiated, is always an alternative and will almost always involve, for most individuals, a less awful, and less rights-violating, outcome than being killed. A focus on the extreme case may obscure the risks and disadvantages of being forcibly defended. If the rights lost through nonresistance or surrender would be relatively insubstantial and the risk of more profound losses as a result of mounting a defense would not be insubstantial, then institutions mandated to secure our rights should do so by *not* mounting a forcible defense. Jack Benny's doubts to the contrary notwithstanding, it is often rational and most in accord with maintaining one's rights that one hand over one's wallet rather than risk one's life. As long as the risks of military confrontation and war, in terms of the security of rights, are significant, avoidance of confrontation and war must play a major controlling role in any rational defense policy. No extended argument for a right to engage in defensive acts, including acts that indirectly kill bystanders, should lead one to forget the dangers of exercising that right to self-defense.

Implications: Alliances and Interventions

In this section and the next, the moral goals for and the moral constraints upon U.S. defensive policies are clarified through application to real-world policy decisions about, for example, protection of overseas resources, alliances, aid to liberation movements, and U.S. nuclear strategy. The emphasis throughout is on the moral dimensions of these decisions. Where the nonmoral, empirical dimension is itself complex and controversial, as in the decisions about continued U.S. participation in our North Atlantic Treaty Organization (NATO) and Japanese alliances, extensive evaluation is deferred to the relevant special chapter, for example, chapter 5 on alliances.

The first standard for evaluating any U.S. defense policy must be whether it really does increase the security of the rights that it is the mandate of a freedom-oriented U.S. government to protect. Moral theory endorses this standard over competing standards such as the enhancement of national prestige while it remains an empirical matter to determine whether, in fact, a given policy does increase this security. The second evaluative standard is whether the policy proceeds by morally permissible means—that is, whether it avoids the direct infliction of injury and death on nonthreats to these rights (and, consistent with this, minimizes injury and death to innocent threats). Moral theory identifies what counts as impermissible means, while it remains an empirical matter to determine where such means are in fact employed.

Overseas Resources

To clarify the first standard we must recall what a rational national defense policy for the United States does not aim at accomplishing. It does not aim at the establishment of the U.S. government as a "global power" or as "the leader of the [so-called] free world." It does not aim at national prestige or a world-historical role for the American people or our aspiring "statesmen." It does not aim at economic prosperity. Nor does it aim at the protection of the rights of other peoples (much less their "interests"), no matter how much some of us may sympathize with one or another (putatively) endangered group. To this list of nonaims one more is to be added. The protection, by military means or the threat thereof, of overseas holdings of U.S. individuals and firms (even rightful holdings) is not an aim of a rational national defense policy. For such protection inevitably involves a vast forced subsidy by most taxpayers for overseas investment. If individuals or firms choose to carry on businesses with certain extraordinary costs, for example, the costs of suppressing nationalization movements or the costs of repelling takeovers by the neighboring Marxist outpost, then it is *their business* to bear these costs. (And if they do, of course, they have every right to their higher-than-average profits from such risky endeavors.) Individuals and firms will choose to bear these costs if and only if, in the light of nationalizing pressures, their protective enterprises still make economic sense. It makes no more sense to allow individuals or firms to fob off this sort of business expense on others than it does to allow them to fob off the costs of credit or labor.

There are numerous other factors that argue for disengagement from the protection of foreign investments by military measures. In the case of large-scale investments involving accords between U.S.-based companies and foreign states, the legitimacy of the resulting property holdings will usually be dubious. More likely than not the U.S. government would be coming to the defense of some unholy alliance of local oppressors and their (perhaps reluctant) corporate partners. Common vehicles for bringing pressures against foreign regimes in the name of protecting "our" interests include various statist economic devices—international quasi-government banking institutions, national tariff or quota systems, and so on. But rather than embracing such vehicles, we should be striving to abolish them. Another alternative for exerting influence is for the U.S. government to promise arms shipments to those who will adopt the U.S. policy of the moment, or to the enemies of those who continue to disturb "our" interests. As a consequence, among the actual costs of protecting "our" foreign investments are the costs of vast boondoggles for U.S. weapon manufacturers, the costs of the resulting economic misallocations within the United States, the costs of subsequent U.S. military involvement with regimes that the United States has sought to influence, and so on. It is not uncommon for the U.S. government to protect "private" U.S. interests against an economically statist regime by becoming that regime's economic and military bedmate. In the process the United States becomes coauthor and abetter of the rights-violating activities of that regime.

A final policy alternative for protecting overseas investments would be direct military action. In principle and in the abstract, there would be no objection to a low-cost surgically precise zapping by U.S. (volunteer) forces, of the wicked Minister of Nationalization who is about to expropriate the property of the morally upright U.S.-based business. In principle what is done in such a case in no respect differs from what is done to the aspiring domestic thief. But there are great dangers connected even with authorizing the government of a free society to intervene only in low-cost ways for the sake of protecting legitimate overseas holdings. For any such authorization will call forth demands for protection of both legitimate and illegitimate holdings, and the inherent difficulties of distinguishing among these demands will generate opportunities to pass off illegitimate demands for high-cost protection as legitimate demands for low-cost protection. Moreover, any authorization for intervention against other governments will present a powerful temptation to political leaders, whatever their avowed principles, to flex military muscle and play the role of world statesman. Finally, when deciding whether or not to act under such an authorization, any group of officials on the spot is likely to overassess their power to effect the result they favor and to underassess the chances of being caught up in a vastly more extensive, complicated, and morally dubious operation than even they first envisioned.

These remarks, along with the point that it is not the business of the U.S. government to employ military means to (attempt to) ensure prosperity, may erroneously foster the image of a U.S. economy increasingly cut off from foreign trade and resources. But such an image is the product of the view, usually proclaimed by enemies of U.S. "imperialism," that only capitalist societies gain from international trade. This image is contradicted by the fact that "nationalist," "revolutionary," and "Marxist" regimes everywhere are quite happy to sell "their" natural resources to Western companies and governments. The additional economic costs (reductions of which are not, in any case, legitimate goals of U.S. military activity) of dealing with such regimes are miniscule alongside the escalating and uncontrollable personal, economic, and moral costs of the maintenance and employment of Rapid Deployment Forces and their like. (As an empirical aside, it is useful to remember that those *political* decisions by foreign regimes that have disrupted temporarily the U.S. economy have been reactions to the U.S. interventionist policies, for example, the massive support of the Shah of Iran.)

Alliances

Two types of criticism, based respectively on the two standards cited, and each decisive, have potential application to U.S. alliances. The first is that a particular alliance does not provide us with added security against some independently existing threat (a threat not itself fostered by the alliance) or that the security added by the alliance against an independently existing threat does not outweigh the added risks to us from the alliance. The second criticism is that the alliance, perhaps only gradually and inadvertently, makes us coagents of the evil done by our alliance partners, either to their subjects or to other peoples.

Any plausible critique of our current NATO and Japanese alliances will proceed predominantly in terms of the first standard. It must focus on questions about the extent to which these alliance partners contribute to our defense and about the risks to us of such entanglements, especially in an age of nuclear weapons. A large part of such an analysis is an estimation of the likelihood of the worst possible outcome upon a U.S. withdrawal—namely, that Western Europe and Japan would become satellites of the Soviet Union and an estimation of how dangerous this would be to our rights. The difficult and complex empirical case for withdrawal from these alliances is made in chapter 5. The relevance of the current chapter is to establish that, as noble as such goals as preserving Western civilization or freedom throughout the world may be, these are not the sort of goals by which the defense decisions of a limited constitutional government of a free society are to be gauged. (Nor does the advocate of the free society believe that any government *could* engineer such grandiose goals.)

A plausible critique of our current alliances and military aid agreements with other regimes throughout Latin America, Africa, and Asia can proceed in terms of both the first and the second standard. With respect to the first standard, it is difficult to find any one of our military commitments or programs of aid, training, and technological support to all those regimes throughout Latin America, Africa, and Asia professing to be "moderate" or "anticommunist" that plausibly, in fact and in the long run, renders the relevant rights of Americans more secure. Such security is not enhanced when a central African butcher remains in power rather than his opponent, who is for the moment receiving weapons from Moscow, nor when the established crew of despots in the Philippines or South Korea remains in power rather than Soviet-dominated competitors. Even less are our rights better secured when our attempts to maintain various brutes in power fail—as they typically do. Nor even would a legitimate aim of U.S. governmental policy be endangered were Israel (along with its rivals) denied further military aid and hence required to reach an accommodation with its neighbors. Moreover, numerous of these alliances have destroyed or threatened to destroy the very rights the U.S. government should secure. One need only recall the Korean and Vietnamese wars and the ongoing danger of conventional and nuclear war posed by our commitments to, for example, South Korea and Israel.

The point is not that the peoples of these countries would be better off without U.S. military involvement, though sometimes they would be. Rather it is that, awful as certain political changes in the world may be for the people who directly suffer them, these changes pose no threat to the aims of a rational U.S. defense policy. It should be added, of course, that just as people who are particularly fond of their African uranium mines or their Arabian oil fields have every right to finance and organize resistance to a violation of their rights, so too do sympathizers with unjustly threatened peoples have every right to rush to the defense of these peoples. Noble as these sympathies may be, however, there is no reason why their expression should be confused with the task of our common defense.

In terms of the second evaluative standard, these alliances with and commitments to Latin American, African, and Asian regimes often have involved the U.S. government as aider and abettor of a government's aggression against its own people. Even if we count only the most serious, undisguised, and systematic violations, we would have to conclude that the vast majority of regimes supported by the U.S. government in the name of the rights definitive of a free society are criminal violators of those rights. It is common for assurances of U.S. military aid and cooperation to encourage a regime's repression of its own population and to set in motion forces that lead to a more corrupt, vicious, and ultimately unstable, regime than would otherwise have existed. U.S. clients would not so often need escalating U.S. aid against rebellious populations were they not U.S. clients to begin with. And as these regimes have grown in viciousness, the U.S. government, at least as often as not, has become a more active and controlling, and hence more blameworthy, partner in heavy-handed attempts to subdue dissident populations. Although envy, spite, moral barbarism, and economic infantilism are major contributors to anti-American sentiment throughout the world, the contribution of U.S. government support of murderous regimes should not be underestimated.

The application of the two standards, then, tends strongly toward the rejection of our existing alliances, especially alliances that commit the United States to the defense of other peoples and, worse, their unwholesome rulers. However, it should remain clear that the moral goal of and the moral constraints upon a free society's defense do not, in principle, rule out alliances. In particular, limited treaties that facilitate the deployment of important warning devices or weapons systems may well be rational and morally permissible. For example, a wide-ranging and hence relatively invulnerable submarine-launched missile system may well require worldwide servicing and communication facilities, as might a space-based antimissile system. Similarly, overseas sites may be crucial for the gathering of intelligence about a potential aggressor. Treaties designed for these genuinely defensive purposes can be justified as long as they do not themselves generate risky commitments or blameworthy support of unjust regimes.

Given the ease with which such caveats have been ignored and the even greater ease with which limited arrangements can slide into full-scale domestic and international support, any such proposed agreement must be scrutinized with the utmost care. Since the only principled geographical limitation on the placement of U.S. defensive installations is that they not violate well-grounded property rights, there is no principled objection to defensive operations and installations anywhere in the open seas or in space. The dominant issue is the empirical one—which operations and installations most enhance our security—with the dangers of prospective confrontations and entangling alliances always kept fully in mind.

Intelligence and Subversion

In order to defend a free society effectively its government needs intelligence about the intentions and capacities of those posing a threat to that freedom. No particular justification is needed for using orbiting satellites to survey Soviet military bases. But intelligence operations may include stealing state documents or bugging dachas. Beyond intelligence *itself,* even acts of sabotage (e.g., of experimental weapons) must be considered. In order for the agents of a free society to be justified in such actions, the subject of those actions must already be threatening or overtly preparing to threaten directly and aggressively that free society. The presence of Soviet or Soviet-controlled operatives in, for example, some Third World country, does not justify U.S. intelligence operations there. The more grave the developing (or even potential) direct threat, the more justified the intelligence operations will be. The justification for cleverly sabotaging the development of a new Soviet missile guidance mechanism would be greater than for disrupting the development of an improved infantry rifle. Given the typically speculative character of the need for any given intelligence operation, limits *at least* as strict as expressed in the Just War Defense doctrine should apply to their conduct. Moreover, the important historical-empirical rules of thumb developed in chapter 9 demand extreme caution about the extent of a free society's tolerance for intelligence operations. Their secrecy, expense, ineffectiveness, counterproductivity, and susceptibility to all forms of corruption must give us more than pause.

These dangerous features also characterize counterintelligence agencies, agencies designed to thwart intelligence against our defensive capabilities. In general, counterintelligence and counterespionage should be approached as a matter of enforcing the normal and relatively well-defined criminal law against the theft of blueprints and information, against bribery, and so on, rather than as enforcing ill-defined antitreason or antiespionage law. And all the normal protection for individuals against criminal investigations must be strictly respected. Excepted from these constraints are known agents of a threatening aggressor. In principle, just as these agents may be subject to normally unacceptable surveillance and interference within their own countries, they may be subjected to such treatment during their missions to free societies. This point, of course, does not determine what level of counterintelligence is cost-effectively feasible and whether it is valuable to assure the diplomatic corps of hostile nations a degree of genuine privacy.

Two final cautionary points must be emphasized. The first is that counterintelligence must be limited strictly to thwarting an aggressor's military intelligence. No counterintelligence action of any sort can be justified by the suspected or real political affinities of its target. The long and sometimes brutal abuse of the politically and even merely socially disaffected by local and national counterintelligence units is profoundly unworthy of a free society. The second is that no designer of counterintelligence programs should even imagine that some conceivable set of measures is available that would protect a free society's military secrets as well as they can be protected in unfree societies. To discover such secrecy-protecting measures would be to discover a plan for the internal subversion of the free society.

We have noted that it is not part of the mandate of a limited government of a free society to ensure that regimes in other societies are just. And alliances cannot be justified with regimes or their revolutionary opponents in the name of the righteousness of their programs. But if an unjust and oppressive regime seriously threatens our survival as a free people, help short of war to dissidents against such a regime falls within the ethical mandate of the government of a free society. The wisdom of aid to freedom fighters and the limits of such aid are discussed in chapter 10. Suffice it to say here that extreme scrutiny and caution are necessary to guard against dangerous, spiraling, and morally compromising adventures in which support for revolutionaries might render us responsible for injustices subsequently perpetrated by them.[10]

Implications: Strategic Defense

We must always recall war avoidance as a method of securing the rights that the U.S. government should seek to protect. Since any form of nuclear defense against nuclear threats (in particular, the threat presented by the Soviet Union's military) poses the risk of nuclear war and massive violation of American rights, it behooves us to examine, as a policy for securing these rights, the abandonment of any such defense. The more moderate and conventional version of this option is bilateral abandonment of nuclear forces through explicit or tacit agreement. Unfortunately, while the reliable mutual destruction of all nuclear armaments (and all means of quickly assembling replacements) would be a lovely thing, the prospects for such an arrangement are exceedingly dim. Besides the more objective difficulties of coordinating a mutual, confidence-sustaining process of reduction, there are the more subjective factors that everyone knows (that everyone knows) that international agreements are always broken and that an atmosphere of international confrontation can be highly advantageous to the rulers of the confronting states. Nevertheless, serious good faith efforts must be made. Otherwise, it can never reasonably be claimed that more forcible defensive measures are *necessary* for the securing of rights.

While reliable mutual nuclear disarmament may not be within the power of the U.S. government to effect, unilateral disarmament is. An examination of the case for unilateral disarmament will tell us what is risked by engaging in less than fully reliable programs of mutual disarmament. This discussion assumes that if the United States were to engage in a unilateral nuclear disarmament, it would also forgo any attempt to guard against Soviet conventional forces. The latter attempt would be purposeless because whatever demands the Soviets might make would be backed by their monopoly on nuclear power.

Pragmatic Surrender

An interesting case can be made for unilateral disarmament, or in other words implicit surrender, in terms of the standards developed within this chapter. The first standard is whether the proposal on balance increases the security of our rights. In this context the expected loss of rights associated with nonresistance must exceed the suspected loss of rights (among those being protected) associated with employing the defensive system in question. Of course, both extent and probability of possible losses must be considered.[11] The second standard is that the operation of the defensive system in question must not proceed by means of the direct, intentional killing of nonaggressing individuals. The second standard speaks directly to the moral status of defense by countervalue deterrence.

One can imagine costs of surrender sufficiently benign that the employment of any expensive defensive system that falls short of *guaranteeing* protection would be irrational. Suppose, for example, that the cost to U.S. taxpayers of unilateral disarmament were to be the annual payment, in tribute to the Soviet Union, of exactly what the U.S. defense budget would otherwise have been. The paying of this tribute, we are imagining, completely eliminates the risk of conventional and nuclear war. (I ignore third-party complications.) Under these circumstances, surrender would be eminently rational. We would get everything we were previously hoping to get for exactly the costs we were willing to incur *and* the risks of war would be totally eliminated. If the risks to us of employing the best available defensive system were substantial, then tribute payments significantly *exceeding* the projected costs of maintaining that system would be rational—*as a means of best securing our rights* (except for our rights to the resources transferred as tribute, which are, however, hypothesizd to be valued less than the security of rights gained by the tribute payments).

The point of this extortion example is that the case against disarmament requires that the costs to us of disarmament be very substantially higher than tribute payments of several hundred billion dollars a year. Such significantly higher costs are, indeed, likely. The tribute payments or other terms that would be imposed (perhaps only gradually) by the Soviets should the U.S. government disarm would generate widespread resistance. A tribute-paying U.S. government would have to demonstrate its "friendship" to its Soviet protector by suppressing such opposition. This in turn would breed further resistance and oppression. The growing general subservience by the U.S. political structure to the Soviet Union would foster an acceleration of collectivist economic legislation—designed, perhaps, more readily to link U.S. production with Soviet needs—which would progressively undercut the economy.

As the less productive economy faltered, the burdens of tributary payments or transfers would be more and more difficult to bear. Moreover, those who would rise to the top of the political heap in such circumstances would be sure to meet economic difficulties with further despotic inroads on economic freedom and on the civil liberties associated with and dependent upon economic freedom. Such a downward spiral would reenforce the spiral of protest, resistance, and repression. An increasing prospect of failure to meet tribute or transfer quotas or to appreciate the "comradely" relationship with the Soviet Union, would foster suspicion among Soviet leaders and demands for tighter controls. Western social, economic, and political institutions, as examples of non-Soviet alternatives, are dangerous to the Soviet regime. As exhibited willingness to protect Soviet interests in a nonrestive, tribute-paying United States became the condition for success in U.S. politics, the U.S. political leadership would become more inclined to dismantle these provocative institutions from our bourgeois past. At some point in these processes our more progressive leaders might well have to issue the conventional appeal to Soviet forces to save the country from the forces of reaction.

It is often argued that were the U.S. government to disarm, the Soviet dictators would be embarrassed by no longer having an excuse to offer to their own population for their military spending and, more generally, for their economic and spiritual oppression. But this argument, if anything, embodies a reason for pessimism about the consequences of a unilateral U.S. disarmament. A disarmed and tribute-paying United States that was nevertheless still more prosperous and less oppressive than the Soviet Union would be an affront to the Soviet regime in the eyes of its subjects. But it is implausible to conclude that, under such circumstances, the response by the Soviet leaders would be radically to liberate their regime so that it would compare better to the still relatively prosperous United States. Rather, if such comparisons in the minds of their subjects matter to them, the likely response of the Soviet rulers would be to attempt to increase the transfer of wealth from the United States to the Soviet Union or, if that were not possible, to undermine further the liberal capitalistic institutions that remained in the United States and that were the source of its continued relative prosperity. The Soviet rulers would much rather see a decline in U.S. prosperity (even at some cost to the prosperity of their own subjects) than a diminution of their own totalitarian powers.

There are reasons for thinking that this process, over time, would go significantly further than Finlandization. As the perceived ultimate rival of the Soviet Union, the United States would be a candidate for permanent economic and social incapacitation—perhaps being subject, over time, to something like a Morganthau plan.[12] Such an incapacitation would, in Soviet eyes, be a fitting fate for the homeland of the institutions and ideas that communism is concerned with destroying. The long-term prospect of U.S. unilateral disarmament could easily be something as bad as East European satellization.[13]

Permissible Strategic Defense

Assuming costs of this sort in the abandonment of defensive systems, there is room for the justified adoption of a less-than-perfect defensive structure. But before describing the features of such a system, we should clarify the constraints on a justified defensive system that flow from the proscription of direct, intentional, killing of bystanders. Our current form of defense against a Soviet nuclear attack is the legacy of policies based on wholehearted preparation for directly inflicting massive destruction upon the Soviet population. Although during the last decade there has been some shift, both in targeting doctrine and in weapons characteristics, toward Soviet military and related targets, it is difficult to see the current U.S. policy as a genuinely counterforce policy that conforms to a Just War Defense doctrine. It is far from clear that current targeting decisions are systematically and fully dictated by (sufficiently narrowly defined) counterforce considerations. Moreover, it is not enough to satisfy a Just War Defense doctrine that weapons originally designed indiscriminately to maximize deaths be retargeted toward military objectives. A true counterforce policy satisfying a Just War Defense doctrine requires a sustained effort over time toward minimizing nonaggressor deaths. Such a policy requires counterforce weapons, in other words weapons themselves designed, to the greatest feasible extent, to strike discriminately at aggressors. Although there has been some movement toward lower yields and more precisely delivered warheads, it is doubtful that this has been pushed toward its maximally feasible extent or that this transition has been guided by a firm policy of striking only at aggressors.

(The argument against countervalue deterrence is not based on its being wrong to threaten countervalue retaliation. It might well be permissible to create the *deceptive* impression that one would carry out a murderous retaliatory attack. But if the impermissibility of the *use* of such a capacity comes to be more widely acknowledged, as it should, the maintenance of this capacity will itself become more and more politically infeasible. The impermissibility of the use of such countervalue strikes undermines the capacity to generate credible deterring countervalue threats.)

A plausible alternative to the current countervalue nuclear deterrence strategy would combine two basic elements. The first would be a purely protective system designed to ward off Soviet missiles, bombers, and so on. The moral virtues of such a system are obvious. Its direct purpose would be to protect the rights of the U.S. populace and at least many elements of such a system might operate without any (even indirect) killing of Soviet bystanders. Recent advances in, for example, computer and laser technology, enhance the feasibility of such a purely protective system.[14] While the development and deployment of such a system might require cancellation of treaty clauses by which the United States and Soviet rulers have handed over to each other as hostages their respective populations, this is hardly grounds for objection to such a system. Moreover, the proposed "weapons" in space would be limited to devices designed to destroy already activated or launched Soviet delivery systems.

Another possible element within a purely protective structure would be a revitalized civil defense. If the active portions of a protective system work reasonably well, but not perfectly, then a system of shelters and stored supplies may further secure people's rights. While assessing the feasibility of a civil defense program is beyond the scope of this chapter, it is important to note both that the coercion and regimentation involved in a state-mandated program of civil defense would be offensive to the values of a free society and that an optimal level of civil defense might be generated by individuals' free choices in the market. (The present low production of privately produced shelters may well represent rational choice under our current defenseless circumstances.)

If a protective system were fully protective no further defensive structures would be necessary. Unfortunately, this is extremely unlikely. Given less than perfect protection, a potential aggressor could pose a serious threat with the only prospective cost to the aggressor being the expenditure of its weapons. For this reason any purely protective system must be supplemented with a counterforce capacity sufficient to deny an aggressor the power gainfully to follow up any initial attack. The justifying aim of such a counterforce capacity is the destruction of the military machinery the aggressor has set into motion. The hope is that the combined prospect of a fairly successful protective system and a counterforce reaction will deter any aggressive assault.

While a counterforce defensive system reduces to zero the number of bystanders intentionally killed, no doubt the reduction, relative to a countervalue system, in the number of bystanders unintentionally killed by its use would be less dramatic. Nevertheless, a good-faith effort to focus a U.S. reactive attack on elements of the aggressor's military structure, including a good-faith effort to develop weapons specifically appropriate to this counterforce strategy, should significantly reduce the number of bystanders killed by a nuclear counterattack. Moreover, a known, long-term, counterforce policy shifts the moral responsibility for the deaths of bystanders killed by defensive counterforce strikes to the rulers of the aggressor state.

Since the proposals put forth here are squarely within the tradition historically defined by Catholic Just War Theory, it is natural to inquire how they relate to the positions taken in the recent pastoral letter of the National Conference of Catholic Bishops.[15] In its final form this letter embodies deep ambivalence both toward Just War doctrine and in its actual recommendations. The document at first acknowledges the possibility of the morally acceptable use of force for the sake of "preserving the kind of peace which protects human dignity and human rights," while adding the traditional requirements that the defensive force be discriminate and proportionate. It thus quite properly condemns the use of nuclear weapons "for the purpose of destroying population centers" and it further condemns even the intention of such use as part of a deterrence strategy. In accordance with traditional doctrine, the bishops maintain that a counterforce strike may be rendered morally unacceptable by the loss it would indirectly inflict on innocents being disproportionate to the benefit expected. For the bishops, then, the acceptability of a given counterforce nuclear strategy should depend upon a careful analysis of the expected benefits of that strategy against its expected costs. Such an analysis of the overall defense orientation of this book would find it to be morally acceptable. For this strategy, including confrontation avoidance, purely defensive systems and strictly counterforce weaponry, by both reducing the risks of nuclear war (and of bystander casualties in the event of war) and enhancing the security of our valued freedoms, does not seem to involve expected evils disproportionate to the expected evils it would thwart.

Unfortunately, the bishops do not carry out this analysis. Instead, in effect they abandon their own theoretical tradition by maintaining that any counterstrike that would kill a sufficiently large number of innocents must be considered indiscriminate. This, of course, is to renounce the idea that intention makes a significant moral difference. Indeed the pastoral letter even goes on to suggest that the use of the notions of counterforce and indirection bears the taint of "perverted . . . moral casuistry." The bishops arrive, then, at the highly restrictive, if not quite principled, position that even defensive warfare that is completely targeted against aggressors will be morally unacceptable if *too many* innocents (however many that may be) will be killed.

This restrictive principle demands the abandonment of our current deterrence strategy—as does traditional Just War doctrine and the position espoused here. However, this new restrictive principle also condemns *all* feasible strategies of forcible national defense. Nevertheless, the bishops do recognize that major reliable bilateral arms reductions are, at best, many years away and that some defensive strategy is needed for the interim. Their compromising solution is "a strictly conditional moral acceptance of nuclear deterrence." Yet this seems to constitute an acquiescence, for the foreseeable future, not merely to counterforce defense but to full-fledged countervalue deterrence. Having adopted an unsoundly overrestrictive principle, the bishops' only defense against their own doctrine is to pretend that it does not exist.

Another widely discussed, albeit less sophisticated and more politically naive, treatment of these issues appears in Jonathan Schell's *The Fate of the Earth*. According to Schell, any decision to maintain any strategic weaponry must be viewed as a decision to render likely the extinction of mankind, while the only end improved by such a fateful decision is the existence of sovereign nation-states. Given this choice, Schell has little problem condemning all defensive measures and endorsing a "solution" wherein "mankind, acting for the first time in history as a single entity, can reorganize its political life."[16] Schell shows no concern for what evils such a political life might bring, either for us or our descendants, nor any concern for strategic protection against such evils, protection which at the same time would lower the current danger of nuclear destruction.

The proposals suggested here and developed and further vindicated throughout this book represent an alternative both to sustained and even intensified nuclear confrontation and countervalue terror and to the surrender of our rights to some ominous global political "solution." This suggested defensive orientation would not have unduly grandiose aims. It would be devoted to the protection of the core rights, respect for which defines a free society. It should lessen the likelihood of war, allow us to wash our hands of sometimes criminal and almost always dangerous alliances, while preserving the freedom that is our central political inheritance. The adoption of such a system would involve a rejection of the idea that the U.S. government has the capacity, wisdom, or prerogative to fine-tune the world, an idea that is ludicrous enough in its more modest domestic incarnation. By reminding us that the rights of individuals are at stake, rather than some vague collective goal such as world leadership or victory in the Cold War, this defensive posture is less likely to turn our minds away from the search for viable disarmament schemes. And the purely protective element in this defensive structure may someday greatly facilitate such a scheme by providing a necessary alternative to reliance on Soviet goodwill.

Notes

1. John C. Ford, "The Morality of Obliteration Bombing," reprinted in *War and Morality,* ed. R. Wasserstrom (Belmont, Calif.: Wadsworth, 1970), p. 15.

2. See, of course, John Locke's *Second Treatise* in *Two Treatises of Government,* ed. Peter Laslett (Cambridge, England: Cambridge University Press, 1960). For three quite divergent contemporary statements see Tibor R. Machan, *Human Rights and Human Liberties* (Chicago: Nelson-Hall, 1975); Robert Nozick, *Anarchy, State and Utopia* (New York: Basic Books, 1974); and Murray Rothbard, *The Ethics of Liberty* (Atlantic Heights, N.J.: Humanities Press, 1982).

3. The so-called Principle of Fairness upon which this type of argument turns is subject to a powerful critique in Nozick, *Anarchy, State and Utopia,* pp. 93–95. Arguments for conscription as the only (or best) feasible method of recruiting for the military are dealt with in chapter 8.

4. Just one of the oversimplifications of this discussion is the contrast between the nonproduction and the production of the public good

rather than between the prospect of its underproduction if financed voluntarily and its overproduction if financed coercively. On financing public goods noncoercively see David Friedman, *The Machinery of Freedom* (New Rochelle, N.Y.: Arlington House, 1978), ch. 34. A different approach, based on quite different premises appears in Tibor R. Machan's "Dissolving the Problem of Public Goods," in *The Libertarian Reader,* ed. T.R. Machan, (Totowa, N.J.: Rowman and Littlefield, 1982).

5. A commitment to something like doctrine 4 is present in J.J. Thomson's "Self-Defense and Rights," Lindley Lecture, 1976 (Lawrence: University of Kansas Press, 1977). Thomson, however, eschews any theoretical explanation for her various case-by-case intuitions.

6. At least 300,000 civilians were killed in Germany through strategic air strikes. Perhaps that many were killed in the infamous strike against Dresden alone. Of course, different individuals and policy-setting groups put forward different and changing bombing strategies and justifications (both technical and moral). But to a substantial degree, British strategic bombing strategy was guided by the goal of indiscriminately striking at German city dwellers and their homes. Even less clear in the strategists' minds was what further goal would be achieved by "area" or "morale" bombing. Among the many discussions, see, e.g., B.H. Liddell Hart, *History of the Second World War* (London: Cassell, 1970), ch. 33; B. Barrie Paskins and Michael Dockrill, *The Ethics of War* (Minneapolis: University of Minnesota Press, 1979), ch. 1; and George Quester, *Deterrence before Hiroshima* (New York: John Wiley and Sons, 1966), chs. 7 and 9.

7. See James T. Johnson's *Just War Tradition and the Restraint of War* (Princeton, N.J.: Princeton University Press, 1981). In R. Wasserstrom, *War and Morality,* see Ford's "The Morality of Obliteration Bombing," which condemns Allied anticity attacks of World War II, and E. Anscombe's oracular "War and Murder." The literature on the central element in Just War Theory, the Doctrine of Double Effect, is immense, much of it associated with other types of putatively just killing, such as abortion. For one critical treatment, see H.L.A. Hart's "Intention and Punishment," *Oxford Review* 4 (1967). For more favorable treatments see Germain Grisez's ambitious and difficult "Toward a Consistent Natural Law Ethics of Killing," *American Journal of Jurisprudence* 15 (1970), and Joseph Boyle's "Toward Understanding the Principle of Double Effect," *Ethics* (July 1980).

8. See the discussion of alternative justifications of self-defense and their implications for proportionality in George Fletcher's *Rethinking the Criminal Law* (Boston: Little, Brown, 1978), pp. 855–875. A full theory of justified defense would consider separately the choice

between enough force and no more force than produces proportionate injury, as that choice applies respectively to guilty aggressors, innocent aggressors, and bystanders.

9. Jan Narveson, "Pacifism: A Philosophical Analysis," in Wasserstrom, *War and Morality,* p. 72. Also see Narveson's "Violence and War," in *Matters of Life and Death,* ed. Tom Regan (New York: Random House, 1980).

10. The advisability of U.S. governmental support for anti-Soviet freedom fighters defended in chapter 10 gives less weight to this condition regarding morally compromising endeavors.

11. Neither here nor in what follows do I endorse any particular decision-theoretic model. If one accepts the premises that being red is better than being dead and that fewer would be killed under the worst possible postdisarmament regime than under the worst possible nuclear war, and if one also accepts a minimax decision rule, one has to favor unilateral disarmament. The weak link here is the minimax rule, though the premises are also dubitable.

12. This viciously punitive plan, formulated by Roosevelt's Secretary of the Treasury, Henry Morgenthau, Jr., and sometimes endorsed by Roosevelt, would have permanently suppressed all industrial activity in postwar Germany, converting what was left of that country "into a country primarily agricultural and pastoral in its character."

13. This outline of a scenario embodies fairly harsh judgments about Soviet (or, some would emphasize, Russian) intentions and capacities. Moreover, it envisions, perhaps suspiciously, a possible world domination for the Soviet Union more complete than history has ever seen. On the other hand history has never seen either the current technological capacities for world domination or the unilateral disarmament of the major rival to an aspiring world dominator.

14. See, e.g., Lt. Gen. Daniel O. Graham, *High Frontier: A New National Strategy* (Washington, D.C.: Heritage Foundation, 1982).

15. *The Challenge of Peace: God's Promise and Our Response,* adopted by the National Conference of Catholic Bishops in Chicago on May 2, 1983—excerpts printed in the *New York Times* on May 5, 1983.

16. Jonathan Schell, *The Fate of the Earth* (New York: Alfred Knopf, 1982), p. 219. Despite its pomposity and obscure moral argument this book has some virtues, including its depiction of the horrors of even Hiroshima-scale nuclear warfare and its critique of countervalue deterrence theory.

2 Empirical Basis of Defense Policy

R.J. Rummel

Why war? How peace? Science has now given us empirically well-supported answers to these questions, but these answers have yet to inform the defense policy debate. Indeed, when it comes to assumed generalizations about cooperation and conflict, the balance of power, the causes of war, arms races, and the like, the need for well-established empirical-based knowledge and understanding is not even widely acknowledged despite its critical importance to policy. Real-world assumptions underlying the defense debate seem to be accepted without question, as for example that

1. Conflict and cooperation are opposites—the more conflict the less cooperation, and vice versa.
2. Increasing trade, aid, cultural and scientific exchange, and diplomatic interaction with another state decreases the possibility of war with it.
3. There is and has been a Soviet–American arms race.
4. Arms races lead to war.
5. Power parity means stability, which means peace.

Probably most participants in the defense debate would identify at least four of the preceding statements as true; at least three of the statements would likely be considered undoubtedly true. Yet, for all five, empirical findings and tests are generally negative.[1] If defense policies are to secure the nation and protect freedom, they must be factually and empirically sound, consistent with known social laws and principles of human and group behavior.

Certain empirical assumptions about defense are fundamental to the complex defense debate and underlie the most important policies. One set of assumptions concerns the nature of international conflict and its relationship to cooperation, such as trade, aid, cultural exchange, joint scientific efforts, and so on. A second key set of assumptions involves war and peace, especially the conditions and causes of war; the nature of the global and regional military threat; and which defense-related policies will help maintain peace and reduce the risk of war, but also defend a nation should war occur. A third set of assumptions pertains to power, its nature and function in preserving or protecting a country, and the efficacy of various assertions of power. National defense is, after all, basically the management and use of naked power—force and coercion. A fourth set of assumptions, perhaps most evident in the public debate on defense, concerns arms races in general, and a presumed Soviet–American arms race in particular.

Two sets of assumptions that focus on the intentions and capabilities of other states also underlie the current defense policy debate. The first set concerns which states are a threat to U.S. survival as a free society, particularly through their aggressive pursuit of regional or global domination. The second involves the capability of these states actually to endanger American interests and ultimately to check or defeat the United States in war.

These key assumptions of the defense debate, whether about war and peace, arms races, or hostile states, really comprise a system of beliefs, a *defense perspective,* that informs and orients people in their position on major defense issues. The "dove" versus "hawk" labels, although much overused and abused, do reflect such different perspectives on defense.

To be clear, it is not the purpose here to argue or show that one defense perspective or another, as such, better fits reality. Rather, the focus will be on the key assumptions themselves. In particular, this chapter will bring out those related empirical propositions about conflict, war, and peace that have, so far as our knowledge has developed, the greatest confirmation; and those related principles of human and group behavior that provide the soundest relevant understanding.[2] General empirical propositions about conflict and cooperation will first be presented, followed by an integrating overview and perspective on the process of conflict. The propositions about the major threat—Soviet intentions and capability—affecting U.S. security will be more appropriately covered in the next chapter, but will be assumed here in order to illustrate and apply the propositions about conflict and cooperation, especially war and peace. Before presenting the substance of the chapter, however, some discussion of the empirical basis and sources of these propositions and of their limitations is necessary.

Irenology—The Science of Peace

Since the 1930s there has been a growing literature of scientific research on peace and war. This work has involved extensive and systematic data collection, quantitative analyses, and mathematical models. Much of it is abstract and general, with little obvious relevance to immediate defense policy issues. Even when relevant, most of this literature is technical, demanding a knowledge of particular statistical and mathematical terms and assumptions. Indeed, specific studies are often opaque even to the scientist, unless he or she is skilled in the particular techniques, methods, or models used in a study.

Hundreds of scientific studies on international conflict now exist. These cover all states, all recorded wars and periods of peace, all kinds of conflict behavior for which data can be collected, and most conceivable causes and conditions of war. No established statistical technique has been neglected; no applicable scientific research design ignored; no reasonable relevant natural or social science model or theory unexploited.[3] All this research constitutes an emerging scientific field.

The name of this field remains in dispute. Some favor "peace research," but this label has become associated with political movements, especially on the left. "Polemonology," or the science of war, is a possibility, but this leaves out nonviolent conflict, as well as the study of peace. Another possible name is "irenology," or the science of peace (from Irene, the goddess of peace), which has been adopted here. For in order to understand peace, irenology must concern not only the nature and conditions of peace, but also the transformation of peace into conflict, violence, and war; and their transformation back into peace.

Irenology of course begs many questions about the limits and role of science in analyzing peace and conflict. Especially crucial are questions about the best balance between science on the one hand, and on the other hand philosophy, insight, personal experience, and wisdom.

Surely there are limits to irenology. Conflict and peace are often contextual, partially dependent on unique individuals and the accidental conjunction of events. Great uncertainty permeates human affairs. Violence and war, perhaps above all, most depend on an invisible roulette wheel. And yet there are certain commonalities to cooperation and conflict, peace and war. There are patterns, trends, and probabilities that often comprise the unstated assumptions underlying our assessment of foreign and defense policies. And science is the best method man has developed to determine and assess generalities.

A judgment on the value of irenology need no longer be speculative. The accumulated literature now shows the applicability and value of scientific methods for determining commonalities, patterns, and trends in conflict and peace, and for predicting or forecasting the same. The question is no longer whether there can be a science of peace. It is now how irenology bears on this or that defense policy issue and what it has to say. Nonetheless, this literature has been generally ignored in the public debate on foreign and defense policies.

There may be several reasons for this. Early scientific work was heralded by much trumpet-blowing about the presumed value of science and the Neanderthal quality of traditional scholarship, even though the heaves and sighs of the scientific elephant often brought forth an abstract mouse. However, irenology has progressed far beyond this stage, and much useful work is carried on with quiet competence and an appreciation of the essential partnership between science and scholarship, intuition and method, real-world experience and theory.

Of course, irenology is still abstract and technical. Few have been willing to translate their findings into policy terms and also able to make the significance of their results clear. Even when results have been related to foreign and defense policies, they have been buried in the more technically oriented journals and books; and even if the interpretations are published in plain English in a policy-oriented journal, its readers may be forgiven their skepticism. After all, the data and methods will be unknown and may have been juggled to force out a congenial conclusion.

Regardless of the reason, there has been a growing and unfortunate gulf between scientific findings on peace and war and defense policy analysis. Above all, there has been little utilization of such scientific findings to assess the course of and options for Soviet–American relations.

Sources and Bases

The empirical propositions presented in this chapter are based on a screening of nearly 1,000 published and unpublished books, articles, research reports, and papers. Of these, 368 studies contained 682 competent and relevant scientific analyses of international conflict, violence, war, or peace.[4]

To capture the flavor of these analyses, several are described briefly here:

F.H. Denton and Warren Phillips factor analyzed the patterns in 375 wars between 1480 and 1900.

Maurice East determined the dependence of violence on the international status quo for about 120 states and 381 conflicts between 1848 and 1961.

Wayne H. Ferris analyzed the relationship to the power of states of 42 wars between 1850 and 1966.

Matthew Melko assessed the characteristics and causes of peace in 52 peaceful societies in recorded history.

Andres Onate analyzed the relationship between international and internal conflict for all states between 1950 and 1970.

Robert Randle statistically assessed the nature and causes of the outcomes of 500 wars between 1500 and 1971.

Michael D. Wallace studied the dependence of war on capabilities and change between 1820 and 1964.[5]

Though these studies represent only a fraction of the total analyzed for this chapter, they illustrate the variety and nature of the available scientific investigations of war and peace. These analyses constitute a reservoir of scientific findings, but their prodigious detail and diversity may overwhelm most defense policy analysts. One study, for example, presents over 30,000 correlations and over a dozen parameters for more than 236 attributes and behaviors of states.[6] Clearly, some scheme for organizing such findings, especially when multiplied across a large, varied literature, is essential.

Elsewhere, a field theory of international relations has been elaborated and tested along with 56 related empirical propositions on the phases, causes and conditions, and nature and termination of international conflict, violence, and war.[7] These propositions provided an ordering of the results of the 682 analyses in irenology and sharply defined a number of statements about conflict and peace for which there was strong scientific support. From these, only those that have found the most support from irenology and are most important for defense policy, particularly securing peace with freedom, are included here.

Caveats

A number of caveats on the propositions here and in chapter 3 should be made explicit. First, though to ignore sound and consistent scientific findings on a question is unwise, to make a judgment solely on scientific grounds is equally unwise. Truth stands on a three-legged stool, of which science is only one leg. The second is reason; and the third includes insight, intuition, and imagination. But what in the end is the best defense policy for a free society is a matter of both morality and practicality. Irenology is valuable as one necessary, but not sufficient, ingredient in any final assessment of policy options.

A second caveat is that, while the propositions are precisely worded and the scientific analyses related to them usually are systematically or quantitatively done, the interpretation of their relevance to defense, particularly to Soviet–American relations, must rely on traditional scholarly analysis.

Finally, although the propositions are presented and discussed singly, the international relations of war and peace constitute a field, a gestalt, an organic whole. As in analyzing the liver and lungs separately from the human body, the propositions really divide out factors, causes, and conditions for analysis that are holistically interrelated and play an interdependent role in, say, Soviet–American relations. For analysis, the propositions must be divided out; but *for a full final assessment, the propositions must be considered as a totality.* Such an integrative analysis is given in chapter 3.

A final word of caution: In scientific work and its translation into practical policies the scientist grows to appreciate the room for error and the impossibility of empirical certitude, always aware that by future standards and knowledge, today's science may be considered primitive. However, today's science is the only science we have. And in areas in which subjective judgment and emotion reign, this science can at least help to improve our forecasts and policies. This is not to say that science is or can ever be the sole source of truth. But the prudent analyst and policymaker should certainly take into account scientific analysis of peace and war.

Conflict, War, and Peace

1. Conflict is a balancing of powers, and cooperation depends on expectations aligned with power.[8]

What causes international conflict, including violence and war? Surely interstate relations involve a complex subjective field of perceptions, expectations, interests, and capabilities. Any putative cause or condition of conflict, whether ideology, aggressive goals, power parity, bad leaders, population or resource pressure, or geopolitical forces and the like would operate within this field. Such possible causes and conditions would form a whole, a process, and an equilibrium. In short, as part of a field between two states, the causes and conditions of conflict are *contextual.* And this context and the larger subjective field within which context is shaped evolve out of a *process* of interstate interaction.

First, states are specific complexes of decisionmakers operating within particular historically evolved and politically balanced bureaucratic and organizational forces and restraints and through diverse interests and expectations. Moreover, each state has its own national character, or cultural matrix, through which its leaders see the world and interpret the intentions and capabilities of other states. In this sense each state is unique, a different subjective universe. What matters is not so much the objective content of an event, attribute, or behavior, but its subjective meaning and value within the particular perspective of a state's leaders.

Second, there is no way the intentions of another state's leaders can be known with certainty, nor can the state's real defense capabilities be assessed except in rough terms outside of the ultimate test of war. Moreover, intentions and capabilities can be severely compromised by a weakness of will and interests, both variables exceedingly difficult to judge.

Third, states (meaning the diverse individuals and groups in a state relevant to international relations) therefore evolve among themselves a structure of relations as porcupines learn to sleep together on a cold night: gingerly, through trial and error. This process is a discontinuous series of mutual adjustments involving relatively harmonious periods of cooperation interspersed by periods of confrontation and conflict.

Fourth, through contention and confrontation states learn to read more accurately each other's field of expression, the totality of clues that communicate each other's interests (goals and means), capabilities, and will (including credibility). Through this reality-testing they adjust their perceptions of each other and develop a balance among their respective interests, abilities, and will to use diverse powers (among which coercive, authoritative, bargaining, and raw force are most important).

This results in a balance (equilibrium) of powers, where power equals interests times capability times will. If any one of these components of power is zero, a state's power is zero. Capability alone is useless unless there are clear interests to give it direction and the will to apply it. Similarly, will or interests without capability can achieve or secure nothing. Through conflict, states grow to appreciate and adjust to each other's peculiar combination of interests, capabilities, and will.

Fifth, conflict hammers out a more realistic structure of expectations between states. A state's expectations are subjective, perhaps unconscious or unarticulated predictions as to the outcome of its policies and behavior regarding other states. As a result of conflict, states develop norms and rules, formal and informal understandings, treaties and agreements concerning the issues in dispute. All these constitute a structure of expectations, a region of order, agreement, and cooperation in their relations.

This structure of expectations that develops out of conflict is based on the balance of powers determined by the conflict. An international conflict thus produces two distinct but connected components of international relations: a structure of expectations (a cooperative order) associated with the complex of rules, norms, agreements, and the like, evolving from and perhaps even terminating the conflict; and a balance of powers—of interests, capabilities, and will—undergirding these expectations.

2.   A gap between expectations and power causes conflict.

Change is the constant of life. Interests shift, wills alter, capabilities vary, and the mutual balance of powers diverges in time from the structure of expectations it supports. Expectations, whether embodied in treaties, formal agreements, or informal understandings, change slowly and usually through accumulated interpretations and evolving interaction. However, the balance of powers can alter rapidly and sharply, as when a state's leadership is tossed out, or its political system is overthrown; or when a dissatisfied state militarizes.

Since interests, capabilities, and will can change much more rapidly than expectations, a gap can form between the underlying balance of powers and the associated structure of expectations. The larger this gap, the more strain there is toward revising expectations—toward a change in who has and gets what—which will be more in accord with the changed balance of powers. The larger this gap, the more it is like explosive gas seeking a spark. All it needs is one trigger event—an assassination, a border raid, the sinking of a passenger liner—to disrupt the increasingly unstable expectations, to end the period of cooperation, and thus to initiate a new period of conflict. This renewed conflict behavior then functions to determine in fact what the changed balance is, and to adjust expectations to the new reality of what the states really want, can, and will do.

3.   Conflict and cooperation are not opposites, but complementary; artificially increasing cooperation with another state will not be likely to reduce or avoid conflict and may even increase it.[9]

As shown, conflict and cooperation, war and peace, are phases in the process of mutual learning and adjustment among states. Through conflict, violence, and war, states adjust to changing realities. Structures of expectation, and at its widest extent, the prevailing cooperative order, then reflect what specific adjustments are made between states;

and the expectations are undergirded by the associated balance of powers. It is the gap between this balance and expectations that creates a risk of conflict, and the larger this gap, the greater this risk.

Conflict-cooperation-conflict, and so on, is then a continuous process in the interaction of all individuals, groups, and states. But this is not a cycle. It is a helix, since all learn about one another from previous conflicts and cooperation. There is a successive dampening of conflict as a result, and peace lasts longer. The process is a coil ascending in accumulated learning through time. Thus newlyweds learn to live together; postrevolutionary periods settle into law and order; states learn to coexist competitively as have the United States and Soviet Union since World War II.

Assumed here is the usual scientific "all other things constant." Conflict decreases and peace lasts longer only as long as the bases of a relationship remain constant. Let a new baby be born into a family, a coup change a postrevolutionary power balance, and a new party assume control over foreign policy, and family, state, and interstate relations will undergo a new process of adjustment. In the international life of states, therefore, the ideological change in leadership, the intervention of a Big Power in a state's affairs, a breakdown in the international economic system, or a producer's boycott (as with oil in 1973) affecting all states, can create new conditions and require a whole new process of power-balancing and reordering of expectations between the parties.

If the conditions of Soviet–American relations were stabilized, therefore, an increasingly cooperative and less conflictual coexistence should develop. Such did in fact appear to occur in the moderation of Soviet–American relations from the deep Cold War years of the early 1950s to the détente of the early 1970s. But underlying the détente of the 1970s was a shifting in the balance of power toward the Soviet Union and a consequent increase in the risk of war, which will be discussed in chapter 3.

The policy of détente saw cooperation as the lever to lessen conflict. The backbone assumption of the Nixon-Kissinger foreign policy of détente, continued essentially through the Ford and Carter administrations, was that cooperative activities with the Soviet Union would entangle it in a web of beneficial bonds, difficult to break by aggressive or tension-increasing behavior. In sum, cooperation would reduce conflict, and, it was hoped, the risk of war.

However, empirical research does not support any such general connection between conflict and cooperation.[10] Cooperation is an *outcome* of the adjustment process through which expectations are aligned with what states can, will, and want to do. Cooperation that is not organic to this process, but plastered over an underlying conflict, eventually may only intensify the overt conflict behavior necessary to adjust to changes in the balance of powers.

In any case cooperation does not alter the risk of war. The existence of much more Soviet–American cooperation in the late 1970s—the fruit of détente—did not prevent a marked increase in the risk of war, actual and perceived, by 1981. Nor would more cooperation necessarily have reduced this risk. As will be shown subsequently, it was not lack of cooperation but the considerable shift in the balance of powers underlying the Soviet–American structure of expectations (and core status quo) that increased this risk of war.

Violence and War

    4.   Violence assumes a disrupted status quo.[11]

The status quo is the existing division in rights and duties, of what is "ours" and "theirs." It is the hard core of any structure of expectations, usually well defined, and the major values in any interaction.

In international relations the status quo is defined by who has sovereignty over, control over, or the actual or implied allegiance of the people living in a territory. A conflict may be over a border area (Vietnam versus Cambodia in 1977–1978); the independence of a colony (the Algerian War, 1954–1962); the independence of a state (the Israeli–Arab War, 1948); or the control of a state (the Soviet invasion of Czechoslovakia, 1968). Moreover, a territorially defined status quo is often the source of conflict, as over the rights of Greek versus Turkish Cypriots.

"Ours" and "theirs" may refer to the allegiance or ideology of territorially defined peoples. We "lost" Cuba to the Soviet Union; they "gained" Angola and Ethiopia. The "free world" now consists of countries x, y, and z; NATO will be "weakened" if Italy has a communist government. And so forth.

The disruption of the status quo may not cause violence. A new status quo may be determined nonviolently, as in the Panama Canal Treaty negotiated by the United States and Panama and the granting of independence to many former colonies. However, the status quo defines the high stakes—it defines what is worth violence. A disrupted status quo is a necessary condition of violence.

What constitutes non–status quo expectations? This is the entire complex of implicit and formal understandings, agreements, and treaties governing relationships and interactions between parties that do not define who has what rights and duties over what territory. Trade agreements, consular understandings, disarmament treaties, diplomatic norms, and the like, constitute the non–status quo part of our international structures of expectations.

> 5.   A gap between the status quo and the balance of powers causes war.[12]

As with violence generally, a breakdown in the status quo is a necessary cause of war. War is fought over territorially defined sovereignty, control, or influence. There are always those states that support a status quo (call them the Status Quo Powers) and those that desire to change it to their benefit (the Anti–Status Quo or Revolutionary Powers). What maintains the status quo structure between these opposing forces is the inertia of established expectations and the underlying balance of powers: those that wish to change the status quo do not have the interests, capabilities, or will to overcome the resistance of the Status Quo Powers or to accept the perceived costs compared to the expected gains.

However, as this balance of powers supporting the status quo rapidly alters to favor the Revolutionary Powers, the prevailing status quo gets out of alignment with the supporting balance. And pressure builds up toward alteration in the status quo. Finally, some trigger event disrupts the status quo and war will most likely occur. War then serves to reorder the basic status quo more in line with the actual balance of powers among states.

Conflict and associated structures of expectations, war and its related status quo, are analogous to earthquakes and consequent stability in the earth's crust. At any moment the stability of the earth's surface is a balance of multiple underlying geological forces. However, these forces change, and while the crust itself may move slowly, perhaps an inch or two a year, in response to these forces, pressures may nonetheless increase in a particular areas. Finally the stress and strain on the crust reaches a point where a sudden slippage in one place is rapidly transformed into a wholesale readjustment of the crust to these forces, and the earth quakes. Wars are the earthquakes of international relations, the sudden readjustment among states to pressures on the status quo due to changes in underlying forces.

It is this insight that provides understanding of the recent increase, evident to all since 1980, in the risk of Soviet–American war. Of course, there is much room for informed disagreement on the nature and course of the conditions underlying Soviet–American relations. The conditions themselves need not be defined here, but only those factors they must influence in order to affect Soviet–American relations. The three elements especially important in a relationship are interests, capability, and will. The product of these defines a state's overall power; a balance of powers between two states is a balance among these elements. A radical change in the conditions of a relationship, then, would be felt through their impact on the interests of the parties, their capabilities (economic, military, organizational, leadership, and the like) to achieve these interests, and their will to use their capability to pursue them.

With this in mind (as will be described fully in chapter 3), there has been a critical shift in the conditions of Soviet–American relations, resulting in a sharp alteration in relative interests, capabilities, and wills and constituting a highly significant change in the balance of powers in the Soviet favor. Whether this change is perceived as good or bad in some sense is irrelevant here. The point is that this power shift far exceeds any change in the structure of expectations framing Soviet–American relations or the global international system. The status quo still mainly reflects the Western faith in free trade, diversity and pluralism, and the sovereignty and independence of states. But this Western international order is no longer consistent with the weakened interests, capability, and will of the Western leader, the Unites States, and the strengthened Anti–Status Quo Power, the Soviet Union. Why then should a Revolutionary Power continue to accept an order that manifestly contradicts its beliefs and professions when it perceives that the chief protector no longer has the same interest, capability, and will to defend this order?

The result is a strain between the underlying factual Soviet–American balance of powers and the status quo, a strain toward a fundamental readjustment more in line with the underlying reality. Some trigger— a crisis, a coup in a sensitive area, a new Soviet leadership—may disrupt this unstable structure and precipitate an attempt to realign expectations and the status quo. And in this readjustment lies the greater risk of war. In short, the great change in the Soviet–American balance of powers has increased the risk of violence and war between them. Indeed the risk of this war may soon, if not now, be at least as great as during the deepest Cold War years.

Escalation

6.   Power parity makes escalation to war more likely.[13]

A conflict that has reached the stage of violence (but not yet war) is always over deeply held status quo interests. Already costs have been incurred, the stakes are high, and further successes or losses depend on the balance of coercive power or forces. If one side is clearly superior in will and existing military capability and potential, the other side is likely to avoid escalation, if necessary by negotiating a resolution to the conflict. Of course, if the stakes warrant it, the stronger side is likely simply to threaten war in order to pressure the other into making concessions.

Power parity presents an ambiguous situation of coercive power in which each side simultaneously can believe that it will be victorious; or at least, that it will not lose. War clears up this ambiguity.

As will be discussed in the next chapter, though many experts contend that Soviet military strength is superior to that of the United States, there is sufficient ambiguity about their superiority to say that there *is* a rough parity in Soviet–American power. Thus the likelihood of escalation of a Soviet–American confrontation to war is increased. That there will be Soviet–American crises cannot be doubted. What is uncertain is when, where, and why. Regardless, as long as neither side is clearly superior, these crises probably will involve a greater risk of escalation to war than we have seen in a generation.

7. Credibility at stake risks escalation in violence.[14]

The more a state's credibility for defending its interests or meeting its commitments to defend others is at stake in a conflict, the more intense and prolonged the conflict may become. If the conflict is violent, the status quo is certainly involved; it is the status quo that is being fought over. Also at stake is a state's *reputation for power,* however, the image it projects of a will to protect its interests and follow through on threats. For leaders realize that what a state does in a current conflict is recorded on an international ledger to be consulted by others interested in pushing their own status quo interests. To show weakness of will, like the child in the schoolyard who submits, crying, to the taunts and slaps of a bully, is to invite a broad assault on many of one's interests. States fight not only to win a current conflict, but to avoid or reduce the costs of the next. The credibility stake, for example, became a major variable explaining U.S. military involvement in Vietnam under President Lyndon Johnson.

Currently, through formal alliances and treaties, the United States is politically committed to defend its allies if attacked by communist powers. These commitments are worthless, however, unless there is a *perceived* U.S. capability and will to meet these promises if attack does in fact occur. Moreover, even where formal U.S. commitments do not exist, many states maintain relations with the United States under an assumed protective umbrella of U.S. power. Finally, whatever overall foreign or defense policies are pursued, there will be certain irreducible American interests (such as protecting U.S. commerce on the open seas, safeguarding American diplomats abroad, or peacefully resolving disputes with other states) that can only be maintained or pursued within the framework of an American reputation for power.

Then, of course, there are the actuality and the image of the mailed fist behind Soviet control over Eastern Europe (witness Poland) and the uneasy status quo along the Sino–Soviet border. Moreover, the perceptions of growing Soviet power relative to the United States have probably eased the passage of Soviet arms and influence into the Third World.

For both the United States and Soviet Union there is much at stake in maintaining their credibility for the use of power. Let that credibility be questioned, as it was perceived by U.S. leaders to be in the Vietnam War, and violence and escalation to war become more likely.

For the United States, there is an increasing likelihood that future crises will be seen as such a test of American power. The events of the 1970s, so damaging to U.S. credibility, may have passed into history. The "loss" of South Vietnam, Laos, and Cambodia; the perceived relative American "inactivity" during the 1975 communist push in Portugal; the "submission" to the 1973 Arab oil boycott and blackmail; "withdrawal" from confrontation in Angola in 1975; and "acceptance" of Cuban-Soviet intervention elsewhere in Africa are now matters for historians to debate. But recent subdued or low-key responses to the Soviet invasion of Afghanistan and intervention in Poland, and Cuban-Soviet armed and possibly organized rebellions in Central America, coupled with the continued weakness of U.S. military capability, may be perceived as a loss or defeat of U.S. interests and will in continuing as the Western leader and pillar of the noncommunist world. The pressure is therefore increasingly on U.S. leaders to be tougher, to refuse to back down, to draw the line. Once established, a reputation for power requires only that it be maintained by the occasional and prudent exercise of power. Once lost, however, only the use of naked power remains.

8.   Abrupt perception of opportunity, threat, or injustice risks
      catalyzing and escalating conflict behavior.[15]

"Surprise" is a characteristic of events whose occurrence triggers perceptions of opportunity, threat, or injustice. These are the crisis creators, the disruptors of the status quo, the stiffeners of will. They are the immediate, the proximate causes of violence, escalation, and war. What such a trigger may be is unpredictable. It could be an assassination, a terrorist hijacking, a ship blown up, a sighting of dangerous weapons secretly mobilized in neighboring territory, a unilateral change in the status quo, a coup d'état, and so on.

Events that provoke *perception* of status quo territorial opportunity or threat can create a Soviet–American confrontation; sudden events that sharply alter this perception toward seeing greater opportunity or threat can cause an escalation toward or an increase in violence. The probability of such an event occurring is related also to the size of the gap between the status quo and the balance of powers, and the time over which this gap exists. When this gap is large (and possibly getting larger), as may currently be the case, the probability of some event within a Soviet–American crisis or confrontation triggering an escalation to violence and war is increasing.

Arms Races

    9.   An arms race may increase or decrease the risk of war.[16]

All this can now be focused on the very widely held belief that an arms race necessarily leads to, or increases the risk of, war. An arms race is the sequential, interrelated military buildup of two antagonistic states, each trying to keep up with or outdo the other in military power. Since 1840 there have been thirteen major arms races between major powers, only five of which ended in war.

The previous propositions provide understanding of why and when arms races may lead to war or peace.[17] An arms race cannot be isolated from the balance of powers and its relationship to the status quo. If an arms race really maintains the congruence between the balance and status quo, as when both sides to an arms race keep in pace with each other, *a stable peace will continue.* If, however, a Revolutionary Power is overtaking the Status Quo Power through an arms race, a large gap between power and status quo looms, creating a dangerous threat of war. This is especially true if, after allowing a one-sided arms buildup by the Revolutionary Power, the Status Quo Power undertakes to rectify the imbalance by beginning an arms race. This is the situation we are in now, and it will be addressed in the next chapter.

Whether one should accept or reject a defense policy involving an arms race with the Soviet Union thus depends on the overall balance of powers, Soviet intentions, and the Soviet–American status quo. Fear of an arms race itself is irrational and may actually lead, through a further loss of power, to the very war that provokes that fear.

Fostering Peace

> 10. War does not occur between democratic states, and vio-
>   lence very rarely; the more democratic a state the less its
>   foreign violence and war.[18]

This proposition is less relevant to Soviet–American relations and
defense than it is to the long-run foreign policy goal of a peaceful and
secure world. It is included here because defense is concerned not only
with security but also with peace; and not only peace with the Soviet
Union, but ultimately a global peace in which armaments are no longer
required. Is such a peace a dream? No, for it is solid in theory and well
verified empirically that the more freedom the people of a state have,
the less likely they will engage in foreign violence or war; and that war
does not occur between established free—democratic—states.

For evidence, just consider that of all the many wars fought all over
the world in the last two centuries, and of all the different kinds of
states that have made war on each other, in no case has this involved
war between two liberal democracies.[19] Democracies do not even arm
against each other. The long, unarmed border between Canada and
the United States is exemplary of the relations between democracies.
Moreover, regardless of the wide prevalence of low-level international
violence other than war, even this is practically unknown between democracies. In the almost forty years since World War II, there have
been only two marginal cases of violence: the so-called Cod War over
fishing rights between Iceland and Great Britain in 1973; and the controversial attack by Israel on the USS *Liberty* during the 1967 Arab–
Israeli War. And statistical tests show that this lack of war or violence
among democracies is highly significant: hardly a matter of chance,
hardly due to a lack of common borders, or hardly because there are
only a few democracies. Actually, according to Freedom House[20] there
were fifty-four democracies and twenty-seven related territories in 1982,
or 36 percent of the world's population. That one-third of the world's
nations should thus be free from war and interstate violence among
themselves is extremely significant.

The imperative of this proposition should be obvious. Supporting
and furthering freedom in the world is to nurture a global peace; furthering a democratic world is the route to a lasting global peace.

> 11. Polarity stimulates intense violence, while inhibiting non-
>   violent conflict behavior and low-level violence.[21]

The previous proposition notwithstanding, developing a world of free societies is a very long-run policy. But there is an intermediary peace-fostering goal that gets us halfway there and significantly lessens the risk of global war and the overall magnitude, if not the frequency, of international violence. By moving from the current bipolar system toward a pluralistic *multipolar* world, one of many and diverse centers of military and economic power, of overlapping and cross-pressured groups and interests, of countervailing checks and balances, the risk of war may be diminished. That is, by generalizing to the international level the reason why democracies engage in the least violence—by creating international pluralism, interest groups, and a horizontal distribution of power (this is not the same as creating a democratic world, for multipolarity allows for the coexistence of authoritarian and totalitarian states), peace may be enhanced.

Polarity is a political concept describing the centralization and dispersion of political power (including authority, coercion, and force). A *unipolar* world would be a world state, a global empire, or an effective global domination by one state. The present global system is *bipolar,* with the economic and military size of the United States and Soviet Union, and particularly the sheer destructive capability of their nuclear weapons, dominating any other combination of states. For this reason only these two are called superpowers. A *multipolar* world would have more than two dominating powers. Such would be, for example, an international system of Western Europe, Japan, the United States, the Soviet Union, and China, were they roughly equal in power.

The proposition asserts the following: As polarity in the system increases, the amount of conflict and the number of wars should *decrease,* but the *intensity* of wars and violence when they occur should *increase.* That is, a bipolar world compared to a multipolar one has fewer wars, but when they occur they carry the risk of involving the superpowers and thus being nuclear and global. This same principle operates within states, as can be seen in comparing pluralistic democracies to highly centralized (and polarized) states. Democracies have frequent internal nonviolent conflict, cases of isolated violence, and sometimes low-level generalized violence. For authoritarian and totalitarian states, however, there will be less conflict across society, but when it occurs it risks involving basic interests of the central government and escalating to revolution and internal war.

Similarly, a true multipolar world would lessen the danger of World War III and decrease the total of the world's population killed from lesser wars; but in the absence of a world of free societies, the continued existence of authoritarian and totalitarian states in a multipolar world would mean a higher frequency of war itself. Most people would probably agree that it is better to have more low-level wars, with a lesser risk of global war, than a few intense wars, each possibly escalating to involve everyone, everywhere, with every weapon.

Summary and the General Conflict Process

As described in propositions 1–5, conflict is a means through which states adjust their different interests, capabilities, and wills; it is a trial-and-error, mutual learning *process* that achieves an accommodation of some sort between what states want, can get, and are willing to get. These accommodations, whether forced or negotiated, explicit or implicit, written or unwritten, constitute a *social contract* delineating the status quo: who owns, controls, or influences what. And this status quo is based on a *balance of powers* (such as between the capability of states to bring force to bear, to make credible threats, to bargain) achieved by the conflict.

The picture of this process for hostile confrontations, deep crises, violence or war, is shown in figure 2–1. The vertical coordinate reflects the increase in mutual learning and adaptation between states; the horizontal coordinate measures the time passed. At the lower left, the jagged line pictures the process of hostile conflict between two states; it zigzags upward as the conflict drives home a mutual appreciation of each state's intentions and goals, military and economic capability and resources, leadership and morale, and character and resolution. Out of this is forged (1) accommodations and adjustments that define a partly explicit, partly implicit status quo; and (2) a supporting, congruent balance of powers (the triangle in figure 2–1).

In time interests, capability, or will may alter between the states in a way to favor the one—the revolutionary state—that wishes to change radically the status quo. Then the balance of powers is no longer supportive, as illustrated by the "gap" in Figure 2–1. The wider this gap, the more tension and hostility, and the greater the probability that some trigger will precipitate violence and war.

This violence and war will in turn end in a new status quo and balance of powers. Although this process seems cyclic and unending, conflict actually can become less intense and frequent. If the geopolitical and technological environment changes only slowly, such that there is no radical political change in relevant states and alliances, and technology does not alter the conditions of a relationship (as by a new mode of transportation neatly cutting distances, or a new product sharply altering economic relations), this process of learning and adaptation will gradually lessen the duration and intensity of conflict and lengthen and deepen the periods of peace. This process can be seen in operation

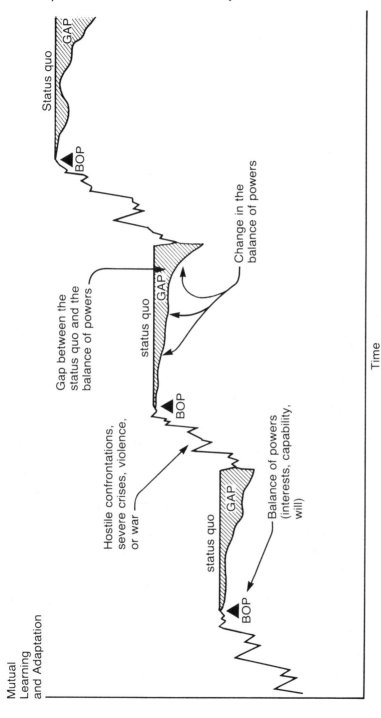

Figure 2-1. The Process of Conflict

between newlyweds, for whom the first year of marriage is one of frequent and intense conflict as they adjust to each other; but in time, barring a great change in situation (a child, a radical move, a change in career), the relationship becomes increasingly harmonious and conflicts decrease.

Such is the general process of conflict. In chapter 3 it will be applied to Soviet–American conflict, strategic trends, and the risk of war.

Notes

1. Assumptions (1) and (2) are treated under proposition 3 in the text of this chapter; assumption (3) is discussed under proposition 2 in the next chapter; assumption (4) is related to proposition 9, in this chapter; and why assumption (5) empirically fails is answered by proposition 6 in this chapter.

2. The propositions are largely discussed and tested in R. J. Rummel, *Understanding Conflict and War,* 5 vols. (Beverly Hills, Calif.: Sage, 1975–1981); the relevant principles are developed throughout these volumes and made explicit in volume 4 (1979).

3. A comprehensive survey of this scientific literature is given in Rummel, *Understanding Conflict and War* (especially vol. 4, app. 3). For other summaries or overviews of this literature, see William D. Coplin and Charles W. Kegley, Jr., eds., *A Multi-Method Introduction to International Politics* (Chicago: Markham, 1971); Karl W. Deutsch and Dieter Senghaas, "The Steps to War: A Survey of System Levels, Decision Steps, and Research Results," in *Sage International Yearbook of Foreign Policy Studies,* ed. Patrick J. McGowan, vol. 1 (Beverly Hills, Calif.: Sage, 1973), pp. 275–329; Michael Haas, "Societal Approaches to the Study of War," *Journal of Peace Research* 4 (1965): 307–323; Susan D. Jones and J. David Singer, *Beyond Conjecture in International Politics* (Itasca, Ill.: F. E. Peacock Publishers, 1972); Patrick J. McGowan and Howard B. Shapiro, *The Comparative Study of Foreign Policy: A Survey of Scientific Findings* (Beverly Hills, Calif.: Sage, 1973); Michael P. Sullivan, *International Relations: Theories and Evidence* (Englewood Cliffs, N. J.: Prentice-Hall, 1976); John A. Vasquez, "Statistical Findings in International Politics: A Data-Based Assessment" (Paper presented to the annual meeting of the American Political Science Association, San Francisco, Calif., September 2–5, 1975), and "Statistical Findings in International Politics: A Data-Based Assessment," *International Studies Quarterly* 20 (June 1976): 171–218; Quincy Wright, *A Study of War,* 2d ed. (Chicago: University of Chicago Press, 1965);

and Dina Zinnes, *Contemporary Research in International Relations: A Perspective and a Critical Appraisal* (New York: The Free Press, 1976).

4. For those interested in consulting some of these studies, the following references, as well as those described in note 5, are suggested. See, for example, Edward E. Azar, James P. Bennett, and Thomas J. Sloan, "Steps Toward Forecasting International Interactions," *The Papers of the Peace Science Society (International)* 23 (1974): 27–67; Richard E. Barringer, *War: Patterns of Conflict* (Cambridge, Mass.: MIT Press, 1972); Francis Beer, "How Much War in History: Definitions, Estimates, Extrapolations and Trends," *Sage Professional Papers in International Studies* 3 (Beverly Hills, Calif.: Sage Publications, 1974); William D. Coplin and J. Martin Rochester, "The Permanent Court of International Justice, the International Court of Justice, the League of Nations, and the United Nations: A Comparative Empirical Survey," *American Political Science Review* 66 (June 1972): 529–550; E. R. Dewey, "A New Cycle in War Discovered," *Cycles* 13 (February 1962): 33–40; "The 17.7-Year Cycle in War: 600 B.C.–A.D. 1957," *Research Bulletin 1962–64* (Pittsburgh, Pa: Foundation for the Study of Cycles, 1964); "More About Cycles in War," *Cycles* 20 (April 1969): 91–95; "Evidence of Cyclic Patterns in an Index of International Battles, 600 B.C.–A.D. 1957," *Cycles* 21 (June 1970): 121–158; William A. Gamson and Andre Modigliani, *Untangling the Cold War: A Strategy for Testing Rival Theories* (Boston: Little, Brown, 1971); Michael Haas, "International Subsystems: Stability and Polarity," *American Political Science Review* 64 (March 1970): 98–123; Ole R. Holsti, Richard Brody, and Robert C. North, "The Management of International Crisis: Affect and Action in American-Soviet Relations," in *Theory and Research on the Causes of War* (Englewood Cliffs, N. J.: Prentice-Hall, 1969), pp. 62–79; Ib Martin Jarvad, "Power versus Equality," *Proceedings of the International Peace Research Association, Second Conference*, vol. 1 (Assen, Netherlands: Van Gorcum, N. V., 1968), pp. 297–314; Robert B. Mahoney, Jr., "American Political-Military Operations and the Structure of the International System, 1946–1975" (Paper presented to the annual meeting of the section on military studies, International Studies Association, Ohio State University, October 1976); Raoul Naroll, Vern L. Bullough, and Frada Naroll, *Military Deterrence in History* (Albany, N. Y.: State University of New York Press, 1974); Sophia Peterson, "Events, Mass Opinion, and Elite Attitudes," in *Communication in International Politics,* ed. Richard Merritt (Urbana: University of Illinois Press, 1972); Robert F. Randle, *The Origins of Peace: A Study of Peacemaking and the Structure of Peace Settlements* (New York: The Free Press, 1972); J. David Singer and Melvin Small, *The Wages of War, 1818–1965: A Statistical Handbook* (New York: John

Wiley and Sons, 1972); R. Ko-Chih Tung, "International Structure, Inter- and Intra-State Violence: A Causal Model Analysis of Change," *Proceedings of the International Peace Research Association, Fifth Conference* (Oslo, 1975), pp. 229–257; U.S. Department of Defense, Office of Naval Research, *United States Naval Operations in Low-Level Warfare,* prepared by Bendix Aerospace Systems Division, December 1968; Richard Van Atta and Dale B. Robertson, "An Analysis of Soviet Foreign Economic Behavior from the Perspective of Social Field Theory" (Paper presented at the annual meeting of the Midwest Political Science Association, Chicago, 1975); John Voevodsky, "Quantitative Behavior of Warring Nations," *Journal of Psychology* 72 (1969): 269–292; Quincy Wright, "The Escalation of International Conflicts," *Journal of Conflict Resolution* 9 (December 1965): 434–449; and Dina Zinnes, "An Analytical Study of the Balance of Power Theories," in *Conflict Resolution: Contributions of the Behavioral Sciences,* ed. Clagett G. Smith (Notre Dame: University of Notre Dame Press, 1971), pp. 364–379.

5. These studies are found in F.H. Denton and Warren Phillips, "Some Patterns in the History of Violence," *Journal of Conflict Resolution* 12 (June 1968): 182–195; Maurice A. East, "Status Discrepancy and Violence in the International System: An Empirical Analysis," in *The Analysis of International Politics,* ed. James N. Rosenau, Vincent Davis, and Maurice A. East (New York: The Free Press, 1972), pp. 299–318; Wayne H. Ferris, *The Power Capabilities of Nation-States: International Conflict and War* (Lexington, Mass.: Lexington Books, 1973); Matthew Melko, *52 Peaceful Societies* (Oakville, Ontario: Canadian Peace Research Institute, 1973); Andres D. Onate, "The Conflict Interactions of the Peoples' Republic of China, 1950–1970," *Journal of Conflict Resolution* 18 (December 1974): 578–594; Robert F. Randle, *The Origins of Peace: A Study of Peacemaking and the Structure of Peace Settlements* (New York: The Free Press, 1972); and Michael D. Wallace, "Status, Formal Organization, and Arms Levels and Factors Leading to the Onset of War, 1820–1964," in *Peace, War, and Numbers,* ed. Bruce Russett (Beverly Hills, Calif.: Sage, 1972), pp. 49–69.

6. R. J. Rummel, *Dimensions of Nations* (Beverly Hills, Calif.: Sage, 1972).

7. R. J. Rummel, *Field Theory Evolving* (Beverly Hills, Calif.: Sage, 1977). In brief, the theory is that international relations is a social field, whose medium is the meanings, values, and norms of states. This medium is the seat of diverse forces potentially affecting international behavior. Which forces in fact will affect what states in which way depends in part on the position of states in the field, as defined by the field's space-time components. These are primarily wealth, power, to-

talitarianism, and authoritarianism. Field forces are in equilibrium when states interact within a structure of expectations congruent to a balance of power. If a gap develops between expectations and the balance of power, the equilibrium may be disrupted. Conflict in the field is then a signal that such a breakdown has occurred and a mechanism for rebalancing field forces and creating congruent expectations. The empirical propositions were tested in Rummel, *Understanding Conflict and War,* vol. 4.

8. This and the following proposition sum up the process theory of conflict as a helix. Only two empirical studies are directly relevant to the conflict helix, and both are supportive. However, from the theory over fifty specific empirical propositions have been derived, each of which is supported by the greater majority of empirical work. These propositions include those numbered 3 to 8 in this chapter. On all this, see Rummel, *Understanding Conflict and War.* On the specific test of the conflict helix, see Rummel, *Understanding Conflict and War,* vol. 4, appendix 18A.1, prop. 18.1

9. Out of fifty-one relevant empirical studies, sixteen are strongly positive on this relationship, twenty-one are positive, six are negative, and two are strongly negative. For the list of studies, see Rummel, *Understanding Conflict and War,* vol. 4, appendix 18A.1, prop. 18.2.

10. Ibid.

11. Of ten relevant empirical studies, all support this proposition, four strongly.

12. Of ten relevant studies, all empirically support the proposition that violence assumes a disrupted status quo. See Rummel, *Understanding Conflict and War,* vol. 4, app. 16B, prop. 16.10.

13. Of thirty-seven empirical analyses relevant to this proposition, twenty-four are supportive (eleven strongly); nine are negative (one strongly). See Rummel, *Understanding Conflict and War,* vol. 4, app. 16B, prop. 16.21).

14. Two relevant empirical studies have been done, both of which support this proposition (one strongly). See Rummel, *Understanding Conflict and War,* vol. 4, app. 16B, prop. 16.17.

15. Of two relevant published empirical studies, both are supportive (one strongly). See Rummel, *Understanding Conflict and War,* vol. 4, app. 16B, prop. 16.28.

16. See Samuel Huntington, "Arms Races: Prerequisites and Results," *Public Policy* 8 (1958): 41–86. Huntington provides still one of the best historical and analytical analyses of arms races in the literature. He lists twelve arms races; the Soviet–American conventional-nuclear arms race, 1946–1967, has been added here. Of course, how many arms races there have been and their relationship to war depends on how

they are measured, no easy or uncontroversial matter. Empirical studies of arms races have so far had mixed results, with most being seriously flawed by definitional or methodological problems.

17. This proposition also follows from the previous ones, and their empirical support reflects on this one as well.

18. See Rummel, *Understanding Conflict and War,* vol. 4, app. 16B, props. 16.11 and 16.27. That freedom promotes peace is the overall conclusion to Rummel, *Understanding Conflict and War* (1975– 1981). For additional empirical tests of this proposition, see R. J. Rummel, "Libertarianism and International Violence," *Journal of Conflict Resolution* (March 1983).

19. There are two marginal exceptions: a briefly democratic France fought a briefly democratic Rome (Papal States) in the Roman Republic War of 1849; and a democratic Finland joined Germany in her attack on the Soviet Union in 1941, which formally involved Finland on Germany's side against the allied democracies like Great Britain and France. However, there were no hostile engagements between Finland and the democratic allies.

20. See Freedom House's *Freedom at Issue* (January-February 1982), pp. 3–14. They classify all nations and territories in terms of their civil liberties and political rights. The tests of the proposition that democracies do not have wars between them have taken as given the many classifications by political scientists as to whether nations were democratic or not. Indeed some of the classifications used have been by those hostile to the proposition. For example, see R. J. Rummel, "Libertarianism and International Violence," *Journal of Conflict Resolution* (March 1983).

21. A variety of related propositions support this. See Rummel, *Understanding Conflict and War,* vol. 4, app. 16B, props. 16.11, 16.15, 16.19, 16.21, 16.23–24, 16.27, and associated evidence. See particularly figures 16B.1 and 16B.2 for a description of the relationship between polarity, violence and war.

3 Current Strategic Realities

R.J. Rummel

In his March 31, 1982 news conference, President Ronald Reagan shocked reporters by quietly admitting that the "Soviets' great edge is one in which they could absorb our retaliatory blow and hit us again." That is, the American nuclear deterrent, based on the threat of destroying the Soviet Union if attacked, is no longer effective: the Soviets could survive an American retaliatory blow, either because of the buildup in their defenses or because of the number of American weapons they destroy in a first strike or both; enough of their weapons would survive the American retaliation for them to hold American cities hostage to American surrender.

Such in fact is the present strategic situation. How and why did we get into this dangerous condition, and how do we understand this in the light of the previous chapter? In answer this chapter will first present and discuss three propositions about Soviet intentions and capability, the major threat facing the United States. This threat then will be related to the Soviet–American process of conflict since 1945, and this in turn will provide a systematic background for understanding past American strategic policies and doctrines and the present strategic situation. Keep in mind the analysis of chapter 2; the implications of all this for defense policy will be discussed in the concluding section.

Soviet Intentions and Capability

1. Soviet strategy and tactics aim at a global victory for Soviet Marxism-Leninism and the transformation of the international system of sovereign states into a global socialist government directed from Moscow.

How do we know a ruler's intentions? As a psychological variable, intentions are latent in actions but never themselves manifest; they are hidden in a ruler's head. However, there are some things we generally know about intentions that will help us assess the intentions of Soviet leaders.

We "read" others' intentions by their assertions, actions, and character. The professed aims, correlated behavior, and character of individuals communicate their intentions. Similarly, to understand Soviet intentions, we must look at and determine the correlation between what Soviet rulers say, do, and are. To provide context for understanding their statements and deeds, consider their character first.

Table 3–1 classifies the character of Soviet rulers into decisional, ideological, and personal traits; the aspects of each; and their implication for the intentions of Soviet rulers. In sum the character of Soviet rulers *disposes* them toward a view of conflict and violence as basic to state relations between capitalist and socialist systems, a struggle that socialism is bound to win but that can be nudged along by Soviet rulers. Military power and force are crucial to the struggle and closely tied into politics, and military superiority plays an important political role.

General war is to be avoided, but should be prepared for as a contingency forced onto the Soviet Union in the last extremity by dying capitalism. World forces favor communism, however, and unnecessary risks need not be taken. Opportunities still should be seized, nonetheless. The struggle against capitalism should be waged ceaselessly by whatever means that does not endanger the progress toward eventual socialist victory.

Finally, Soviet rulers have wide flexibility in *high-level* strategies and tactics due to their centralization and totalitarian control. If they consider doing so profitable, they can reverse policy. Any policy requires careful articulation down the hierarchy, however, so that rulers and cadre, propaganda and actions, at all levels march in step. Policy lines and attendant public justification or rationales must be communicated. By totalitarian necessity, Soviet rulers themselves help provide a clear mapping of their general intentions.

Taking up this last point, then, what do Soviet rulers *say?* Table 3–2 classifies a number of representative quotes, which clearly are not only consistent with the Soviet character outlined in table 3–1, but the two tables also support and illuminate each other.[1]

Finally, what do Soviet rulers do? Table 3–3 sketches the main outlines of Soviet actions, which, as can be seen, are consistent with their pronouncements (table 3–2) and character (table 3–1).

But table 3–3 is impressionistic, intuitive. What has been found by attempts to analyze scientifically diverse Soviet behavior toward other states? This work has been brought together elsewhere, but here can be noted the following.[2] First, Soviet actions fall into clear empirical patterns reflecting an ideology of struggle, an emphasis on "peaceful coexistence," support for national liberation movements, military dominance, and separately, reliance on economic and political power.

Table 3–1
Character of Soviet Rulers

Aspects	Implications for Intentions (Goals and Means)
Decisional	
Hierarchical and highly centralized control	High-level flexibility.
	Responsiveness to perceived threats/opportunities.
	Possible long-range strategic planning.
Longevity of rulers	Accumulated tactical experience and reality testing.
Bureaucratic	Low- and middle-level policy inertia.
	Low and middle level standardized responses or initiatives.
	Declaratory policies.
	Necessity to ensure hierarchical congruency in statements and actions.
Noncompetitive politics	Insulated intentions.
	Ingrown perceptions and expectations.
Ideological	
Marxist-Leninist	War for communist victory is just.
	Perceives world as an arena of conflicting opposites.
	Conflict between capitalism and socialism nonnegotiable.
	Capitalism perceived as the enemy and the U.S. as the pillar and arsenal of capitalism.
	Align means with the irresistible forces of history.
	Expect West to collapse.
	Revolution and violence (short of general war) may hasten final victory of communism.
	Communist victory inevitable but prepare for dying struggle of capitalism.
Clausewitzian	Politics, military power, and force are alternative closely linked means to the same goals.
	Military victory is possible and possibly profitable.
	Perceives U.S. desires détente because of Soviet power.
	Superiority has a crucial political function and will aid transition to communism.
Revolutionary and crusading	USSR perceived as leader and arsenal of the world communist revolution.
	Exploit and create opportunities to spread communism and/or defeat capitalism.
	International and strategic stability not a goal in itself.
Personal	
Aged leadership	Rigid and conservative: basic worldview formed in the revolutionary and Stalin years.
Path to rule is through cutthroat and deadly power struggles.	Basic power orientation: trust based on power and fear.
	Ends justify means.
	Manipulative and coldly calculating.
Personal experience with Stalin's purges and terror, and World War II; leadership of system using mass concentration camps	Life is cheap, human rights nonexistent.

Table 3–2
What Soviet Rulers Say

Concerning	Typical Quote
Ideological Struggle	"not even the most successful talks and the best agreements change the unpleasant fact that a tense class struggle will continue to be waged between the world of socialism and the world of capitalism."[a]
Inevitability	"The total triumph of socialism the world over is inevitable."[b]
Politics and war	"It is well known that the essential nature of war as a continuation of politics does not change with changing technology and armament."[c]
Foreign policy Détente	"We make no secret of the fact that we see détente as the way to create more favorable conditions for peaceful socialist and communist construction."[d]
Peaceful coexistence	"Peaceful coexistence promotes the development of the revolutionary movement of the working class in the capitalist countries and creates conditions for successful struggle by oppressed nations against colonialism, for freedom and independence."[e]
National liberation movements	"the defense of the socialist fatherland is closely tied to giving comprehensive assistance to national liberation movements."[f]
Success	"No impartial person can deny that the socialist country's influence on world affairs is becoming ever stronger and deeper."[g]
Military Doctrine Nuclear war	"the Armed Forces should be capable of stopping a surprise attack by the aggressor in any situation and use rapid, crushing blows to destroy his main nuclear missile weapons and troop formations, thus securing favorable conditions for further conduct of and victorious conclusion to the war."[h] "If in the past the strategic end-result was secured by a succession of sequential, most often long-term efforts . . . today, by means of powerful nuclear strikes, strategy can attain its objectives directly."[i]
First strike	"Surprise attack has always been an important principle of military art and has frequently given the attacker decisive advantages in achieving victory."[j] "The strategic Missile Forces have the combat ability which allows them in the shortest time to solve simultaneously the task of destroying the enemy's military-economic potential, to destroy his strategic means of nuclear attack, to smash his main troop formations. . . . Massive nuclear strikes by strategic weapons allow the attainment of the political aims (of war) in a short period of time."[k]
Military superiority	"We are all witness to the way the CPSU Central Committee takes care that in terms of military and technical facilities, we have an unquestionable superiority over the armies of the most powerful capitalist countries."[l]

Table 3–2 continued

Concerning	Typical Quote
U.S. concept of deterrence	" 'Peace based on a stable balance of deterrence' would differ but little from the cold war. It would be a 'cold peace' that could easily revert to a tense confrontation depressing the consciousness and life of the peoples, and fraught with the danger of a world-wide conflict."[m]
Use of military power	"The strategic course of U.S. policies is now changing before our very eyes from 'pax Americana' . . . to a definite form of necessity for peaceful coexistence. We must clearly understand that this change is a *forced* one and that it is precisely the power—the social, economic, and ultimately, military power of the Soviet Union and the socialist countries—that is *compelling* American ruling circles to engage in an antagonizing reappraisal of values."[n]

[a]Report on the June 14 Moscow City Party Organization Aktiv Meeting, "Along the Leninist Course," *Moskovskaia Pravda,* June 15, 1972.

[b]L. Brezhnev, General Secretary of the Soviet Communist Party and President of the Soviet Union, CC-CPSU Accountability Report to the 24th CPSU Congress, *Pravda,* March 31, 1971.

[c]V.D. Sokolovskii, *Soviet Military Strategy* (Rand Corporation, 1963), p. 99.

[d]Brezhnev, "Excerpts from Brezhnev's Keynote Speech at Soviet Party's 25th Congress," *The New York Times,* February 25, 1976, p. 14.

[e]*V.I. Lenin on Peaceful Coexistence,* 2d ed., 1967.

[f]Army General A. Yepishev, Chief of the Main Political Administration of the Soviet Army and Navy. *Mogucheye Oruzhiye Partii,* Voenizdat, Moscow, 1973.

[g]Brezhnev, CC-CPSU Accountability Report.

[h]Colonel I. Forofonou. "The 24th CPSU Congress on Missions of the Soviet Armed Forces in the Current Phase," *Kommunist Vooruzhennykl Sil* 15 (August 1971): p. 77.

[i]"Methodological Problems of Military Theory and Practice," (Metodologicheskie problemy voennoi teorii i praktiti) Moscow, Ministry of Defense of the USSR, 1969.

[j]Army General Kulikov, Chief of the General Staff, *Kommunist Vooruzhennykh Sil* 6 (March 1973):15.

[k]Bagramian et al. *Istoriia Voin i Voennogo Iskusstva,* pp. 489, 495.

[l]Army General S. Sokolov, First Deputy Minister of Defense, "The Beloved Creation of the Party and People," *Sovetskaia Rossiia,* February 23, 1971.

[m]Brezhnev speech before the Moscow World Congress of Peace-Loving Forces, October 26, 1973, *Pravda,* October 27, 1973.

[n]Cited in Leon Gouré, D. Kohlerfoy, L. Harvey Mose, *The Role of Nuclear Forces in Current Soviet Strategy* (Miami: University of Miami, Center for Advanced International Studies, 1974), p. xxiii.

Second, the relative power between the Soviet Union and other states highly predicts Soviet behavior (much more so than for other states), and its conflict behavior can be most reliably predicted. Third, a model of Soviet actions that assumes the Soviet aim is to destroy or

Table 3–3
What Soviet Rulers Do

Concerning	Actions
Ideology of struggle	Continuous, internal and external hostile, anti-Western, anti-capitalist propaganda and disinformation—unabated by détente. Massive covert spying and destabilization activities directed against non-communist countries, and especially American allies.
Foreign policy Peaceful coexistence	Détente at the interstate level; arms control negotiations and agreements. Military and economic aid to pro-Moscow, Marxist, and anti-American regimes. Fomenting or acquiescing in major destabilizing wars or actions against the United States or its allies.
National liberation movements	Military and economic aid to Marxist and procommunist guerrilla movements; involvement by proxy in guerrilla and civil wars.
Military doctrine Nuclear war	A massive conventional and nuclear arms buildup consistent with waging and winning a general nuclear-conventional war.
First strike	A strategic weapons offensive and defensive buildup and deployment in conjunction with a civil defense that will make a first strike credible.
Military superiority	Have surpassed the U.S. in most weapons categories, with trend lines leading to superiority in others.
Use of military power	Buildup of military bases outside of Warsaw Pact; increased showing of the flag and overseas deployment; direct intervention in Angola and Ethiopia; the explicit threat of intervention in the 1973 Middle East War; invasion of Afghanistan; use of maneuvers and mobilization of forces along the border to intimidate Poland.

disunite the West, but that tactically the Soviet Union frequently will test the West's resolve, avoid or try to lessen extreme conflict while maintaining Soviet credibility, try to discourage Western firmness, and reward Western conciliation—a model of alternating periods of conflict and détente—predicts Soviet behavior much better than alternative models of primarily Big Power or defensive and consolidationist aims. Finally, as the subsequent propositions will point out, the Soviets have in fact engaged in a massive military buildup; and they have developed a significant nuclear first-strike capability. In sum, the empirical evidence supports table 3–3: Soviet actions do correspond to their character and their words.

What then can we say about Soviet intentions? Predominantly, Soviet goals and means are organized around the struggle to defeat capitalism and make Soviet communism globally dominant. This is a revolutionary and crusading goal, whose attendant policies apparently involve six elements. First, the United States is perceived as the main enemy and arsenal, whose defeat or neutralization would assure the final goal. Second, the policy of peaceful coexistence is a means for pursuing the struggle short of general war by establishing peaceful, *interstate* relations—even with capitalist nations. And détente was and is a tactic (now focused on Europe) to inhibit Western reaction to the successes and advances of the anticapitalist struggle. Third, support for national liberation movements and anticapitalist states ("progressive peoples") is an integral part of the struggle, not to be sacrificed for détente. Fourth, the buildup of an unambiguous military superiority is seen as a currency convertible into political pressure and as the backbone of peaceful coexistence. Fifth, as an ingredient in military superiority and in case the Soviet Union must be protected against the dying spasms of the West, a nuclear war-waging, war-winning strategic capability is believed necessary. Finally, any ideological competition to the Soviet vision of a communist world, such as that China presents, eventually must be eliminated.

Moreover, these elements are reflected in the multitrack nature of Soviet actions, whose empirical dimensions reflect struggle against the West and the simultaneous pursuit of peaceful coexistence (détente), military superiority, and success for national liberation movements. And the character of Soviet intentions can be seen in its systematic dependence on power and ideology.

2. The Soviets have engaged in a long-term, massive military buildup to achieve military domination, but although now ahead they have yet to gain a decisive war-winning conventional or NATO-theater superiority.

There are four ways of assessing the Soviet–American military balance. This can be in terms of long-run military trends, the quantitative and qualitative balance at the present time, military capabilities to carry out missions and goals, and a first-strike capability. Though these have been analyzed in detail elsewhere, the conclusions of that analysis can only be summarized and illustrated here.[3]

First, the Soviet Union has been involved in a long-term buildup to wage and win a conventional and nuclear war. This buildup massively increased around 1968 and has been moving steeply upward thereafter.[4] The success of this arms drive can be gauged by a one-to-one comparison of Soviet and American weapons systems and indicators, as done in table 3–4; and in table 3–5 for NATO versus the Warsaw Pact. As can be seen, the Soviet Union surpasses the United States on well over a majority of indicators and weapons systems, in many cases by over three to one. And when the comparison is done by including major allies in NATO and the Warsaw Pact, serious actual and potential disparities favoring the latter also appear. After reviewing these data for the European theater the International Institute for Stratetic Studies concludes that the

> numerical balance over the last twenty years has slowly but steadily moved in favour of the East. At the same time the West has largely lost the technological edge which allowed NATO to believe that quality could substitute for numbers. One cannot necessarily conclude from this that NATO would suffer defeat in war, but one can conclude that there has been sufficient danger in the trend to require urgent remedies.[5]

Even in 1977 these disparities in the European theater and in the global Soviet–American balance were already critical. In a comprehensive review of the quantitative and qualitative military balance, trends in the balance since 1962, and U.S. and Soviet missions and requirements, John M. Collins in 1978 found that

Table 3–4
The Soviet–American Military Balance, 1982–83[a]
($ billions)

Indicators, Weapons, Systems	United States	Soviet Union
Overall		
Defense expenditures	215.9	289[g]
Defense expenditures as a		
percentage of GNP	6.1[c]	12–14[b]
Armed forces personnel	2,116,800	3,705,000[d]
Reservists	899,600	5,000,000[e]
Paramilitary	125,300	560,000
Strategic		
ICBM	1,052	1,398
SLBM	520	989
Nuclear missile submarines	32	83

Table 3–4 continued

Indicators, Weapons, Systems	United States	Soviet Union	
Long-range bombers	316	150	+100[f]
Medium-range bombers	60	435	
IRBM and MRBM	0	606	
Nuclear bombs and warheads	9,268	7,300	
Interceptors	258	2,225	
ABM	0	32	
SAM	0	10,000	
Air defense surveillance radars	91[g]	7,000	
Army			
Personnel (+marines)	982,800	1,838,500	
Tanks	12,130	50,000	
Armored fighting vehicles	20,000	62,000	
Artillery	5,459	20,000	
Mortars	6,300	7,200	
Multiple rocket launchers	68	4,000	
SSM	144	1,300	
Navy			
Personnel	553,000	450,000	
Major combat surface ships	204	290	
Cruise missile submarines	0	69	
Attack submarines	90	204	
Aircraft carriers	14	4[h]	
Cruisers	27	34	
Destroyers	84	69	
Frigates	79	183	
Amphibious warfare ships	65	84	
Combat aircraft	1,350	755	
Air Force			
Personnel	581,000	475,000	
Combat aircraft	3,650	4,480	
in combat wings	1,941	3,800[i]	
Tactical reconnaissance	126	640	
AWACS	26	10[j]	
Tactical aircraft	114	NA	
Heavy transport craft	231	600	

NA = not available

[a] From *The Military Balance 1982–1983* (London: The International Institute for Strategic Studies, 1982).

[b] Estimate based on *Department of Defense Annual Report FY 1982* (1981); and *The Military Balance 1982–1983*, p. 12.

[c] 1981.

[d] Excluding about 560,000 border troops, internal security, and railroad and construction troops.

[e] Available reserves could be as high as 25 million.

[f] These are Backfire bombers, a number of which may have a long-range capability.

[g] From *Department of Defense Annual Report FY 1982*.

[h] Including 2 ASW helicopter carriers.

[i] Fighters, including ground attack.

[j] Modified Tu-126 Moss.

Quantitative changes since the Cuban missile crisis favor the Soviet Union, with scattered exceptions. U.S. *qualitative* superiority, less pronounced than in the past, is slowly slipping away. As it stands:

— High manpower costs inhibit force modernization much more in the United States than in the Soviet Union.
— U.S. technological supremacy shows signs of perishability that results more from policies than potential.
— Soviet nuclear strength increasingly endangers our static force of ICBMs and undefended cities.
— Only a handful of U.S. divisions are free to contend with contingencies without undercutting U.S. capabilities in Europe.
— The U.S. Navy is poorly prepared to cope with Soviet antiship cruise missiles, which severely constrain its mission capabilities.
— The U.S. Merchant Marine could support small-scale contingencies, but even modest attrition from Soviet attacks would sap it quickly.
— Emerging Soviet offensive strength is creating a new range of threats against NATO, whose forces cannot stand large losses.

Mutual Assured Destruction seems less mutual than it was in the last decade. America's land, sea and air forces alike would be hard pressed to support NATO plans at existing levels and deal concurrently with large-scale diversons, including those caused or sustained by the Kremlin in spots that contain U.S. lifelines.

In short, current trends curtail U.S. freedom of action. The upshot abridges abilities of U.S. armed services to deter attacks on the United States, defend this country effectively if deterrence should fail, and safeguard associates whose security is closely linked with our own.[6]

While the margin of Soviet superiority since these words were written has grown, the Soviets have yet to gain a clearly decisive conventional edge. General war with the United States still would be a very risky venture, with victory by no means assured. However, the shift in military power to the Soviet Union continues, with its pace only so far slowed by the Reagan administration.

But what about a Soviet nuclear first-strike capability? And is not all this meaningless in a nuclear-armed world? Would not a nuclear war leave both sides utterly destroyed? Or is a nuclear war winnable, in some sense? These questions are covered by the next propostiion.

3. The Soviet Union is nearing, if it has not already achieved, a nuclear first-strike capability.

In a news article in the March 11, 1982 *Baltimore Sun,* Charles W. Corddry wrote that

Table 3–5
NATO-Warsaw Pact Military Balance, 1982–83[a]

	NATO			Warsaw Pact	
	Less U.S.		Total with US	With USSR	Less USSR
	N. Europe[c]	S. Europe			
Manpower (000)					
Military personnel	1,670	1,211	4,998	4,821	1,116
Reserves (all					
services)	2,050	2,129	5,079	7,138	1,938
Total ground forces	998	931	2,720	2,618	793
Divisions					
In Europe and					
manned in					
peacetime[b]	38-⅓	41	84-⅓	79	37
Manned and					
available for					
immediate					
reinforcement	1-⅔	7	16	8	0
Extra divisions					
available on					
mobilizing reserves	22-⅔	8	45	88-⅔	21-⅔
Total divisions	62	55	145-⅓	171-⅔	58-⅔
Ground force					
equipment					
Main battle tanks	7,531	7,098	17,629	27,300	14,300
				(+19,200[d])	
Artillery, multiple	4,100	5,167	9,829	10,300	5,300
rocket launchers				(+10,000[d])	
Antitank guns	850	146	996	1,978	1,300
				(+ 1,746[d])	
Antitank launchers	3,000	1,000	4,644	1,437	1,150
(crew served)				(+ 385[d])	
Antiaircraft artillery	3,500	1,587	5,207	3,586	2,500
				(+ 2,900[d])	
SAM launchers	1,202	280	1,662	3,151	1,400
(crew served)				(+ 3,142[d])	
SSM launchers	163	96	403	620	348
				(+ 685[d])	
Navy					
Cruise missile					
submarines	0	0	0	54	0
Attack submarines	100	38	184	174	8
Carriers	6	1	13	4	0
Cruisers	1	2	15	27	0
Destroyers	42	32	109	53	1
Frigates	111	37	175	111	4
Amphibious	180	191	404	206	82
Naval and maritime					
aircraft					
Bombers	0	0	0	280	0
Attack	90	0	294	132	42
Fighters	31	0	157	0	0
ASW	16	20	96	125	0

Table 3–5 continued

	NATO			Warsaw Pact	
	Less U.S.		Total with US	With USSR	Less USSR
	N. Europe[c]	S. Europe			
Land attack aircraft and fighters					
Bombers	88	0	88	425	0
Fighters, ground attack	1,069	758	2,355	1,685 (+ 900[d])	585
Fighters	42	96	138	700 (+1,000[d])	0
Interceptors	407	207	614	4,382	1,502
Reconnaissance	213	96	348	564 (+ 400[d])	164
Armed helicopters	460[e] (+180)	5[e] (+460)	795[e]	756 (+ 650[d])	56
Theater nuclear					
Ballistic missiles			342	1,436	
Warheads available[f]			243	1,410	
Warheads arriving[g]			146	818	
Air deliver inventory			1,301	2,688	
Warheads available[f]			556	887	
Warheads arriving[g]			129	267	
Total warheads arriving			275[h] (563)	1,085	

[a]Same source as Table 3–4.
[b]Includes the Trans-Caucasus.
[c]Includes French forces and Canadian forces in Europe.
[d]Estimated additional from western and southern USSR.
[e]Known totals. Figures in parenthesis below are additional potential.
[f]Considering warheads per system, utilization, and serviceability.
[g]Considering warhead survivability, reliability, and penetration.
[h]Excluding 400 U.S. Poseidon warheads available to SACEUR for NATO targeting. The result of including these is shown in parenthesis below.

Defense Department analyses show that the United States will be dangerously inferior to the Soviet Union in stratetic nuclear power for the remainder of this decade despite efforts to close the much-publicized "window of vulnerability," an administration official said yesterday.

In one of the gloomiest assessments yet of the nuclear balance, the official said analyses were conducted separately by the Joint Chiefs of Staff, the Air Force and the Defense Department's systems analysis office and research and engineering staff—"and they all showed that the United States is inferior." . . .

The findings on the strategic nuclear balance—suggesting it is in such

a state that the Soviets might have an incentive to strike in a crisis—
have been laid before the Senate and House Armed Services committees in closed-door testimony.

How are we to understand this "gloomiest assessment?" On what could
it be based? In answer, there are a number of points to be made about
strategic nuclear weapons. First, a nuclear war *could be won;* the gains
could outweigh the costs in lives and property. Consider: if the Soviets
gain a sufficient nuclear superiority to attack suddenly with half their
weapons and destroy virtually all our intercontinental ballistic missiles
(ICBMs), long-range bombers, and missile submarines, we would likely
be deterred from retaliating by a Soviet threat to then also attack our
cities; or if we did retaliate with the small force of surviving weapons,
the damage inflicted on the Soviets could be acceptable to them as a
cost of the final victory over capitalism. In any case the war would be
over, the Soviets would still have a large arsenal of strategic weapons
left with which to threaten American cities and military installations,
while the United States would have almost none. The Soviets would
thus win, and at a cost in lives now most likely less than that of World
War II.

Second, the Soviets do conceive and prepare their forces in terms
of a first strike, as shown in table 3–2. Moreover, in the words of John
Erickson, expert on the Soviet military:

> The current and potential organization of the Soviet strategic forces
> also provides much food for thought; in brief, force structures will
> continue to be configured to furnish what Western analysts describe
> as a first-strike capability or to circumvent the neutralization of Soviet
> systems, both goals part of the Soviet "disarming strike/survival/war
> waging" posture.[7]

And third, one must prudently accept a nuclear first-strike as a
realistic Soviet option, under certain conditions and given certain relative strategic capabilities. As former Secretary of Defense Harold
Brown pointed out:

> The coordination of a successful attack is not impossible, and . . .
> the "rubbish heap of history" is filled with authorities who said some-
> thing reckless could not or would not be done. Accordingly, we must
> take the prospective vulnerability of our ICBM force with the utmost
> seriousness for planning purposes.[8]

The question is, of course, under what conditions would the Soviets
attack? What relative strategic capabilities would tempt the Soviets
seriously to consider, if not launch a first strike?

Though much complex analysis has been used to examine this question thoroughly elsewhere, here only the pertinent results need be summarized in answer to several relevant questions.[9] Generally, this analysis has calculated uncertainties in the U.S. favor, with assumptions about U.S. strategic strength in the early 1980s being overly optimistic. Estimates of Soviet strategic missile capabilities, on the other hand, focus on levels actually already achieved by 1981.[10] Although it is impossible to specify with certainty the total number of Soviet missiles, bombs, or warheads, it is still possible to make general conclusions regarding the comparative strengths of Soviet and U.S. strategic capabilities. (See chapter 4, on arms control, and chapter 9, on intelligence operations, for an understanding of the difficulties in assessing Soviet arms capabilities.) Regardless of whether the numbers themselves are disputed, the destabilizing trend in the comparative strategic strength of the United States and the Soviet Union should still be apparent.

Would the Soviets suffer unacceptable destruction in return if they launched a first strike on U.S. strategic forces? Soviet weapon developments and growing U.S. strategic vulnerabilities have seriously undermined a U.S. retaliatory nuclear strike against Soviet urban-industrial and military targets. Using Soviet fatalities as an indicator of U.S. retalitory capability, in the late 1970s a first strike on *alerted* U.S. strategic forces (ICBMs, bombers, and missile submarines) would have most likely resulted in at least 11 percent of the Soviet population— almost 30 million people—dying in the resulting retaliatory blow. For the reason given below, by the early 1980s this U.S. deterrent capability has been drastically weakened: without assuming Soviet urban evacuation, they could suffer as few as around 7 percent fatalities from a U.S. retaliation, or about 19 million dead and 35 percent industrial destruction, which is less than the cost of World War II in dead and loss of industrial capability to the Soviet Union. If they were to launch a surprise first strike on U.S. forces, Soviet fatalities from a U.S. retaliation could be reduced further to about 14 million people (and 30 percent of Soviet industry destroyed). And these calculations are based on conservative assumptions favoring the United States.

Quite clearly, then, U.S. nuclear deterrence is collapsing. At best the United States now has an unstable minimum deterrence of a Soviet first strike, and under current weapons programs the United States will become more vulnerable, deterrence more uncertain and unstable, until at least the late 1980s.

What weapons are most responsible for this? It is the Soviet implacement of very accurate multiple independently targeted reentry vehicles (MIRVs)—the warheads on the SS-18/19—and the sharp, numerical increase in its modern submarine-launched ballistic missile

(SLBM) fleet; and the consequent vulnerability of U.S. ICBMs and bombers. During this period no new U.S. nuclear weapons systems became operational and the absolute number of bombers and SLBMs declined.

Would not the inevitable uncertainty of nuclear war and urban holocaust still deter a Soviet nuclear attack? Given that the Soviets can define the range of operational uncertainties, confidently assume no U.S. launch under attack, and conservatively calculate they would destroy most of the U.S. nuclear capability, the primary uncertainty that still might deter them involves the human and social effects of nuclear explosions on the Soviet Union.[11] They do have Hiroshima and Nagasaki and numerous megaton bomb tests to study, but these may be as the match to the forest fire when nuclear strikes involve dozens of warheads over modern, densely populated cities. These effects cannot be known in detail ahead of time. Therefore, would the Politbureau risk a posible holocaust? Many American analysts and policymakers believe that regardless of the "game outcome," this nuclear hell will deter a Soviet attack.

The rational choice facing Soviet rulers is whether the decisive global victory of Soviet communism is worth very high costs. Historically, aggressive rulers deemed lesser goals worthy of devastation and extensive losses. Before World War I some thought that the enormous fatalities and great destruction of the American Civil War and the capability of the new weapons and logistics developed thereafter foretold the end of European culture and civilization, were a general European war to occur. Before World War II, the development of the bomber and poison gas was generally believed in the 1930s to lay open all cities to utter devastation, their populations to annihilation. "All that has been written about future wars since Hiroshima merely repeats and amplifies what was said between the two world wars."[12] Yet, World War II occurred.

Throughout history rulers have risked, rationally, all they held dear, as well as the horrible death by mutilation, torture, and fire of whole urban populations, including every man, woman, and child. Simply consider in classical and medieval times the rather common massacre of all inhabitants of cities refusing to surrender before siege. Yet rulers made war, knowing these consequences of defeat; and urban heads refused surrender. Could one argue that Soviet rulers are psychologically, morally, and politically different?

Soviet rulers saw Russia survive ruin from the post-1917 civil wars (about 18 million people killed); the social devastation of Stalin's brutal purges and agricultural collectivization (conservatively, about 30 million killed); and the massive destruction of Hitler's invasion (20 million killed). While nuclear holocaust may still deter them regardless of any strategic calculations, to count on this is to hang U.S. security and world freedom on this uncertainty alone.

Does failing deterrence imply the Soviets will launch a first strike? Not necessarily. A first-strike capability is the ultimate persuader, like the gun in a policeman's holster. Once the capability is there, its threat can empower a spectrum of strategies to achieve political dominance through U.S. fear of nuclear war and the Finlandization of U.S. allies. Already Soviet leaders are more willing to pressure directly the global status quo and are more inclined to test U.S. and Western European will. And as growing Soviet strategic superiority and first-strike capability eventually become clearly overwhelming, U.S. and allied leaders probably will shrink from tests of will and avoid crises and conflict that could escalate to involve Soviet strategic forces.

With these propositions about the Soviet threat as background, we can now turn to an outline of the Soviet–American balance since World War II, and the related American strategic policies and doctrines.

Soviet–American Conflict, Status Quo, and the Balance of Powers

Figure 3–1 shows the Soviet–American process of conflict. The time period covered, 1945–1983, is but a single step (conflict to status quo plateau) in figure 2–1 of chapter 2. Also shown in figure 3–1 are the relevant wars, interventions, crises, and Soviet advances (as defined by *net* increase in satellites, strong allies and ties; gains that they later lost are not shown, e.g., China, Egypt, and Albania). These conflict events and net Soviet advances roughly index the conflict that established the Soviet–American global status quo, one fundamentally delineating the nature of the contemporary international system, including whom the United States or Soviet Union controls, is allied with, or influences.

The period from the end of World War II through the Korean War saw deep Soviet–American conflict and the danger of outright war. But through this conflict a new post–World War II understanding of the status quo was forged that was based on an equilibrium between Soviet and American global and regional interests, military and economic strength, will and credibility. This balance held firm in the late 1950s and was reaffirmed through several crises and confrontations involving the status quo. However, the withdrawal from Vietnam that began in earnest after 1968, the subsequent Vietnam syndrome that began to block any strong U.S. involvement elsewhere, and the consequent sharp unilateral reduction in the absolute defense effort, se-

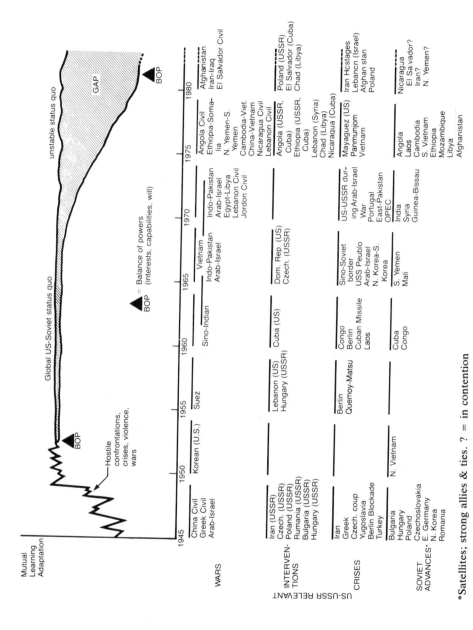

*Satellites; strong allies & ties. ? = in contention

Figure 3–1. U.S. Status quo and Balance of Powers

riously altered the balance of power in favor of the Soviet Union; leaving the status quo hanging in air, as shown in figure 3-1. The resulting large gap, so well evidenced in the figure by the upsurge in related wars, interventions by the Soviet Union or its proxies, and crises, has destabilized the status quo. And this instability is itself manifest by the upsurge in Soviet advances since 1975. This large gap between the balance of powers and the status quo has produced the greatest risk of Soviet–American war since at least the early 1950s, if not since World War II.

As by now should be clear, changes in Soviet–American military capability do not alone account for the gap shown in figure 3-1, which also reflects shifts in national interests and will. However, these shifts do significantly affect U.S. military expenditures and forces. Thus changes in the Soviet–American military balance provide a rough empirical estimate of the overall change in their balance of powers. How this military balance has changed relative to the overall balance of powers can be seen by comparing figures 3–2a and 3 2b to figure 3–2c.

First, in figure 3–2a the critical trend in the strategic balance is indexed by four indicators.[13] One is megatons, the overall explosive power of nuclear weapons on each side. While taking into acount the number and size of warheads and bombs on both sides, this measure can be misleading in favoring the Soviet inventory of many very large warheads contrasted with a far more numerous U.S. force of very small warheads. Strategic analysts, therefore, often use equivalent megatons (EMT) as a better indicator, since it takes into account the greater explosive efficiency of smaller warheads.[14] For both megatons and EMT, the trend has been negative; for the former the balance shifted to the Soviet Union in 1968, while for the more realistic EMT this occurred in 1977.

A third indicator is throw weight, or the useful weight that the boost stages of a missile can put into trajectory toward a target (or targets). The aggregate throw weight of a strategic force is often considered the best measure of its general capability. As can be seen, for throw weight the balance shifted toward the Soviet Union about 1969 and is now about three to one in their favor.

The fourth indicator is strategic nuclear warheads (including bombs). This is the most popular indicator of the strategic balance, but the most flawed of the four: it does not take into account the yield of the warheads

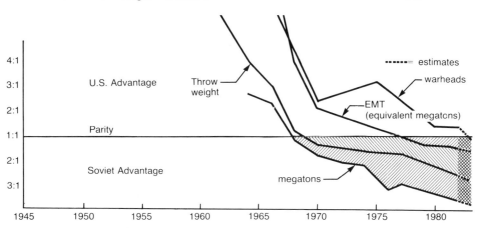

Figure 3–2a. Strategic Force Indicators

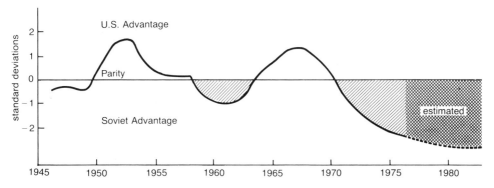

Figure 3–2b. Overall Military Balance

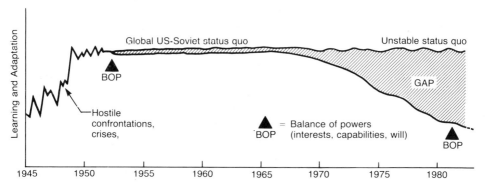

Figure 3–2c. U.S. Status quo and Balance of Powers

(a large majority of American warheads have yields of 50 kilotons or less, while the yields of Soviet warheads are usually 700 kilotons or more), nor the greater destructive efficiency of smaller warheads. The former deficiency is compensated for by the megatons indicator, the latter deficiency by EMT. Regardless, while the most optimistic of the four indicators, the downward trend of warheads is still similar to the others.

Of course, these are static measures of the strategic balance and must be supplemented with the dynamic first-strike analysis described for proposition 3, above, and by former Secretary of Defense Brown.[15] In sum, a dynamic analysis shows trends in a Soviet first-strike capability and postexchange strategic forces similar to that for the static indicators; all more or less parallel the change in the balance of powers shown for comparison in figure 3–2c.

What about overall military forces? In answer, figure 3–2b plots a (standardized) composite of twenty-three military indicators.[16] As shown, the Soviets had a relative overall advantage in the immediate postwar period, which was overcome in the 1950s as a result of the huge U.S. arms buildup catalyzed by the Korean War. However, with the conclusion of the war, President Dwight Eisenhower increasingly cut into U.S. relative capability, which was overtaken in the late 1950s and early 1960s as a rapid growth in Soviet strategic forces was added to its continuing large conventional capability. However, the subsequent rearmament program of President John Kennedy, later cojoined with the Vietnam War buildup, served to rebalance military forces in favor of the United States. Then, beginning in 1969, with the gradual withdrawal from Vietnam and Vietnam-engendered frustration and isolationism, increasingly large cuts were made in conventional forces and a decline in relative strategic capability accelerated. This relative *disarmament* continued until the late 1970s, when Congress and President Jimmy Carter were persuaded by events and the massive Soviet buildup to increase real (relative to inflation) defense expenditures and upgrade conventional and strategic forces. Although still underway, the relative effect of this new buildup has probably been no more than to level off the negative trends in the Soviet–American military balance.

In total, then, the hypothetical gap in the balance of powers shown in figure 3–1 not only correlates with an increasing instability in the status quo and growing Soviet net political advances, but also reflects the actual shift in the strategic and overall military balance of power. All this tends to support the validity of the gap shown between the balance of powers and status quo in figure 3–1. Now we can turn to those strategic policies that partially account for and partially reflect this shift in the balance of powers.

U.S. Strategic Policies, Doctrines, and Objectives

Figure 3–3 relates Soviet and American foreign and strategic policies, leadership, and wars and interventions to changes in the balance of powers. In this way changes in the balance for one period can be correlated with the associated policies, leadership, and violence. The balance of this chapter will give an overview of changing U.S. strategic policies, referring where possible to the related parts of figure 3–3. Throughout, figures 3–1 and 3–2 also will be used.

1945–1947: Demobilization, the Baruch Plan, and City-Busting

The defeat of Germany and Japan in World War II and the subsequent collapse of colonialism created power vacuums in Europe, Asia, and Africa. Only the United States and Soviet Union remained with the means, interests, and will to establish and support a new status quo— a new, central international order.

The 1946 Iranian crisis and outbreak of the Greek Civil War, the 1948 Marshall Plan and communist coup in Czechoslovakia, the 1948– 1949 Berlin blockade, the 1949 NATO Pact, the 1950–1953 Korean War, the 1956 Soviet intervention in Hungary, and the 1958 Matsu- Quemoy crisis and American intervention in Lebanon, and other numerous confrontations, threats, demands, accusations, denunciations, tests, probes, and military alliances all served to establish and maintain through conflict, engagement, and adjustment a global status quo that the United States would and could support, and a status quo that the Soviet Union was willing to tolerate. Except mainly for Eastern Europe under Soviet control, the status quo gradually forged out of post–World War II Soviet–American conflicts and largely hardened in the early 1950s still retained the major ingredients of the pre–World War II state system. Its pillars remained the formal sovereignty, independence, and equality of states; its relationships were largely based on a regulated free exchange and an international division of labor; and its government remained a loose confederation of states, with the new name of the United Nations. This was and is to this day an international order the United States largely accepts and supports.

Turning now to American policy, with the defeat of Japan in 1945, Americans largely believed that a new era of international harmony and cooperation had been created. And although difficulties and confrontations with the Soviet Union began to trouble Washington deeply, the popular cry was "Bring the boys home." By mid-1946 the United

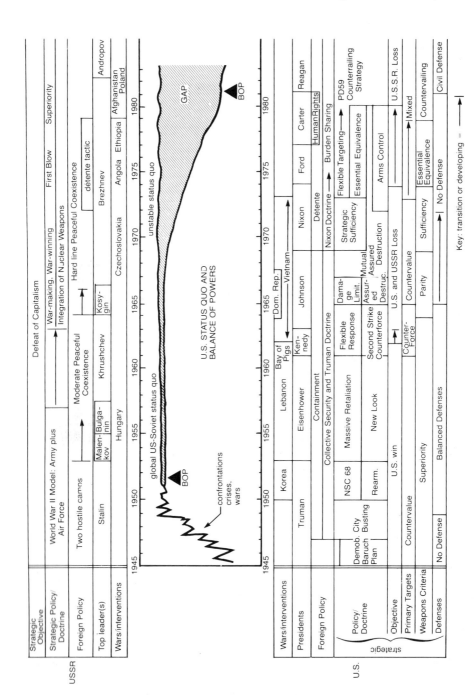

Figure 3–3. Soviet–American Policies, Events, Conflict, and the Balance of Power

States almost completely demobilized its forces, leaving the Soviets with more than five times the American effective ground forces. In defense expenditures the United States declined from nearly twice the Soviet effort to less than half theirs by 1948.

Nonetheless the United States had a monopoly on atomic weapons and a strategic air force that many believed could devastate Soviet industrial capability and seriously retard an invasion of Western Europe. But this could only be a temporary monopoly, and it was believed by defense and intelligence analysts that by the mid-1950s the Soviets would have their own atomic weapons. This, among other reasons, led the United States to propose the Baruch Plan to the United Nations in 1946, which would involve the internationally supervised abolition of atomic weapons and the creation of an international authority with a veto-free monopoly of nuclear research and development of nuclear energy.

The hope was to save mankind from the horror of nuclear war while strategically stabilizing the status quo. Since the United States would not have to destroy its weapons for several years under the plan and would in any case still have the know-how, it still preserved a U.S. atomic deterrent to a Soviet takeover of Europe. But the Soviets opposed the plan and counterproposed an immediate ban on the production of atomic weapons and the destruction of existing stockpiles within three months of a formal agreement, but without any real system of inspection and verification. The question of verification and the Soviet demand for a veto at critical administrative points defeated the Baruch Plan.

Militarily the Pentagon increasingly emphasized the air force and atomic bombing as the best available means to defeat quickly Soviet military forces, especially by destroying their support facilities and economic-industrial base. And since much of this support and industrial capability was in and around Soviet cities, such a strategic air offensive would amount to World War II–style *city-busting*. During 1945–1947, however, strategic bombing as a balance against Soviet conventional might was more a matter of faith and proposal. In 1946 the United States had few B-29 bombers outfitted to carry A-bombs, fewer crews trained to fly atomic weapons, and even fewer specialists to assemble them.

1947–1950: City-Busting

The years 1947 and 1948 were high points of the Soviet military advantage during the early postwar years. The American public was becoming increasingly anticommunist and alarmed at perceived Soviet aggression and hostility; the Truman Doctrine ("to support free peoples who are resisting attempted subjugation by armed minorities or by outside pressure") was proclaimed in 1947; and containment—containing Soviet expansion—became official policy.

For the country as a whole and for Congress, 1948 was a watershed. Any illusions remaining about Soviet–American cooperation, or of a long-term international stability ensured by an American atomic monopoly, were destroyed by the communist coup that brought Czechoslovakia under Soviet domination; and particularly by the Soviet–East German blockade of Berlin begun in 1948, the most serious Soviet–American war crisis between World War II and the Cuban missile crisis of 1962. The first postwar, real increase in defense expenditures was proposed; the Strategic Air Command (SAC) began to be significantly strengthened. And shaped by the worst-case belief that the Soviets could overrun Europe, the Persian Gulf, Korea, and North China before the United States could mobilize, new war plans by late 1948 turned primarily on a single, massive industrial—city-busting—atomic attack.

Finally postwar events convinced the Truman administration that the United States must depart from its historical avoidance of entangling peacetime alliances and build a wall of collective security treaties around the growing Soviet empire. The Treaty of Reciprocal Assistance (Rio Pact), which obligated all North and South American nations to mutual defense against aggression was signed in 1947; the Czechoslovakian coup and Berlin blockade were instrumental in creating the North Atlantic Treaty Organization (NATO) alliance in April 1949, the first U.S. peacetime European alliance.

In sum, the immediate postwar years were a time of continuing confrontation and severe crises. It was a time of flux; a stable Soviet–American status quo reflecting a mutually understood balance of national interests and will, and particularly of military capability and potential, had yet to solidify, as shown in figure 3–1. It was therefore a most dangerous period. Uncertainty about mutual intentions and the lack of reliable expectations about each other's behavior meant a high risk of Soviet–American war. And war would come, but in a most unexpected place and against a most unlikely Soviet ally: North Korea.

1950–1953: National Security Council (NSC) 68 and Rearmament

Throughout the previous years there was no high-level, official strategic doctrine. But the Soviet atomic bomb test of 1949 and the Chinese conquest of mainland China forced the first full examination of U.S.

postwar national security policy. The resulting document, labeled NSC 68, saw a great and growing Soviet danger and estimated that by 1954 the Soviets would be able to launch a devastating nuclear attack on the United States. It proposed an immediate military rearmament and an almost threefold increase in the defense budget. However, there was insufficient public and congressional support for greater defense expenditures, not to mention the expensive rearmament program advocated by NSC 68.

All this changed on June 25, 1950, when North Korea invaded South Korea and unleashed an across-the-board American mobilization. Congress eagerly granted Truman all he asked for to deter or, if necessary, fight a war with the Soviet Union, approving a defense budget jump from $13.3 billion in 1950 to $56.9 billion in 1951.

The Korean War enabled the United States finally to mobilize the capability not only to destroy Soviet cities, but also to balance Soviet conventional forces, as shown in figure 3–2b (both in conventional and in strategic forces the United States reached a superiority over the Soviets by 1953 never again to be achieved). It also focused American national interests and resolutely unified the American public and Congress against aggressive Soviet policies (notwithstanding the later decline in public support for the war) and showed that Americans would actually rearm and fight, thus proving the U.S. commitment to the Truman Doctrine and containment. But most important the Korean War, when added to the defeat of the Berlin blockade, the formation of NATO, and numerous lesser acts expressing U.S. resolve and commitment, hardened and stabilized the status quo in the early 1950s: a balance in Soviet–American national interests, capability, and will had finally been achieved. After 1950 those events indicating instability in Soviet–American relations dropped off sharply, as can be seen in figure 3–1.

1953–1961: The New Look and Massive Retaliation

The year after Dwight D. Eisenhower was elected president, the Korean War was over and Stalin died, creating hopes of new, more moderate Soviet policies. Eisenhower thus initiated a "New Look" in military policy, one viewing the Soviet threat as both military and economic, the latter more serious in that a continuing huge defense burden could destroy the American economy. This required balancing both the military and economic threats, with military forces being primed and configured for the long haul. The existing military balance appeared stable and the possible development of a meaningful Soviet strategic nuclear strike capability was downplayed. But strategically most important, policy shifted away from conventional forces. It was assumed that any large-scale limited or total war would be waged with nuclear weapons.

With 1,400 modern medium-range bombers, many deployed on overseas bases around the Soviet Union, and a considerable and versatile stockpile of possibly 2,500 nuclear bombs, in 1954 the United States achieved its greatest strategic superiority over the Soviet Union. Moreover U.S. air-defense capability was rapidly improved as the Nike-Ajax system for intercepting Soviet bombers began to go up around American cities, and in 1955 a crash construction program was undertaken in northern Canada to give three hours warning of a Soviet bomber attack.

In 1954, Secretary of State John Foster Dulles announced the policy of massive retaliation. This policy tried to deter both a Soviet–American international war and regional-local aggression by the threat of massive nuclear retaliation. It depended on an ability to retaliate quickly, whenever and wherever the United States chose; and meant to shape the military to fit U.S. policy rather than Soviet initiatives. It assumed the United States would win any nuclear war, since it was backed by a clear quantitative and qualitative strategic superiority, a multifaceted counterforce capability, and a growing air defense.

However, the Soviets were beginning to make significant strategic inroads on the U.S. advantage. Still the United States maintained a clear dominance through the 1950s. In 1960 Eisenhower's last year in office, the United States had 500 long-range bombers to a Soviet 147; 1,171 medium-range bombers to a much inferior 1,000 for the Soviets. In warheads and bombs, the United States had 7,592 to a Soviet 637. In ICBMs the Soviets seemed ahead, 35 to 18, but this slight advantage would shift the next year as the United States deployed many new missiles; the United States already had 32 Polaris SLBMs at sea to nothing similar for the Soviet Union. And the year 1960 would be the peak in U.S. megatonnage, reaching 52 times that of 1953.[17]

The great increase in U.S. strategic forces during this period hardly affected their targeting, however. The dominant concept was that of an *optimal mix* of industrial, military, and government control targets. Precedence still was given to urban-industrial targets and the launching of all weapons upon a war's outbreak because of their vulnerability to counterattack. But now Soviet nuclear forces also were targeted.

The policy of massive retaliation favored strategic over conventional forces; and conventional forces already slighted and reduced under the New Look were under additional downward pressure by the significant easing of Soviet–American tensions in 1955 and 1956, particularly with the new, post-Stalin leadership of Nikolai Bulganin and Nikita Khrushchev declaring that a fatal war between capitalism and socialism was no longer inevitable. By 1957 a revised New Look recognized this new spirit and, especially, acknowledged a new strategic "balance of terror," in which a general nuclear war could destroy both sides.

Consequently, while overall defense expenditures were virtually unchanged in constant dollars from 1954 to 1961 (the year of the last budget submitted by Eisenhower), total armed forces decreased from 1954 to 1960 by 25 percent; with most of the decline concentrated in the army and marines (36 percent); fighter and attack plane production was down 83 percent; naval forces off 27 percent.

In sum, from 1953 to 1961 a large U.S. strategic superiority remained, even though the Soviets developed a politically significant ability to attack the continental United States with hundreds of nuclear weapons. In conventional forces, there was a sharp initial decline from the Korean War high of 1952 and a slow but significant annual decline after 1955. Overall, figure 3–2b shows that the quantitative advantage during this period shifted slightly toward the Soviets, largely due to the rapid increase in relative Soviet strategic forces and the relatively great decline in U.S. conventional forces.

This slippage in conventional power was not reflected in American interest or will. Throughout this period the United States had stood firm during several Berlin crises and threatened counteraction if the Chinese followed through on their threat to invade Matsu and Quemoy, the offshore islands controlled by Chinese Nationalist forces. True, the United States stood by while the Hungarian revolutionaries were defeated by Soviet forces in 1956, but intervention in the Soviets' front yard would have meant war; and the United States did intervene in the Lebanon crisis of 1958, putting 14,000 men ashore. American interests in containment were clear; American will appeared resolute; and the Soviet-American balance of powers, as shown in figure 3–1, continued to buttress the bipolar global status quo.

1961–1964: Second-Strike Counterforce and Flexible Response

John F. Kennedy assumed the presidency in 1961 promising to correct a perceived "missile gap." Although once in office the gap was found to be in rhetoric, not strategic forces, he moved to accelerate the buildup in strategic missiles and the development of new programs that would strengthen the U.S. second-strike capability while deemphasizing nuclear weapons overall. The strategic objective was more precisely defined as deterring an attack on the United States or its allies, with the secondary objective of limiting damage to the United States if deterrence failed.

The outline of these major strategic policies was articulated by Secretary of Defense Robert McNamara, who argued for nuclear flexibility, with the principal targets being military, not civilian; cities should be held hostage to residual forces in order to pressure negotiation. The emphasis was therefore on a survivable *second strike* that could provide a selective and adaptive retaliation.

To second-strike counterforce was added the policy of flexible response—that is, beefing up and diversifying conventional forces to meet any threat short of a nuclear attack on the United States or its allies. There must be, Kennedy argued, some option between suicide and surrender. Conventional forces were reemphasized, with a selective buildup in those that helped to avoid finally resorting to nuclear weapons. Especially, it was believed, there was a necessity to prepare for fighting a limited conventional and unconventional war. Indeed, limited war was the principal concern—not nuclear war. The Soviet use of subversion and indigenous communist guerrillas and movements to slice off one piece of the "free world" at a time was seen as *the* great threat. It was fear of this that led Kennedy to increase sharply U.S. military involvement in South Vietnam in 1961 and 1963. With the vigorous new Kennedy defense effort, therefore, the overall military balance shown in figure 3–1 began to shift back toward the United States.

As to the overall balance of powers, there were some events that might have caused American will and interest to be questioned, such as the U.S. agreement to neutralize Laos, a solution that favored the communist Pathet Lao and North Vietnamese; the invasion of Cuba at the Bay of Pigs in 1961 by U.S.-helped and U.S.-trained anticommunist Cuban refugees, who were defeated while the United States stood by; and American acquiescence in the erection of the Berlin Wall.

However, these events were far overshadowed by the Berlin and Cuban crises and Vietnam. In 1961 Khrushchev gave Kennedy an ultimatum: the United States was given six months to agree to Soviet arms, or the Soviets would unilaterally sign a separate peace treaty with East Germany and turn over the access to West Berlin to them—in effect, closing off West Berlin. In response President Kennedy announced a significant strengthening of U.S. military capability and drew the line (again) over Berlin; if necessary, the United States would go to war to protect the status quo. Khrushchev soon withdrew the ultimatum.

But the most important event was the Cuban missile crisis. In 1962 Khrushchev tried to alter significantly the military and political balance by secretly setting up forty-two medium and twenty-four to thirty-two intermediate-range nuclear missiles in Cuba. Upon discovering and confirming this Kennedy acted resolutely, setting up a quarantine around Cuba and threatening nuclear war if the United States or any nation in the Western Hemisphere were attacked by any nuclear missile launched from Cuba, and signaled determination through alerts, mobilization, and military movements. Fortunately Khrushchev backed down.

Finally there was Vietnam. Suffice it to say that the United States saw the communists using a new kind of warfare to slice away the status quo; the victory in South Vietnam would encourage similar tactics elsewhere. Moreover Kennedy and, subsequently, Lyndon Johnson both believed that the United States was committed to protect South Vietnam by a separate protocol to the South-East Asia Treaty Organization (SEATO) agreement and the Truman Doctrine. To shun this commitment would undermine America's credibility, the chief support of U.S. defense alliances around the Soviet empire. By 1964 the United States had 23,000 military, noncombat personnel in Vietnam, an act of containment supported at this time by public opinion, Congress, and the intellectual establishment; and gave undeniable evidence at the time of a focused U.S. interest and will to maintain the Soviet–American status quo.

In conjunction with U.S. military power, the result of the Berlin and Cuban crises and Vietnam intervention was to maintain the Soviet–American balance—to keep status quo and supporting powers congruent, as shown in figure 3–1.

1965–1967: Assured Destruction and Damage Limitation

By 1965 McNamara believed that the United States had lost its first-strike capability against the Soviet Union and that the air force's desire to assure a U.S. first strike should be denied. He thought this would only threaten the Soviets, driving them to negate this advantage and resulting in an endless action-reaction arms race. The better policy, he argued, was to assure a second strike, *unilaterally* restricting U.S. weapons to make clear to the Soviets that the United States not only did not want a first-strike capability, but was actually incapable of such.

In 1965 McNamara brought declaratory strategic policy in line with this basic philosophy through the policies of assured destruction and damage limitation. Henceforth the United States would deter a nuclear first-strike attack on itself or its allies by threatening to launch a second strike that would create unacceptable damage. This destruction would be assured by protecting and configuring American strategic forces against a Soviet first strike and by making sure that U.S. warheads and bombers could get through to their targets. Moreover the United States would select such targets as would limit third-strike damage to itself.

Under this strategic policy any major nuclear war-fighting capability was scrapped. Soviet urban-industrial targets were reemphasized; and counterforce targeting was primarily to suppress Soviet strategic defenses, so that the full retaliatory blow could get through. Counterforce power per se was shunned and civil defense or ballistic missile defense was denied for fear the Soviets would perceive that the United States was preparing for a first strike. By 1967 the administration reached its assured destruction planned number of missiles: 1054 ICBMs, and 656 SLBMs in 41 nuclear submarines. By comparison the Soviets then had only 460 ICBMs and 130 SLBMs. Moreover, reflecting the growing emphasis on strategic missiles, the United States began gradually to decrease the number of long-range bombers from the high of 630 B-52s in 1966 to 600 in 1967 and 545 in 1968.[18]

During this period the United States committed itself to large-scale war in Vietnam. U.S. conventional forces were sharply increased, and by late 1967 U.S. forces in Vietnam reached 485,600 personnel, with 15,902 killed. The willingness of the United States to bear this burden, coupled with the landing of U.S. marines in the Dominican Republic in 1965 to prevent a communist takeover, communicated a continuing U.S. dedication to the status quo.

1967–1969: Mutual Assured Destruction

In 1967 McNamara annunciated a mutuality of assured destruction that assumed: (1) if either the Soviets or Americans launched a first strike against the other, the other's second strike would destroy the attacker; (2) neither could attain, foreseeably, a first strike able to defeat this retaliatory capability; (3) both aimed to avoid a nuclear war by emphasizing second-strike deterrence. This policy of Mutual Assured Destruction (MAD) saw the Soviets as similarly motivated, wishing to achieve a stable balance of terror, and thus aiming only for strategic parity with the United States. The Soviets were also believed to be interested in negotiated agreements that could halt the arms race and assure stability.

In conformance with all this, McNamara limited the size and capability of American strategic forces. The number of ICBMs and SLBMs reached in 1967 became an absolute upper limit. Missiles were modernized of course, the efficiency and accuracy of warheads gradually upgraded, and other improvements made in strategic forces, but the basic second-strike force size and configuration were maintained.

The relative effect of this on the strategic balance is clear in figure 3–2a: the Soviets either had or would soon achieve parity in megatons and throw weight, while the trend in EMT was rapidly approaching parity. From 1967 to 1968 the Soviets almost doubled their ICBMs (460 to 800), while increasing the inventory of nuclear warheads and bombs from 1,000 to 1,200.[19] Of course the United States still remained the dominant nuclear power and when conventional buildup related to the Vietnam War was included, it was the overall dominant military power as well (as shown in figure 3–2b). But strategic trends were adverse, and once U.S. conventional forces began to be cut, as would occur after 1968, eventual military inferiority was down the road.

The strategic trend did not worry the Johnson administraton, however. Indeed, it was desirable and planned. For perhaps as early as 1964 this administration undertook purposely to give up American strategic superiority in order to enable the Soviets to achieve parity and MAD. The belief was that the Soviets would then not feel threatened by U.S. strategic capability, that this would stabilize the nuclear balance and end "the nuclear action-reaction arms race." That the Soviets in their pronouncements and literature ridiculed MAD was thought only a manifestation of their insecurity and lack of sophistication in strategic thought.

Besides MAD this period also saw the 1968 Tet (Lunar New Year) North Vietnamese-Vietcong offensive in South Vietnam. It was decisively defeated, but the communists' ability to launch the offensive demonstrated that they were hardly near defeat and that the war might drag on indefinitely, even were the American commitment sharply escalated. This offensive was the turning point of the war. Disillusionment, fatigue, and frustration over the war led many former supporters to oppose further involvement. This spiritual withdrawal from Vietnam was followed by a gradual withdrawal and demobilization of U.S. military forces beginning in 1969. The effect on the overall military balance is shown in figure 3–2b. After 1968 the military balance began to decline sharply in the Soviets' favor. And although dating this is surely a risky subjective judgment, the beginning of a gap between the Soviet–American global status quo and balance of powers began in 1968 as well, as drawn in figure 3–2c.

Finally 1968 was also the year that Soviet military growth significantly accelerated: now close to strategic parity and helped by an American administration wanting them to achieve it, the Soviets became manifestly engaged in a massive military buildup whose goal could only be overall superiority.

1969–1974: Strategic Sufficiency
and Mutual Assured Destruction

With the Soviets thus threatening to achieve strategic parity, President Richard Nixon took office in 1969 and inherited the Vietnam War when mounting public, intellectual, and congressional opposition was spilling over onto global U.S.defense programs and commitments, demanding reduction in defense expenditures and resignation as the world's policeman. This Vietnam-induced antimilitarism and isolationism—or Vietnam syndrome—was the most fundamental fact of Nixon's administration before the Watergate scandal in 1973. Even were the Nixon administration desirous of recovering American strategic superiority (however defined), or even maintaining the present slight lead, Congress and the public would not have concurred.

Nixon therefore entered into preliminary discussions on strategic arms limitation talks (SALT) with the Soviets in 1969, ultimately seeking a means of restricting further Soviet growth; he pushed the Safeguard antiballistic missile (ABM) system to reduce the growing vulnerability of U.S. ICBMs, and decided to deploy multiple independently targetable reentry vehicles (MIRVs). Originally undertaken in 1965 to defeat Soviet ABMs, MIRVs now become a "cheap" way of maintaining a second-strike deterrence (assured destruction) against the Soviet buildup.

Regarding policy, Nixon abandoned victory in Vietnam, began troop withdrawals, and declared the Nixon Doctrine: while keeping treaty commitments and providing a nuclear "shield" for allies or nations vital to U.S. security, the United States would otherwise expect those nations directly threatened to provide the manpower for their defense. The Truman Doctrine and its open-ended promise to defend nations threatened by communism was officially scrapped.

Moreover Nixon initiated the foreign policy of détente, an attempt to embed the Soviet Union in a number of cooperative relationships and commitments that would restrain Soviet aggression and "adventurism" for fear of rupturing these profitable bonds and encourage negotiation and compromise on divisive issues.

In 1969 Nixon also proposed the doctrine of strategic sufficiency: American strategic weapons exist to prevent other nuclear powers from imposing their will on the United States or its allies; and to create unacceptable risks for a nuclear attack on the United States, for nuclear blackmail, or for acts that could escalate to nuclear war (such as an invasion of Europe). This required a second strike that would deter a Soviet first strike and required a rough equality in the urban-industrial damage each could suffer. In effect strategic sufficiency continued MAD.

However, U.S. strategic options were increasingly curtailed by growing Soviet capability. By 1970 they had overtaken the United States in ICBMs, 1,300 to 1,054; and by 1975 they would surpass the 1967 U.S. level of 656 SLBMs.[20] The overall effect of such Soviet growth on relative strategic force indicators can be seen in figure 3–2a for the years 1969–1974. The upshot was that three choices faced the president in a crisis or nuclear attack on U.S. strategic forces: do nothing; launch a large-scale counterforce attack (but increasingly with the growth in Soviet strategic power, this would leave them relatively *stronger* after the U.S. attack than before); or launch an attack primarily against urban-industrial targets (which meant, however, an assured Soviet retaliation on U.S. cities and the death of perhaps 100–120 million Americans).

During 1969–1974, U.S. Vietnam-related *and* general conventional forces were demobilized, cutting deep into the pre-Vietnam War capability. Compared to the pre-Vietnam War year of 1962, the total armed forces in 1974 were down 653,000 personnel; defense expenditures went from 43.6 percent of the federal budget before the war to 27.9 percent, from 8.9 percent of gross national product (GNP) to 5.9 percent; and the navy was reduced from 850 active ships to 327 after the war.[21] All this occurred during the period the Soviets were accelerating their conventional buildup. As shown in figure 3–2b, by 1974 the United States conceded the greatest military advantage to the Soviet Union since World War II. Truly this can be called unilateral disarmament.

This critical shift in military power was paralleled by the transformation and confusion of American interests associated with the Vietnam defeat; by the weakening of an American will to support the global status quo; by a highly self-critical questioning of American values, goals, and priorities; and by Americans turning away from foreign commitment, intervention, and countervention. This increased the shift in the balance of powers away from the global status quo, enlarging the gap between the international order and what the United States was *nationally* willing, able, and desirous of supporting. This created increasing political uncertainty and instability in Soviet–American relations, with the consequent growth in relevant crises and war, and the Soviet advances listed in figure 3–1.

1974–1980: Flexible Targeting, Essential or Rough Equivalence, and Mutual Assured Destruction

Nixon was unhappy with the choice between killing Soviet citizens, knowing U.S. citizens would be killed in return, or doing nothing. More strategic flexibility was sought, but not until 1974 would Secretary of Defense James Schlesinger announce flexible targeting, a change in nuclear plans to allow for more numerous, less-massive options. Strategic targets now would be grouped into small operational packages, some designed to support theater forces (e.g., NATO), some involving small attacks to limit collateral civilian damage, some reserved for an assured destruction-type deterrence of an attack on U.S. cities (by targeting Soviet cities). Nontargets were also defined, which were places or things the United States could withhold from attacking to avoid escalation or to hold hostage to negotiations. And there was a renewed emphasis on counterforce. The strategic framework for flexible targeting was the doctrine of essential equivalence, which involved two requirements: maintaining essential equivalence between the forces of the Warsaw Pact and the strategic forces of the United States and, secondarily, its allies; and maintaining a full range of conventional forces in order to assure a rough military balance and to avoid attacks below the nuclear threshold.

Although in the next two years under President Gerald Ford there was a growing perception of Soviet superiority in conventional forces, of a Soviet civil defense undercutting an American countervalue strike, of an increasing vulnerability of American ICBMs, and of a Soviet intention to achieve strategic superiority, when Jimmy Carter came into office in 1977 the policy of essential equivalence was basically continued, although sometimes called rough equivalence. The Carter strategic posture was, as since the mid-1960s, to avoid seeking a first strike as long as the Soviets did, to promote crisis stability, and to assure that a U.S.second strike would cause unacceptable damage to the Soviet Union.

As with Nixon and Ford before him, but with greater idealism, Carter incorporated arms control into his strategic program. He was determined to shape strategic policy around arms control and, after over two years of negotiation, signed with Leonid Brezhnev the SALT II treaty limiting strategic weapons. However, because of the widespread feeling that the treaty would not curtail a further substantial Soviet buildup, its ratification by the Senate was in question. In any case the treaty was shelved in the first days of 1980, a week after the Soviets invaded Afghanistan. It must be noted, however, that both the Soviet Union and the United States subsequently declared that they would follow the SALT II limits, a policy that has been continued by the Reagan administration.

A key year in the Soviet–American balance was 1980. Supported by the Iranian government, "students" seized the American Embassy and fifty-two American citizens in November 1979. For over a year the

United States could not get the hostages released or respond to related humiliations—a traumatic experience nationally. But also in late December 1979 the Soviet Union invaded Afghanistan and was soon confronted with a wide-scale national rebellion, a people's war. In the United States this invasion triggered a new confrontational climate, a common public and official feeling of a new risk of Soviet–American war. This, along with the national anger over the American hostages held by Iran, hammered home the realization that the United States was too weak to defend what many perceived as its vital interests, as in protecting the oil lifeline of Europe and Japan in the Persian Gulf. There was new support for the military and a big increase in defense expenditures (Congress subsequently adopted a budget resolution setting the defense budget authority at $171.3 billion, the biggest annual peacetime jump in military spending) and renewed interest in America's intelligence and covert action capability. And officially and unofficially, détente was dead.

Still, in 1981–82 the gap in the military balance remained large (see tables 3–4 and 5); and the balance underlying the status quo was still trending downward, as shown in figure 3–2b. Instability in the status quo was and still is critical, as manifested in the wars and Soviet advances listed in figure 3–1. And the gap between the status quo and balance of powers suddenly became clear in 1980 with the newly perceived risk of a possible Soviet–American war.

1980–Present: PD 59, Countervailing Strategy, and . . .

In 1977 Carter initiated a comprehensive review of existing concepts that led to Presidential Directive (PD) 59 in 1979. In part the new directive only modified the basic nuclear exchange and targeting plans, shifting emphasis from industrial targets to military targets (but still retaining attacks on cities among the options). But PD 59 also recognized that nuclear deterrence could be strengthened beyond simply threatening massive urban-industrial destruction by targeting that which the Soviet regime considers essential to continue its political control or maintain its borders. And PD 59 recognized that U.S. command, control, and communications (C^3) could not at that time support a sustained nuclear war.

Perhaps most important, however, PD 59 codified an "evolving" strategic doctrine called countervailing strategy. Previous strategic policies had relied on deterrence through making the goals too costly; punishment was the aim. The new strategy tried to prevent the Soviets from achieving their goals altogether. Moreover there was a concomitant change in concepts. The goal of ensuring a surviving second strike that could be launched in a single, preplanned attack was demoted; the focus was now on being able to wage a nuclear war of indefinite duration and comprising a number of nuclear exchanges.

In sum countervailing strategy emphasized strategic flexibility in options and targets and in escalation control. Its key was the survivability and endurance of strategic forces and C^3. It attempted to make clear to the Soviets that no use of nuclear weapons at any level or stage of a conflict could enable them to win. Operationally it meant being able to destroy any Soviet target, especially what the Soviets most value, including their political and military means of control over their own people.

As initially formulated by McNamara, MAD is no longer the basis of U.S. strategic policy. Assured destruction is no longer the primary strategic goal, and MAD is no longer seen as the sine qua non of stability by the Reagan administration. Nevertheless the basic principle of preserving stability and keeping alive the nuclear balance of terror by forswearing any sort of ABM system is still widely accepted in the arms control community. Their continued acceptance of MAD is especially ironic since it has become clear that the Soviets have never believed in MAD, following instead a doctrine emphasizing the first blow and a war-waging, war-winning capability.

Apparently the Reagan administration is adhering to the countervailing strategy and seems committed to developing at least a nuclear war-fighting capability, if not a nuclear war-winning capability as well. In any case as with the last years of the Carter administration, the Reagan administration insists on denying the Soviets any possibility of victory through the use of nuclear weapons. Survivability of American nuclear weapons remains the key; controlled flexibility in targets and different kinds of options for the president remain the operational guides.

The Current Strategic Situation

What about the current Soviet–American balance of powers? Figure 3–2c shows this leveling off, but still trending slightly away from the status quo. And from figure 3–1 we can see the instability already associated with the current gap, the greatest since immediately after World War II.

While defense expenditures have risen significantly and short-term steps are being undertaken to redress glaring U.S. military weaknesses,

American interests are still too unfocused and confused, the national will too weak. This is not entirely the fault of the Reagan administraton, whose leading members came into office with a world view and will that would help redress this imbalance. But the public, intellectual establishment, and Congress are not yet persuaded of the great danger and of the effort required—the effects of the Iran hostage crisis and the Soviet invasion of Afghanistan have faded—and the Reagan administration itself is divided over the threat in a way to weaken its impact on the balance of powers. The difficulties of the administration in trying to counterbalance communist intervention in El Salvador, America's backyard, exemplify the public and congressional mood. Its internal divisions are shown by the low-key public support for the Afghanistan people in their war against the Soviet invaders, and particularly by its relatively mild response to covert Soviet intervention in Poland in 1981.

Nonetheless there is in place an administration sensitive to Soviet intentions and the new risk of war. Moreover this administration does intend to end U.S. strategic military inferiority and overcome weaknesses in conventional forces. What is now required is also a new public and intellectual awareness of the great disparity between that which we support globally by treaty, agreement, and declaration, and what the Soviets and Americans want, and can and will get or defend.

Implications

If the risk of war from the current large gap between expectations (treaties, rhetoric) and reality is to be reduced, what kind of policies should the United States pursue? The empirical findings of chapters 2 and 3 suggest several major guidelines for policy. These implications can only be sketched out here; subsequent chapters will fill in color and detail.

The protracted struggle between the United States and the Soviet Union has reached a newly dangerous level. In the near term the large gap between the Soviet–American balance of powers and the associated global status quo poses the dual risks of nuclear war and global Soviet domination. How to avoid both mortal dangers is *the* primary near-term problem. The solution must involve both reformulating the status quo and strengthening American power.

Reformulate the Status Quo

A mindless defense of the status quo creates an unnecessarily high risk of war and defeat. In the nearly four decades since the end of World

War II, much more has changed than simply the relative power of the United States and the Soviet Union. Our once devasted allies have become wealthy and prosperous under the shelter of the U.S. nuclear umbrella, with gross national products approaching ours. And various Third World countries (e.g., Brazil and Saudi Arabia) are now able to influence world events in their own right.

Consequently U.S. defense policies must take into account these changes. Our principal military allies in NATO and Japan must assume their rightful roles as military (as well as economic) superpowers. And other U.S. defense commitment, explicit or implicit, must be carefully rethought. Unless essential to American security, let the dictatorship that denies its people basic rights or the democracy unwilling to provide for its own defense or protect its own resources fend for itself.

Revising American commitments and alliances (and implicit understandings about American interests) must be done slowly and prudently, with careful attention to diplomatic nuances, image, and perception, and in close consultation with affected states. But the vector of action should be clear. To continue to try to support a status quo determined decades ago, in spite of changes in global and domestic political forces and capabilities, is simply to continue an unnecessary and burdensome high risk of confrontation and war and to drain resources and popular support best husbanded for really critical crises.

In the long run a more pluralistic, multipolar world order can be midwifed into being by strong U.S. leadership. The United States must, by policy and by action, make clear that democracies able to defend themselves must not depend on the United States to do it for them. (One way of bringing about his transition is set forth in chapter 5.) Those requiring American assistance must still bear the major burden for their own defense. The United States must be willing to provide these democracies with the military know-how and means to build or procure the most advanced weapons, including nuclear weapons. Realistically a multipolar world would have to be a multi-nuclear-polar world. In such a world the danger of both global nuclear war and Soviet domination would actually be much less than under today's bipolar balance between nuclear superpowers.

Strengthen American Power

Power still equals interests times will times capability. All three of these, even if redefined, must be addressed. The balance of power has shifted too much in the Soviet direction. To strengthen capability, as chapter 4 explains, we must reduce this country's extreme vulnerability to nuclear attack by building both active and passive defenses against ballistic missiles. In addition, our retaliatory forces must be modernized and tailored more precisely to a strictly counterforce role. While arms control should remain a goal (and must be sincerely, continuously, and prudently sought), we must not allow the legacy of MAD to override such crucial needs as developing defenses against ballistic missiles.

To strengthen interests and will, Americans must be reeducated about both the reality of the Soviet threat and the value of living in a free society (as discussed in chapter 11). A more realistic and morally defensible American role in world affairs and a reaffirmation of this country's historic policy of voluntary recruitment of armed forces personnel would go a long way toward restoring popular support for U.S. defenses. In addition, as argued in chapter 10, a carefully defined and limited policy of *countervention*—aiding dissidents against communist regimes or providing military aid to threatened allies deemed essential to U.S. security—would be far more sustainable than today's open-ended treaties and rhetorical commitments.

Overall, chapters 2 and 3 imply moving toward an international structure that would lessen the dual risks of global war and Soviet domination and convert the protracted struggle into a multilateral conflict. This means actively encouraging a more pluralistic, multipolar international order. U.S. policy should help Western Europe, Japan, and other potential centers of global power to catch up with the superpowers in military capability. As chapter 2 pointed out, other superpower democracies would pose no security danger to the United States and, as near-equal centers of power, would help diffuse, contain, and cross-pressure international conflict and violence, while enormously complicating Soviet decision making and global designs.

Finally American policy must also look toward a more peaceful future for Americans and mankind, one in which war is no longer the expectation. The strong implication of chapter 2 is that such a world is one in which democratic freedom and respect for individual rights is globalized—in which all nations, while separated by political boundaries, cultures, religions, and ideologies, have become free societies. Therefore policy should marshal the positive and spiritual forces of mankind for freedom.[22]

Man must be *for,* not simply against something. An international order in which each nation and people are free to realize their own destiny and individually consistent with a similar right for all others is a realistic dream all, not only Americans, can defend and promote against the alternative of a global totalitarian state.

Notes

1. These are taken mainly, but not exclusively, from the material in Foy D. Kohler, Mose L. Harvey, Leon Gouré, and Richard Soll, *Soviet Strategy for the Seventies: From Cold War to Peaceful Coexistence* (Coral Gables, Fla.: Center for Advanced International Studies, University of Miami, 1973); and Leon Gouré, Foy D. Kohler, and Mose L. Harvey, *The Role of Nuclear Forces in Current Soviet Strategy* (Coral Gables, Fla.: Center for Advanced International Studies, University of Miami, 1974).

2. See for example, R.J. Rummel, *Understanding Conflict and War,* vol. 4 (Beverly Hills, Calif.: Sage Publications, 1979), app. 9A; and "Soviet Strategy and Northeast Asia," *Korea and World Affairs: A Quarterly Review* 2 (Spring 1978): 3–45.

3. See R.J. Rummel, *Peace Endangered: The Reality of Détente* (Beverly Hills, Calif.: Sage Publications, 1976); *The Dynamics of Power: The U.S.–U.S.S.R. Arms Field* (Honolulu: Department of Political Science, University of Hawaii, 1977); *Is Strategic Deterrence Collapsing?* (Honolulu: Department of Political Science, University of Hawaii, 1979); "Preparing for War? The Third Reich versus the Soviet Union," *International Security Review* 4 (Fall 1979): 207–230.

4. This has been calculated using a technique called component analysis. For the plot of this trend and comparison with U.S. trends (and with Germany before Hitler invaded Poland in 1939), see ibid.

5. *The Military Balance 1982–1983* (London: International Institute for Strategic Studies, 1982), p. 131.

6. John M. Collins, *American and Soviet Military Trends since the Cuban Missile Crisis* (Washington, D.C.: Center for Strategic and International Studies, Georgetown University, 1978), pp. 395–396.

7. John Erickson, "Soviet Military Policy in the 1980's," *Current History* 75 (October 1978).

8. *Department of Defense Annual Report FY 1980* (Washington, D.C.: January 25, 1979), p. 81.

9. Rummel, *Is Strategic Deterrence Collapsing?* 1979.

10. It was assumed that by the early 1980s the Soviets would have 308 SS-18 and 300 SS-19 deployed, with an upper range CEP for the SS-18 and 19 of 600 feet (see Rummel, ibid., Table 6, p. 27). Except for the SS-19's accuracy (for which they give no estimate), these are

the exact figures that *The Military Balance 1980–1981* (London: International Institute for Strategic Studies, 1981) gives for 1981.

11. See Rummel, ibid., sec 4. In sum it is argued that launch under attack would be unlikely because of the breakdown in command, control, and communications (which itself would likely be attacked by Soviet SLBMs), the short ten- to fifteen-minute decision time, and the credibility of a Soviet threat to attack U.S. cities if theirs are hit.

12. I.F. Clarke, *Voices Prophesying War: 1763–1984* (London: Oxford University Press, 1966), p. 164.

13. The data for these indicators are based upon Jacquelyn K. Davis, "SALT and the Balance of Superpower Strategic Forces," *NATO's Fifteen Nations* (February/March 1978); Charles Fenyvesi, "The Man Not Worried by the Bomb," *Washington Post,* April 11, 1982, p. B-1; Justin Galen, "The U.S. Learns the Final Score, The SALT II Debate and Strategic Balance," *Armed Forces Journal* (October 1980): 52–64, especially Table 2; David Jones, "Statement on Military Posture" in *Hearings on Military Posture and H.R. 2614 and H.R. 2970 before the Committee on Armed Services,* U.S. Cong., House of Representatives, 97th Cong., 1st sess. pt. I, 1981; James McCartney, "U.S. Soviet 'Superiority' Is Numbers Game," *Philadelphia Inquirer,* April 5, 1982, p. 1; *The Military Balance 1982–1983,* 1982; *New York Times,* March 21, 1982, p. 1E; *Newsweek,* March 29, 1982, p. 20; Ben T. Plymale, "The Evoluton of U.S. Declaratory Strategic Policy," *Journal of International Relations* 2 (Fall 1977). The latest data for megatons vary by source from a low of about 1.7 to 1 for the Soviets to a high of about 5 to 1. Judging the quality of the source, the past trend, and consistency with other strategic data, the higher (not highest) figures were used.

14. See the glossary for the formula used.

15. *Department of Defense Annual Report FY 1981* (Washington, D.C.: January 19, 1982), charts 4-2 and 4-3.

16. See note 4.

17. Rummel, *Peace Endangered: The Reality of Détente.*

18. Ibid.

19. Ibid.

20. Ibid.

21. Ibid.

22. To be clear, there is no implication that freedom should be imposed upon other nations, or that the United States should be the world protector of democracies. Rather, what is meant here is a policy fully utilizing the pacific arts: leadership, organization, articulation, example, persuasion, and education.

4 Rethinking Strategic Defense

Sam Cohen

The development of nuclear weapons and the subsequent development of intercontinental means of their delivery instituted a revolution in warfare, the full consequences of which are seldom fully appreciated in this country. Strategic defense refers to those policies and systems that involve countermeasures against threats to survival of the entire nation arising from this revolution in warfare. As chapter 3 has pointed out, U.S. strategic doctrine has evolved in a rather ad hoc fashion, without any moral framework and lacking a coherent plan for fighting a nuclear war, should one arise.

Deterrence of nuclear war has been the linchpin of U.S. strategic policy. In the early years of the nuclear era, simply possessing the largest arsenal of such weapons proved sufficient to deter a nuclear war. Since the development of large-scale nuclear arsenals in other countries, especially the Soviet Union, deterrence has become a more elusive strategy. Paradoxically, in order for deterrence itself to succeed, what has been called a nuclear war-fighting capability must be in place and believable in the eyes of potential enemies. To dissuade others from launching a nuclear attack on the United States in other words, a credible plan for prosecuting the very war the United States hopes to deter through the use of its own nuclear weapons is logically required. In short, to avoid the horror of nuclear war, the United States must have a credible strategy for fighting a nuclear war and the means to implement that strategy.

Three basic ingredients are essential in formulating such a strategic doctrine: understanding the nature of the threat, possessing the technological capabilities, and adhering to the moral constraints inherent in the commitment to being a free society. The principal threat, as set forth in chapter 3, is the possibility of nuclear attack by the Soviet Union. For the rest of this century it is unlikely that any other nation will possess both the means and the motive to pose a serious threat of nuclear annihilation. Yet U.S. strategic doctrine must also recognize and be prepared to cope with lower order nuclear threats, including the possibility of nuclear blackmail by a secondary nuclear power that may threaten to wipe out a few American cities. The possibility that a nuclear missile may be launched by accident remains. At present the United States is defenseless against such threats, due to its reliance solely on deterrence in place of defensive policies.

Strategic defense technology is advancing at a rapid pace. Recent developments in microelectronics and computer technology make it possible to target weapons with incredible accuracy. The potential of outer space as a territory from which to enhance U.S. defense has just begun to be examined seriously. The prospects seem highly promising. Advances in what are called "directed-energy" weapons offer real hope of breakthroughs that can provide truly effective *defense* against ballistic missiles.

Finally the application of the moral constraints described in chapter 1 offers a way to select from among the technological possibilities so as to focus defense developments in a morally acceptable direction. When taken to mean indiscriminate mass destruction, nuclear warfighting is properly condemnable. But when devised in a framework of Just War principles, nuclear weapons can be turned into tools of surgical precision. Today's, and tomorrow's, technology will permit us to develop a morally sound strategic defense.

What are these technologies and how can they be utilized in a coherent strategic manner? Strategic defense consists of three essential elements: alerting, which includes providing means of communicating with and controlling various weapons systems; defense, which includes both active and passive measures to shield against the attack; and retaliation, systems intended to destroy the enemy's remaining war-making ability. In addition, because it is an important consideration in the strategic equation, any discussion of defense must necessarily address the subject of arms control.

Alerting

In order to activate defensive measures and to launch retaliation, a system of collecting and disseminating information must exist. The general term for such systems is command, control, and communications, often shortened to C^3. While seldom receiving the popular attention given to bombers, submarines, or ballistic missiles, C^3 is nevertheless essential, amounting to the nervous system of strategic defense.

The general requirements of C^3 are relatively straightforward. Reconnaissance capabilities are needed to detect any possible precursors of an attack. Some precursors can now be observed by reconnaissance satellites during daylight and in clear weather. The development of spaceborne sensors that can observe reliably at night and through cloud cover would provide further capability to detect such precursers of an attack.

Even today the most likely attack would be a missile attack launched without definitive precursor activities. Warning satellites can detect the heat of rocket exhausts as the missiles are launched, providing about twenty-five to thirty minutes of warning in the event of land-based missiles (ICBMs) and about five to fifteen minutes in the case of submarine-launched ballistic missiles (SLBMs). Ground-based radar installations are also used to detect SLBMs launched from the oceans and to track ICBMs as they transit the Arctic regions. Additional radar systems should be added to detect and track bombers and cruise missiles.

To be effective, most of these warning systems must be located on outside territory. Outer space provides an ideal location for reconnaissance and warning satellites, some of which are over the Soviet Union at all times. To relay messages from these satellites, other satellites and ground stations are required, the latter in some cases in other countries. In addition, line-of-sight warning radars are located in Canada. To attempt to get by without any of these extraterritorial ground stations would entail a significant price (in terms of decreased effectiveness). Thus agreements with other governments regarding these ground stations will continue to be necessary for the foreseeable future. And the ability to locate military satellites in earth orbit is absolutely essential, well-meaning proposals for "demilitarizing space" notwithstanding.

Every essential element of our strategic system can be expected to be a target for enemy attack, and military satellites are no exception. Throughout the 1970s the Soviet Union pursued the development of antisatellite weaponry and, by the dawn of the 1980s, many analysts believed such capability was becoming operational. It is thus crucial that the vulnerability of our satellites be sharply reduced.

Attack by a Soviet "killer satellite," which would maneuver into the vicinity of a U.S. satellite and then explode, constitutes a major threat. Defense against such attacks could be based on a combination of decoys and active defensive countermeasures that would destroy enemy satellites that come within prohibited zones. Just as Soviet warships cannot sail through U.S. coastal waters with impunity, the Soviet Union should be put on notice to keep its vehicles clear of U.S. military satellites—or to risk their destruction.

Once warning of an attack has been provided, the information must be assessed and verified in strategic command centers. Command authorities must then authorize both active defense and retaliatory measures. To implement those commands, messages must be sent to the various weapons systems involved. Here again, both the command centers and the communication links are potentially vulnerable and must be protected, by redundancy, mobility, and concealment as well as by defensive measures.

Communications links to land-based systems (ICBMs, bomber bases) include both land lines and electromagnetic (radio) channels. By contrast, other systems—airborne, spaceborne, or oceangoing—can now only be reached electromagnetically. Most such links are vulnerable to electromagnetic pulse (EMP) effects, although the transmitting and receiving equipment can be hardened.[1] But the preferable solution to the EMP problem is to shift, wherever possible, from electromagnetic communications to communicating via light waves. Fiber optic cables can be substituted for telephone lines and cables. Signal-modulated laser beams can be used in place of radio links, relayed from place to place by satellites.[2]

In particular, laser/satellite systems offer a better means of communicating with missile-carrying submarines. At present those submarines must rise to just below the surface of the ocean periodically, trailing an antenna, in order to listen for messages. (This significantly increases their vulnerability to detection and tracking.) At normal operating depths they are cut off from communications. The U.S. government's present plan is to build an extremely low-frequency (ELF) radio system in northern Wisconsin that would send out a paging signal, alerting the submarines so that they could come to the surface for messages. But the frequency low enough to penetrate ocean depths also results in extremely slow transmission times (e.g., fifteen minutes for a three-letter code). Blue-green laser light can penetrate the oceans to normal submarine operational depths, making it possible to send entire messages, not just a paging call, to submerged submarines.[3] Once this technology is operational, it should be possible to communicate with SLBM commanders as rapidly as can now be done with ICBM bases. The submarines themselves would thereby be rendered much less vulnerable. Such laser/satellite systems could also be used to communicate with land-based vehicles, surface ships, and aircraft carrying missiles.

In addition to giving retaliatory systems their marching orders, it is also necessary to guide them accurately to their destinations. Guidance system technology has made tremendous strides over the past two decades. While ICBMs could be used only against physically soft targets in the 1960s, today's ICBMs, using advanced inertial navigation (based on exact knowledge of the coordinates of the launch point, precise measurements of enroute movements via accelerometers, and correction for gravitational anomalies encountered enroute) permit ICBMs to hit their intended targets within a few hundred feet.

Until the 1980s SLBMs could not approach this sort of accuracy. But recent developments in space-based radio navigation (triangulation) systems (e.g., the NAVSTAR Global Positioning System) will soon permit SLBM accuracies of the same degree of precision. Both inertial and triangulation systems can be supplemented with star-tracking (celestial) systems of the sort used to guide deep-space probes.

A third development is being applied both to cruise missiles and to medium-range missiles (e.g., the Pershing II). This is terrain contour matching, in which reconnaissance radar maps of particular targets and the terrain along the way are stored in a missile's on-board computer. Radar sensors on board the missile compare actual scenes with the stored pictures to enable the missile to avoid obstacles and locate its particular target within a hundred feet or less.

In short, today's guidance system technology has made it possible to assign missiles—ICBMs, SLBMs, and cruise missiles—to very specific targets. When combined with relatively low-yield warheads (kilotons rather than megatons), such missiles can be used with precision strictly against military and command structure targets. Technology, in short, has given us the means to fight a nuclear war in accordance with Just War principles.

Defense

Active Defense

Thus far in the nuclear age the U.S. approach to the active nuclear defense of its population primarily has been to place nuclear warheads in rockets and missiles for purposes of retaliation. At the beginning, when the entire threat consisted of Soviet bombers, it was decided (probably properly so) that the bulk of the limited Soviet nuclear weapon stockpile would be directed at U.S. urban-industrial areas, these areas being the most lucrative targets. In this context early nuclear air defense systems consisted of manned interceptors armed with nuclear-tipped air-to-air rockets and surface-to-air guided missiles with nuclear warheads.

All these systems are now long gone, a decision having been made that the principal future threat from the Soviet Union would consist of ballistic missiles. Not only are the nuclear air defense weapons gone, but so are most of the rest. The United States is now defenseless against air attack, whether by bombers or cruise missiles, at a time when the Soviets are known to be operating a fleet of Backfire bombers, which have the capability to conduct nuclear attacks against the United States, and have been testing a new bomber having B-1 capabilities.

In 1970 the United States set about to develop and deploy the Safeguard antiballistic missile (ABM) system to protect the population and key military installations. In 1972 this program effectively came to an end with the signing of the SALT I ABM treaty. Although the treaty permitted each side to construct two ABM sites—one for the capital city, the other for an ICBM field—the United States chose to disband its program.

We are now essentially defenseless against attack. This situation is one of design in accordance with the unrealistic policies the United States has adopted in the nuclear age. It has been rationalized on the basis that, by having the capability to mount a devastating nuclear counterattack, the United States will remain successful in deterring nuclear war. Despite the overwhelming historical evidence showing that the introduction of new weapons never has succeeded in preventing wars, some of which have been at least as destructive on a relative basis as the nuclear war we dread, U.S. nuclear deterrence has come to be regarded as essentially absolute. The Soviets have not attacked the United States, *we* proclaim, for fear of the terrible reprisal in store. Not only does this arbitrary assertion leave our fate in the hands of Soviet leaders, it also leaves this country vulnerable to lesser nuclear threats: for example, those posed by China or by a missile launched accidentally.

It is interesting to note that the Soviet Union has not emulated our absolute faith in deterrence. Not only have the Soviets maintained and modernized the ABM systems allowed them under the ABM treaty; in addition they have developed and continually modernized an extensive air defense system that consumes approximately half their strategic nuclear budget. This system comprises thousands of jet fighter-interceptors and between 10,000 and 12,000 surface-to-air missiles (SAMs) and more than 6,000 radar systems to defend against bombers and cruise missiles.[4] Some defense analysts also suspect that the Soviet SA-5 SAM, though nominally an air defense missile, has actually been developed with ABM capabilities, as well.

Many Americans, because of doubts over the viability of the 1960s-technology Safeguard ABM system, retain the impression of ABMs as Rube Goldberg affairs that cannot really be made to work. In fact substantial technological progress has resulted from the $20 billion spent on ballistic missile defense research over the past fifteen years. Improvements in data-processing capabilities, interception strategies, and detection, designation, and discrimination technologies have all been quite significant.

The currently favored analytical concept is multilayered defense. The idea is to utilize two or more layers of defense, some outside the atmosphere (exoatmospheric) and others at shorter range within the atmosphere (endoatmospheric). The incoming reentry vehicle would have to pass through each successive layer in order to reach its target, but the different layers would use different means of detection (radar, optical, infrared) and different means of kill (both nuclear and nonnuclear).[5] Such redundancy increases the likelihood for successful interception of the actual warheads (as opposed to decoys) and provides against both operational failures of some part of the system and against unanticipated breakthroughs in the enemy's reentry vehicle technology. According to computer simulation studies, two-level systems using present-technology radars, missiles, and data processing produce a high degree of attrition of incoming reentry vehicles, though no prototype systems have yet been built and tested.

One low-cost concept for the lowest-level (terminal) defense is known as Swarmjet. It would utilize thousands of foot-long high-velocity rockets, fired at incoming reentry vehicles in a swarm, guided by a simple range-only radar. Such a system has been advocated as an essentially off-the-shelf means of defending ICBM silos, pending development of more sophisticated systems.[6]

One multilayered system is the proposed High Frontier project.[7] This system would provide for a three-layer defense, with the first two located outside the atmosphere based on satellites and the terminal layer consisting (at least initially) of Swarmjet projectiles. The other two layers would seek to intercept ICBMs in, respectively, the boost and midcourse phases of flight. The initial space-based portion would consist of 432 orbital platforms, each equipped with forty to forty-five interceptor missiles, guided by infrared, with nonnuclear warheads. The orbital platforms would provide continuous coverage of both the Soviet Union and the ocean areas where Soviet SLBMs operate.

A second-generation orbiting system could make use of some form of directed-energy weapon. High-energy lasers or beams of subatomic particles could function literally as death rays, vaporizing a portion of the ICBM booster or reentry vehicle and thereby destroying it. Both U.S. and Soviet defense agencies are researching these technologies. Although the Soviets apparently began serious particle-beam weapons research first, the United States may have a substantial edge in laser technology and, perhaps more important, in the sensor and data-processing technologies needed to turn a promising concept into an effective weapons system. Research and development on directed-energy weapons is of the utmost importance, since the successful deployment of such systems could significantly strengthen deterrence of nuclear attack.

It is not yet clear whether space basing will be optimal for directed-energy ABM weapons. The strength of an energy beam is limited by its power source, and since ICBMs can be hardened to some extent against such beams, very large-scale power requirements could result, calling for very large, expensive satellites. In addition, of course, satellite battle stations might be vulnerable to attack, and their communications links might be vulnerable to interference. On the other hand most directed-energy beams propagate with least dispersion and energy loss through the vacuum of space and are attenuated by passing through the atmosphere. Clearly trade-offs of various sorts will have to be made.

Thus another approach would be to utilize earth-based directed-energy weapons. Basing the system on the ground would permit a straightforward, brute-force approach. Compared with orbiting battle stations, there would be no stringent constraint on power supply because of launch-vehicle payload limits. Compared with an interceptor missile, once again there would be no comparable limit on size or performance.

An earth-based system would also lend itself to use of a nuclear explosive as the power source for a directed-energy weapon. There are some indications that the Soviet particle-beam weapons research and development program is using nuclear explosives as the power source, given that the experiments are being carried out in the huge Semipalatinsk nuclear testing area and that high radiation levels have been detected in connection with those particle-beam experiments.[8]

Use of a nuclear explosive to power such a weapon need not pose a danger to the surrounding populace, however. The device would be of "clean" design, producing very little radioactivity. It would be exploded underground, with the heat and radiation mostly absorbed by the soil, but with the kill-mechanism effects directed upward in the beam toward the incoming reentry vehicles. One such underground nuclear device could be used to launch a huge number of small, high-velocity projectiles—a sort of nuclear shotgun or nuclear Swarmjet.

The point of this discussion is not to specify precise system designs. Rather, the purpose has been to demonstrate that technology exists and is continuing to develop for defense against ballistic missiles. All that prevents us from having such a defense is the political will to do so and the provisions of SALT I's ABM treaty, to which we will return in the chapter's final section.

Passive Defense

If there were to be nuclear war with the Soviet Union, unless we sought to commit suicide by deliberately bombing Soviet cities, bringing about retaliation in kind, there is no evidence that the Soviets would deliberately seek to attack the U.S. population. To the contrary, Soviet targeting priorities in nuclear war long have been known; in the main they constitute military facilities.

Included in the target list would be that part of the U.S. economy directly supporting the war. Although such attack may indirectly bring about large-scale urban devastation and casualties, by no means does this imply that most of our populace will be directly at risk from the destructive effects of Soviet nuclear weapons. Relatively few U.S. cities contain industrial facilities relating critically to the prosecution of a strategic nuclear war. This strongly suggests that those urban-industrial centers that might come under direct attack should be protected by a combination of active defense and civil defense against the effects of nuclear bursts not directly employed against the population per se. The rest of the country should be protected by cheap underground fallout shelters.

How realistic is such civil defense? After all, the common impression, from such popular writers as Jonathan Schell and Helen Caldicott, is that a nuclear war would exterminate life itself.[9] Such statements have had a huge negative effect on U.S. civil defense efforts to date. If global extinction is inevitable, so is our national extinction, in which case efforts to ensure national survival are hopeless.

Responsible scientific studies show that even with a very heavy nuclear exchange, the human race and its ecology can survive. For example, in 1975 the National Research Council issued a report examining the global effects of a massive thermonuclear exchange, involving a total yield of 10,000 megatons.[10] (Included in the exchange were 500 to 1,000 weapons of 10 to 20 megatons each, far larger than most of those in today's arsenals.) The principal question asked was whether the biosphere and the species, *Homo sapiens,* would survive. The response of the study was "Yes."

One very common fear is that a nuclear war would so seriously deplete the ozone layer that over a period of several years ultraviolet radiation would produce large-scale damage to plant life and seriously burn exposed humans and animals. What this argument neglects is that significant ozone depletion happens only when extremely high-yield warheads, greater than 10 megatons, are detonated.[11] The trend in both U.S. and Soviet strategic warheads has for some time been in the direction of smaller and smaller yields. (Promoting this trend is the

Threshold Test Ban Treaty, which precludes testing of devices larger than 150 kilotons.) In the near future all U.S. strategic warheads, in ballistic and cruise missiles, will have yields well below 1 megaton, whose mushroom clouds will not rise to the level of the ozone layer. Similarly, as the Soviets increasingly arm their ballistic missiles with multiple warheads (MIRVs), it can be expected that their warhead yields will also be reduced to fractional-megaton levels.

Unfortunately the Reagan administration has based its entire proposed civil defense program on a concept called "crisis relocation," evacuation of cities into nontarget areas. This program is premised on the expectation that a nuclear war would develop out of a major crisis, providing ample time for evacuation. To embark upon such a program would be highly unadvisable, for two reasons.

First, in implementing a crisis relocation program, it would be necessary to conduct training evacuation drills. Yet it is doubtful whether anything approaching the full cooperation of all Americans would be achieved and it is highly likely that such drills would evoke considerable resistance and antagonism. There would certainly be much resentment against the disruption of normal urban functions. Moreover, even were the bulk of a city's populace to comply and evacuate, if they returned and found some number of their homes and businesses looted, a political boomerang would result. For these reasons alone, evacuation appears to be a dubious prospect.

Even if cooperation in these evacuation drills were forthcoming, it is unlikely that a nuclear war would develop out of a major crisis, providing the necessary time for evacuation. Instead it is more likely that a nuclear war would commence with a surprise attack. Realistically, warning time for civilian survival would be on the order of five to twenty minutes—only enough time for a significant fraction of the urban population to get to shelters immediately at hand. Clearly the only feasible solution for protecting civilians in a nuclear target area would be a system of underground shelters. Such shelters can be made highly resistant to blast and radiation. Underground sheltering offers the possibility of drastic reductions in civilian casualties, a point that has not been lost on the Chinese, the Swedes, and the Swiss, all of whom have developed extensive systems of underground shelters.[12]

The Swiss civil defense system has focused on providing blast and radiation protection, allowing purely local movement to a protected site.[13] Capitalizing on their generally mountainous terrain, the Swiss have constructed enormous underground shelters. In other cases underground construction for other purposes has been modified to provide occupation facilities in the event of war, one prime example being the modification of Lucerne's Sonnenberg tunnel, which can accommodate

20,000 people. The larger shelters are fully stocked with essentials to permit extended inhabitation and contain extensive medical facilities. For example, the Sonnenberg shelter contains central ventilation, electrical generators, kitchens (with refrigeration), water supplies, medical facilities (including two rooms for surgery and more than 300 hospital beds), and so on. And keep in mind that Switzerland has a long record of avoiding war.

How effective an underground shelter program may be in saving lives given the imponderables of nuclear war and human behavior is impossible even to estimate. At issue here are such indeterminable factors as Soviet nuclear strategy, the efficiency of shelter occupation, the nature of urban construction in the immediate vicinity of shelters, how protected shelter occupants may be from fires that may be raging at the surface and the degree to which the shelters were stocked in the event of prolonged surface radioactive contamination. Although different studies, holding to different assumptions, predict different levels of casualties, they nevertheless show that national survival can be greatly enhanced.[14]

Perhaps the most important factor affecting the efficacy of civil defense is the Soviet targeting strategy. In this respect there has been a proclivity on the part of many civil defense opponents to take upon themselves the task of deciding Soviet strategy, choosing to ignore what the Soviets themselves may have decided. Having become self-appointed Soviet targeting analysts, they then proceed to evaluate U.S. civil defense in the context of horrendously large warhead yields being directed at the heart of major U.S. cities; for example, 25 megatons detonated over downtown Los Angeles, which not only erases downtown Los Angeles, but probably most of its shelters as well.

There is nothing in the Soviet doctrine to indicate that such monstrous attacks against civilians are at all seriously considered. To the contrary there is ample evidence pointing to a rational desire to avoid excessive civil damage. A paper in *Military Thought*, the official journal of the Soviet General Staff, makes this point clear:

> The objective is not to turn the large economic and industrial regions into a heap of ruins . . . but to deliver strikes which will destroy strategic combat means, paralyze enemy military production, making it incapable of satisfying the priority needs of the front and rear areas and sharply reduce the enemy capability to conduct strikes.[15]

Since the Soviet Union might absorb terrible punishment to its own urban-industrial fabric, why would it wish to deprive itself of the economic contribution a reasonably intact defeated United States might make toward its postwar recovery?

Regarding the specifics of Soviet targeting strategy, the Soviet military has made it very clear that they are primarily interested in defeating and occupying the United States in a nuclear war, not in exterminating it.[16] In this connection, if the Soviets intend to occupy a defeated United States, why would they wish to produce a postwar aftermath of such horrendous devastation and contamination of urban areas as to make occupation extremely difficult or even infeasible? This is not to say that the war would not be brutal; it most certainly would be. Rather, it is to say that the Soviets do not regard nuclear war as a means of exterminating the enemy populace and economy.

On the other hand this massive destruction could result from a Soviet response to a U.S. second strike against Soviet cities, were the United States to retain its Mutual Assured Destruction strategy, and actually implement it during the war. Even then, however, if reason were to prevail over passion in the Soviet leadership, it would be rational for the Soviets to stick with their peacetime targeting doctrine; and, for the reasons listed before, at least to be able to exploit an undevastated U.S. economy to help rebuild a devastated Soviet Union.

In evaluating an underground shelter civil defense system, as best possible a realistic risk assessment must be made; balancing the probable benefits (which can be huge; although accompanied by high costs, perhaps eventually approaching $100 billion) against the possibility that the Soviets will deliberately attempt to defeat such a system (a possibility which, taking the Soviet strategy into account, seems quite low). Based on the arguments presented here, such an assessment would rule heavily in favor of civil defense, despite its costs, *provided* that the United States becomes equally realistic in assessing the risks of continuing with its present policy of containing Soviet aggression in Europe and Asia. Giving up this highly unrealistic objective would make funds available for the direct defense, both active and passive, of the United States.

Retaliation

No nation can be defended for long simply by shielding itself from attack. Even were our ABM and civil defense capabilities developed to the fullest possible extent, a nuclear attack would still cause considerable damage. Moreover the attacker would be free to regroup his forces and try again, and again, until eventually the defenses were exhausted. Thus as chapter 1 makes clear, Just War principles sanction retaliation so as to destroy the enemy's ability to attack again.

Just what that retaliation should do is the subject of war-fighting doctrine. Unfortunately what passes for U.S. strategic war-fighting doctrine today reflects a failure to accept the realities of a nuclear warfare environment. To a considerable degree U.S. strategic doctrine is still premised on the concept of deterrence per se; should deterrence fail, there would be no rational or moral strategy spelling out how to use our nuclear weapons and therefore how many and what type we need. Yet as noted earlier, the paradox of deterrence is precisely that unless U.S. enemies *believe* that a war would produce unacceptable consequences to them, they are unlikely to be deterred. Thus a *credible* deterrent must be one that is based on a credible doctrine for use of nuclear forces to wage war.

How should strategic nuclear weapons be used in retaliation? From chapter 1 we know that they must not be aimed deliberately at civilians; the Mutual Assured Destruction idea of smashing cities must be ruled out. What should be hit, instead, are the enemy's military bases, naval vessels and harbors, weapons factories and storage depots, training camps, command centers, communications links, and so on. In addition, the Soviet government's apparatus for controlling its populace—and its satellite nations—can and should be targeted. As noted in the previous section, the guidance-system technology exists and is largely operational to specify and hit targets within 100 feet or less. Thus it is quite possible to target specific buildings throughout the Soviet Union— planning ministries, KGB offices, Communist Party facilities, even Black Sea dachas of the Kremlin leadership—with low-yield nuclear explosions, producing but a small fraction of the collateral damage inherent in the current strategic arsenal.

One potential target has not been emphasized in the foregoing list: missile silos. It is well-known that many Soviet missile silos are designed for "cold launch" of ICBMs (using compressed gas, rather than the missile's own rocket engines), making the silos reusable. Current defense planning in the United States places great emphasis on being able to destroy such silos, in order to (1) destroy any ICBMs not launched in the first-wave attack and (2) to render the silos unusable for subsequent launches. Three requirements for U.S. ICBMs emerge from this targeting doctrine: quick response, large warheads, and accuracy. Quick response is justified on the assumption that the Soviets may wait quite a while before launching a second wave from the remaining silos or that reloading of silos used in the first wave will take quite a while. Large warheads are needed because missile silos are "hardened" in an effort to make them survivable. And accuracy is needed because a missile silo is a very small target. The requirement to destroy Soviet silos was the principal justification for the very large MX missile system.

Yet the case for retaliation against Soviet missile silos rests on shaky ground. As will be discussed later in this chapter, without on-site inspection there is no way of knowing how many of the Soviet Union's official silos (which can be observed, in daylight, by U.S. reconnaissance satellites) even contain ICBMs at all. Modern Soviet missiles like the SS-18, SS-19, and SS-20 can be stored in and launched from self-contained cannisters that can be moved from place to place. There is no need for them to be housed in fixed silos. Thus a policy of attacking silos—especially if that policy uses up a major portion of our strategic retaliatory resources—may accomplish very little while costing a great deal. Because we would be unable to destroy the bulk of Soviet ICBMs in any retaliatory strike—either they would have already been launched in the Soviet first strike or they would be concealed elsewhere—it makes little sense to devote nearly half the destructive force of our strategic weaponry to Soviet silos. Those same resources could accomplish far more if targeted largely against the Soviet military and command infrastructure.

Making such a shift would be more risky if the United States were to continue to forswear defense against ballistic missiles. Given the active and passive defense systems outlined earlier, however, such a shift of targeting makes sense. Moreover, by revising its strategy regarding MX-type silo-busters, the United States would be removing the suspicion that such weapons might someday be used in a first strike against the Soviet Union. This would knock the props out from under the Soviet claim that its own weapons buildup is merely defensive.

What, then, *are* the requirements for strategic retaliatory weapons systems? Clearly they must be able to survive a nuclear attack so that they can be used. They must also be able to survive attempted interference with their command, control, and communications systems enroute to their targets. And they must have a high probability of getting through to their intended targets. Finally they must be designed with sufficient accuracy to hit their targets as precisely as possible and with a warhead yield sufficient to destroy the target with as little collateral damage as possible.

Present U.S. strategic weapons consist of three principal types, comprising the so-called Triad. These are (1) land-based intercontinental ballistic missiles (ICBMs); (2) submarine-launched ballistic missiles (SLBMs); and (3) manned bombers. A fourth component is now entering the arsenal: the nuclear-armed cruise missile, which may be launched from aircraft, surface ships, or submarines. (Cruise missiles can be launched from land, as well, but since they lack intercontinental range, for U.S. strategic defense they must be carried to within range of the Soviet Union by some sort of carrier vehicle.)

The basic idea of the Triad is a sound one: to enhance survivability, to reduce C³ vulnerability, and to increase the likelihood of reaching the target by using a *mix* of weapons systems having *different* technological characteristics. Unfortunately interservice rivalries produce strong tendencies to cling to particular systems (e.g., manned penetrating bombers) even when they begin losing their effectiveness and better systems such as the cruise missile come along. The point is that while avoiding putting all your eggs in one basket is prudent, the traditional Triad is certainly not sacred. A suitable mix of strategic systems must be derived from the requirements of retaliatory war-fighting, not some mystical devotion to three traditional systems.

Table 4–1 compares ICBM, SLBM, bomber, and cruise missile capabilities against a number of system requirements. In addition to the four requirements already discussed, three others often advanced in discussions of the Triad are listed: (1) speed of response (generally raised in connection with taking out missile silos); (2) payload capability (also raised in discussing the need to destroy hardened targets like silos); and (3) recallability, the ability to call off an attack after the button has been pushed.

As can be seen, no system ranks highest on all requirements. In the past five years land-based ICBMs in fixed silos have become vulnerable to attack, due to increases in missile accuracy. Missiles on submarines remain highly invulnerable, at present, though this may change as research in antisubmarine warfare progresses. Bomber survivability is listed as "moderate" based on two assumptions. The first assumption is that the bomber force be kept on continuous alert, in aircraft capable of quick (several-minute) launch. The second assumption is that the bomber fleets not be based near the seacoast. The principal threat to bomber survivability is SLBMs, with their short five- to fifteen-minute flight time.[17]

It should be noted also that a coordinated enemy strike could *not* succeed in destroying both bombers and ICBMs in their silos. If Soviet ICBMs and SLBMs were launched simultaneously (aimed, respectively, at our ICBM silos and bomber bases), even if no bombers could be launched by the time the ten-minute SLBM flights had elapsed and the warheads were destroying the airbases, there would still be twenty minutes of Soviet ICBM warhead flight time left, during which our own ICBMs could be launched. (This would *not* be "launch on warning," since the destruction of our bomber bases would be proof positive that the war had begun.) Alternatively if the Soviets timed both ICBM and SLBM salvos to arrive *simultaneously* on target, once our warning satellites had detected the ICBM launches (in the first five minutes), there would still be twenty-five minutes to launch the bombers—again, without going to a hair-trigger "launch [of ICBMs] on warning" policy.

Table 4–1
Strategic Weapons Characteristics

	Survivability (Preemptive)	C³ Survivability	Penetration	Accuracy	Payload	Speed of Response	Recallability
ICBMs							
Fixed-site	Moderate[a]	High	High	High	High	High	No
Land-mobile	High	Moderate	High	High	Moderate	High	No
Sea-mobile	Moderate	Moderate	High	High	Moderate	High	No
SLBMs							
Current guidance, C³	High	Low	High	Low	Mod-High	Moderate	No
Future guidance, C³	High	Moderate	High	High	Mod-High	High	No
Bombers							
Gravity bombs	Moderate[a]	Moderate	Low	Low	High	Low	Yes
Precision-guided bombs	Moderate[a]	Moderate	Low	High	High	Low	Yes
Cruise missiles							
Air-launched	High	Moderate	Moderate	High	Low	Low	Yes
Ship-launched	Moderate	Moderate	Moderate	High	Low	Moderate	Yes
Submarine-launched	High	Low	Moderate	High	Low	Moderate	Yes

[a]As explained in text, either bombers or ICBMs are likely to survive a preemptive strike, but not both.

On the requirement for invulnerable C^3, fixed-site weapons launchers are the most secure, since they can be alerted via fiber optic land lines, invulnerable to EMP or electronic jamming. Any mobile systems are somewhat less secure and submerged ones are the least secure of all, at least until direct communications techniques are perfected.

On the third parameter, the probability of actually penetrating to the target, at present both ICBMs and SLBMs rank high, with cruise missiles probably less likely to get through, due to the Soviet Union's extensive air defense system. That applies even more strongly to bombers, which must now be ranked as the least likely to get through. Even the new stealth techniques, designed to reduce radar visibility, can be applied equally well to cruise missiles, thereby preserving their relative advantage over bombers in penetrating air defenses.

Five years ago, the column labeled "accuracy" would have listed only fixed-site ICBMs as having high accuracy (cruise missiles not yet being available). Today with the availability of the precision guidance systems discussed earlier, SLBMs and cruise missiles can also be rated as highly accurate. While conventional gravity bombs are unacceptably inaccurate, bombers can now be equipped with "smart" precision-guided bombs, raising them into the highly accurate category, as well.

Relative payload capabilities are compared in the fifth column. Fixed-site ICBMs and bombers can carry the largest payloads, followed by SLBMs on large submarines. Mobile missiles, based on land or surface ships, generally have to be smaller and lighter in order to be mobile and hence can carry less payload. Finally cruise missiles are small and can carry only small payloads.

As noted earlier, systems having high speed of response may not be as important as Triad supporters generally maintain, due to the possibility that Soviet preemptive or deceptive measures may deprive them of a large fraction of their targets. Nevertheless the sixth column shows how the systems compare on overall response time—from decision to launch to arrival of the warhead on target. ICBMs are the quickest, but once direct undersea communications has been perfected, SLBMs will become equally rapid. The systems slowest to respond are bombers and air-launched cruise missiles.

Finally, as emphasized by their advocates, bombers and cruise missiles are "recallable"—that is, they can be launched upon warning of an attack *without* being irrevocably committed. While not of overwhelming importance, this capability can in some circumstances permit increased flexibility and survivability.

Given the mix of attributes depicted in table 4–1, what mix of weapons systems makes the most sense? Focusing on the most important requirements, in the first four columns, we can eliminate bombers on the grounds of their being least likely to get through to their targets. (Note that we are here talking about the bomber itself as a penetrating weapon; we have not excluded bomber-type aircraft as cruise missile carriers, in which case only the missile itself would attempt to penetrate enemy air space.) We can also eliminate current-generation SLBMs as being far too inaccurate to be acceptable. That leaves us with some possible mix of ICBMs, SLBMs, and cruise missiles, with various possible launching modes for the first and third.

In view of the increasing vulnerability of fixed-site ICBMs, there is much to be said for switching to mobile ICBMs. Survivability would be improved by switching to large numbers of much smaller missiles, widely dispersed, based on road-mobile vehicles, on surface ships operating in protected coastal waters, or both. By shifting the hardened-target payload requirements to SLBMs, the new ICBM could be made as small as 20,000 pounds (compared with 80,000 pounds for the Minuteman and nearly 200,000 pounds for the MX), thereby making it readily mobile over ordinary highways on standard commercial heavy trucks. The missile would carry a single warhead.

Widespread dispersal of nuclear-armed missiles, rather than confining them to relatively small numbers of submarines or missile bases, raises potential concerns over accidents, unauthorized launch, and even capture by terrorists. Although stringent security and command-and-control techniques would be employed, one way of reducing these vulnerabilities would be to divide each missile into three components, to be assembled only after war had broken out: the rocket booster, the reentry vehicle, and the nuclear material itself. The rocket boosters themselves could be moved about on commercial-type tractor-trailer rigs or offshore patrol boats. The reentry vehicles and nuclear materials could be kept on small aircraft with vertical/short take-off and landing (V/STOL) capabilities, operating out of secure military bases. Upon receipt of an alert, specific V/STOL aircraft would rendezvous with predesignated rocket carriers, where the reentry vehicles and nuclear material would be assembled. While this system would not have the same speed of response as preassembled mobile ICBMs, it must be remembered that speed of response is not a prime requirement and that SLBMs would continue to provide a fast-response capability (once equipped with undersea communications capability).

Overall, then, a preferred strategic retaliatory capability would consist of (1) mobile ICBMs, based on land or on small surface ships or both, (2) SLBMs with improved guidance and communications systems enabling the submarines to communicate in real time with command authorities and with SLBM accuracies comparable to those of current ICBMs, and (3) some mix of cruise missiles in air, sea, and submarine-launched modes. This mix of systems would be highly survivable, both against preemptive strikes and attempts to interfere with C^3. All of its components would be highly accurate. Some, the SLBMs, could still respond rapidly, but a large force of ICBMs and cruise missiles would be available after this initial strike for more adaptive responses. Both hardened and softer targets could be hit. And one component, the cruise missiles, would be recallable.

One of the most important aspects of this revised mix of weapons systems is its impact on Soviet doctrine and strategic posture. The Soviets' highest priority targets are U.S. strategic nuclear weapons. In the kinds of strategic weapons the Soviets have developed and deployed, the basic design goal has been an effective attack on U.S. land-based strategic weapons. The resulting huge and continually modernized Soviet force of ballistic missiles represents the great bulk of the Soviet strategic force investment, designed against a clearly perceived target system in the United States, a system that so far has become increasingly lucrative to Soviet strategic planners, who seem to have planned all too well. Were this priority target system to be taken away from the Soviets through the shift to mobile systems, Soviet planners would have to question whether they had developed the wrong doctrine and deployed the wrong kind of strategic weapons and whether they had overdesigned and overproduced weapons whose primary targets have mainly disappeared.

One possible way to achieve strategic nuclear arms control is to deprive the Soviets of their target list. If this were accomplished by facing them with mobile missile forces that could not be successfully attacked by their vaunted ICBMs, an incentive might exist to discontinue production of these missiles, or even begin to reduce their numbers. Two birds would have been killed with one stone: such mobile missile systems not only would best enhance strategic force survivability, they also could provide a compelling reason for the other side to freeze or reduce its own strategic force. Properly conceived and designed, new strategic weapon developments may be a better way to bring about reductions in the other sides' weapons, and in U.S. weapons as well, than years of frustrating and unproductive negotiations.

Arms Control

The strategic systems advocated in this chapter—mobile land-based and sea-based missiles, nuclear-armed cruise missiles, and ABM systems—all share one common characteristic. Although they are in accord with the Just War moral principles of chapter 1, they violate the current precepts of arms control, premised on the logic of Mutual Assured Destruction. Mobile missiles and cruise missiles are inherently unverifiable by "national technical means of verification" (reconnaissance satellites). And new ABM systems explicitly violate the SALT I ABM treaty, from which the United States would have to withdraw in order to implement such systems.

All this gets to the very heart of the nuclear arms control process, which is held by its proponents to offer the best prospects for U.S. national security and for avoiding nuclear war. What can be said about this process?

If one attempts to defend strategic nuclear arms control based on the record thus far, there is little that can be advanced to show that U.S. national security has increased while two treaties—SALT I and II—have been consummated and their terms observed by the United States. At the time the United States decided to enter into the SALT I negotiations, it held a significant lead over the Soviet Union in strategic nuclear systems, quantitative and qualitative. Today, as shown in chapter 3, the Soviets hold a substantial lead in the number of systems. Qualitatively their weapons appear to be at least the equal of those of the United States.

At the same time that the United States, in the arms control atmosphere of the 1970s, was allowing the Soviets to achieve superiority in offensive strategic nuclear capabilities, it also was allowing the Soviets to establish a virtual monopoly in defensive capabilities. As Secretary of Defense Caspar Weinberger pointed out:

> While the Soviets have emphasized both offensive and defensive forces, the United States has largely neglected defense preparations. The Soviets have also continued development of and paid increasing attention to civil defense and a wide variety of measures, designed to enhance the prospect of survivability of key elements of their society after the outbreak of a nuclear war.[18]

Based on the actual record of strategic arms control to date, there is little to suggest that the arms control process has seriously slowed down the so-called arms race; that it has increased stability and thereby decreased the probability of nuclear war; or that it has increased U.S. national security. In fact largely the opposite has been true. This is not to suggest that we discard arms control as a national policy objective (though that is probably a political impossibility) but, rather, to suggest that we address the issue realistically.

The fundamental problem stems from a 1972 decision, in furtherance of the SALT process. Until that time U.S. policy was to insist that any arms control treaty provide for on-site inspection to verify compliance. But to verify the SALT I treaty provisions, the United States agreed to rely on reconnaissance satellites and other remote sensing devices (e.g., electronic listening posts in places like Iran and Turkey), the so-called national technical means of verification. The problem with these devices is that we can see only what the Soviets want us to see.

As noted earlier, reconnaissance satellites cannot even see in the dark or through clouds and fog. They certainly cannot see through the roofs of Soviet defense plants and warehouses, beneath the ground, or even under camouflage netting. Although they enable us to count missile silos—holes in the ground—they give us no clue to the actual number of ICBMs the Soviets have produced or even deployed in some other mode or location. Missiles can be hidden in warehouses, factories, caves, or mines. They can be stored in their launching cannisters, ready to be erected for launch at a location chosen by the Soviets and not known in advance for us to target. The Soviets have perfected a cold-launch technique using compressed gas to launch ballistic missiles from cannisters in silos; it is similar to the technique used for launching our own SLBMs from their submarine tubes. We have no way of knowing how many such encapsulated Soviet ICBMs have been produced and secretly deployed, invisible to our eyes in the sky. Nor, for that matter, do we know how many Soviet silos may be empty, serving simply as false targets.

Both SALT I and SALT II limit only the number of launchers, *not* the number of missiles. Thus the Soviets might be in technical compliance with the terms of both, having precisely the number of silos they claim, while having large (unknown) numbers of additional ICBMs stored in cannisters at unknown locations. The existence of Soviet cruise missiles, much smaller and easier to conceal, only compounds the problem.

Once it is understood that we *cannot* count numbers of Soviet weapons, the validity of national technical means of verification disappears. Even more disturbing, differences in weapon quality cannot be "verified" at all. And the progress of technology continues to improve weapons quality.

The U.S. arms control approach has been a numbers game played in the context of verification by national technical means; not an attempt to achieve treaties based on a realistic assessment of each side's actual military capabilities, which would have to include both offensive and defensive weapons. (In terms of overall capabilities the Soviet advantage over the United States may exceed very considerably the admitted advantage they have in offensive weapons.) In this context it is *impossible* through national technical means alone to make an assessment that safeguards U.S. security interests.

If the Soviet Union and the United States truly want nuclear peace, they will both be willing to let one another know their respective capabilities. Thus the United States should propose unlimited continuous inspection of all nuclear installations, known or suspected, of the other without notice, day or night, by an army of legal Soviet spies for our installations and an army of legal American spies for theirs.

The inspections would not be limited to declared nuclear installations because nuclear weapons may be concealed elsewhere. The offer would make acceptance by the Soviet Union a precondition of arms control negotiations. Each side would have to give a complete report to the other of all nuclear weapons. Then the legal spies would arrive and have the access required. They would stay in the other country with replacements from time to time. Meanwhile negotiations could proceed and be continuous, with treaties resulting from time to time, subject to cancellation on short notice.

The unlimited inspections would not cease with the treaty. They would continue subject to cancellation with an agreed period for notice. The inspections would be a greater service to peace than any treaty. A treaty can be broken in an instant. The inspections would provide confidence in the other side's intentions. Even such an arrangement possibly can be foiled if loopholes are allowed. Thus it is essential that the proposal not be hedged in any way: no limit on inspections and no notice required.

There is a solid historical precedent for such an arrangement. In the 1919 Treaty of Versailles, ending World War I, the Germans gave the victorious allies detailed promises that they would not rearm. To verify these pledges, the Allied Control Commission was stationed on German soil and given unlimited access to every installation in the country, twenty-four hours a day. (Unfortunately the Germans were able to begin rearmament anyway, concluding secret agreements by which the Soviet Union began producing weapons for Germany. And in 1927, the commission was withdrawn, in the spirit of Locarno—the détente of the 1920s.)[19]

Objectors to this proposal will say that it is just a ploy to kill arms control negotiations. The reason we settled for scientific surveillance was that the Soviet Union would not permit on-site inspections. They are hardly likely to permit an army of bourgeois spies.

The way to find out is to offer. If the offer is accepted, the chance of nuclear peace is enhanced. If the offer is rejected, we will know that for the Soviet Union arms control is a game to gain an advantage and act accordingly.

The offer would unite the country. The American people have far more sense than their guardians acknowledge. If the president makes the offer and the Soviet Union rejects it, the president can forge a national consensus for peace through armed strength rather than through paper chains.

Some will object that the Soviet Union would use the knowledge they obtain under the agreement against us after cancelling the arrangement. But because of our open society, the Soviets now know much more about our nuclear strength than we know about theirs.

But with nuclear war a very real possibility, most Americans would follow the president's lead. We have heard much about risks for peace that urge us to buy a pig in a poke. Why not an offer for peace that gives us what we truly require: full disclosure and inspection?

The United States certainly need not worry about how such a proposal would appeal to our allies, who are urging negotiations at any cost. And the proposal would be a proper answer to foreign and American demonstrators for peace. The proposal need not put conditions on the outcome of the talks; let them await the bargaining table. Meanwhile let's take the Soviets at their word, assume they want to avoid nuclear war, and make the offer in good faith, hoping for acceptance.

Notes

1. William Broad, "Nuclear Pulse," pt. 1, *Science* (May 29, 1981): 1009; pt. 2 (June 5, 1981): 1116; pt. 3 (June 12, 1981): 1248.

2. Philip J. Klass, "Laser Communications Plan Studied," *Aviation Week and Space Technology,* September 3, 1979, p. 73.

3. Philip J. Klass, "Studies Weigh Approaches in Blue-Green Laser Use," *Aviation Week and Space Technology,* June 21, 1982, p. 70.

4. Roger D. Speed, *Strategic Deterrence in the 1980s* (Stanford, Calif.: Hoover Institution Press, 1979), pp. 51–56.

5. See, for example, Colin S. Gray, "A New Debate on Ballistic Missile Defence," *Survival* 23, no. 2 (1981): 62, and Clarence A. Robinson, Jr., "Layered Defense System Pushed to Protect ICBMs," *Aviation Week and Space Technology,* February 9, 1981, p. 83.

6. *Swarmjet Final Report, Phase III* (San Ramon, Calif.: Tracor MBA, June 30, 1981).

7. Lt. Gen. Daniel O. Graham, *High Frontier: A New National Strategy* (Washington, D.C.: Heritage Foundation, 1982).

8. Clarence A. Robinson, Jr., "Soviets Push for Beam Weapon," *Aviation Week and Space Technology,* May 2, 1977, p. 16.

9. See Jonathan Schell, *The Fate of the Earth* (New York: Alfred Knopf, 1982); and Helen Caldicott, *Nuclear Madness* (New York: Bantam Books, 1980).

10. U.S. National Research Council, *Long-Term, Worldwide Effects of Multiple Nuclear Weapons Detonations* (Washington, D.C.: U.S. Government Printing Office, 1975).

11. Carsten M. Haaland, "Developments in Strategic Nuclear Weapons," *Journal of Civil Defense* (October 1982): 6.

12. Cresson H. Kearny, *Nuclear War Survival Skills* (Aurora, Ill.: Caroline House, 1981).

13. Will Brownell, "Civil Defense Swiss Style," *Survive* (March/April 1983): 28.

14. U.S., Department of Defense, *United States Military Posture for FY 1979,* prepared by George S. Brown (Washington, D.C.: U.S. Government Printing Office, 1978), pp. 39–40.

15. M. Shirokov, "Military Geography at the Present Stage," *Military Thought* 11 (November 1966).

16. See, for example, Joseph D. Douglass, Jr., and Amoretta M. Hoeber, *Conventional War and Escalation: The Soviet View* (New York: Crane Russak, 1981); and the series of volumes entitled *Soviet Military Thought* by various Soviet authors, translated and published by the U.S. Air Force from 1970 to present.

17. See Speed, *Strategic Deterrence in the 1980s,* pp. 45–51 for a discussion of bomber survivability.

18. Caspar Weinberger, *Annual Report to the Congress, FY 1983* (Washington, D.C.: U.S. Government Printing Office), p. II-11.

19. Lawrence W. Beilenson, *Survival and Peace in the Nuclear Age* (Chicago: Regnery/Gateway, 1980) p. 87.

5 Military Alliances and Far-Flung Forces

Laurence W. Beilenson

During the administration of President Harry Truman, as part of a policy to contain communism by force, the United States began in peacetime to make military alliances, to station military forces overseas, and to give large subsidies to many countries. These actions reversed the course followed by the United States ever since George Washington said in his farewell address: " 'Tis our true policy to steer clear of permanent alliances, . . . Taking care to keep ourselves . . . on a respectable defensive posture, we may safely trust to temporary alliances for extraordinary emergencies."

The heresy of the late 1940s has become the foreign affairs orthodoxy of the United States. In 1982 Secretary of Defense Caspar Weinberger, in justifying military subsidies to American allies, said, "It is so obviously to the advantage of the United States . . . to have a strong network of alliances that no further advocacy should be required."[1] So far has the United States departed from its previous policy that it now promises to help defend some forty nations around the globe against the Soviet Union and its surrogates. To carry out this commitment, at heavy cost, the United States stations abroad—principally in Europe, Japan, South Korea, and adjacent seas—approximately 500,000 American soldiers, marines, sailors, and airmen, supported by some 150,000 civilian helpers with their dependents.[2] The bulk of the rest of the large American military establishment is dedicated to preparation for fighting overseas wars, including one in the Persian Gulf, some 7,000 miles from our shores. Subsidizing American allies and friends with huge sums has become routine.

All this the United States has done and continues to do, not out of an abundant surplus in its treasury, but out of borrowed money. These fiscal actions, accompanied by large spending at home on the "general welfare," have debased U.S. currency by inflation and the printing press.

This policy does more than commit dollars and lives; it has put the survival of the United States as a free nation at stake in the containment game. The United States promises its European allies that if the Soviet Union attacks conventionally in Europe and the allied conventional

123

forces are not holding back the Soviets, the United States will make a first nuclear strike against the Soviet Union. Meanwhile at home the United States has no active or passive defense against nuclear missiles and has denuded itself of air defense. In this posture, if nuclear war should come, it would claim the lives of millions of Americans; at least 20 million; in some circumstances 160 million or more.

Even granted that the 1940s policy decision was wise in the prevailing situation, these disturbing results require a reassessment of the policy's continuing wisdom. Should the United States terminate any or all of its alliances? Should we bring the boys back home?

History of Containment

Before Truman's administration peacetime military alliances and the far-flung disposition of our forces were equally alien to the American tradition. The founding fathers wanted no part in Europe's perennial wars. The United States abrogated its Revolutionary War treaty with France by Jay's Treaty with England in 1795. From then until 1942 the United States made not a single alliance treaty.[3] While the Monroe Doctrine warned the nations of Europe against further conquests in the western hemisphere, the United States entered into no alliances, stationed no troops abroad, and fought no wars in support of the doctrine. Minding its own business, the United States expanded to the Pacific and thrived mightily.

The occasional forays of the United States into Central America were undertaken without allies in pursuit of so-called dollar diplomacy, later giving way during Franklin D. Roosevelt's administration to the good-neighbor policy. Military ventures far from our borders were only sporadic. The United States acquired the Philippines in the Spanish–American War, again without allies. Although the United States later returned the islands to the Filipinos, it maintained a base there which Japan attacked in World War II. American troops helped suppress the Boxer Rebellion in China; Americans did not, however, join the Europeans in seizing Chinese territory. The United States fought World War I under an ideological banner—"To make the world safe for democracy"—but made no alliance treaties with its war partners.[4] Disillusionment with the peace so firmly committed the United States to isolation that it took the Japanese attack on Pearl Harbor to bring Americans into World War II.

Notwithstanding this tradition, the climate after the war was ripe for a change. While high hopes for the United Nations were being dashed, one world and collective security still exerted a strong pull.

The Soviets' delay in withdrawing their troops from Iran, their clamp on the European satellites, their presence in North Korea, the communist rebellion in China, the conflict in Greece, and the Soviet demands on Turkey all seemed to herald that another expansionist power was stepping into Hitler's shoes. If the Europeans, joined by a United States under arms, had halted Hitler at the outset—we reasoned—together they might have prevented the later carnage. Appeasement and the shame of Munich were still fresh in our minds and on our conscience.

The Truman administration began U.S. military alliances to execute its policy of containing the Soviet Union, expounded with authority in a 1947 pseudonymous article by George F. Kennan of the State Department.[5] If the policy has become a mistake, its error does not stem from the article's misapprehension about the true face of Leninism. Having captured power in Russia, V. I. Lenin and his heirs mapped and have waged a protracted global campaign, designed to persist until success, to place communist parties in control of all governments.

Kennan then realized the historical unreliability of any treaty promise, accentuated in the Soviet case by a lack of belief in fidelity. "If the Soviet government," he wrote, "occasionally sets its signature to documents which would indicate [a community of interest with capitalist powers], this is to be regarded as a tactical maneuver permissible in dealing with the enemy (who is without honor) and should be taken in the spirit of *caveat emptor*." The United States should enter upon, Kennan said, "a policy of firm containment, designed to confront the Russions with unalterable counter-force at every point where they show signs of encroaching upon the interests of a peaceful and stable world."[6] The United States fought the Korean and Vietnamese wars for no gain save containment of communism.

Our system of alliances, overseas troops, and subsidies has hardened into an orthodoxy, while our policy of containment, despite variations, has persisted. The ideological tinge blurred somewhat when Truman gave generous subsidies to Tito's Yugoslav communist dictatorship after its break with Joseph Stalin. This caved in the levee. Since then, not content with largesse to its supposed friends, the United States has extended its giving to foes as well.

China became one of the countries to be contained when Mao Tse-tung triumphed in 1949, only to have Richard Nixon tarnish the moral and ideological gloss on the policy by embracing Mao. Each of Nixon's successors has accepted his China shift.

Although from the date of U.S. withdrawal from Vietnam, U.S. commitment to containment has been hardly steadfast, Nixon's détente and Jimmy Carter's human-rights emphasis were superimposed on containment rather than displacing it; the military alliances and overseas troops remained in place. Ronald Reagan reasserted a firm policy of containment.

Almost unnoticed, the United States has broadened the purposes of containment and of its military forces abroad to include a so-called national interest in protecting American access to oil and other raw materials. During the administration of Dwight D. Eisenhower, Prime Minister N. Mossadegh of Iran nationalized British oil companies. In response the United States stopped the shipment of Iranian oil, flew the shah out of the country, paid money to start trouble in the Tehran streets with the connivance of the Iranian army, which, as arranged with the United States, overthrew Mossadegh and brought back the shah.

Any reader of the annual Military Posture Statements by the U.S. Joint Chiefs of Staff has become familiar with a standard argument for means of "projecting our power" far from our shores: to ensure access to raw materials we do not own. Under Gerald Ford, Henry Kissinger rattled our sabres about oil. Ford and Carter each asserted that the United States was an Asian power and would remain so. Carter thundered war to ensure the flow of Persian Gulf oil, saying in his 1980 State of the Union message that the United States would use "military force" against "an attempt by any outside force to gain control of the Persian Gulf region." Thereby he threatened either a conventional war 7,000 miles away against the Soviet Union that the United States cannot win or a catastrophic nuclear war. Subsequent discussion of the Carter Doctrine has broadened those against whom we will fight for oil we do not own to include surrogates of the Soviet Union, such as, according to the State Department, Libya, Ethiopia, and South Yemen, and even to internal troublemakers creating "instability" in this unstable region. To gain bases, we widened our allies to include the Sultan of Oman. Carter created a rapid deployment force (RDF) to implement his new doctrine. The Reagan administration placed the RDF in the forefront of U.S. preparation to equip and transport American troops to wherever on earth U.S. "interests" are threatened.[7]

Pursuant to containment, under eight presidents since World War II, four Democrats and four Republicans, the U.S. system of military alliances, overseas troops, and foreign subsidies has become settled U.S. policy, solidly endorsed by our foreign-affairs and military establishments. Accepting this orthodoxy, Reagan, in sober honesty, requested Congress to vote the money to start closing the tremendous gap between these worldwide commitments and the conventional forces with which to fulfill them. With that it is hard to find fault. If there is an error, it lies in the continuance of containment policy itself.

History of Military Alliances

Whether the United States should terminate its alliances and recall its overseas troops cannot be decisively determined by reviewing the history of military alliances alone. Like all other political pacts, the wretched history of military alliance treaties chronicles their habitual breach, with fidelity seldom taking precedence over interest. Athens and Sparta signed a fifty-year alliance to close the first phase of the Peloponnesian War; seven years later they again started to fight each other. So it has been ever since; a few examples illustrate the norm. The founding fathers broke our 1778 alliance treaty with France; the United States and Britain broke their 1942 alliance pact with Poland. Throughout European history breach of alliance treaties has been the rule. By invading Czechoslovakia in 1968, the Soviet Union and four of its satellites each broke the multiple-party Warsaw Pact alliance treaty and also five bilateral alliance treaties with Czechoslovakia, plus the United Nations Charter to keep the peace.

From the long history of military alliance treaties, the following patterns emerge: (1) the treaties have been regularly broken, hence unreliable; (2) despite that fact, they have been often relied upon; (3) frequently, allies have fought each other. For example, from 1689 to 1802, England and France fought five long wars (forty-five years total), before each of which they were allies. Even when an ally deserted during war, however, the soldiers it furnished helped the common cause while they fought, and strong defensive coalitions sometimes have deterred attack, at least for a while. Not every military alliance can be summarily characterized as an ineffective tool of statecraft. George Washington scarcely could have so regarded our French alliance, which proved to be our salvation in the War of the American Revolution, even though we broke the treaty when it no longer served our purposes.[8] The question, then, whether to continue U.S. alliances and the global disposition of U.S. forces becomes a question of judgment.

Containment Policy Reassessed

The pursuit of any course abroad usually has advantages and disadvantages. In grave questions such as the one posed, the decision depends on whether the policy furthers or retards our paramount objective: the survival of the United States as a free nation. Thus whether containment is wise turns on whether the actions and inactions taken to carry out containment contribute more than they detract from this aim.

That is often lost sight of; policies tend to acquire their own momentum to run over our chief goal. This is strikingly illustrated by the Vietnamese tragedy; the pursuit of containment became sacrosanct, superseding the supreme objective. Truman started U.S. involvement in Vietnam early in his administration by heavily subsidizing the French effort to suppress the Vietnamese rebellion led by Ho Chi Minh. Never mind that the French were white foreign conquerors; the revolt was led by a communist, and U.S. policy was to contain communism. Eisenhower continued the subsidy but refused American military intervention to save the French. When they lost, he subsidized Ngo Dinh Diem as ruler of South Vietnam and stepped up the ante by adding military advisers, a few of whom were killed in battle during 1959. President John F. Kennedy raised the ante again; he increased the number of military advisers to 4000, and in 1963 connived in the coup that overthrew Diem, whose continued rule Kennedy believed imperiled U.S. containment policy. Lyndon Johnson pushed in a big stack of chips; he went to war, which the United States waged under Johnson and Nixon strictly as a containment war, never invading North Vietnam.

U.S. containment policy in Vietnam so strongly generated its own momentum that attention to the paramount objective became lost. It makes no difference whether the United States should or should not have waged war in Vietnam; both sides agree that the war as conducted was disastrous to the United States. Containment influenced not only the original intervention, but also the war as it was fought. And the aftermath of Vietnam still lingers on as one of the intangibles affecting American public opinion.

In determining whether American military alliances and overseas forces should be retained three factors should guide the decision: (1) the paramount objective of the United States; (2) the situation, which includes the strengths and weaknesses of each side and the surrounding circumstances; and (3) historical experience—using the past as a beacon to light the future.

Americans all sail in the same ship of state, sharing a common danger. Any reappraisal of policy ought to be discussed in this spirit. Such a spirit is hampered by critics who, inveighing against American greed, militarism, and imperialism, find no difference between the so-called superpowers and damn them both while advancing specious reasons to excuse Soviet actions. This attitude disregards the conduct of the Soviet Union for two-thirds of a century. There may have been some excuse for believing in Soviet mellowing in the 1920s; such a belief in the 1980s is a case of "none so blind as those who will not see." Soviet leaders continue to justify their dictatorship at home by the necessity of the triumph of communism abroad and continue to employ violence and fraud as their means. Nor is the United States the same as the Soviet Union in lack of ethics. Though since World War II the United States has not been a moral paragon abroad, generally its actions have been unaggressive and directed toward the hope of a peaceful world sharing in abundance. The United States also has been generous to a fault in helping friends and former foes. What territory has the United States conquered? What country has the United States extorted? While the United States has talked about protecting raw materials it does not own, it has seized none. If a change in U.S. policy is desirable, it is not because there is no real ethical difference between the two sides, but in spite of the very real ethical difference.

Nonetheless, it is high time for a reassessment. The paramount aim—survival as a free people—has not altered, but the passage of more than three and a half decades warrants another look at the U.S. situation to ask whether its differences from 1947 are material enough to justify terminating some or all of U.S. military alliances and bringing the troops home. In the reexamination, we also are entitled to retest the pillars of containment on which the alliances and far-flung U.S. military presence abroad rest.

The Changing Nuclear World

We live in the nuclear age, when a Soviet-American nuclear war threatens U.S. survival as a free nation. The likelihood of a nuclear war has been present since the invention of the atomic bomb, as becomes apparent from two historical patterns. Whatever have been the causes of war, its constant throughout the ages has been its recurrence. Add another pattern to which there never has been a single exception, prior to and including atomic weapons: man has used every type of weapon he has ever devised. The sum predicts nuclear war somewhere sooner or later. As the possessors of the two most formidable nuclear arsenals, the United States and the Soviet Union are probable belligerents.

With so many nuclear weapons in existence, somebody is apt to use one. War by accident could happen, especially with the short time for reaction, the danger of launch on warning, and the propensity to errors of humans and the machines they manufacture and operate.

Because of the horrendous damage nuclear war would inflict, it has become customary to say that only a madman would start a nuclear war: an unwitting prediction of such a war. Many crazy rulers have presided over the affairs of nations, to which add the risks entailed by gambling rulers such as Napoleon III and Kaiser William II, ideologues such as Mao, who believe the triumph of their ideal is worth any cost in lives, and just plain fools. Any of these types is a candidate for the

first to push the button, but the pusher may be a lamb turned lion—
or who knows?

A candid survey of history deepens the gloom. The military, diplomatic, and political history of the world has been steeped in blood
and anointed with chicanery. The ideological contest between the communist-ruled states and the coalition led by the United States is an
added potential cause of war.

These deep-seated potential causes of nuclear war were present in
the late 1940s but were lessened for the United States by the atomic
weapons situation at the time. In 1947 the United States was the sole
possessor of the atom bomb. When the Soviet Union became an atomic
power in 1949, the United States had the long-range bombers needed
to deliver the explosive on the target, while the Soviet Union did not.
Thermonuclear intercontinental ballistic missiles (ICBMs) have revo-
lutionized the character of war. Every American is in the front lines
subject to annihilation. For a long time we had clear nuclear superiority
over the Soviet Union, which we calculated would offset Soviet conventional superiority in Europe. The balance now, as noted in chapter
3, tips toward the Soviet side.

Nuclear war would imperil U.S. survival as a free nation, not only
as a result of the death of countless millions of Americans. In addition,
the chaos following such a war probably would bring to power a dictator.

Later this chapter will show how in practice U.S. alliances and far-
flung conventional forces reduce its nuclear deterrent and defense. Here
it is enough to say that U.S. alliances and far-flung conventional forces
do not materially increase our nuclear deterrent. The United States is
in no danger of invasion. The major peril to U.S. survival comes from
the possibility of a nuclear attack, the only kind of war that could destroy
the United States as a nation. The British and French nuclear arsenals
are too small to count in the scale of the American deterrent, and the
United States could replace those arsenals many times over if it were
freed of the expense of defending its allies.

The present U.S. posture largely increases our chance of fighting
a disastrous nuclear war. When the United States began stationing
troops in Europe, the government justified them by saying that it was
better to fight on foreign soil than in the United States, and our Military
Posture Statements have been parroting this assertion ever since as part
of a so-called "forward strategy." It is true that if the Soviets attack
conventionally in Europe and the United States and its allies defend
conventionally, prepositioning troops and supplies would be better than
trying to ferry them across an ocean prowled by Soviet submarines.
But this assumes no use of nuclear weapons—the basic error in the
whole strategy.

The forward strategy to defend Europe had some apparent validity in the 1940s when the Soviets were not a formidable nuclear power. If they were to attack at all, a conventional attack was the type to be reasonably anticipated. In the 1980s a forward strategy has become unrealistic, especially when joined with the other U.S. strategic doctrine: flexible response. Those who advocate the two strategies envision this scenario: the Soviet Union attacks conventionally in Europe; the allied forces defend conventionally. If they succeed in holding the attacking Soviet troops, happy days. If they do not, the United States fires tactical nuclear weapons. If these weapons hold the attacking Soviet conventional forces, happy days. If the tactical nuclear weapons do not defeat the attack, the United States makes a first strategic nuclear strike against the Soviet Union.

Soviet doctrine regards war as indivisible, to be waged by all weapons—nuclear and conventional; surprise and the first blow are of the essence. Apart from these doctrines, either before or concurrently with a Soviet invasion of Europe, the Soviets would be fools not to make a first nuclear strike on the most formidable nuclear arsenal that can blast them—that of the United States. Knowing the American doctrine of flexible response, the Soviets would be doubly fools not to hit the United States first because of the great advantage the first blow confers. And even if an American president solemnly renounced the flexible doctrine, the Soviets would not believe him.

Thus the U.S. military presence in Europe ensures that any war there will become nuclear and that the United States will be the major target. Our European allies have always intended it to be so. In addition to an occasional admission to that effect, their actions so demonstrate; they have never been willing to spend the money for a credible conventional defense. They regard U.S. forces in Europe as a trip wire to ensure U.S. involvement. This is not because our allies are villains, but because they regard the American nuclear arsenal as the best deterrent to a European war. If the deterrent fails, however, as it may, the Soviet nuclear missiles hit the United States.

The presence of U.S. troops in Europe does not stop the Soviet missiles from going far over their heads to hit the United States. But that presence continues to pose a major risk of a Soviet–American war with American and allied forces confronting the Warsaw Pact armies in a region that for centuries past has been one of the cockpits of the world.

Americans have never fully accepted the nuclear age. To suppose that each of two adversaries whose passions have been sufficiently aroused to go to war will fail to use its most effective weapon is to deny experience and reality. The firebreak is not between conventional and nuclear war; the firebreak is in preventing a Soviet–American war of which our alliances and far-flung forces increase the risk.

Far-Flung Forces to Keep the Peace

History does not support the proposition that far-flung military forces prevent war. On the contrary, the Roman Empire, a prime example, was constantly fighting. The most pertinent modern precedent is the British Empire from 1815 to World War I. On the Continent, where Britain maintained neither bases nor troops, Britain fought little; in Asia and Africa, where Britain maintained troops and many bases, Britain fought incessantly. More recently, American bases in Japan and the Philippines failed to deter the Korean War. In spite of U.S. military presence in Taiwan, China bombarded Quemoy and Matsu and made one abortive attempt to take them. Although the United States could have delivered a naval and air assault on China from its bases in Japan, China conquered Tibet and attacked India.

A 1910 conversation between the British General Henry H. Wilson and the French General Ferdinand Foch illuminates what military presence abroad signifies. Wilson asked how many British soldiers needed to be stationed in France in peacetime to reassure the French. Foch answered that one would be enough, and in the event of war the French would see to it he was killed.

Wherever U.S. forces are deployed in a foreign country, if a war occurs there, the United States is necessarily in it. The American people do not want to fight another Korean War, but if war starts in Korea, our presence there ensures that we shall be a belligerent.

The Fiscal Facts

U.S. alliances, far-flung military forces, and foreign subsidies have cost and continue to cost U.S. taxpayers an enormous amount of money. This not only weakens the United States financially; it adds greatly to the danger that the United States will be devastated by nuclear war. If we continue our present policy, thereby unconsciously—but nevertheless realistically—we are deciding not to maintain as strong a nuclear arsenal as we are capable of fielding. It is also a decision not to lessen by civil defense the number of Americans killed if nuclear war occurs, and it is deciding not to spend the necessary money to create a defense that will ward off incoming missiles before they hit the United States. In short, the United States is concluding that its own safety is promoted to a greater extent by U.S. conventional forces abroad than by maintaining a stronger nuclear arsenal and a nuclear defense, civil and active, to deter and protect the United States from the only war that can destroy it: nuclear war.

Hyperbole? On the contrary, sober truth. Where U.S. safety is concerned, expense should be immaterial. But since the darkest days of our revolutionary war, expense never has been immaterial in the real world, and to expect it to be immaterial in our world is a grave mistake. That unlimited funds to undertake every project do not exist is a political fact of life.

"Contrary to the general opinion," wrote Niccolo Machiavelli, "the sinews of war are not gold, but good soldiers; for gold alone will not procure good soldiers, but good soldiers will always procure gold."[9] He was correct in the sense that gold without iron does not offer security; it is instead an invitation to plunder. But gold, protected by iron, always has been a significant sinew of war from earliest times to the present. Only rich states could afford chariots, the first cavalry and decisive arm in battle. Since the industrial revolution, armed might of quality in quantity has rested on science and technology, transformed into weapons by factories, which in turn requires a strong industrial base. The United States needs both arms and wealth, each useless without the other.

The U.S. national debt at the close of World War II was approximately $260 billion; as these lines are written, it had crashed through a trillion-dollar ceiling. In 1947 the United States was by far the strongest nation on earth financially and industrially. "Sound as a dollar" was accurate; U.S. currency was stable. Our financial balance sheet has become a sea of red ink. We have lost our industrial preeminence; we are challenged in trade by Japan, Europe, and even South Korea and Taiwan.

But it is not only a total financial collapse that jeopardizes the United States; it is the fact that we will not spend the nuclear funds we need because they are crowded out by our appropriations for conventional warfare, which go primarily for the defense of U.S. allies. Defense funds in peacetime have not been abundant. In our entire history we have entered every war except Vietnam woefully unprepared and have lost many American lives as a result. When Truman was pledging a fight to protect freedom everywhere, the United States had neither the necessary number of atom bombs nor the means of delivery, and U.S. conventional forces had declined to rock bottom, as was revealed when we entered the Korean War and had to buy back at exorbitant prices rifles and machine guns we had sold as surplus. We corrected our deficiencies after the Korean War and have never again hit such a bottom. But U.S. nuclear superiority over the Soviet Union started to erode to its present state (see chapter 3) during the Vietnam War to contain communism. The heavy cost of conducting the Vietnam War crowded out expenditures for nuclear weapons.

The record for civil defense is even bleaker, as are its prospects for the future. Unlike the Soviet Union, Switzerland, Sweden, and China, the United States has no civil defense.[10] A civil defense that will save many millions of American lives if nuclear war comes would require a shelter system in place, schooling, training, and a corps of trained professionals, costing upward of $100 billion. In pursuing an expensive containment policy with dubious benefits, the United States is unable to afford a civil defense system for the direct protection of Americans.

Nor can the United States afford the necessary defensive weapons to protect itself against nuclear attack. The United States ought to have in progress a project like the Manhattan project to devise and deploy a defense to ward off incoming missiles. Such a project would cost a good deal because it is necessary to spend funds on several systems without being sure which will be effective. That kind of "waste" is exactly what we should be doing to preserve our safety; for nuclear war sooner or later may mean tomorrow. Yet the United States is plodding along at a snail's pace on all nuclear defense because we cannot afford it given the costly pursuit of containment.

The United States still has money for foreign aid, the great bulk of which has not been sweet charity, but subsidies designed to strengthen countries that are not communist, which the United States embraces as allies in containment. On May 18, 1982 Senator Jesse Helms (North Carolina) inserted into the *Congressional Record* statistics gathered by the Library of Congress from annual appropriation bills and the Treasury Department. Total foreign aid from 1946 through fiscal year 1981 equaled $286.5 billion. With interest calculated at the prevailing rate for each year—in 1946 the rate was below 2 percent, and it did not reach 3 percent until 1960, or 4 percent till 1967 or 7 percent till 1978— the true cost of foreign aid to the United States was $2 trillion, 304 billion, 257 million, 900 thousand. It is fair to include interest because the aid was paid out of borrowed money.[11]

While foreign subsidy has been and is an integral part of present U.S. policy, the defense budget alone tells the same story. Contrary to popular assumption, the United States has been spending only $1.00 for nuclear forces for every $7.00 for conventional forces. The nuclear ratio is slightly higher currently, but the one-to-seven ratio is the average. The major portion of defense spending goes for manpower and maintenance, both large factors in conventional forces, but relatively small components of nuclear forces, thus accounting in part for this ratio.[12]

Most U.S. conventional forces are either deployed or earmarked for defense of U.S. allies. Since the inception of U.S. containment policy, we have been spending well over half our entire military budget for this purpose. If we brought our troops home and disbanded ground forces not necessary for the defense of the United States, leaving an ample margin for error, we would have no trouble finding the money for increased nuclear deterrence and civil and active nuclear defense.[13] To say we should provide more nuclear weapons and civil defense for ourselves as well as field the conventional forces for global defense is no answer. The United States has not done so in the past nor is it likely to do so in the future, given that unlimited resources simply are not available for defense spending.

The Strength of American Allies

The economic condition of American allies has vastly improved since the 1940s, but this change has not been adequately reflected in the sharing of the financial burdens of U.S. military alliances. The Japanese case is the most egregious. Through an alliance treaty, the United States has agreed to protect Japan, but incredibly Japan has not agreed to protect the United States. Because Japan was unable to afford the costs of its defense, the United States bore practically all of them at the outset. Though Japan has become a financial and industrial giant, the United States still bears a substantial part of the expense entailed by the presence of U.S. troops in Japan. U.S. military expenditures shrank before Reagan took office to about 5 percent of the U.S. gross national product (GNP), but during most of the years of the Japanese treaty, the percentage has been substantially higher. Upon taking office, President Reagan began increasing military expenditures to around 7 percent of the GNP. By comparison the defense budget of Japan has been steadily less than 1 percent of its GNP and still is. To U.S. pleas to raise their defense expenditures, the Japanese reply that their World War II experience converted them to pacifism. The Japanese have become wealthy in part owing to their thrift, hard work, and ingenuity. It is no less true that Japan has become rich because the American taxpayer has borne the cost of Japan's defense. The Japanese have invested their money in their civilian industries and have outstripped the United States because we did not. The U.S. treaty with Japan is outrageously unfair to the United States in the 1980s when Japan has ample manpower and wealth to defend itself.

The same is true of South Korea, which became a U.S. ally after the Korean War. South Korea is prosperous and has more than twice the population of North Korea. Yet over thirty years after the Korean War armistice, the United States finds it necessary to maintain a large garrison in South Korea to protect it from North Korea.

After World War II Europe was prostrate; it has become prosperous. For a large part of the duration of the alliance, the United States contributed the lion's share of the expense of the North Atlantic Treaty Organization (NATO). NATO still costs about half of the U.S. defense budget. While the U.S. military budget under Carter was slightly over 5 percent of GNP, our NATO European allies averaged about 3.5 percent. Despite the huge U.S. increase in defense spending, its allies are standing still, led in this respect by prosperous West Germany, the front-line country. During the 1970s we spent a much larger percentage of our GNP on our military in every year than the Germans did on theirs, while they invested a much larger percentage of their GNP in nondefense industry than the United States did. The German "economic miracle," like Japan's, occurred partly because of thrift, industry, and wise management, but also because the American people shouldered a major load of West Germany's defense. The European NATO nations are capable of defending themselves; they almost equal the Warsaw Pact nations in population and far exceed them in GNP and capital.

Apologists for NATO emphasize the benefit to the United States from adding many European troops and weapons to our own. This begs the question: Who is defending whom? Because of geography it is the European allies, not the United States, who are in danger of a Soviet invasion, and the threat of a Soviet nuclear attack on the United States arises primarily because our nuclear arsenal protects these European allies.

It is not only in the major U.S. alliances that the sharing is unfair. To other U.S. alliances all around the globe, Europe and Japan contribute nothing. The United States needs oil from the Persian Gulf only to a small degree; Europe and Japan need it greatly. Who is preparing the rapid deployment force for the Persian Gulf and at whose expense? The United States.

In his report to Congress (January 19, 1981, just before he left office) Secretary of Defense Harold Brown, a staunch defender of U.S. military alliances said:

> Many of our allies appear . . . unwilling to assume their share of the common defense burden. During the years in which Western Europe was being rebuilt (in no small measure with U.S. help) and during

the era of unquestioned U.S. strategic superiority, the American people always willingly assumed the great bulk of the burden of European
defense. Today, when the common threats are larger, the aggregate
economic strength of our NATO and Japanese allies—in spite of the
severe common scourges of inflation and unemployment—has become
immense (in terms of GNP, Western Europe exceeds the United States,
and Japan alone equals about one-third of our GNP). And as the
American people are asked to spend more on defense, they—and
their elected representatives—will surely demand a more equitable
division of labor with the Allies. They will not long tolerate a situation
in which the security of our allies is assumed to be more important—
and thus allowed to be more costly—to Americans than it is to our
allies themselves, a situation in which U.S. defense budgets (already
consuming a larger percentage of GNP than in the case of any other
NATO ally and five times that of Japan) are growing faster than those
of any other member of the NATO Alliance.[14]

As these lines are written, the disparity grows worse.

U.S. allies around the world are not linked to each other except
through the United States. The United States is the ally that bears the
burden in Europe without help from Japan; in Japan, without help from
Europe; in Australia without help from either; the same in Brazil. And,
though somewhat loosely, the United States holds its nuclear umbrella
over the world.

The U.S. departure from its traditional stance in the 1940s came
during an unusual situation; there was nobody else to pick up the
burden. In a completely different world, economically, financially, and
militarily, U.S. leaders still load on the backs of 225 million Americans
the defense of the noncommunist world. Because of its obvious unfairness, if we persist in such a course, we shall break down our home
front, the most vital in our long contest with the communist-ruled
nations.

Containment—Success or Failure?

The defenders of present U.S. policy are not jingoists. They believe
the 1940s posture has endured because it has contributed to U.S. security. While there have been many wars since World War II, there
has been no world war and no nuclear war. Nor does the communist
party yet rule in Western Europe, Greece, Turkey, Italy, Portugal, or
Spain. Noncommunist Europe, Japan, and South Korea still are U.S.
allies. In short, say the defenders, the policy has been a success for
over thirty-five years. Why change it?

In order to believe an alteration is required, it is unnecessary to
attack the policy as a mistake in the 1940s; for, as has been related,

the situation has vastly changed. The claim of long success, however, is overstated. The real deterrent never has been the inadequate allied conventional forces; the real deterrent has been the nuclear arsenal of the United States. For most of the period, the United States enjoyed nuclear superiority; for only a few years has there been a shift in favor of the Soviet Union.

For succeeding in the announced 1947 goal—to prevent noncommunist countries from becoming communist-ruled—the scoreboard of U.S. policy scarcely is impressive. Since the United States proclaimed the Truman Doctrine, Czechoslovakia, China, Cuba, North Vietnam, South Vietnam, Laos, Cambodia, Mozambique, Angola, and Afghanistan have become communist-governed. Probably South Yemen should be added, Ethiopia perhaps; Nicaragua is in flux, and there are other question marks. No communist-ruled government has been overthrown: the Allende government in Chile, a possible exception, was still in transition. By the Brezhnev Doctrine the Soviet Union has announced that once a country comes under communist rule, the Soviet Union will use force to ensure the perpetuation of such rule. U.S. alliances and far-flung forces have failed to stop the spread of communist-ruled government.

Fiscally the policy has been a disaster. And the fortitude of the U.S. home front has weakened in the contest the Soviets have forced upon the United States. In 1947 the United States had just concluded a victorious war; Americans were confident of their ability to take care of the world. The United States had never lost a war, and only the war of 1812 against Britain, a great power, had been a draw. Looking back in the 1980s on the two most recent wars waged by the United States against weak powers reveals a different picture. The Korean War was a draw; the Vietnamese War was a humiliating defeat. In 1947 Kennan concluded his article with a stirring appeal that fitted the U.S. attitude then:

> The thoughtful observer of Russian-American relations will find no cause for complaint in the Kremlin's challenge to American society. He will rather experience a certain gratitude to a Providence which, by providing the American people with this implacable challenge, has made their entire security as a nation dependent on their pulling themselves together and accepting the responsibilities of moral and political leadership that history plainly intended them to bear.[15]

No thoughtful observer can honestly so characterize the American national mood in the 1980s.

Nor is the U.S. home front likely to be strengthened by the attitude of American allies. Realizing that countries with nuclear arsenals are targets for a first strike, Japan, Denmark, and Norway refuse to allow nuclear weapons to be stationed on their soils. Let the United States be a target, not them. A similar fear prompted European NATO's rejection of enhanced radiation weapons (the neutron bomb). Although such weapons are the best way to overcome the overwhelming conventional superiority of the Soviet Union, our European allies refuse to allow even American troops stationed in Europe to deploy such weapons. The Soviet theater nuclear superiority is immense. When, in response to a European request, the United States proposed to offset the Soviet advantage with theater nuclear weapons (and some disparity still would remain), European NATO demanded and obtained arms control negotiations on theater nuclear weapons before NATO's deployment would be consummated. England and France maintain nuclear arsenals, but the West Germans, Dutch, Danes, Belgians, and Norwegians apparently hope that any nuclear war will bypass them, while the Soviet Union and the United States fire over their heads.

Some Defects of Containment

In considering a claim of success, the inherent defects of containment policy, as they have appeared in execution, are germane. In retrospect the United States could now have been much better armed without the drain on its purse resulting from its pursuit of containment policy. Nor can it be good strategy to pit Americans against Soviet surrogates all over the world, draining U.S. blood and solvency. The Soviets sit back, smile, and increase their nuclear arsenal, while the United States allows its arsenal to decline because of the war's expense. This is precisely what happened during the Vietnam War.

Strategists agree that while defense to hold the enemy is essential, effective defense must include local counterattack followed eventually by assuming the offensive. Containment is purely a holding action.

The most persuasive argument for maintaining U.S. alliances is that the Soviets try to break them up on the same bipolar opposing-coalitions model that the United States follows, with each side trying to add allies to its own side while detaching allies from the opponent. That has been the general historical course of such struggles. The advocates of the policy usually add one of the standard clichés of foreign affairs: The balance of power keeps peace.

As the sanguinary story of nations shows, power never has stayed in balance for long, and the classic method of correcting imbalance has been war. Yet one nuclear war can be catastrophic. The opposing-coalitions theory, even though the Soviets follow it, is hardly comforting for averting the horror of nuclear war. Though alliances sometimes have deterred war for a while, despite the habitual unrealiability of allies, the long-range record of alliances is not reassuring for prevention of a fatal nuclear war. Customarily alliances have brought into existence an opposing coalition; presently for us it is the Warsaw Pact. The frequent outcome has been war between the leading members of the opposing alliances; for example, Athens against Sparta in the ancient world; in the modern, the incessant coalition wars in the age of Louis XIV, the same during the French revolutionary and Napoleonic era, the Triple Alliance versus Triple Entente ending in the slaughter of World War I, and Allies against Axis in World War II.[16]

If we cease to defend West Germany and Japan, we cannot object to their acquiring nuclear weapons; for they cannot defend themselves without them. Both have been bellicose in the past, and one day's allies frequently have become the next day's enemies. There is indeed some risk that Germany or Japan will become a future enemy of the United States. But practically every policy has its drawbacks, which in this case are heavily outweighed by the risk we run of sliding down the slope to nuclear war by freezing our present posture. Nor is it true that the acquisition of nuclear arsenals by Germany and Japan would probably increase U.S. peril. The likely result of a German or a Japanese nuclear arsenal, or both, is not a minus, but a tremendous plus for the United States. These nations, having experienced political and economic freedom, are scarcely likely to welcome the embrace of the Soviet bear. One of the worst features of present U.S. policy is that the Western allies plus Japan are not applying their full power against the Warsaw Pact nations because the United States is bearing a disproportionate share of the load. Deterrence would better deter with strong nuclear arsenals in the United States, France, Britain, Germany, and Japan. In such a situation, furthermore, the United States would cease to be the sole magnet for a Soviet first strike.

More often the defenders of present U.S. alliances argue the opposite line: if the United States does not continue to protect Europe and Japan, they will allow themselves to be Finlandized—to have to dance to the Soviet tune abroad—and then let themselves be conquered by the Soviet Union because they will not defend themselves. That too is possible; so suppose the worst possible case, a Soviet-conquered Europe. The United States still would be in less peril of nuclear destruction than it is under containment policy. The United States would have removed the tension point and thereby made nuclear war less likely.

Freed of the expense of defending the world the United States could field a much stronger nuclear arsenal, certainly have fine civil defense, and probably achieve the ultimate in safety: an active defense that would ward off incoming missiles. Nor would the nuclear missiles that threaten the United States be increased. The Soviets do not allow their satellites to control any nuclear weapons because the Soviets justly fear the satellite troops may turn their weapons on the Soviets. Much less would the Soviets trust nuclear weapons to conquered nations that have known freedom.

Conquest, however, is not the probable outcome. Japan and the nations of Europe have defended themselves against outlanders for many centuries. The people have seen the ugly face of Soviet communism; they value their political and economic freedom. Why then posit that without the United States these nations that for so long have fended for themselves will surrender their liberty?

It was such a specter of surrender unless Americans defended against communists all over the world that caused the original basic error of containment. The policy allows the opponent to pick the battlefields far from U.S. shores and to choose our surrogate opponents. When we announced we would fight everywhere, the results was either loss of credibility from not fighting or long conventional wars in faraway places, which drain our substance and weaken our home front. The United States remains in that position.

Containment was premised on the false notion that the noncommunist world was free and the United States was preserving that freedom. While some of the noncommunist world was free, most was not.

Containment implicitly presumes that if a country becomes communist-ruled it will join in a holy war against the United States. History does not support the thesis. Nationalism has been more potent as a motive for the conduct of nations than any ideology, not to mention the most powerful motive of nations, the desire for power.[17] If all the countries of the world became communist-ruled, they would then fight over which was top dog, and one of those wars probably would be nuclear. There is no historical basis for the belief that ideology is the main motive for alliances or that countries ideologically incompatible will not join against a common threat. For example, absolute-monarchist France and Spain joined the fledgling United States revolting against its monarch in the War of the American Revolution because of power rivalry against England, and in spite of ideological incompatibility with the United States. In the long contest between the Reformation and the Counterreformation, sovereigns shifted sides despite their religious beliefs. In the final phase of the Thirty Years' War (1618–1648), Catholic France allied itself on the Protestant side with Sweden to defeat the Catholic Holy Roman Emperor. While bitter antagonism between Catholics and Protestants persisted during the Age of Louis

XIV (1661–1715), Catholic Spain, the Catholic Emperor, and many of the other Catholic states were in the coalitions against Catholic France, while Louis had Protestant allies, among them Sweden and Denmark. Up to 1701 Catholic Spain and Catholic France were always antagonists. In the War of the Spanish Succession (1702–1713), Catholic Austria joined Protestant England and Holland to fight Catholic France and Spain.

During its entire history the United States has been a democratic nation. During that same period of time—except for the interlude from the March 1917 revolution to the Bolshevik November 1917 revolution—Russia has been governed by tyrants and has been expansionist. Despite this pronounced ideological incompatibility the United States has never fought Russia aside from a small flare-up at the end of World War I.

Communist countries are not necessarily Soviet allies; they are just as likely to fight each other. The Soviet Union and China are highly antagonistic. China and Vietnam fought a recent war against each other, as did Vietnam and Cambodia—all communist-ruled countries. Aside from its incursion into Afghanistan, the only wars the Soviet Union has fought since World War II have been against its own communist-ruled satellites to prevent them from throwing off their totalitarian yoke.

In addition to attributing to ideology an ahistorical importance in the formation of alliances, containment theory errs in assuming that U.S. involvement in wars around the globe is the best way to resist Soviet efforts to spread communist rule. If the notion ever had any validity, ICBMs outmoded it. The belief that the American people would willingly be the fighters for freedom everywhere while their allies in other parts of the world sat by and applauded (or criticized) ascribed a quality to the United States that no nation ever has sustained over a long period.

That every conquest by the Soviet Union advances its ultimate triumph is the ultimate fallacy of containment. Suppose the Soviet Union finally subdues the resistance and imposes communist rule in Afghanistan. Will the Soviets really have gained against the United States? Although the Soviet Union will have acquired another satellite, it also will have evoked more hatred against it in Afghanistan and abroad and will always need troops nearby ready to maintain its control. To the Soviets, the European satellites (with the possible exception of Bulgaria) are sources not of strength, but of weakness, ruled by fear and loathing the Russians and all they stand for, ready to turn against them when the opportunity arises, and creating an apprehension and uncertainty in their conquerors, not to mention requiring large military establishments for the suppression of internal disorders. And even if the satellite soldiers do not turn against their masters in the event of war, the Russians never can be sure of their allegience. In the nuclear age, furthermore, conventional forces are not going to be the decisive factor.

With this in mind, look again at a Soviet-conquered Europe. Poland would seem a dream of tranquility compared to such a situation. No conqueror ever has been able to rule Europe for long. The European nations, which have known freedom, would be in perpetual resistance, erupting into revolts. Communism in Europe, including in the Soviet Union, would die from a fatal case of indigestion.

Even more fallacious is the perversion of containment, in which it is contended that the United States must fight wars all over the earth to protect its worldwide "interests." The perversion erases any U.S. claim of morality and puts the United States in the same power-seeking imperialist class as the Soviets. This interpretation of containment is not only immoral; it is not in our self-interest. According to this variation, the United States is fortunate to have Japan and South Korea as allies; they afford the United States the bases for garrisons to prevent the Soviets from dominating Asia and defeating U.S. interests as an Asian power. We cannot afford to let the Soviet Union strangle us by gobbling up raw materials such as oil needed for the industrial machines of our allies and ourselves. The United States must not only keep the raw materials in friendly hands; it much also keep global "choke points"—straits and the like—out of hostile grasp. The purpose of U.S. alliances and troops abroad is to prevent these dire events, with war as the ultimate preventer.

This perversion of containment for material profit fails to weigh benefits against cost. We are told of U.S. trade with Asia. But the absence of alliances would not interfere with this secondary aim of prosperity through trade. The United States traded widely for most of its history without either troops abroad or alliances, as do Japan, West Germany, and Sweden in the 1980s. The communist-ruled countries would like to broaden their trade with the United States.

A war for material benefits defeats its purpose if the war costs more than the material benefits obtained from its prosecution. Wars for raw materials and preparing for such wars are expensive alternatives, both in money and in blood, to stockpiling needed raw materials in large quantities and devising substitutes.

The Rapid Deployment Force (RDF), exemplary of the kind of military preparations ensuing from the perversion of containment, makes even less sense in the light of the real situation. The Soviets need not invade Iran to stop the flow of oil from the Persian Gulf. The gulf is in easy bombing range of the Soviet Union. The Soviets need drop only one bomb and miss; the insurance rate for tankers entering the gulf would stop the flow of oil.

What material good does it do the United States to be an Asian power? Such a role only encumbers the United States with the expense of defending Japan, South Korea, and Southwest Asia. Before the United States "lost" Indochina, it used to add Southeast Asia to this list.

Chapter 2 shows that in relations between nations periods of stability alternate with periods of instability, with the latter making war more likely statistically. The sad fact is, however, that wars have been endemic. Aside from wars with the Indians, during our history we have been at war at least every twenty-five years on the average. During fifty of the sixty-seven years of George Washington's life, war was being waged in Europe. From 1500 through 1972 (473 years) France was at war with another European country 42 percent of the years. If wars with non-European nations had been counted, the percentage would have been even higher.

A Proposal for Change

Those who would stand pat on the present U.S. policy of alliances and far-flung forces warn the United States not to rock the boat and make war more likely by creating instability. Of course there would be a diplomatic upheaval if we changed our course; there usually is in such a case. But that it would cause war does not follow. In the nuclear age, the real deterrent to an American–Soviet war are nuclear arsenals.

Such a dare-not-change attitude would lock the United States into the present policy forever, with the consequent danger of nuclear war previously noted. Nor did the originators of U.S. alliances expect them to last forever. To reassure Europe of a long time to recover, the original North Atlantic Alliance was for twenty years. Thereafter any nation could withdraw on one year's notice, a provision still in effect. All other U.S. alliance treaties have a one-year termination-by-notice clause except the Rio Pact, which requires two years' notice. The American creators of these alliances provided a way out of them.

The present U.S. posture does not array the full strength of the allies against the enemy. The allies against the Warsaw Pact nations have an overwhelming preponderance of resources with which to create military forces of sufficient strength to be superior to the Warsaw Pact. They are inferior because the United States is carrying more than its fair share of what should be the common burden. U.S. leaders have complained to and exhorted our allies in vain. As long as the United

States clings to the policy that "the temple of the alliance" must be preserved, the United States will fetter itself in preserving its survival as a free nation.

The United States should promptly terminate all its alliance treaties, telling its allies that the United States will remain their friend but has decided to bring all its troops home. The United States should state its willingness to do so gradually, giving time for replacement of its troops, if in the interval the allies will bear their total cost. From that position the United States can negotiate. Its chief concern should be rearming the United States to protect itself. If, and only if, Europe is willing to defend itself with tactical and strategic nuclear weapons, the United States should help it attain that capacity, not with money, but with a free exchange of its nuclear knowledge. The United States should leave the shape of European NATO to European determination.

The United States has no proper place as an Asian power. Except for Alaska, U.S. shores are far distant. The U.S. "national interest" in Asia consists of obligations to defend Japan, South Korea, and the Philippines against the Soviet Union and China. About the Philippines, it is possible to differ reasonably. The U.S. base in the islands is not close enough to either the Soviet Union or China to be a point of friction, and U.S. military presence there might afford some assurance to China. It can be persuasively argued on the other side that U.S. withdrawal should be total to induce Japan and China to take their natural place as the major military powers in the Far East. Aside from perhaps the Philippines, the United States should withdraw its military forces from Asia.

The U.S. Rapid Deployment Force should be scrapped. Stockpiling oil and other needed natural resources is much cheaper in money and blood, as noted earlier.

The United States has no alliance treaty with either Israel or Egypt, nor should it make any. Israel requests none.

Bases for tracking enemy missiles are useful. Such bases as the United States needs should be on islands and not exposed to enemy forces. To obtaining such bases for money there is no objection; alliance, however, is too high a price to pay. Naval bases are convenient; if the price is right, the same comment applies.

In failing to grasp the full implications of the nuclear age, it is understandable that well-intentioned sensible American leaders look at the worst case, shudder, and decide we must tolerate the unwillingness of American allies to shoulder their share of the load in fear of a greater evil by abandoning U.S. military alliances. Those leaders assume that this is their only choice. A more realistic reading of the situation foretells that the real choice is between a phased withdrawal soon or a hasty retreat later. "There can be no greater error," George Washington warned, "than to expect or calculate upon real favors from Nation to Nation."[18] The way people act is as much a part of any political situation as the guns on each side. Champions of U.S. Atlantic ties are fearful of and tender about the attitude of the Europeans. They would be better advised, even in the interest of Europe, to pay more attention to the American home front. Americans will not forever put up with the disparity of sacrifice between their country and its allies. The present situation will not endure. The choice is between an orderly withdrawal soon or a precipitate retreat later, as occurred in Vietnam. Wise leadership anticipates.

Long ago Charles DeGaulle called the alliance that required the United States to risk its own destruction to save Europe unnatural. More recently Harold Macmillan has said that a recovered Europe should assume its own defense.[19] That, however, is a choice for Europe when the United States gives notice of its withdrawal or before.

In any estimate of the situation, the strength of U.S. forces must be assayed, including an assessment of the willingness of the American people to fight all over the earth. All indications show either unwillingness, or at least deep division, hardly the sentiment necessary to support such wars.

Even those American leaders who advocate continuing current U.S. alliances admit that U.S. allies are neglecting their obligations. An alliance that arrayed a strong nuclear Germany, France, and England allied to a strong United States would be better for the United States than the present posture, for it would add greatly to deterrence. But only a notice of termination is likely to bring that about. Even if the result of termination were no alliance, the United States would still be better off.

By ending its alliances and bringing American troops home, the United States would become isolationist only in the sense that it would not fight wars all over the globe to contain communism. It would still trade worldwide, exchange cultures, and wield all the other tools of statecraft, including diplomacy. It would build up, rather than decrease, its military power, but for its own defense. Shedding all sacrosanct policies—total isolation as well as containment—chapter 10 will suggest wielding another offensive tool against the Soviets.

Permanent peacetime military alliances and far-flung disposition of American forces to contain the Soviet Union was an aberration in the history of the United States adopted to meet the situation of the late 1940s. In light of the different situation in the 1980s and the inherent defects of containment, it is time for a change.

Notes

1. *Annual Defense Department Report FY 1983,* p. I-31.
2. *Annual Defense Department Manpower Report FY 1983,* p. XI-10. The number of civilians is taken from earlier reports.
3. Indian treaties excepted.
4. That made a difference. Usual wartime treaties among allies include promises against a separate truce or peace and provisions for division of the spoils. See Laurence W. Beilenson, *The Treaty Trap* (Washington, D.C.: Public Affairs Press, 1969), passim.
5. George Kennan, "The Sources of Soviet Conduct," *Foreign Affairs* 25 (July 1947): 566. Excerpted by permission of *Foreign Affairs.* Copyright 1947 by the Council on Foreign Relations, Inc. Though Kennan has been backtracking ever since, his article remains the accepted description of 1947 U.S. policy.
6. Ibid., pp. 572, 581. For Kennan's sweeping statement about the unreliability of promises by a nation, see his *American Diplomacy 1900–1950* (Chicago: University of Chicago Press, 1951), p. 95. His later statements at variance have no historical basis.
7. The RDF has been renamed the Rapid Deployment Joint Task Force (RDJTF), *Annual Defense Department Report 1983,* p. III-103. For defense, of one thing there has been no dearth—names for the various doctrines.
8. Beilenson, *The Treaty Trap,* pp. 2, 7–8, 18–29, 41–42, 63–65, 192–193, and passim; Alexander Hamilton, *The Federalist,* No. 15.
9. Niccolo Machiavelli, *Discourses,* bk. 2, ch. 10.
10. "Crisis relocation" has been largely paper pushing.
11. U.S. Congress, Senate, *Congressional Record,* 97th Cong., 2d sess., v. 128, no. 60, Washington, D.C., May 18, 1982.
12. *Annual Defense Department Report FY 1981,* p. 123: "The total Department of Defense [DoD] request for Strategic [nuclear] Offensive Forces in FY 1981 is approximately $10.2 billion. This is about 6 percent of the DoD budget. Allocating overall support costs among functional areas gives an estimate of about twelve percent." *Annual Defense Department Report FY 1977,* pp. 50–52, put the cost of nuclear forces at 10 to 15 percent of the whole military budget. Secretary of Defense James Schlesinger's *Statement before the Senate Armed Services Committee on the FY 1975 Defense Budget and FY 1974 Supplemental Request, DOD,* February 5, 1974, p. 15, said, "Strategic programs . . . for FY 1975 come to only 8.4 percent of the total [military] budget, as compared to . . . in 1964 . . . 16.7 percent." See also, *Annual Defense Department Report FY 1983,* p. I-17–18 in which Weinberger said, "At

present we spend 85 percent of our total defense budget on non-nuclear forces. Nonnuclear capabilities would . . . receive an even higher priority" if it were not necessary to cope with severe inherited inadequacies. See also ibid., p. I-39.

13. For FY 1983 the money required for conventional (all-purpose) forces that the United States devoted to defense of Europe consumed half the U.S. defense budget; with Asia added, the percentage came to 65 percent (Earl C. Ravenal, "Reagan's 1983 Defense Budget: An Analysis and the Alternatives," *Policy Analysis,* Cato Institute, Washington, D.C., April 10, 1982, pp. 1, 7, 8). My own calculations substantially correspond. Ravenal reached about the same result by analyzing the FY 1976 defense budget ("After Schlesinger: Something Has to Give," *Foreign Policy* 22 (Spring 1976): 78–83). To the same effect concerning NATO, see remarks of Senator T. Stevens (Alaska) on the continuing appropriations legislation for FY 1983 (U.S. Cong., Senate, *Congressional Record,* S. 15138, Dec. 16, 1982, 149, pt. 3) and Congressman Ron Paul (U.S. Cong., House, *Congressional Record,* H.R. 3316, June 9, 1982). See also Jeffrey Record, "Beyond NATO: New Military Directions for the United States," in *U.S. Strategy at the Crossroads: Two Views,* Institute for Foreign Policy Analysis, Washington, D.C., 1982, pp. 2, 6, 29; William Greider, "It's Time Congress Re-Examined Our Military Priorities," *Norfolk-Virginia Pilot,* March 8, 1983, p. 2, pp. 7-F, 8-F. In "Moral Clarity in the Nuclear Age" (*National Review* 35. April 1, 1982, pp. 380–381), Michael Novak gathered data from varied sources supporting the same conclusion. I note these citations for the figures only; not for their consequences, about which the authors disagree. My own views on the consequences are in the text.

If the United States withdrew all forces from overseas, it would not follow that the defense budget could be cut 65 percent. As I pointed out in *Survival and Peace in the Nuclear Age* (Chicago: Regnery-Gateway, 1980, p. 104) soldiers brought home "still would have to be paid, fed, housed, and clothed unless disbanded. Therefore, to make a large savings we would have to bring home substantially all our ground forces and disband some of them." By doing so and cutting our ground forces in half with a corresponding reduction in civilian helpers, maintenance, conventional weapons, and overhead, we would still have enough money from the savings to increase our nuclear forces, to create an excellent civil defense, and to spend the necessary money to develop and deploy an active defense. The air force brought home would provide additional defense against bombing. Further savings in conventional expenditures could be made depending on what wars the United States prepared to fight or deter.

14. *Department of Defense Annual Report FY 1982,* p. vi.

15. Kennan, "The Sources of Soviet Conduct," p. 585.

16. The period 1815–1913 is often cited on the coalition—balance-of-power road to peace. While there were wars elsewhere and some on the Continent, 1815–1913 marked the most peaceful period on the Continent for twenty centuries. But this comparatively peaceful period is no testimonial for alliance treaties as keepers of the peace. Unlike previous epochs, from 1815 to 1854 there were no facing coalitions. Then a coalition led by Enlgand and France entered the Crimean War to defeat Russia. The Treaty of Paris ending the war created a coalition to defend Turkey, which did not end in war because it was shattered by breach. The beginning of the Triple Alliance was an 1879 alliance treaty between Austria-Hungary and Germany, joined by Italy in 1882. The Triple Alliance was not opposed by a coalition until the French-Russian alliance treaty of 1893, which England never formally joined until 1914. Perhaps the balanced strength of the unfriendly coalitions prevented war from 1893 to 1914, but the result was the carnage of World War I.

17. Nationalism itself may be called an ideology.

18. George Washington, Farewell Address.

19. William F. Buckley Jr.'s *Firing Line* national telecast on December 7, 1980 by Public Broadcasting System, transcript published by Southern Educational Communications Association, P.O. Box 5966, Columbia, S.C. 29250, no. 44, p. 12. (Interview with Harold Macmillan).

6 Naval Forces and Freedom of the Seas

Michael J. Dunn

A standing navy has been an inseparable part of American history, ever since the formation of the Continental navy on October 13, 1775—more than eight months before the Declaration of Independence was signed. Although disbanded following the Revolutionary War, the navy was reestablished by Congress in 1794 to subdue the Barbary pirates. It has remained in service to this day, having grown in size and strength to become a powerful instrument of national defense and foreign policy.

Yet what purpose does this navy serve? Neither historical tradition nor institutional inertia are sufficient justification for its perpetuation. The object of this chapter is to show that a nation's geographic and economic circumstances must provide the rationale for keeping a navy; that maritime commerce directly and indirectly contributes to national defense; that a navy must fight according to a strategy responsive to these facts; that new tactical environments dictate the nature of war at sea; that naval forces must be composed according to the requirements of these environments; and that a navy must be structured to defend American domestic and maritime rights against the naval forces of its most threatening enemy, the Soviet Union.

The Geographical and Economic Setting

The first foreign policy concern of any nation is territorial security, the integrity of its frontiers and coastlines. The frontier of the United States consists of 7,458 miles of undefended border with Canada and Mexico, with whom we have enjoyed peaceful relations since 1814 and 1848, respectively.[1] Moreover, Canada and Mexico are militarily less powerful than the United States and represent no significant aggressive threat to American citizens and territory.

By contrast the coastline of the United States extends 12,383 miles along the two largest oceans of the world, open to any foreign navy. Modern weapons would enable an aggressor to threaten a coastal zone 300 miles deep with amphibious invasion, shore bombardment, aerial attack, or missile attack with nuclear weapons. If traced along U.S. coastlines, this zone would include:

26 of the 50 states, including Washington, D.C.

63 percent of the U.S. population

37 percent of U.S. territory

65 of the 100 most populous metropolitan centers

80 percent of U.S. petroleum production capacity

58 percent of U.S. electrical generating capacity

21 percent of U.S. cropland[2]

39 percent of U.S. raw steel production capacity

56 percent of U.S. manufacturing capacity.

Our vulnerability to foreign aggression therefore lies at our shores. Instead of conceiving the United States to be essentially a continental nation, it should more accurately be regarded as a *maritime* nation where national security is concerned.

This conclusion is underscored by the geographic separation of U.S. territorial commitments. For example, Alaska comprises nearly one-fifth of all U.S. territory, yet is 500 miles distant from the lower forty-eight states at its nearest point. From Seattle, it is 1,600 miles to Anchorage, and over 3,000 miles to Prudhoe Bay. Alaska's protection from aggression requires the security of the Beaufort, Chukchi, and Bering seas, as well as the Gulf of Alaska. But protection of sea and air *access* to Alaska requires the security of the Canadian littoral of the Pacific Ocean. As remote as Alaska is from most Americans, it is separated from the Soviet Union only by the 40-mile gap of the Bering Strait.

Situated 2,200 miles from California, near the center of the North Pacific Ocean, Hawaii presents an even more extreme case of geopolitical estrangement. Although comprising less land area than New Jersey, Hawaii is dispersed throughout an oceanic area as large as Texas. Hawaiian vulnerability to foreign aggression was demonstrated by the attack on Pearl Harbor on December 7, 1941. Protection of Hawaii requires the security of the surrounding waters, but protection of the sea- and airlanes to Hawaii requires the security of a triangular region of the Pacific Ocean linking Honolulu, Seattle, and Los Angeles, a region half the size of the continental United States.

In addition to national territory, the United States is responsible for the protection of Commonwealth and Trust territories located in oceanic regions. One such group includes Puerto Rico, St. Croix, and the Virgin Islands, all of which lie more than 1,000 miles from Miami. Their protection, in conjunction with the protection of the Gulf Coast states, requires the combined security of both the Caribbean Sea and the Gulf of Mexico. Note also that Cuba straddles the main sealanes of communication to these areas. Cuba has initiated close military relations with Nicaragua which is building the military infrastructure to support tactical airborne operations. Once established, such forces could constitute a military threat to the entire Caribbean Basin. The remaining protectorates include Guam, American Samoa, Micronesia, and miscellaneous individual islands—all of which are scattered through 5 million square miles of the Western Pacific Ocean between Hawaii, the Philippines, and New Zealand (see figure 6–1).

Moreover the maritime character of the American economy emphasizes the need for secure coastal waters. The commercial fishing industry generates $2.2 billion annually from deepwater operations in the Atlantic and Pacific oceans, and in the Gulf of Mexico. Nearly one-sixth of domestic petroleum is produced by the Prudhoe Bay fields and must be transported by tankers to mainland refineries. The Eastern Seaboard receives the majority of its refined petroleum products (heating oil and gasoline) from the Gulf Coast states via the Straits of Florida. The Caribbean sealanes are high-density oil routes over which 65 percent of the total crude petroleum imported to the United States must pass.[3] The superior economics of oceanborne transport confer great benefits to American commerce, but simultaneously expose the workings of our economy to interference on the high seas.

This maritime vulnerability is significant. In 1980 the United States received $240.8 billion of imports and delivered $220.7 billion of exports, for a total value of $461.5 billion in international trade. Such trade is a direct extension of the American domestic economy, comparable to more than 17 percent of the U.S. gross national product (GNP). Approximately 60 percent of this trade is oceanborne, a value nearly six times greater than the cost of maintaining the entire U.S. Navy.[4] An interruption in international trade would not simply contract our GNP. The American economy, based on an advanced technological infrastructure, is currently heavily dependent on mineral imports that

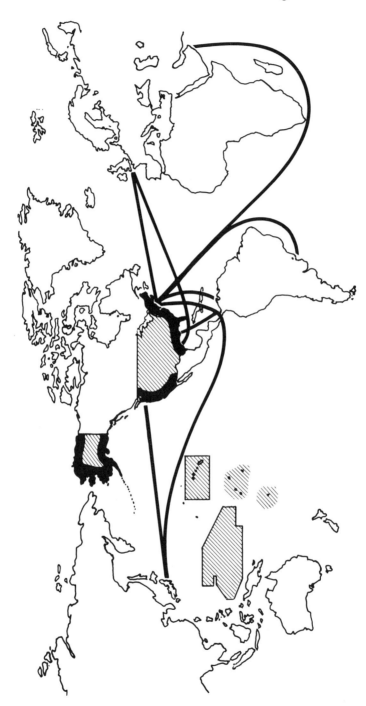

Figure 6–1. Maritime Vulnerability of the United States

are an integral part of that infrastructure. Though American commercial and military manufacturing could adapt to a sustained interruption in the supply of these imports through stockpiling, recycling, development of domestic resources, and so on, the overall costs of such adjustments would be considerable. Simple economic prudence provides an argument for protecting this trade.[5]

These concerns about maritime trade highlight the importance of maintaining *freedom of navigation in international waters*. This is a prerequisite for all peaceful maritime pursuits ranging from pleasure sailing to shipping, fishing, seabed mining, oceanography, and thermal power extraction, to name a few. As with other political rights, freedom of navigation can be preserved only through vigorous assertion by word and deed. If the United States fails to assert its navigational rights in the oceans of the world, it will forfeit its freedom of the seas to any nation that chooses to extend its sovereignty over international waters.[6] In particular the Soviet Union would dominate the seas if it were not counterbalanced by a powerful U.S. Navy.

Therefore, naval forces are necessary for three purposes: (1) to protect and preserve the integrity of the United States and its Commonwealth; (2) to open and secure the sealanes for peaceful commerce; and (3) to preserve freedom of navigation on the high seas. The remaining question, then, is how to define their jurisdiction of operation.

The ideal basis for establishing sovereignty in a free society is by the consent of the affected parties. For example, if landowners wished to affiliate with a national government, their consent would empower that government to exercise jurisdiction over their property. The totality of all lands voluntarily affiliated with a national government would then constitute the sovereign territory of that government.

By extension of this principle, other forms of property could be included under the definition of sovereign territory: islands, seabed mining sites, seamounts, offshore drilling platforms, and vessels of any description. The concrete manifestation of this principle would require maritime property owners to document their affiliation with the national government of their choice (registration) and to display a conspicuous insignia of that nation for purposes of identification in international domains ("flying the flag" on the high seas).

At present U.S. flag registration subjects a vessel to the laws of the United States, which mingle regulation of commercial activities with various forms of maritime welfare. It would be more in keeping with the doctrine of a constitutional republic to reinterpret flag registration as a covenant whereby American political rights are protected for the registered vessel on an equal basis with U.S. territory.

This would transform flag registration into a contractual agreement, in which naval protection would be extended to the registrant in return for annual fees (possibly based on the degree of risk entailed by the registrants, as well as on the geographic remoteness of their routes). Sovereign protection would then be negotiated as an explicit service, which any shipowner would be free to decline. Correspondingly the U.S. government would be equally free *not* to offer protection to shipowners who do not uphold civil rights aboard their vessels or who elect to travel in exceedingly dangerous regions of the globe (where provision of protection would be militarily untenable). This proposal might require a constitutional amendment since transformation of flag registration into a contractual arrangement may conflict with the present wording of the Constitution, which states that the government will provide for the "common defense." If this is interpreted to signify the defense of the persons and property of all citizens, wherever they may be, the U.S. Navy would not have the option to deny protection to any U.S.-owned vessel, and the supposed contractual nature of the relationship could not depend on considerations of undue risk or military inconvenience. The possible need for a constitutional amendment should not, however, discourage the effort to implement better policy.

If we accept flag registration as the legal basis for extending sovereign protection over commerce vessels and recognize U.S. economic and military dependence on the security of maritime trade, it follows that it would be desirable for U.S. flag carriers to predominate in the import trade.

Alas, the exact opposite is the case! Figure 6–2 illustrates the precipitous decline of the U.S. merchant marine's share of overseas trade over the past sixty years. From 1950 to 1979, the fraction of trade carried by U.S. flag vessels fell from 42.3 percent to 4.3 percent despite a sixfold increase in total tonnage traded during that interval. Considering only nonpetroleum commodities (minerals), the 1979 portion falls to 1 percent.[7] (By way of comparison, the Soviet merchant marine carries 60 percent of all imports to the Soviet Union, which is largely independent of mineral imports to begin with.[8]) In short, 99 percent of U.S. strategic mineral imports are shipped in vessels it has no legal basis for protecting.

U.S. maritime commerce is carried either by foreign national lines (e.g., those of Japan, Greece, Norway, or the United Kingdom) or by private vessels operating under flags of convenience (e.g., Liberia, Panama, Honduras). In 1979, for example, Panamanian and Liberian vessels accounted for 37.2 percent of all U.S. foreign commerce.[9]

This circumstance entails several potentially serious threats to U.S. maritime security.[10] First, strategic mineral imports are constantly vulnerable to naval attack. The vulnerability of flag-of-convenience ship-

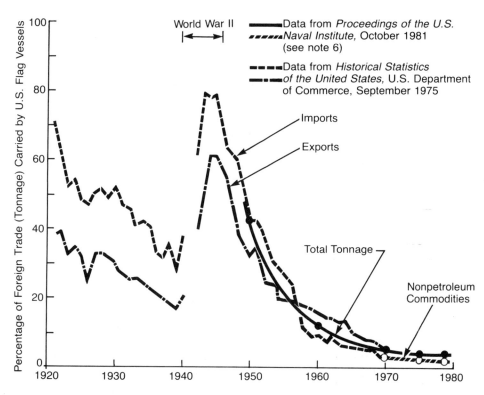

Figure 6–2. The Decline of the U.S. Merchant Marine

ping to military action is exemplified by the 1971 seizure by the Cuban navy of the *Lylia Express* and *Johnny Express* in international waters. Both vessels were U.S.-owned, but under Panamanian registry. The Cuban navy shelled and rammed both vessels and captured a U.S. citizen. Second, flag-of-convenience nations may interfere with or prohibit the transport of strategic commodities in time of war. During the Middle East crisis of 1973-1974, the late Liberian president, William Tolbert, issued a proclamation banning all Liberian-registered ships from transporting munitions to the Middle East. Only U.S.-owned ships were affected by this proclamation, and nothing could be done to circumvent it. Considering the increasing political volatility of flag-of-convenience nations, which could develop into treaties of friendship with the Soviet Union, or emerge as anti-American revolutionary regimes, Tolbert's proclamation sets a precedent for the interruption of U.S. oceanborne commerce by a boycott of flag-of-convenience nations. Should a shipowner attempt to circumvent the first two problems by registering under a new flag, a flag-of-convenience nation might preemptively nationalize all private flag registrants to thwart this. Flag-of-convenience operations are thus strategically untenable.[11]

The irony (and tragedy) of this situation is that U.S. maritime policy has itself created the economic incentives for shipowners to prefer foreign registry—by subjecting U.S. registrants to antitrust legislation, unfavorable capital depreciation allowances, and compulsory union crewing. The United States is unique among nations in restricting its flag fleet owners from pursuing exclusive or bilateral shipping agreements with foreign ports or trading nations, on the grounds that such agreements constitute "restraint of trade."[12] In addition the United States provides only a 14½-year depreciation period for shipping assets. Europe and Japan generally provide much shorter periods, for example, six years. In the United Kingdom vessels can be depreciated in *one* year. Naturally, shipowners would prefer to register with nations that encourage an economic return on their investment.[13] U.S. flag vessels also must recruit personnel through union hiring halls. A seaman's document proving U.S. citizenship and security clearance, among other things, is prerequisite for shipboard employment.[14] Furthermore U.S. policy actually impairs the success of those ships already flying the U.S. flag by granting construction and operating subsidies to shipowners. The construction subsidies perpetuate inefficient and outmoded ship design and construction practices, saddling owners with noncompetitive vessels. The operating subsidies disguise inefficient performance and insulate the shipowners from economic incentives that otherwise would impel them to adopt more productive methods. Moreover U.S. flag-ships are spared from competition with each other by route-protection legislation that grants exclusivity to a single carrier on certain routes. The predictable result of these policies has been the disintegration of the U.S. flag fleet.

These appalling facts notwithstanding, the U.S. merchant marine could survive and prosper with appropiate remedial action. It is worth noting that the American shipping industry's most profitable carrier, Sea-Land Industries, is also the nation's sole *unsubsidized* carrier. U.S. maritime policy should be revised to: (1) revoke all antitrust regulations on oceanborne commerce; (2) drastically truncate the tax depreciation period for shipping assets; (3) abolish compulsory union crewing requirements; and (4) terminate all subsidies and protective restraints on competition. To be sure, some domestic shipping lines would suffer in an unprotected market environment, but whenever a free market has been allowed to function, the long-run consequence has been revitalization and growth in stagnant industries. If these measures are not taken, the U.S. merchant marine faces extinction.

A merchant marine is necessary in the event of war in order to form convoys to maintain essential overseas trade and to provision U.S. fighting forces, or to become an auxiliary in support of naval operations. Passenger liners can be converted to troop carriers and hospital ships (as were the *Queen Elizabeth II* and the *Canberra* during the Falkland Island dispute). Oceanographic research vessels equipped with advanced sonar can serve as antisubmarine pickets. Fishing vessels can be outfitted as minelayers or minesweepers. The possibility of direct involvement in military activities raises the issue of how wartime obligations of this nature are to be established among private shipowners and the U.S. Navy.

At present any U.S.-owned vessel can be requisitioned by the Department of Defense upon a presidential proclamation of national emergency. Whether U.S.-owned vessels of foreign registry could effectively be recalled during hostilities is a matter of conjecture. One can understand why shipowners, particularly foreign shipowners, would be unwilling to adopt U.S. registry if their vessels would be liable to requisitioning by the U.S. Navy. After all, in wartime there is an excellent prospect of being damaged or sunk by enemy action, and insurance companies traditionally do not honor claims resulting from acts of war. This requisitionary power is a product of confused priorities; merchant vessels are valuable assets and should be safeguarded from chance destruction, not thrust into jeopardy. A merchant vessel should be free to suspend commercial operations if the perceived risks exceed the anticipated revenues. Such a decision may fortuitously preserve a number of ships for employment at a later time, when other vessels have been lost or when the resumption of peace would permit the reconstruction of overseas trade. In any event it is doubtful whether requisitioning could actually marshal enough sealift to meet potential military needs when the existing merchant marine is in a state of decline and when foreign-flag-registered vessels may be prevented from answering the summons.[15]

The need for merchant or auxiliary vessels to support wartime naval operations can best be satisifed on a contractual basis. Several working arrangements are conceivable, whereby the U.S. Navy could build ships expressly for military support purposes and lease them to contractor-operators for service as commercial carriers.[16] For example, they could be equipped with heavy-duty powerplants and electrical generating systems; provisions for underway refueling; upgraded navigation and communication gear; a capability to handle break-bulk cargo; submarine-detection sonar; complete protection against chemical/bacteriological/nuclear environments; deck mountings for self-defense weaponry; hull armor belting; or even nuclear propulsion. Application of nuclear propulsion would provide military benefits (independence from refueling and the ability to sustain high speeds, e.g., in excess of 25 knots) that would translate into powerful commercial advantages. Upon the outbreak of war ownership prerogatives would revert to the navy, who could then crew the vessels with civilian or naval reserve personnel.

Or the navy could arrange with private shipowners to finance the installation and associated operating expenses of military-specific equipment installed on their ships, under an agreement that would release such vessels for navy use during hostilities (similar to the working arrangement of the Civil Reserve Air Fleet between commercial aircraft owners and the U.S. Air Force). As another alternative, the navy could lease commerical vessels as needed in time of war. The viability of this option would be improved if the navy could encourage shipowners to employ ship designs that would have dual suitability for commercial and military shipping, or to incorporate construction standards that would facilitate later shipyard conversion to military use in the event of war. Premium lease rates could be offered for such vessels, in preference to vessels of purely commercial design, because they would save precious time in outfitting.

To recapitulate: The immediate geographical and economic nature of the United States requires the security of adjacent oceans and the formation of a strong, nationally registered merchant fleet by which to protect the import of strategic minerals. The next issue is what strategy should be followed in the event of an attack upon U.S. maritime assets.

Naval Warfare—Objectives and Threats

A nation's ability to survive and repel aggression depends fundamentally on how rapidly it can convert from a state of peace to a state of war, and whether its armed forces are ready for battle. Thus standing military forces equipped and maintained in peacetime at combat readiness are indispensible for deterring aggression.

An adequate military force requires a capacity for defense as well as for retaliation. Defensive warfare attempts to preserve the defender's population, territory, economic resources, and military capability by diverting the aggressor's attacks, rendering them ineffective in the field, impeding their execution on all fronts, and disrupting their lines of supply. A popular misconception is that defensive warfare is alone sufficient to contend with aggression. Unfortunately, protracted combat on the defensive will inevitably evolve into a siege, wherein attrition will weaken and breach defenses, and the continued violence of enemy assaults will penetrate to wreak terrible damage, especially if nuclear weapons are used. It is therefore crucial not merely to defend against enemy attacks, *but to prevent such attacks from continuing.*

Retaliatory warfare attempts to destroy the aggressor's means of waging war by disrupting or capturing his armed forces and compelling his leadership to surrender. It is always militarily preferable to shift the battlefield to enemy territory. And, because there is no rational or moral excuse for permitting an aggressor to retire from battle to prepare for further attacks, the ultimate objective of retaliation is to vanquish and extirpate the sources of aggression. Thus a successful military campaign depends on a nation being able to convert from the defensive to the offensive while under the press of attack.

An initial defensive posture is one that can be constantly maintained in peacetime. For naval forces, this would consist of two missions. The first is to *guard U.S territory,* whereby the ocean approaches to the continental United States and outlying jurisdictions would be patrolled and monitored for the presence of hostile forces (e.g., surface fleets, bomber squadrons, or missile subs). The second mission is to *protect the sealanes* used by the U.S. merchant marine with vigorous patrols and/or escort of merchant vessels. (Self-protection of the navy fleet is presumed, but not to the detriment of these primary missions.) The purpose of these missions is twofold: (1) to deter aggression by maintaining a conspicuous and credible naval warfare potential; and (2) to enable the United States and its maritime assets substantially to survive the outbreak of a war, after which a transition to retaliatory missions including strategic retaliation, sea control, power projection, and logistic support should be effected as soon as circumstances permit. The urgency of resorting to strategic retaliation, referring to the use of nuclear weapons promptly to destroy the aggressor's nuclear arsenal and fixed military assets, would depend upon the particular military scenario. In a worst-case situation in which the Soviet Union engaged in a preemptive central war against the United States, prompt strategic retaliation would very likely be essential. Under other circumstances strategic retaliation would be postponed as much as possible to avoid an escalation of conflict.

In virtually all scenarios of naval warfare, a *sea-control* mission would be undertaken by locating and destroying the naval forces of the aggressor. Failing complete success, *sea denial* could be attained by forcing an aggressor's naval forces to withdraw into closed bodies of water. *Power projection* entails bringing sufficient air power and bombardment capability to an aggressor's coast for the destruction of ground forces and the establishment of local air superiority. This would be followed by amphibious assault to breach the aggressor's line of defense and provide a beachhead for invading tactical forces. All fleet operations, invasion efforts, and expeditionary campaigns would, of course, require *logistic support.*

Although not all of these missions would be required in every instance of aggression, they follow a sequence appropriate to the resolution of a full-scale central conflict with the Soviet Union. Forward-deployed naval forces would engage an aggressor far from U.S. shores, forcing the aggressor to expend a major portion of its resources to breach the U.S. line of defense, yet without immediately jeopardizing U.S. territory. In this way the attack may be either repulsed or obstructed to an extent that would enable U.S. reserve forces to gather for the strengthening of the defense or the formation of a counteroffensive. Once on the offensive, U.S. naval forces would sweep the aggressor from the seas (and skies), drive the aggressor back onto its own territory, and then mount an expeditionary invasion to secure final control over the aggressor's forces.

Knowing the objectives of naval warfare is but one part of a successful military strategy; the other part is knowing the enemy and its weapons. The military threat to American maritime interests may be divided into three levels of severity: piracy, regional conflict, and central war.

Piracy

Piracy is robbery, extortion, or terrorism conducted on the high seas. An archetypic example is the piracy of American merchantmen by Muslim corsairs along the Barbary Coast of North Africa during the closing years of the eighteenth century. This episode led to the institution of permanent U.S. naval forces by act of Congress. Subsequently piracy of U.S. vessels generally has been deterred by the progressive growth of American military power and the implicit promise of reprisal against pirate forces.[17]

The availability of relatively inexpensive, yet highly effective antishipping missiles (ASMs) may, however, alter the status quo. Without investing in a major naval fleet, a small nation can obtain missile gunboats and thus be in a position to inflict serious damage to unarmed ships. Many Third World nations lying adjacent to vital U.S. shipping routes already possess such weapons. Should an anti-American regime come to power in one or more of these countries, it could threaten U.S. flag vessels for ransom, emulating the Barbary priates of old. An avaricious potentate may not be deterred by the threat of reprisal if he could inflict more damage or inconvenience on a wealthy victim than the victim could threaten against him in retaliation.

Such threats of extortion (or outright plunder) need not even involve the established governments of Third World nations, but could instead proceed from the ambitions of a well-financed revolutionary organization such as the Palestinian Liberation Organization (PLO). Terrorist designs easily could be implemented by demonstrative destruction of oil tankers or passenger liners. Such attacks would be difficult to counter because of the fugitive nature of the perpetrators, the probable remoteness of their operating locale, and the diplomatic problems of pursuing aggressors who attempt to hide under the protection of a "host" nation's territorial inviolacy. Deterrence of piracy therefore requires the capability to respond rapidly to such incidents with sufficient military forces to permit swift and certain capture or destruction of the pirates—and the intimidation of any governments sharing complicity with pirate acts.

Regional Conflict

As well as ASMs, the more prominent of the Third World nations have procured naval forces that include aircraft carriers, submarines, and both major and minor combatant vessels. The distribution of these forces is shown in table 6–1. Using these forces, a regional power may attempt to invade the territory of a neighbor (as in the Indo-Pakistani War and the Iran–Iraq War), occupy the maritime or territorial assets of another nation (as in the Falkland Islands dispute), or establish regional hegemony by forcibly curtailing freedom of navigation in surrounding waters (as in the Gulf of Sidra incident).

America may be involved in such affairs either as the victim of direct attack or indirectly because of its proximity to the disputants. In addition it may be coerced to abandon formerly used sealanes. The appropriate response to these threats is the measured and firm use of conventional naval force to subdue an aggressor or to provide escort defense to U.S.-registered assets. It is worth noting that the Falkland Islands campaign required the Royal Navy to perform sea control, power projection, and logistic support missions, thus demonstrating the importance of maintaining a well-balanced, well-trained, and well-equipped navy with which to deter or resolve even minor overseas aggressions.

Central War

Any discussion of naval warfare must consider the possibility of total conflict with a powerful adversary. For the United States, the Soviet

Table 6–1
Distribution of Naval Forces in the Third World

	Aircraft Carriers	Submarines		Cruisers and Destroyers	Frigates and Corvettes	Gunboats and Patrol Craft
		SSGN	SS			
Libya			5		7	28
Egypt			12	5	3	61
Iran				3	6	17
Pakistan			11	10		24
India	1		8	3		17
People's Republic of China		2	101	13	27	1005
Indonesia			4		21	31
North Korea			19		10	382
South Korea				11	4	44
Cuba			3		10	76
Brazil	1		8	12	1	22
Argentina	1		3	8	6	15
Chile			3	10	3	38
Peru			10	12	5	6
Ecuador			2	2	2	8
Colombia			2	3	1	7

Source: International Institute for Strategic Studies, London, *Air Force* (December 1982).

Union, which steadily has been creating a "blue water" navy designed to attack the American heartland and to defeat its navy, represents such an adversary. The relative strengths of the Soviet and American navies are compared in table 6–2. Soviet naval strategy focuses on two applications of their philosophy of "combined arms": protecting their ballistic missile submarines (SSBNs) with surface forces against U.S. antisubmarine warfare (ASW), and coordinating attacks on U.S. carrier battle groups (CBGs) by patrol bombers and submarines firing standoff antishipping missiles. The latter engagement relies on overwhelming force for success.[18] No longer a coastal defense force, the Soviet navy is a formidable military instrument capable of threatening U.S. territory and naval forces and is forward-deployed in excellent locations from which to attack sealanes vital to the United States.[19]

A war at sea with the Soviet Union would result in a tactical environment differing from previous naval experience: use of nuclear weapons, all-weather battle operations, reliance on space-based systems, and dependence on advanced sensors and computers.

Nuclear Weapons. It is likely that U.S. naval forces would be confronted with tactical nuclear weapons; the Soviet Union recognizes the revolutionary role of nuclear weapons in modern warfare and has im-

Table 6–2
Comparative Naval Order of Battle: Soviet Union versus United States

	Soviet Union	United States
Surface forces		
Large aircraft carriers	0	14
Medium aircraft carriers	4	0
Battleships/heavy cruisers	1	0
Cruisers	33	27
Destroyers	69	84
Frigates	183	79
Aircraft		
Land-based ASW patrol	190	216
Land-based bombers	390	0
Carrier attack fighters	40	734
Submarines		
Ballistic missile (SSB/SSBN)	83	32
Cruise missile (SSG/SSGN)	69	0
Attack (SSN)	56	85
Attack (SS)	148	5

Source: International Institute for Strategic Studies, London, *Air Force* (December 1982).

plemented a corresponding strategy by the copious development and deployment of nuclear-capable naval units. This is further evidenced by their systematic and continual training of crews and forces to fight and operate in a nuclear-warfare environment. The United States seemingly has not admitted to this.[20]

The use of nuclear weapons at sea is not subject to the constraints applying to their use on land. Because nuclear detonations on the high seas would be geographically removed from populated areas, direct injury to civilians would not be an issue and fallout would be minimal. Also such use would not constitute a violation of the territory of the attacked country. Thus the use of tactical nuclear weapons against naval targets would not necessarily entail an escalation of the conflict. If attacked by nuclear weapons, the U.S. Navy must rapidly choose among three alternatives: abstinence from nuclear arms (with a corresponding certainty of defeat), escalation to general nuclear war (with uncontrollable casualties), or reciprocal use of nuclear weapons in tactical combat. Therefore it is vitally important for the U.S. Navy to develop a doctrine for the conduct of limited nuclear war at sea.

Nuclear combat at sea has several important tactical consequences. First, surface forces must be dispersed. A 125-kiloton tactical warhead would sink most ships within a 3,000-foot radius and would result in serious damage to others within 3 statute miles of the detonation.[21] Tactical nuclear weapons do not have to be accurate to be effective. A single such warhead could put several warships out of commission simultaneously, provided they were close together at the moment of detonation.

Second, surface forces must be rapidly mobile. An ICBM targeted against a carrier battle group, using targeting data from reconnaissance satellites, could deliver a 25-megaton warhead which, if optimally airburst, could sink all ships within 4 miles of Ground Zero, immobilize all ships out to 10 miles, and seriously damage other ships to a distance of 20 miles.[22] Given twenty minutes of warning and a flank speed of over 35 knots, a CBG could avoid major losses by departing the target zone and dispersing beyond the range of lethal nuclear effects.

Finally naval forces must be enduring. The ability to withstand tactical nuclear attack is not a conclusive measure of fleet survivability. Nuclear weapons can also strike indirectly at naval forces by destroying fuel refineries, operating bases, shipyards, and supply depots providing logistic support to naval units. Although domestic bases may not be targeted in the context of a purely naval war (because doing so would invite undesired nuclear escalation), such restraint would be less applicable to naval bases in other nations. Therefore foreign bases should be regarded as temporary peacetime conveniences, not as viable wartime assets. Similarly, domestic bases should be augmented by seaborne and airborne means of fleet maintenance, capable of nuclear survivability through mobility and dispersal. Fleet reliance on port servicing should be reduced as much as possible.

All-Weather Operations. Inclement weather conditions (overcast skies, precipitation, wind squalls, heavy seas) will interfere with military operations by impeding ship traffic; degrading radar, optical, and infrared sensor capabilities; reducing the effectiveness and reliability of aircraft and missiles; obscuring surface forces from aerial or satellite observation; and rendering the effects of nuclear weapons uncertain. For these reasons a fleet commander will have strong incentives to cover his operations by inclement weather, both to reduce his vulnerability and to exploit weaknesses in enemy capabilities.

Space-Based Systems. Dispersed surface formations may place vessels beyond line-of-sight communication with each other, underlining the need for secure communication among force elements and for precision navigation data. Though heavily encrypted broadcast communication could be secure, battle circumstances would generally militate against it, in part because broadcasts act as beacons allowing oneself to be detected and located. The alternative, tight-beam communication, will require reliable and enduring satellite communication relays available on a worldwide basis, along with geodetic satellites providing all-weather navigation references accurate to within a hundred feet of true position. If fleet commanders also intend to exploit weather conditions, they will need comprehensive, real-time meteorological data—again, available from special-purpose satellites. Most important, fleet commanders will need intelligence data on enemy fleet movements, composition, and dispositions, leading to a requirement for satellites to perform radar ocean reconnaissance, optical and infrared reconnaissance, and radio communication interception. The adversary who commands the most flexible and responsive constellation of satellite assets will have the advantage in understanding the lay of the battlefield and in maneuvering forces to exert their maximum effect in combat. Loss of these assets could spell a catastrophic defeat. Therefore, because similar space systems will be employed by the Soviet Union, a crucial need will exist for the development and deployment of antisatellite weapons.

Advanced Sensors and Computers. Combat in adverse weather will primarily curtail the use of directed gunfire and manned aircraft, thus favoring the use of guided missiles, remotely piloted vehicles, and radar as the major offensive weapons. The most important characteristics of the guided missiles are the accuracy, reliability, and sophistication of their sensor systems and guidance and control computers. Because increased performance of modern missiles will extend the range at which combat can be joined, remotely piloted vehicles (RPVs) will be required to provide over-the-horizon targeting data and target-damage assessment for surface vessels. A corollary to this fact is that surface combatants will require powerful radars for threat detection and tracking (perhaps deployed on RPVs) linked to computers for signal analysis and synthesis of electronic countermeasures needed to defeat enemy missile radar sensors or enemy aircraft radars. This emphasis on sensors and data processing applies also to antisubmarine warfare, in which the acoustic signatures of enemy vessels must be detected and discriminated from background noise over long underwater transmission distances.

Conducting Naval Missions

The nature of naval forces should correspond to the tactical environment they will experience in the conduct of their missions. For example, the threat of piracy may be contained within the sealane protection, sea control, power projection, and logistic support missions. Because pirate aggressor vessels would be minimally armed (although with ASMs), the sealane protection and sea-control missions mainly could be assigned to minor surface combatants (escorts) equipped with sufficient range, speed, and firepower to convoy merchant vessels, hunt down aggressor ships, and defeat them in combat. Exceptional cases of piracy, bordering on warfare, would require an on-shore power projection capability in order to defeat and occupy pirate/aggressor strongholds. This more advanced mission could be performed by an assault task force comprising a gun battleship for provision of shore bombardment and antisurface-vessel warfare (ASUW) support; amphibious assault ships, each providing one battalion of Marine Corps; and a perimeter defense screen of escorts and submarines. Because counterpiracy actions would not be expected to encounter significant airborne threats (other than ASMs) or to force combat far inland, there would be no requirement for an aircraft carrier capability.

Regional conflict, however, would involve the same missions in a much higher level of conflict, requiring the use of aircraft carriers for their extensive sea-control and power-projection capabilities, and the use of other large surface combatants (cruisers) to protect the aircraft carriers and conduct ASUW operations. Also at this level of conflict, sufficient opportunity and justification may exist to provide direct support of fleet operations by land-based air power, either through ASUW, shore-bombing, fleet air defense, antisubmarine warfare, refueling, or reconnaissance.

Central war between the Soviet Union and the United States would almost inevitably involve tactical nuclear combat, probably making changes in the U.S. fleet capabilities and operations necessary. The Soviet navy poses two threats: (1) a nuclear attack on the continental United States by submarine-launched and bomber-launched missiles and (2) destruction of American surface forces and interdiction of the sealanes.

The first threat can be countered within the scope of land-based air defense and antisubmarine warfare activities involving patrol aircraft, escorts, submarines, mine warfare, and satellite reconnaissance. The second threat is more complicated in that the Soviet navy has been structured to combat and destroy U.S. aircraft carrier battle groups (CBGs) through overwhelming attack by bomber-launched and submarine-launched cruise missiles armed with nuclear warheads. At present CBGs are structured to counter this threat by a defense in depth, whereby the carrier provides long-range detection and interception of the threat, and the supporting vessels provide medium- and short-range layered protection of the carrier. To date, this has been a powerful combination.

Under this operating concept, however, it becomes increasingly expensive to counteract improvements in Soviet cruise missile design and targeting capability. Increased missile range will reduce the effectiveness of long-distance interception and will place a greater burden on medium- and short-range defense capabilities. Increased missile speed and lethality will lead to greater "leak-through" and diminished survival prospects. To counter such threat evolutions will require more extensive provision and upgrading of defensive systems and a greater density and proliferation of screening forces. In this manner Soviet tactical design improvements will compel the U.S. CBG to devote more of its resources to defense while becoming an even larger, more valuable target complex and, at the same time, infringing on the resources to conduct retaliatory missions, thus reducing the CBG threat to Soviet forces. Clearly this is an evolutionary dynamic that is undesirable.

The answer may well be that a tactical nuclear war at sea should *not* be fought with carrier battle groups. These groups should retire (if possible) to the cover of land-based long-range air defense and antisubmarine warfare patrol aircraft, accompanied by a screen of escorts and submarines. Their involvement in battle (sea control and power projection) should be minimized until the major anticarrier threats have been removed.

In place of carriers, the primary combatants in a nuclear sea-control mission should be cruisers, submarines, and land-based aircraft. By dispersing offensive capability among highly mobile forces, vulnerability to Soviet massive-attack tactics would be reduced. Soviet naval bomber bases and surface force elements could be destroyed by missiles launched from any of these platforms. Soviet submarine activity could then be supressed by widespread air patrols, sonar scans by towed hydrophone arrays, and by attack from aircraft, submarines, or escort vessels. Warfare at this level would be based on denial of enemy reconnaissance information and the use of large-scale maneuvers to keep Soviet fleet commanders uncertain of U.S. force locations and attack vectors.

The proposal to rely more on cruisers, submarines, and land-based aircraft than on carrier battle groups in a nuclear sea-control mission diverges radically from traditional tactics. However, nuclear warfare capabilities at sea make CBGs, with their concentration of function, increasingly vulnerable. Though such concentration of military assets worked well in the past, they are unlikely to work well in the future. In a nuclear environment the ability to distill firepower and coordinated effect from dispersed assets that are more homogeneous in character becomes crucial.

Because tactical nuclear combat is a high-risk environment, fleet logistic concepts must emphasize sustainability with a minimum of logistical support. This can be accomplished by eliminating inherent logistical needs by appropriate choice of technologies (e.g., eliminate at-sea refueling by adoption of nuclear propulsion), providing greater on-board redundancy and spare parts supply (e.g., by reducing carrier aircraft varieties), and utilizing air transport as a logistic option (e.g., using seaplanes to evacuate wounded or to replenish shipboard stores). The following discussion will consider the implications that these operating concepts may have for naval weapons design.

Surface Forces

In view of the tactical requirements of a central war with the Soviet Union, U.S. naval forces should be designed with structural and radiological hardening to nuclear weapon effects, a flank speed in excess of 35 knots for surface combatants, and nuclear propulsion for major combatants (aircraft carriers, cruisers, and battleships) and selected auxiliary vessels. Nuclear hardening would contribute directly to survival of surface vessels in tactical nuclear engagements. Increased flank speed would further enhance nuclear survivability and would provide tactical maneuver advantages. Nuclear propulsion would permit the main elements of a fleet to operate even if refineries and fleet oilers had been destroyed in the first salvo. Reactor cores can last for years even when operated continuously at maximum power levels. Fleet replenishment would then be limited to the provisioning of food, medicine, spares, munitions, and aircraft fuel.

Aircraft Carriers (CVNs). Although aircraft carriers are recognized to be a tremendously flexible weapon, large nuclear-powered aircraft carriers have recently been criticized as being too costly for the purpose served and unduly vulnerable to cruise missiles and nuclear warheads. The suggested alternative is to dispense with such large vessels and subscribe to smaller, more numerous, oil-fueled carriers.

While it is true that aircraft carriers are large and costly ($2.1 billion for a 95,000-ton *Nimitz*-class carrier[23]), it is not true that smaller and more numerous replacements would be less expensive overall. Because a CBG's offensive capability is measured by the number (and kind) of aircraft it can commit to battle, the cost of providing a given number of aircraft will be largely independent of the number of vessels among which they will be distributed—but distributing them among a larger number of vessels will result in *increased* costs of duplicating shipboard service facilities. The importance of large aircraft carriers, then, is that they exploit economies of scale. This point may be illustrated by example. Herschel Kanter has estimated that an *Essex*-class, 42,000-ton carrier would cost $0.7 billion (1982 dollars) to construct compared with $1.2 billion for an 80,000-ton *Kennedy*-class carrier. However, if one wished to provide an *Essex*-class fleet equal in total displacement (i.e., volume available for aircraft storage) to three *Kennedy*-class carriers costing $3.6 billion total, six *Essex*-class carriers costing a total of $4.2 billion would be required. Thus the large carrier is economically preferable. The inclusion of nuclear propulsion would accentuate this trend, as it would make small-displacement carriers disproportionately more expensive than large-displacement carriers. Lack of nuclear propulsion would render a carrier vulnerable to disablement in a major war because of interruption of fuel supplies. Furthermore smaller carriers would be *more vulnerable* to cruise missiles and nuclear warheads (because being smaller results in a less robust hull) and *less capable* of self-defense (because, having less displacement, they would be unable to mount as many defensive weapons). The currently developed, large-displacement, nuclear-powered aircraft carrier is therefore the logical development for this ship type.[24]

As discussed previously, the liability of the aircraft carrier lies not in its size but in its operational concept during a central war scenario, a liability that would be even more critical for less capable and more numerous carriers. In this regard modifications in carrier design should include more extensive self-defense systems, embracing long-range, antiaircraft warfare (AAW) systems and robust close-in point-defense weapons (such as high-energy lasers[25]). This requirement may actually mandate a slight increase in carrier displacement (2,000–3,000 tons) to accommodate the additional defensive systems.

Gun Battleships (BBs). No longer suitable for sea-control missions, the gun battleship's impressive firepower would be a decided advantage in power-projection missions (such as amphibious assaults), in many cases eliminating the need for an aircraft carrier to provide the equivalent firepower.[26] Thus, even though a battleship requires a large crew (but reduced from World War II levels by increased automation of equipment), it is economically preferable to an aircraft carrier requiring an even larger crew.

The current program to refit and recommission the 57,000-ton *Iowa*-class battleships is a cost-effective way to attain this mission capability. These ships have high inherent hardness to nuclear attack, are well-armored against nonnuclear weapons, and are capable of 33 knots flank speed. With an 8,000-ton fuel capacity, these ships can travel at slow speeds three-quarters of the way around the world without refueling, and can refuel their own escort vessels in the absence of an oiler. This self-sufficiency is compatible with the requirements of fighting in a tactical nuclear war. The only improvements needed are upgrading of crew accomodations, electronics, missile weapons, and close-in weapon systems. The cost of reconditioning one battleship is comparable to the construction cost of a guided missile frigate (FFG), a vessel one-tenth the *Iowa's* displacement and much inferior in firepower.[27]

The *Iowa*-class recommissioned battleship may be operable into the twenty-first century, but must eventually be retired. A follow-on class of amphibious firepower support ships could combine gun firepower (two forward turrets) with vertical take-off and landing (VTOL) attack aircraft operating from a flight deck at the rear of the ship. Inclusion of nuclear propulsion could increase flank speed to 40 knots and permit the expanded use of fuel bunkers to refuel aircraft and escort vessels. Such a warship might be designed to a displacement of 45,000 to 50,000 tons and would merit a new designation, BVN (battleship, air wing, nuclear). As well as being purposefully designed for the power projection mission, the BVN would have significant sea-control capability as well.

Cruisers (CGNs). At present the U.S. Navy operates a mix of cruisers and destroyers ranging from 6,000 to 17,000 tons displacement (fully loaded), only some of which are nuclear-propelled. The primary mission assigned to these vessels is aircraft carrier protection.

By giving guided-missile cruisers the primary sea-control role in a tactical nuclear war, greater antisurface vessel capability should be provided in addition to antiaircraft and antisubmarine warfare (ASW) weaponry. This would suggest standardization on a 12,000 to 14,000 ton, nuclear-propelled warship to accommodate the necessary weapon systems and mission support aircraft. VTOL aircraft could be utilized for antisubmarine warfare operations.[28] Surface-search radar surveillance and over-the-horizon target acquisition, tracking, and designation could be performed by remotely piloted vehicles. Surface-to-air and ASW missiles should be developed with greater range and speed. Lightweight 8-inch automatic cannon should be mounted as standard dual-purpose secondary armaments.

Currently the most effective antiship weapon is the aerodynamic cruise missile, which utilizes high speed to penetrate enemy defenses. However, it appears that effective countermeasures are within grasp (such as rapid-firing cannon), which would indicate the onset of a classic long-term competition between offensive and defensive systems.

Escorts. Today this class of warship is dominated by guided missile frigates (FFGs) of 3,000–3,500 tons diplacement. They are predominantly oil-fueled, have flank speeds less than 30 knots, and would be extremely vulnerable in nuclear combat. Investment in nuclear propulsion does not appear advantageous in this case, as it would drastically increase the cost and displacement of the escort without increasing hardness or firepower. The essential requirement of escorts is that they should be available in large numbers.

These considerations suggest adoption of hydrofoil vessels instead of surface-riding vessels. Studies by the Boeing Company indicate that hydrofoils of 2,000 tons displacement are technically feasible.

A class of destroyer hydrofoils would be able to travel at 50 knots in even very harsh sea conditions with a range of nearly 4,000 miles.[29] Reduced speeds and surface-running in good seas would result in considerable range extension. High speed would enhance nuclear survivability by permitting rapid escape from Ground Zero and would permit the use of evasive maneuvers as a defense against antishipping missiles.[30]

Destroyer hydrofoils would be armed primarily with antiaircraft and antisubmarine missiles. Surface attack capability could be provided with a single-turret installation of an automatic 8-inch cannon and ammunition capable of homing on targets designated at long range by remotely piloted vehicles carried onboard. Provision of neutron-warhead cannon shells would give a destroyer hydrofoil significant offensive capability against all surface targets (large ships would be defeated from the radiological effects of the weapon, rather than the blast effects) while minimizing collateral effects.

Amphibious Assault-Landing Ships. The current assault-landing ship is equipped to land one battalion of marines by seaborne and helicopter transport. An advanced version, the LHD, will permit the use of air-cushion surface transport of troops to the shore, and also operation of VTOL attack aircraft from the flight deck. VTOL aircraft should be developed for rapid troop transport to the combat zone and behind enemy lines.

Aircraft

Currently naval aviation consists primarily of carrier-based attack, air superiority, and antisubmarine warfare, as well as land-based ASW aircraft. Carrier-based aviation constitutes a carrier battle group's greatest offensive asset, capable of securing control of the skies and inflicting damage on enemy ships or shore installations. Because of the increasing need for sustainability in the face of a central war scenario, it will be desirable to decrease the *variety* of aircraft spares on ship, in order to increase the *inventory* of essential spare parts for extended mission capability. This requirement implies the need for aircraft design commonality or multimission capability. The F/A-18 is a start in this direction, being intended to replace both the F-4 (fighter) and the A-7 (attack aircraft). Since multimission capability often involves performance compromises, it must be pursued with caution. A promising alternative is the use of common subsystems (engines, electronics, actuators, structural subassemblies), so as to reduce greatly the need to maintain separate spare parts inventories for each type of aircraft flown.

Land-based naval aviation should be expanded beyond its current capabilities, as follows:

Antisubmarine Warfare Patrol Aircraft. The requirement here is for long range and long endurance. Replacements for today's turboprop patrol aircraft will probably also be turboprop-powered transport aircraft, but advanced-design dirigibles are also a possibility.

Bomber/Combat Support Aircraft (CSA). Conceptually this aircraft type could comprise B-1 bombers equipped with advanced air-launched missiles. Such aircraft would be used to provide air defense patrols for surface forces and to seek and engage enemy surface forces. Reconnaissance versions of this aircraft could provide real-time data on enemy dispositions as well as over-the-horizon targeting data for U.S. surface forces.

Logistic Support Aircraft (LSA).. The maintenance of supply lines to fleet elements in a central war scenario would be fraught with great risk, due to the presence of hostile bombers and submarines that could impose heavy losses on surface shipping. Although the use of high-speed nuclear-propelled cargo ships escorted by destroyer hydrofoils and having an organic air-defense capability might prove resistant against such threats, their deployment would be limited to a minimum of missions.[31]

An alternative means of transporting items to and from widely dispersed fleet elements that would be invulnerable to submarines and less detectable than a ship, is the large cargo seaplane. Designs have already been proposed for conventionally powered seaplanes capable of transporting 1,000-ton payloads.[32] While such an individual payload sounds small compared to the tenfold larger capacity of surface ships, two factors must be considered: (1) a smaller payload may be more appropriate for servicing widely dispersed fleet elements without forcing them to gather together, thereby becoming an inviting and vulnerable target; and (2) a seaplane travels at least fifteen times faster than an ocean vessel, thus permitting delivery of *as much or more* payload in a given period of time.

Seaplanes could evacuate wounded crewmen; provide crew reliefing; and supply food, medicine, dry goods, spare parts, munitions, and even fuel for aircraft or escort vessels. Transit to and from combat zones could be escorted by a formation of two or three combat support aircraft. Replenishment or service requests from the fleet could be more rapidly satisfied as it would be unnecessary to load exceptionally large cargos before a seaplane could be dispatched. In addition special variants of such aircraft could support power-projection missions by providing air-transportable amphibious troop and cargo delivery.

Submarines

The submarines of the U.S. Navy consist of nuclear-powered ballistic missile submarines (SSBNs), nuclear-powered attack submarines (SSNs), and non-nuclear-powered attack submarines (SSs). The need for ballistic missile submarines has already been addressed in chapter 4; therefore, the subsequent discussion will be limited to attack submarines only.

Nuclear Attack Submarines (SSNs). The U.S. Navy operates sixty-five SSNs, with five converted *George Washington*-class SSBNs currently entering service as SSNs and a reserve of some older-model boats. With a service life of about twenty years, these boats are due now for replacement. Subsequent SSN designs should incorporate more advanced reactor designs and automatic controls in order to decrease the displacement of the boat and increase its speed. Such an advanced SSN might be expected to displace 5,000 tons submerged (compared to 6,900 tons for today's *Los Angeles* class).

Conventional Attack Submarines (SSs). The U.S. Navy has only five Diesel-electric boats in service, and only for fleet antisubmarine warfare training exercises. While it is recognized that nuclear propulsion results in a superior submarine capable of worldwide deployment, it also incurs high construction costs that limit the number of boats that can be built and put into service. The result is a shortage of submarines for important missions that may not require nuclear propulsion. But Diesel-electric boats are effectively crippled by the need for regular resurfacing for battery-recharging and by the extremely limited underwater speed capability of battery-powered propulsion. How can this defect be corrected without recourse to nuclear propulsion?

One approach would be to introduce a new class of attack submarine in the 3,000-ton category, utilizing closed-cycle engines. Closed-cycle propulsion burns a fuel *and* a storable oxidizer (hydrogen peroxide or liquid oxygen) in turbine or piston engines, pumping the exhaust overboard dissolved in seawater. This technology was brought to a state of high development by Germany at the end of World War II,[33] but only minor interest in the concept has been retained since the advent of nuclear propulsion.[34] Such submarines are certainly within U.S. technical capability, and past designs indicate the potential of boats capable of 30 knots submerged for ten hours or more. Occasional surface operation would extend the operating range to several thousand miles.

A representative design would utilize liquid oxygen and could operate from American coastlines or in conjunction with a battleship, when proximity to sources of fuel and liquid oxygen would not be a limitation.[35] The nonnuclear power sources of these boats would lend them well to a dispersed, home-ported naval reserve role, to be called into service upon a threat to the American homeland.

Having thus defined the elements of the U.S. fleet, we must estimate its total size and composition.

Naval Force Levels

The following discussion will develop an estimate for naval force levels based on the six principal missions described earlier. Only four missions will be quantitatively considered though, because the strategic retaliation mission has been addressed in chapter 4 and the logistic support mission involves greater detail of analysis than can be treated here.

Because naval forces cannot be 100 percent available (owing to the necessity of crew liberty and vessel maintenance), the estimate of total forces will be based on a rule of "one forward, two reserve" for major combatant vessels and "one forward, one reserve" for other combatants, aircraft, and submarines. Thus for every major combatant vessel forwarded to a mission, two reserve vessels are maintained in port. The peacetime basis for this rule stems from the fact that a vessel deployed at sea for a month, with the crew working twelve hours daily with no rest days, would have to allow a month's shore leave to approximate the duty cycle of a civilian forty-hour work week. On this basis only half a fleet would be deployed in peacetime, the other half being on leave. When consideration is made of the necessity for vessels to be laid up in shipyards—with full crew—for periodic maintenance and refitting, the available fleet drops to one-third of the whole. Other estimating ground rules and methodological assumptions will be introduced as they apply to specific cases.

Guarding U.S. Territory

A major strategic threat to the United States is preemptive attack on U.S. bomber bases and ICBM fields by submarine-launched ballistic missiles launched from positions near U.S. coastlines. The United States therefore requires an inventory of antisubmarine aircraft to patrol the Atlantic and Pacific coastal and midocean regions for detection of Soviet nuclear-powered ballistic missile submarines. The existing inventory consists of 260 aircraft, which could be increased by perhaps 25 percent to provide additional margin for this mission. Antisubmarine warfare patrol activity should be augmented by increased attention to mine warfare, which can provide substantial protection at modest cost.[36]

Cruise missile attacks launched from Soviet submarines, surface forces, and long-range bombers can also threaten the American mainland. Three comparable countermeasures are appropriate: attack submarines to hunt Soviet submarines and surface vessels, and cooperative forces of destroyer hydrofoils and combat support aircraft to conduct search-and-destroy sorties against Soviet ships and to establish a barrier defense against Soviet bombers. Destroyer hydrofoils and attack submarines should be deployed along the 6,000-mile populated American coastline such that they are able to intercept and engage a surface target within one hour of alert. This would imply an active force of 60 destroyers and 100 attack submarines (or total forces of 120 and 200, respectively). The combat support aircraft can be expected to have a patrol range of about 6,000 miles, corresponding to a fan-shaped path 2,000 miles deep and covering an arc of 60°. At one-hour spacings, 10 aircraft per patrol arc would be required. Coverage of the Atlantic and Pacific coasts would require 2 patrols from each coast, plus 1 patrol each originating from Hawaii and Alaska. This deployment requires 60 active aircraft (or 120 for the total force).

Protecting the Sealanes

The total extent of sealanes traversed by (potential) U.S. flag vessels is tremendous, but roughly can be characterized as covering some 32,000 nautical miles.[37] One criterion for sizing protective forces would be to require a response to a call of distress within six hours. For destroyer hydrofoils operating at 50 knots, this would permit an escort spacing of 600 nautical miles—implying a requirement for 54 active vessels (or a total of 162, using a "one forward, two reserve" criterion to accommodate for time lost in transit to and from mission stations). For this case, the ability to replenish from friendly ports would be quite useful.

An alternative to deploying navy escorts would be to confer escort authority on privately owned and operated vessels that would be armed and could be hired for sealane protective service. Constitutional authority may already be considered to exist for such a plan.[38]

Strategic Retaliation

Requirements for this mission are developed in chapter 4.

Sea Control

The sea-control mission has two phases: the tactical nuclear phase and the conventional phase. Different force compositions will be needed in each case.

The tactical nuclear phase of a sea-control mission would involve cruiser task forces, each nominally comprising 2 cruisers, 1 attack submarine, and 5 destroyer hydrofoils. Assuming conservatively that each U.S. cruiser can defeat one major Soviet surface combatant, we obtain a requirement for about 42 cruisers. This is equivalent to 7 active cruiser task forces, with total corresponding numbers of 14 SSNs and 70 destroyer hydrofoils. Each task force could be supported by 1 squadron of 5 active combat support aircraft (or a total of 70 CSAs), to assist in intercepting Soviet long-range bombers or destroying their bases of operation.

Additionally, it will be necessary to destroy the main strength of the Soviet nuclear-powered ballistic missile submarine fleet, consisting of about 60 boats operating in the Barents Sea and off the Kuril Islands. If it is conservatively assumed that 1 U.S. SSN can effectively destroy 2 Soviet SSBNs, this would require 30 active SSNs or a total force of 60 SSNs.

Once the sea-control mission has alleviated a major part of the tactical nuclear threat, it will be possible to employ aircraft carrier battle groups to sweep the oceans clean and drive the remnants of the Soviet navy into closed bodies of water. For this discussion, a CBG is nominally composed of 1 carrier, 4 cruisers, 8 destroyer escorts, 60 attack fighters, and 3 SSNs. In the judgment of naval professionals, 2 CBGs acting in concert is the minimum requirement for theater operations. Allowing, then, a pair of CBGs on each coast as a minimum requirement, we obtain a total force of 12 aircraft carriers, 48 cruisers, 64 DHG escorts, 720 attack fighters and 24 SSNs. In this event each CBG could expect the support of 2 squadrons of combat support aircraft, leading to a requirement of 80 CSAs total.

Power Projection

As previously discussed, the power-projection mission could be based on an assault task force consisting nominally of 1 battleship, 3 assault transports (LHDs), 5 destroyer escorts, and 3 SS attack submarines. Because only 4 refurbishable *Iowa*-class battleships exist, in the near future the United States can realistically expect to establish only two such active task forces on a "one forward, one reserve" basis. In the event of a central war, 2 assault task forces could be combined with a carrier battle group for reinforced protection against enemy shore forces and to provide regional air superiority. These requirements translate into the following total forces: 3 aircraft carriers, 12 cruisers, 4 battleships (BB/BVN), 12 assault ships (LHDs), 180 attack fighters, 36 DHG escorts, 12 SS boats, and 6 SSN boats. Again, a squadron of combat support aircraft would be allocated to each assault task force, requiring a total of twenty such aircraft.

Logistic Support

Because the requirements for logistic support depend on a postulated invasion strategy and the circumstances existing at the time of invasion, quantitative analysis of these requirements lies beyond the scope of this discussion.

Determining the recommended size of a naval fleet is not an exercise that can successfully be outlined in a few thousand words. While the following analysis is presented as a rough estimate of the needs and requirements of the principal naval missions considered in this chapter, the reader must appreciate the need for greater depth of analysis before reliable fleet-sizing estimates can be obtained.

To make this point clearer, the estimates for the individual missions are presented in table 6–3. From these mission estimates, a minimum and a maximum fleet-sizing estimate may be derived. The minimum estimate is found by taking the maximum number of a given vessel required by any *single* mission; the maximum estimate is found by taking the sum of given vessels required by *all* the missions. In this way we obtain a lower bound on a recommended fleet size, based on the assumption that multiple-tasking of fleet elements can be accomplished. The upper bound is based on the assumption of no multiple-tasking whatsoever. Clearly the appropriate fleet size falls within these bounds.

Since the first two misions are somewhat overlapping, their force allocations could be merged according to the rules of forming the minimum requirement—that is, 162 destroyer hydrofoils, 325 antisubmarine patrol planes, 120 combat support aircraft, and 200 attack submarines. The sea control mission is distinct, but its two components are redundant, giving a combined requirement for 12 aircraft carriers, 48 cruisers, 70 destroyer hydrofoils, 720 attack fighters, 80 bomber/combat support aircraft, and 74 nuclear-powered attack submarines. The power projection mission can be built on everything else, plus the special complement relating to the battleship assault groups: 4 gun battleship/BVNs, 12 amphibious assault-landing ships, 20 destroyer hydrofoils, 12 attack submarines, and 20 bomber/combat support aircraft. Altogether this yields a fleet of 614 ships and 1,265 planes: 12 carriers, 4 battleships, 48 cruisers, 252 escorts, 12 assault ships, 74 nuclear attack submarines, and 212 closed-cycle submarines, plus 720 attack fighters, 325 antisubmarine warfare planes, and 220 combat support aircraft.

Foreign Basing

Examination of the map of figure 6–1 clearly shows the extent to which American maritime interests are spread about the globe. In some cases (e.g., the Western Pacific and the South Atlantic), maintaining a naval presence would be difficult if the fleet had to rely exclusively on U.S.

Table 6–3
Recommended Order of Battle, U.S. Navy

| | Mission Allocations | | | | | Fleet Totals | | |
| | Guarding U.S. Territory | Protecting Sea Lanes | Sea Control | | Power Projection | Minimum Requirement | Nominal Recommendation | Maximum Requirement |
			Nuclear Phase	Normal Phase				
Surface forces								
Aircraft carriers (CVN)				12	3	12	12	15
Battleships (BB/BVN)					4	4	4	4
Cruisers (CGN)			42	48	12	48	48	102
Escorts (DHG)	120	162	70	64	36	162	252	452
Assault ships (LHD)					12	12	12	12
Aircraft								
Attack fighters				720	180	720	720	900
ASW patrol	325					325	325	325
Bomber/CSA	120		70	80	20	120	220	290
Submarines								
Attack (SSN)			74	24	6	74	74	104
Attack (SS)	200				12	200	212	212

bases. This prompts the need for foreign basing arrangements (such as Subic Bay in the Philippines).

The drawback to foreign basing is that, to date, such arrangements have involved the direct support of governments that blatantly transgress principles of civil liberty (such as the Marcos regime in the Philippines). Such support undermines any profreedom foreign policy the United States might wish to practice. How far should the United States permit the naval advantages of foreign basing to intrude on its foreign policy objectives?

The answer must be that foreign basing is never essential; it is only *expedient.* However, without foreign bases more naval forces will be involved in steaming to and from home ports, with a smaller fraction available for duty. Thus while foreign bases are expedient, they are expedient at a fairly high economic discount, probably reducing by a factor of three the total number of forces needed. Nonetheless basing arrangements should be subordinated to foreign policy objectives, even if the cost is higher, because the ultimate objectives of U.S. foreign policy are the deterrence of war and the protection of our freedom. Where foreign bases require supporting regimes that violate the principles of a free society, expedience should not be allowed to dictate foreign policy. Establishment of a foreign base should be strictly a business arrangement between the United States and the host nation, the medium of exchange being limited to U.S. dollars in the form of international purchasing credit. No other form of payment, assistance, or service should be permitted, in order to limit culpability for the actions of the host regime. In the event that a host nation attempts to exercise a monopoly advantage through negotiation of exorbitant rents, the U.S. should terminate occupancy of the base and begin negotiations with competitors. While it is true that natural harbors are a scarce resource, it is also true that a wealthy tenant such as the United States is an equally scarce resource. By consistently refusing to be exploited by undesirable regimes and by maintaining leases at a number of competitive basing locations, the United States could assure itself of adequate overseas basing without jeopardizing its foreign policy objectives. This approach would surely be more expensive than simply sealing a pact with a single dictator, but it is not as subject to the corrosive effects of a foreign policy contradiction.

The United States depends direcly and indirectly on the freedom of the seas for its immediate survival as an independent and free nation. It has a legitimate need to defend its territory and commerce from any form of coercion. Naval forces provide the means of this protection. The United States cannot afford to stint on this protection. If our navy is of inadequate quality, it will not withstand combat; if the navy is insufficient in number, it will fail to vanquish the aggressor. As Theodore Roosevelt stated, "We can hold our own in the future . . . only if we occupy the position of a just man armed."

Notes

1. The 1916 expedition of General Pershing against Pancho Villa does not properly qualify as an act of war; Villa was a revolutionary fighting against the recognized Mexican government.

2. Because American agriculture is heavily dependent on petroleum to fuel its farm machinery, the impact of petroleum interruption would extend far wider than the croplands mentioned here.

3. Imports from Caribbean nations and Mexico amounted to 1.94 million barrels per day, compared to a total of 5.18 million barrels per day imported from all other countries (Department of Energy Statistics, 1980). However, other sources cite much higher estimates for Latin American and Caribbean imports: 6.01 million barrels per day during January to June of 1980. See Timothy Ashby, "Grenada—Threat to America's Caribbean Oil Routes," *National Defense* (May–June 1981): 52–54, 205. Paul Seidenman notes that "the Caribbean sealanes are high-density oil routes. It's the place where heavily laden super tankers, whose cargo of crude is destined for the U.S., must stop and off-load to smaller vessels because there are no American ports which can accommodate the giant oil transports. According to the Caribbean Contingency Joint Task Force in Key West, this trans-shipment of oil accounts for 30 percent of the petroleum transiting the Caribbean. The same shipping lanes are the roads over which 65 percent of the total crude imported to the U.S. must pass." See Seidenman, "The Caribbean: A Sense of Urgency," *National Defense* (March 1981):46–53.

4. Based on comparison of 1979 statistics, imports were $206.3 billion, exports, $181.8 billion *(The World Almanac and Book of Facts, 1982)*. Value of oceanborne foreign trade was $242.1 billion according to David Bess in " 'An Act of Faith and Hope' Revisited," *Proceedings of the U.S. Naval Institute* (October 1981):70–71. Naval appropriations by the federal government were $41.7 billion *(The World Almanac and Book of Facts, 1981* p. 312).

5. For a thorough discussion of the strategic minerals issue, see Michael Shafer, "Mineral Myths," *Foreign Policy* 47 (Summer 1982): 154–171; and Leonard L. Fischman, *World Mineral Trends and U.S. Supply Problems* (Washington, D.C.: Resources for the Future, 1980).

6. The attack on U.S. Navy F-14s by Libyan Su-22s over the Gulf of Sidra on August 18th, 1981 illustrates the relevance of this issue.

See Dennis R. Neutze, "The Gulf of Sidra Incident: A Legal Perspective," *Proceedings of the U.S. Naval Institute* (January 1982):26–31.

7. Bess, " 'An Act of Faith and Hope' Revisited"; and Bennett Caplan and Joseph E. Ryan, "A Critique of Flags of Convenience," *Proceedings of the U.S. Naval Institute* (October 1981):70–85.

8. Norman Polmar, ed., *Soviet Naval Developments* (Annapolis, Md.: Nautical and Aviation Publishing Company of America, 1979), pp. 51–54.

9. Caplan and Ryan, "A Critique of Flags of Convenience."

10. Ibid.

11. See, Albert T. Church, Jr., "Flags of Convenience or Flags of Necessity," *Proceedings of the U.S. Naval Institute* (October 1981):52–57.

12. Charles I. Hiltzheimer, "The Enemy Is Us," *Proceedings of the U.S. Naval Institute* (October 1981):44–49.

13. Ibid.

14. "Merchant Marine of the United States," *Funk & Wagnalls New Encyclopedia,* vol. 16, pp. 191–194.

15. Larry C. Manning, "Sealift Readiness: You Don't Get What You Don't Pay For," *Proceedings of the U.S. Naval Institute* (October 1981):34–43.

16. Erle V. Maynard, "The Case for Nuclear-Powered Merchant Ships," *Proceedings of the U.S. Naval Institute* (January 1981):64–70.

17. Reference to U.S. action against Cambodia in response to the seizure of the U.S. vessel, *Mayaguez,* in the Gulf of Siam, on May 12, 1975.

18. Milan Vego, "Their SSGS/SSGNs," *Proceedings of the U.S. Naval Institute* (October 1982):60–68.

19. See U.S., Department of Defense, *Soviet Military Power* (Washington, D.C.: U.S. Government Printing Office, 1983).

20. See, Linton F. Brooks, "Tactical Nuclear Weapons: The Forgotten Facet of Naval Warfare, *Proceedings of the U.S. Naval Institute* (January 1980):28–33; Floyd D. Kennedy, Jr., "Sea Services: Toward a New U.S. Naval Strategy—I and II," *National Defense* (May-June 1981):10–11; and (July-August 1981):12–14; and Joseph D. Douglass and Amoretta M. Hoeber, "The Role of the U.S. Surface Navy in Nuclear War," *Proceedings of the U.S. Naval Institute* (January 1982):57–63.

21. Brooks, "Tactical Nuclear Weapons," gives damage-range estimates. Vego, "Their SSGs/SSGNs," states that the SS-N-3/12 and SS-N-7/9 cruise missiles can be fitted with 350-kiloton and 200-kiloton warheads, respectively.

22. Letter by Commander P.T. Deutermann, *Proceedings of the U.S. Naval Institute* (April 1980):83.

23. Herschel Kanter, "The Fleet for the 21st Century: At a Fork in the Road" *National Defense* (February 1981):36–40, 65–67.

24. See Thomas B. Hayward, "Thank God for the Sitting Ducks," *Proceedings of the U.S. Naval Institute* (June 1982):22–25.

25. William J. Beane, "The Navy and Directed Energy Weapons," *Proceedings of the U.S. Naval Institute* (November 1981):47–52.

26. See Alfred D. Bailey, "The 16-Incher: Big, Big Gun," *Proceedings of the U.S. Naval Institute* (January 1983):106–108.

27. See Samuel L. Morrison, "The Facts behind the Thunder, *Proceedings of the U.S. Naval Institute* (August 1981):98–101; Floyd D. Kennedy, Jr., "Sea Services," *National Defense* (September 1981):16–17; Joseph C. Antoniotti, "The BB(V)," *Proceedings of the U.S. Naval Institute* (February 1982):99–100; Howard W. Serig, Jr., "The Iowa Class: Needed Once Again," *Proceedings fo the U.S. Naval Institute* (May 1982):134–149; Robin Nelson, "The Born-Again Battlewagons," *Popular Mechanics,* June 1982, pp. 73–75, 141–143.

28. William D. Siruru, Jr., "The Tilt-Rotor: The Best of Both Worlds," *Proceedings of the U.S. Naval Institute* (September 1981):116–119; and Floyd D. Kennedy, Jr., "Sea Services: V/STOL at Sea—III," *National Defense* (May-June 1982):17–19, 204.

29. For example, an ASW hydrofoil design of 1363 tons could operate for 3,600 nautical miles at 50 knots continuous speed and would be able to do so in the North Atlantic for 98.5 percent of all days. See, James D. Hessman, "The Splendid Sprinter: Patrol Hydrofoils," *Sea Power* (October 1974).

30. For a discussion of hydrofoil maneuver tactics against anti-shipping missiles, see Gene R. Myers and J. Thomas Coates, "Tactical Deployment of Hydrofoils," *Naval Forces* (January 1981).

31. See James J. Mulquin, "Arapaho Update," *Proceedings of the U.S. Naval Institute* (January 1983):103–106.

32. See William Welling, "Renaissance for the Seaplane" *Proceedings of the U.S. Naval Institute* (April 1981):64–69.

33. The advanced Type XXI U-boat design, from which the U.S. *Tang* and *Nautilus* designs were derived, was originally developed for a submarine using closed-cycle underwater propulsion. The original version, the Type XVIII, utilized the Walter Cycle powerplant (closed combustion of petroleum fuel with hydrogen peroxide) and had a displacement of 1652 tons. This 1943 design was intended to have a maximum submerged speed of 24 knots and a range, at this speed, of 270 nautical miles. Surfaced, at 8 knots, the range would have been 18,500 nautical miles. See Eberhard Rössler, *The U-Boat: The Evolution and*

Technical History of German Submarines (Annapolis, Md.: Naval Institute Press/J.F. Lehmanns Verlag, English-language version, 1981).

34. Reference to the "endothermic anaerobic" propulsion system for submarines marketed by SubSea in *Military Technology* (July 1982).

35. Liquid oxygen can be produced from transportable (or shipboard) refrigeration apparatus that liquefies and fractionates ordinary air.

36. Floyd D. Kennedy, Jr., "Sea Services," *National Defense* (March 1981):

37. Representative trade routes are as follows:

New York–Southhampton, England	3,189 nautical miles
New York–Buenos Aires, Argentina	5,817
New York–Cape Town, South Africa	6,786
San Francisco–Yokohama, Japan	4,536
San Francisco–Valparaiso, Chile	5,140
San Francisco–Melbourne, Australia	6,970
Total	32,438 nautical miles

(The World Almanac and Book of Facts), p. 140.

38. Article I, Section 8, Item 11: Congress shall have power "to declare war, grant letters of marque and reprisal, and make rules concerning captures on land and water." This can be construed as providing the legal basis for authorizing private vessels to operate with arms as agents of the U.S. government.

7

Effective Land and Tactical Air Forces

Michael Burns

Effective land and tactical air forces are essential for the defense of the United States. We have the opportunity to achieve effective land and tactical air forces. The only question is whether we will take the steps necessary to realize that goal.

Two major forces that can give impetus to our progress toward effective forces are the withdrawal of U.S. air and land forces garrisoned overseas and emphasis on the reserve element as the primary component of U.S. force structure. While it is desirable to take these actions for their own sakes, these actions are doubly important from the standpoint of setting in train forces powerful enough to overcome the grip of bureaucratic inertia that has left the United States with forces clearly inadequate for its defense. Further, the spirit that pervades these ideas can provide a guide as to how American forces should be structured, trained, and provisioned.

But how do these two initiatives permit the evolution of more effective land and tactical air forces? Withdrawing American forces garrisoned overseas contributes directly and indirectly to increasing our forces' effectiveness. The first contribution is the elimination of the need for a large active force, rendered unnecessary because of the elimination of overseas deployment and rotation. Permanent overseas garrisons require people able to sustain long tours of duty, which is to say full-time active soldiers. But even then troops must be eventually brought home, so they must be replaced with other full-time active soldiers. The elimination of this overseas commitment removes a major need for full-time active forces and opens up the way for other options to meet the requirement for larger and well-constituted military forces.

The second positive effect is to broaden the scope of our thinking about who, when, and how we might have to fight. Troops based overseas cause us to overfocus on those areas to which they are deployed. A form of institutional tunnel vision easily takes over, leaving us blind to those other regions where we may actually have to fight. Recall that while we have been in Europe, our forces have actually engaged, unsuccessfully, in two wars far removed from Europe.

The third contribution would be to shake up institutional rigidity.

Major changes could come about from within the services if their own conception of their mission could be broadened beyond a specific theater of expected operation. Relieved of having to justify a service role or mission by pointing to a well-established overseas commitment, the services would be encouraged to examine a variety of potential reponses to new problems. Yet at the same time, because resources are not unlimited, they would have powerful incentives to review, test, and audit their newly derived insights.

Finally, and most fundamentally, a move to withdraw from overseas troop commitments entails a framework of perceptions that would contribute enormously to fostering forces better able to respond to the demands of war. Such a view at the highest policy-making level would recognize that unpredictability and change are the hallmarks of international life and that we ought to prepare to cope with change rather than try to build artificial, predictable relationships. Support for that view could bring about a similar change in orientation in our land and air forces, a point which will be elaborated on later in this chapter.

But what of reliance on the reserves, here understood as the national guard and reserves; how will this contribute to making American land and air forces more effective?

First, it is a realistic way to expand the force, a process that has eluded us for decades. The simple fact is that reserves cost less for the same size force than actives. If the resources now spent on the active troops stationed overseas were to be spent on reserve forces here in the United States we would achieve a fantastic increase in our force structure.

Second, reliance on the reserves would more tightly bind together society, our armed forces, and our foreign policy. This would make it harder for U.S. policymakers to ignore the requirements of the military, yet more difficult to engage in adventuristic foreign involvements.

Next, it would encourage the development of equipment more appropriate to combat. Since the reserves would be numerous, dispersed, and need equipment that can be mastered in short training periods and supported with minimal effort, institutional pressures could be brought to bear to produce such equipment. Equipment that is simpler to train with, cheaper to build and maintain, reliable, competitively prototyped and produced, lighter to move, and susceptible to surge production would equip a force for success in war. Further, because the reserves would be dispersed at home, a rebirth of thinking about mobility, both to get the troops, supplies, and equipment to an airport or a seaport and move the force to a war overseas, would arise.

Another benefit of reserve force emphasis is that physical decentralization and dispersion would permit greater freedom of action in developing new approaches to solving the difficult problems posed by war. The reserves would be freer to innovate, experiment, and evolve into a source of intellectual competition for the remaining active forces. It would further help sharpen our skills for war by making armed forces less amenable to bureaucratic top-down control. The organizational approach would instead have to explore new methods for harmonizing diverse efforts. In all, the environment of a reserve-dominant land and tactical air force would feed an evolution to a more innovative and human, rather than bureaucratic and mechanical, approach to combat and its requirements.

Finally an emphasis on reserves would help build the moral bonds of the force. Coming as the reserve forces would from local areas, and working with each other for long periods of time, would provide the opportunity to build up rich common frames of reference and deep insights into the character of the people of the unit. This is perhaps the single most important potential benefit. Moral bonds and common frames of reference point to the development of implicit interaction, which greatly increases the combat power of a unit or a force.

A final point needs to be made that pulls together these two major ideas. There is a critical need for us to reconsider and reconcile the values we accept as guides for society at large and the values we accept as guides for the armed forces.

Land and tactical air forces do not exist in a social vacuum. Effective forces must be able to preserve a free society from attack while simultaneously helping to preserve and expand the maximum amount of internal freedom. Put another way, U.S. forces should affirm in their make-up, thinking, and provisioning the values of the society they defend. Configuring American forces this way does not jeopardize our safety. Indeed, for a free society it is actually much easier to produce effective forces if its values are applied to that task.

Remember that a free society regards people as responsible moral actors, thinking individuals, as well as physical entities. This belief values, permits, and encourages flexibility, adaptability, rapidity, and harmony in social activity. The economic market presents a good illustration. Free societies understand that the inherently complicated and basically unpredictable process of producing economic wealth requires, if only for reasons of efficiency, the barest minimum of central direction. Contrast this with the command societies' approach. They (communists, socialists, fascists, et al.) emphasize the physical dimension of their people in their thinking. Planning is detailed and top-down. Responsibility is diffused in bureaucracies. Central control is the norm, and, consequently, rigidity the rule.[1] With these two contesting approaches to social organization in mind, which inherently has the better orientation to cope with the stress, confusion, unpredictablity, and rapidity of war?

Finally, effective tactical air and land forces can be evaluated only in totality. To be effective these forces must interrelate their moral, mental, and physical aspects into a harmonious, organic whole. Furthermore society and its tactical air and land forces must cooperatively interrelate at these three levels to form an overall organic whole. Effectiveness is the quality of the whole, not one dimension abstracted from the others.[2]

Moral Evaluation

The primacy of the moral dimension in conflict has been attested to by the great captains and theoreticians of warfare for 2,500 years. Sun Tzu, the great oriental philosopher of war from 500 B.C., considered the moral factor the most important. Napoleon's quote, "the moral is to the material as three is to one," is familiar enough testimony. In our own era General Bruce Clarke, one of General George Patton's most successful commanders, shared this view, as did Herman Balck, a highly proficient German general who fought Patton's Third Army. How is it that such a diverse group would settle on the same conclusion? Most probably the answer lies in that they understood war from a theoretical and practical standpoint and knew what was required most for success.

The nature of war explains the priority of the moral dimension.[3] Fundamentally war is people trying to adapt to rapid and violent change imposed by an enemy while simultaneously trying to overcome that enemy through the application of rapid and violent change. How well a force of people can maintain their internal coherence and organic unity in the face of this rapid and violent change, and how well they can impose such change to disrupt an enemy's coherence and organic unity, will be critical.

Internally it is a question of how well one can maintain the harmony of one's force while presenting an enemy with a variety of threats developed and executed in a rapid manner so as to maintain the initiative and disrupt the enemy's cohesion. Such rapidity, variety, harmony, and initiative is difficult to achieve under the stress imposed by an enemy. But it is required for victory. How then does the moral factor feed these necessary qualities?

Moral force provides the glue that forms the basis of trust, which holds a unit of people together. A moral context of trust permits a force to develop variety, rapidity, harmony, and initiative. Variety is developed through trust by a willingness to permit and undertake experimentation and risk. In order to perform the unexpected in war, knowledge must be gained about what actions are possible and what the advantages and limitations of those actions are. While surprise cannot be guaranteed or eliminated in war, experimentation aimed at producing a variety of possible responses keeps the mind articulate and able to adapt not because the answer to a combat problem had been worked out in advance, but because the habits of mind that support the development of various courses of action were practiced.

Rapidity of action depends on the moral factor of trust. Practice and working through problems together as a unit over time permit accurate intuitions about the ability and limits of others. This permits an unstated but understood appreciation of what superiors and subordinates would do or expect to be done in various situations. This cuts down on the need for direct, explicit, and detailed communication to settle on a particular course of action that is related to the overall military objective. In this sense variety developed through experimentation (and based on trust) contributes to rapidity of execution (also based on trust).

Variety and rapidity without coherence is a formula for disaster. But variety and rapidity cannot be developed without trust. Therefore this suggests that coherence must be based on trust. This coherence is called harmony. As opposed to rigid control, harmony enables a commander to specify his general intent to a subordinate, which in turn allows the subordinate who is closer to the action to decide on the most advantageous and detailed application of rapid and various action. Only by practicing together in an atmosphere of trust to develop war skills can a military organization achieve harmony. In addition it will increase its ability to foster initiative.

Initiative is the willingness to take risks and the ability repeatedly to act against an enemy before an enemy can coherently act or react. In a sense initiative has a moral quality all its own and is based on the moral underpinnings of variety, rapidity, and harmony. Maintaining initiative forces an enemy to limit his responses, to slow his reactions, and to let himself be guided more by the opponent than by himself.

Success in war requires variety, rapidity, harmony, and initiative. These qualities depend on moral bonds for their development. Therefore, developing moral bonds is necessary for successful land and air forces. Furthermore an appreciation of the moral dimension would lead one to recognize that in preparing for war (as in war itself) there is little place for the bureaucratic norms of rigidity, overall and top-down control, and mechanical execution. With this in mind, let us examine U.S. tactical air and land forces to assess their appreciation of the moral factor.

The presence or absence of moral bonds cannot be measured directly. They are not quantifiable. Nevertheless insights can be gained by observing how our army and air forces behave.

In 1980 the Air Force Office of Scientific Research sought to answer the question of why pilots were leaving the air force. When questioned, departing pilots, aged thirty to forty and therefore with sufficient experience in the system to know it well, answered in declining frequency of response: (1) lack of feeling of professionalism; (2) poor leadership; (3) flying is secondary; (4) unsatisfactory overall benefits and working conditions; and (5) pay.[4]

Sometime between 1975 and 1978 the engines of the F-15, the front-line fighter of the air force were trimmed by about 10 percent. The trimming reduced the top speed of the plane, its acceleration, and maneuverability. However, the pilot manual was not changed to reflect these alterations, nor were the pilots alerted. They were finally told by their own service of the trimming after the story broke in the press in 1981.[5]

While there is a strong indication of problems with the moral orientation of the air force, there is a positive side. In 1975 the Red Flag program was begun. Red Flag is a free-play air-to-air mock combat where air force pilots "fight" against a special team of "aggressors" who use Soviet tactics and aircraft similar in size and performance to Soviet aircraft. Pilots are encouraged to experiment and test themselves in Red Flag. Clearly it represents a commitment by the air force to develop moral bonds, trust, and the abilities they foster.

The army presents a similarly mixed picture. The army's internal inability to cope with the stress of the Vietnam War is revealing. The yearly rotation of soldiers, the six-month rotation of officers, and the individual replacement policy all eroded the army's internal cohesion and resulted in near-mutinous conditions. The army took years to heal most of the visible wounds of that period. Some, however, continue to fester.[6]

Personnel turbulence is still a problem, the result of a managerial approach to manpower that overlooks the moral requirements in its quest for efficiency. Even General Edward Meyer, former army chief of staff, had to overcome stiff internal army resistance to modify the manpower approach of his own service. His cohesion, operational readiness, and training (COHORT) program is designed to leave people in place long enough so they can develop moral bonds. Implementation of the program is very slow and threatened by budgetary pressure.[7]

Combat operations are to be "synchronized," say authoritative army documents. The notion of synchronization is mechanical and rigid. With operations conceived of in this way, there is little incentive to develop lower level initiative, variety, rapidity, or harmony. Worse, it suggests there is a lack of appreciation for the basis of developing such traits. But on the positive side, the army has an ambitious training facility at Fort Irwin, which tries to simulate force-on-force brigade-sized combat operations and which will provide at least an opportunity for the participants to develop a feel for combat and their own abilities.

Both services suffer from an overreliance on technical command, control, and communication arrangements. These systems present a great temptation to impose central control and direction of operations at the expense of lower level initiative. As instruments they are neutral, but how they are used and how they are approached is critical. Given the services' present orientation, the most likely effect of these instruments will be to disrupt the organic cohesion of American forces rather than the enemy's.[8]

Finally the services present themselves to the public (and must therefore see themselves at least to some degree) as employers rather than as organizations with a distinct character. As Charles Moskos, a leading manpower analyst, has written, "The critical flaw (with the services' approach to manpower) has been the redefinition of military service in overly econometric concepts and models."[9]

Though this section presents a mixed picture, the discouraging signs outweigh the positive ones. As far as the moral dimension goes, the concern tends to be more on the physical aspects rather than moral ones, with a mechanical outlook rather than an organic one.

To encourage the development of moral bonds that are the basis of variety, rapidity, harmony, and initiative the United States should gradually draw down the budget share going to the active forces for maintaining overseas garrisons and allocate those dollars to force expansion in the national guard and reserves. As Laurence Beilenson has shown in chapter 5, such a withdrawal would be more compatible with the real defense of the United States. Furthermore such a redirection would permit us to expand greatly our pool of combat ready forces and also allow us to create a healthy competition between the reserve and active forces.

In addition to this fundamental restructuring and redirecting of U.S. armed forces to correspond with the overall changes in defense policy deemed appropriate for a free society, other policy changes specific to the armed forces are necessary. First, individuals at all ranks within the armed forces should be held morally responsible for their actions. Second, the COHORT program within the army should be rapidly extended and a similar approach should be supported in the air force as well. Both services should take part in free-play exercises greatly expanded in frequency and scope. Interunit competitions should be undertaken to encourage unit distinction and pride. Finally the national guard could lead by example through exploiting its inherent stability, its ability to conduct joint tactical air and land exercises under one commander, and the lack of burning career ambition among national guard personnel.

While moral bonds must be present within and between services, they must also exist between the services and society. Without those bonds American forces will be ineffective. The Vietnam War illustrates what happens when those bonds are not formed. The Vietnam War was a resource managers' war with insufficient regard paid to the moral dimension of conflict. No attempt was made to consolidate domestic support officially through a declaration of war. The national guard was not nationalized. Anonymous draftees were plucked from society to fight the deadly nonwar. Success was measured by body count and truck kills. The secretary of defense saw the war as a challenge to focus U.S. material forces on the material forces of the North Vietnamese.[10] The result: we had total air, sea, and land superiority. We won every battle. But we lost the war. Why? The North Vietnamese exploited our moral vulnerability, divided us internally by exploiting domestic mistrust, sapped our resolve, severed our moral bonds, and denied us the ability to act in an effective and purposeful way.

That episode was a disaster, though of different intensity, for both South Vietnam and the United States. We should learn the lessons dearly paid for. They are simple lessons, as Sun Tzu observed 2,500 years ago. First, there must be domestic harmony when army and air forces are sent to war. The bonds that unite the people, the government, and the services must defeat all attempts by an alien will to corrode them. Bonds based on trust, and trust that is based on consistent merit, are the most difficult for that alien will to break. But the slightest hint of duplicity from within can rupture the bonds and hand the victory to the enemy. Meriting and maintaining trust is the first requirement for achieving domestic harmony when forces are sent to war. Second, there must be a correct sense of purpose. When forces are engaged and people are dying, what we have is a war; not a police action, not counterinsurgency. The institutional means for recognizing that condition in America is a declaration of war. Declaring war unifies a people toward a common goal and publicly ratifies in law the trust that binds the people, the government, and the services. An attempt to commit troops to action under the guise of calling the action by another name raises the suspicion that the government does not trust the people to support the war. But the people will be expected to bear its physical cost. And as that cost grows, and the mismatch between the burden and trust becomes obvious, the time is ripe for an enemy to exploit the very fear that led the government to avoid asking initially for a declaration of war: the split between the people's will and the government's action.

While the wartime examples of the need for moral bonds are obvious, there are peacetime implications for moral bonds between army and air forces and society. Society must of course support the services in a material way. But if only the material factors are featured in budget deliberations, the services will be seen as just another resource-hungry domestic political faction competing for a portion of the national budget. Air and land forces will of course cost money. But the major argument for resources should be couched in reference to moral values that the services share with society. And how they use those resources should be carefully monitored lest a mismatch arise between how the resources are used and how they are justified.

To foster moral bonds between society and the services so that both are able to cope with the moral requirements of conflict, the United States should bridge the gap between the military and the American public by expanding the force structure in the national guard. Far from making the United States less prepared for combat, this move would make us much better prepared as a society to carry through a war to a successful conclusion. Because the national guard is the citizen soldier's force, increasing our force structure there would force the government to take into account the need to consolidate popular support before a war could be fought. Second, it is essential that a declaration of war be required before an expeditionary force can be sent into conflict. Upon declaring war, the national guard should be mobilized. Since military spending is often the source of considerable friction between the military and the American public in general, debates regarding tactical air and land forces should focus on how to amplify soldierly virtues and meet soldiers' needs rather than on bureaucratic requirements (that is, a larger budget). Related to this, when money is spent, reliable accountability to the public regarding money spent is essential in order to maintain social support. With our force structure expanded in the national guard, a greater openness to review would be possible as would healthy cross-review between the active forces and reserves.

Mental Evaluation

How do U.S. land and air forces understand conflict and what ideas do they offer on how to cope with it? How well do the war-fighting concepts of our air and land forces support a free society's values? What changes in the conceptual orientation of those forces would improve combat effectiveness and how might such a conceptual reorientation be promoted?

A free society places primary emphasis on the value of the free individual for ethical reasons. But this orientation also permits greater social effectiveness because of the way it shapes the mental perception of the problem of social organization and drives a unique response to that problem.

Because life is unpredictable and ever changing for good or ill, freedom is necessary to shape and adapt to those changes. In a free society many independent individuals are allowed to look out for changes, thus providing observations of changes from many perspectives. Freedom permits not only the rapid observation of change, but also the formulation of many responses to those changes.

Individual responsibility encourages an accurate estimate of the observations of change and the development of suitable responses to that change. It also forms the basis for rewarding success and punishing (overwhelmingly unofficial) failure. Aware that actions have direct consequences, free actors have an incentive to think through carefully in a many-sided way their analysis of the problem and their proposed response.

Because many plans are developed to cope with change, and rewards are given for successful resolution of these changes, initiative is encouraged in both a broad and narrow sense. At the macro level many plausible reponses are developed, assuring that at least one will evolve a successful response to a problem. At the personal level initiative amplifies the reward that accompanies responsibility.

In addition to permitting society quickly to initiate responses to ever-changing circumstances, freedom creates a harmonious relationship among the many diverse plans and actors. Free people gauge their actions within a mental context that describes the rules for social action and expectations. The rules are procedural and stated in broad terms. The expectations are intuitively sensed. Therefore, detailed administration is not necessary to produce harmonious interrelations of diverse plans. Free societies also create harmony by specifying broad goals rather than detailed objectives for social action. In an overall sense a free society in action more closely resembles an organism than it does a machine.

This suggests that a free society understands conflict as a dynamic, indeterministic process whereby the moral, mental, and physical dimensions of people must be appealed to implicitly rather than explicitly in order for individuals to observe multiple changes in a variety of ways; to get their bearings and relationship to those changes rapidly; to decide on a course of action that fits their particular situation and the situation of others; and to carry out that action quickly before others do or before new observations make that action irrelevant.[11]

Contrast this view of conflict with that held by a command society. Rather than accepting unpredictability and adapting to it, command societies attempt to control it, determine it, and make it predictable. They devise plans in bureaucratic ways that eliminate individual responsibility. Their plans are not rich and varied but narrow and limited, which removes initiative. Because of their desire to control, to plan centrally limited responses, and to substitute conscious direction for individual initiative, their plans are rigid and their decision-making process ponderous. They are slow to observe, orient, decide, and act. Overall they resemble a large machine, overloaded and laboring. Consequently, in their actions there is a strong emphasis on the physical dimension and a general neglect of the moral side of people. The mental faculty is narrowed to focus on the physical nature of things.

With these contrasting views on the nature of conflict in mind, we should turn our attention to examining the ideas on conflict held by U.S. land and air forces. The historically dominant theme in the army's concept of conflict is to achieve victory through the physical destruction of the enemy, known as attrition. Attrition warfare can be defined as

A managerial approach to war which primarily concerns itself with kill ratios, target servicing, and mutual inventory reduction. War is reduced to a simple mathematical formula; the side with the most men, weapons, and logistics can endure the meatgrinder longer and will eventually win. On the tactical level, objectives are terrain features, attacks are frontal, and defenses linear. Set-piece battles are sought. Maneuver, if any, is more often than not ponderous, muscle-bound, and well telegraphed.[12]

Attrition is a bureaucratic approach to warfare, with its physical management emphasis, presumption of predictability, and relative disregard for the moral factors. It is warfare by the book.

The U.S. Army also has practitioners of another type of warfare, one that is less rigid and directed at destroying an enemy's ability to cope with rapidly developed threats to the cohesion of his moral, mental, and physical organization. Generals William Sherman, George Patton, and Douglas MacArthur practiced this variant. So historically the army was of two minds, the dominant attrition school, and the other minority view. What is the situation today?

The U.S. Army's Operational Concepts Pamphlet, "The Airland Battle and Corps 86," is most revealing.[13] An operational concepts pamphlet describes how combat operations are to be conducted. In this particular pamphlet we are told that the ideas it contains are not new ways to fight but instead ways of applying new technology within old fighting concepts. Some of its highlights are the following: tight coordination of strike assets; concentration of friendly strength against enemy strength (strength understood as physical strength); instruction and emphasis on how to "service targets" (a bureaucratic and military term for killing physical targets); an enemy's intentions are revealed by where he masses his forces (this projects the attrition approach as the enemy's approach); combat is linear (lines are easier to manage than swirling cauldrons of combat confusion); and an understanding of mobility that relates to clearing roads so troops can move. These concepts place this document firmly with the traditional attrition approach.

Another picture of the army's combat concepts emerges on examination of its FM 100-5 Operations paper. This document is "a statement of what the Army must do to win campaigns and battles in contemporary warfare, with guidance on how it must be done." Many of the themes in the FM 100-5 lie clearly outside the attrition perception and are compatible with a free society's understanding of conflict. These themes include a recognition that battle will most often not be linear; cohesion in battle is "inestimably valuable"; cohesion is based on mutual trust, confidence, and esprit; command, control, and communications systems will not permit central control, thus making initiative of subordinate commanders within the overall intent of the superior command vital; a superior should designate the main effort of an operation, communicate his intent through broad mission orders, and expect lower level commanders to feed the overall scheme with local initiatives; operations should appear to an enemy as rapid, unpredictable, violent, and disorienting; our forces should have the initiative and agility to take independent action within the context of an overall plan; and finally, we should focus our strengths against an enemy's weaknesses.[14]

For all its good points, and there are many, the document is conceptually schizophrenic, much like the army itself, by presenting two minds about fundamental approaches to conflict. Like schizophrenia in a person, FM 100-5's conceptual unity is disrupted. Used as a guide to army thinking, the document would contribute to confusion and disharmony in the army as a whole.

Two crippling flaws are evident in the document. The first is the insistance on the synchronization of operation.[15] Synchronization bespeaks a rigid, mechanistic perception and approach to the problem of achieving harmony and coherence. Watches are synchronized; a war, and the people who fight in it, cannot be. If synchronization is pursued it will stifle initiative, reduce agility, and undermine mutual trust, confidence, and esprit. It will reduce cohesion under stress by making the fighting unit inflexible when the synchronized plan is disrupted. It will, to the degree it is used, replace broad mission orders with orders of greater specificity, detail, and constraints.

Synchronization also connotes an emphasis on the physical factors and a corresponding minimization of the moral and mental factors. This tends to suggest that the destruction of an enemy will be accomplished by destroying him physically rather than destroying his ability to exist as a coherent organic whole. This notion surfaces in FM 100-5's statements on maneuver.

Maneuver is understood as combining mobility and fire to attack enemy weaknesses.[16] While attacking enemy weaknesses is a step in the right direction, the document's understanding of what makes up a weakness is flawed. In the FM 100-5 weaknesses are identified as weak points, which are weak in themselves for human (moral), operational (mental), or technical (physical) reasons, and therefore vulnerable to attack. An enemy is vulnerable because he is weak *in detail*. Therefore the cumulative destruction of enemy weak points in detail will ultimately destroy an enemy. Though the document claims this to be maneuver, it is actually a more advantageous form of attrition, or the piecemeal destruction of the enemy.

The objective of maneuver is to confuse, disrupt, or destroy the moral, mental or physical bonds or connections that permit an enemy to exist and function as a coherent, organic whole.[17] Properly executed maneuver focuses on weak points that are an enemy's vulnerable bonds or connections, not discrete weaknesses. Identifying weak points in a maneuver context requires a frame of reference related to the organic unity of the enemy. The FM 100-5 lacks such a frame of reference.

An organic understanding of an enemy's weak points permits a more coherent and effective scheme of attack that need not be centrally managed or synchronized. It permits one to identify weak points within weak points, and weak points within *those* weak points, and so on down to the lowest level of action. The FM 100-5 concept does not permit a similar harmony of focus. Indeed the requirement for synchronization becomes clear in light of this deficiency since without a shared frame of reference to determine what constitutes a weak point, only central- ized determination of what a weak point is and the top-down direction of the force against that weak point will give any degree of coherence to friendly action. The FM 100-5 is a flawed document in which an intellectual version of Gresham's Law operates to let bad ideas drive out or dilute the good.

The air force is a young service and the short history behind its creation provides insights on how it sees itself contributing to a war and how it thinks about that contribution. Early proponents of air power made three arguments. First, aerial bombing of enemy war production centers would collapse an enemy's war effort by directly attacking his ability physically to sustain a war and his morale. Second, by its nature, this mission was independent of ground operations. And third, the above two arguments themselves argued for the creation of a substantial and independent air force to prosecute aerial bombing.[18]

Three notions emerge from these arguments. First, bombing was guided by an attrition approach with moral effects as an undertone. Second, the air war was not prosecuted in association with or directly related to the ground war. And third, any direct involvement with the ground war diverted strength away from the more important aerial bombing mission and jeoparidized the institutional independence of the air force. These notions fed the air force's actions in World War II.

World War II provided an opportunity to conduct a strategic bombing campaign. Great emphasis in the form of men, machines, and thinking was placed on that mission. A fighter force was created for air defense, air superiority, and bomber escort. Contributing to the ground war in a direct way was clearly a secondary mission in the eyes of the army air force, although it did perform the mission and did it reasonably well (exceptionally well in some cases).

In the postwar years, and in great part because of nuclear weapons, the strategic mission orientation continued to dominate air force thinking and the allocation of resources. However, a tactical air (Tac Air) arm did begin to assert itself and to grow, eventually overtaking the strategic air force in squadrons of aircraft by 1964. In concept Tac Air of this period could be seen as a ministrategic air command (SAC). Its focus was on air superiority, tactical nuclear bombing, and deep interdiction. Close air support was assumed to derive from these capabilities.[19]

But the inadequacy of Tac Air for close air support (CAS) was glimpsed in Korea and seen graphically in Vietnam. In Korea the United States did not have an aircraft capable of performing effective CAS. The F-86 was a superb fighter (even though it was designed as a bomber interceptor), but not very suitable for CAS missions. In Vietnam, Tac Air used its F-105, a deep interdiction and tactical nuclear bomber, for CAS. Its inadequacy was quickly evident and the plane was withdrawn from the role to be replaced by a World War II-era navy plane, which proved more effective.

The physical unpreparedness of Tac Air for CAS results from the pursuit of deep interdiction (a tactical adaptation of the attrition-focused strategic bombing idea), and the pursuit of operationally independent missions that separate it from action on the ground. One feeds and reenforces the other. But is this orientation effective?

Tactical air power's deep interdiction orientation is defective at three levels. First, the moral effects of deep interdiction are not properly appreciated. Deep interdiction is often counterproductive from the moral standpoint. In World War II the Germans, instead of cracking under the pressure of strategic bombing (what would be called deep interdiction), solidified their ranks. Indeed, according to the Strategic Bombing Survey, bombing helped improve German war production.[20] It could be argued as well that the British resolve to defeat the Germans was helped rather than hindered by German bombing.

For a future war, say in Europe, it is problematic whether a deep interdiction campaign would help or hinder our effort on a moral level. Bombing targets in Eastern Europe could discourage people who may otherwise be willing to help undermine the rear area security of the Soviet Union. Regardless of where we contemplate a deep interdiction campaign we should ask and answer the question of whether we are building up or draining away the moral integrity of an enemy. Deep interdiction also has domestic moral effects that can undermine a war effort. The example of Vietnam is still fresh enough in the memory and does not need elaboration. Finally, the great error in overestimating the physical effects bombing will have on an enemy rests on the assumption that the physical effect of bombing will be so overwhelming that a defender will be unable to adapt to diminish its effect. But history has shown that this attrition-oriented outlook has not worked. Interestingly, a contemporary of Giulio Douhet (the fountainhead of strategic bombing thinking), Paul Vauthier, a French air power theorist and advocate, wrote extensively on how a determined and ingenious people could adapt to overcome the effects of aerial bombing.[21] Douhet and his followers were misled by an overemphasis on the physical dimension; Vauthier was closer to the truth because his thinking has a more organic twist.

Second, deep interdiction reduces the mental effect of Tac Air. An enemy's plan is rich, complex, and not easily perceived even if looked at in an organic way. Because attrition factors out or reduces the importance of the organic connections between the moral, mental, and physical, it cannot identify those critical connections that must be seen, leaving instead a bewildering array of potential physical targets, each demanding attention. Because genuine weaknesses or vulnerabilities are not seen in a coherent way, attrition-driven bombing can easily lead to a waste of effort and indeed frustrate one's own plan by failing to produce desired effects. Finally the potential for frustrating one's own effort and failing to frustrate the enemy's is heightened by the conception of independent air operations. This fragments our own effort and allows Tac Air to try to divine the enemy's plan and vulnerability where it will be most indistinct and ambiguous to the outside observer—that is, deep within the enemy's own territory. Only when the enemy operation takes on greater definition to an outside observer—when it is interrogated, probed, tested, and unmasked on the ground—can an outsider sort out its complexity and isolate critical vulnerabilities.

And finally, even if we set aside the moral and mental problems, the effectiveness of deep interdiction in achieving its attrition goal is doubtful. The number of enemy targets is large, dispersed, redundant, in many instances hardened or disguised, and defended with varying degrees of intensity. Historically the cost in pilots and planes lost in the attack of deep, hard, fixed, and defended targets is high and grows over time. Furthermore an enemy will adapt to attacks by dispersing, relying on substitutes, rerouting supplies, reassigning forces, and stiffening his defenses to further reduce the effect of air bombardment. Combining these limitations with the shifting value and importance of targets in the course of war and the time that deep interdiction bombing takes to achieve its physical effect, we can see that making deep interdiction the focus of air operations will diminish Tac Air's ability to create menace and fear, shock and disorientation, as well as meaningful destruction.

Even within a concept of air war that has as its goal the destruction of an enemy's organic cohesion, deep interdiction will have a low payoff, be difficult to execute, and be costly to mount and sustain. Focusing Tac Air's effort on deep interdiction would seem to pit weakness against strength.

Much greater effectiveness can be achieved from Tac Air if a mental reorientation allows a shift in emphasis away from deep interdiction and toward close air support of ground operations. Tactical air's greatest strength is its ability rapidly and unexpectedly to concentrate or disperse air power to disorient, disrupt, or destroy the connections that allow an enemy to function as a coherent whole. Close cooperation with the army's operations will magnify that effect. In a moral sense close air support (CAS) can contribute more to building up our sense of confidence in survival, allow us to cope more confidently with uncertainty, and build interservice trust while simultaneously amplifying a sense of menace, uncertainty, and mistrust in the enemy. Close air support can be applied more effectively to attack the enemy's plan by masking and distorting the enemy's picture of our efforts, by probing for and exposing an enemy's vulnerabilities, and by allowing us to threaten and attack many enemy weak points. In a physical sense CAS can more easily achieve its goals, have overall greater effect on the enemy, and cost less to prepare for and sustain. In this sense CAS feeds the strength of air power and directs that strength against an enemy's weak points. Of course what is required for this transition is a turning away from air war conceived as an attrition exercise and moving toward a more organic understanding of the enemy and ourselves.

"You know you never defeated us on the battlefield," said the American colonel. The North Vietnamese colonel pondered this remark a moment. "That may be so," he replied, "but it is also irrelevant."[22] Our objective should be to make this conversation a one-time-only occurrence. Doing that requires a mental reorientation in our thinking about war. To begin that task, we should recognize that successful air and land forces require concepts of war that are compatible with a free society's values. As a basis of such a concept, an organic understanding of our air and land forces should be developed that promotes rapidity, variety, harmony, and initiative by harmonizing our moral, mental, and physical dimensions and holds as our objective the destruction of our enemy's ability to function as an organic whole. Our regular air and land forces should be encouraged to develop these ideas. The national guard should be rewarded for having already adopted these ideas. The regular forces should be given incentives and freedom, not directives, to achieve their own formulation. We should recognize that unless they see the need for these developments (many, and at all levels, do), and move toward them freely as an institution, nothing will change fundamentally. We should also encourage the development of combined air and land forces employment ideas. With a light but perceptible touch we should move the active forces along this path and reward the national guard for already adopting the combined forces concept. We should recognize the national guard as the spearhead of combat-oriented thinking to spur creative intellectual competition between the national guard and the regular air and land forces.

A very effective way to achieve this end would be to support the stated intention of the national guard to develop, refine, and adopt these ideas.[23] By shifting our force structure emphasis to the reserves and making explicit our national support for the new combat ideas of the national guard, we can accelerate the movement away from our present doctrinal orientation and toward a new synthesis.

Further, by removing our forward-deployed active forces we will contribute to breaking the tunnel vision in our thinking, which is born of starting with specific scenarios. Withdrawing these troops and expanding the reserves will permit the services to think in broader terms and be less driven by scenarios.

How could those reserve forces be organized? Manpower analyst Roger Folsom has taken the following cautious look at some potential problems and benefits that could arise.

A key question is how the reserves are to be organized, and how they fit it with the regular forces. One approach would be that in wartime individual reservists would join regular forces to bring undermanned units up to full strength and to replace casualties. The U.S. Navy relies heavily on this approach, because it does not have enough extra ships to permit many to be designated for the reserves, and because many naval reservists live in the central United States far from any oceans, making it impractical for them to man vessels and sail together regularly as ships' crews. With this approach, reservists must be trained as individuals to work well in groups, but there is no need for training to forge groups of reservists into wartime teams because they will be deployed as individuals. One could argue that with this approach there should be little need for any reserve organizational units; individual reservists should train with regular forces on active duty whenever possible.

Another approach is reserve forces organized into the same military units that will be deployed in wartime. Deployable units could be very small: in the case of the army, perhaps as small as a platoon (the smallest unit commanded by a commissioned officer) or a company, but more likely a battalion, regiment, or brigade (several of which constitute a full division). There is some advantage in deploying whatever size unit trains together regularly (typically one weekend a month), because the members of these units will have learned to work together as a team. Moreover, during annual training (typically two weeks) small units can train with and learn from the regular forces. In wartime, small units can be dispersed throughout the regular forces, strengthening all of the major units rather than having large reserve units (e.g., a reserve division) that is conspicuously less competent than the corresponding regular units. And reserve forces deployed in small units may be ready to fight much sooner than if they were deployed in large units. . . . Of course, deployment of small reserve units maximizes the amount of interaction between civilian reservists and regular military personnel, and may be desirable for that reason alone. . . .

The disadvantage of deploying small reserve units in wartime is that there is not much need for high-ranking reserve officers because, . . . the regular forces take care of command and control. For example, if battalions commanded by captains are the reserve unit integrated in wartime into the regular forces, then there is no need for reserve majors, colonels, or generals, except perhaps for peacetime supervision and liaison with regular forces.

Alternatively to integrating the reserve and regular forces, reserve units may be considered cadre forces into which fresh volunteers . . . are added in case of a major mobilization. This training role frees the regular forces for fighting, but unless the reserve forces are very well trained it smacks of the "blind leading the blind." This training role is more likely to be effective if the reserve forces consist largely of former active duty military with at least two years training.

None of these alternative roles for the reserves need be mutually exclusive: perhaps some reserves should be mobilized or deployed as individuals, some as part of small units, others as part of larger units, to be integrated into the regular forces; perhaps some reserve units' role should be that of a cadre which will not be expected to fight until it has grown and developed into a full-strength fully trained force. Unfortunately there is little evidence that these matters have been carefully thought through, analyzed, and then decided.[24]

Physical Evaluation

The moral, mental, and physical categories that have been used for this analysis are aids for sorting out a complex picture and not rigid boxes into which reality must be fit. Indeed all three elements exist within any one of these taken separately. Organic entities are inseparable in their moral, mental, and physical properties. But analysis requires that they be viewed as discrete.

Thus far we have seen the nature of and the relation between the moral and mental dimensions of our air and land forces. Here the physical dimension will be the focus of attention. As a point of departure for this section, attention should be paid to the defense budget, for the budget is a significant determiner of what the physical expression of our forces had been, is now, and will most likely be.

The most important point is that for almost thirty years the defense budget, when the effects of inflation are removed, has been essentially flat. It has exhibited no significant tendency (less than 1 percent) toward growth. This is remarkable since the last thirty years have been a period of rising international tension and domestic turmoil. And while the future cannot be predicted, it would seem that internal domestic economic and general budgetary pressures make it risky to presume that the defense budget either could or will sustain significant long-term (five to ten years) real growth.[25]

Within this overall no-growth pattern, the constant dollar cost of buying equipment has risen. In twenty years, and in constant collars, the price of a tank has risen by a factor of three, as has the price of a fighter.[26] In addition to this increase, the cost of maintaining this new, more complex equipment has risen at a faster pace. The cost of weapon support is going up, as is the demand for more and better trained (and higher paid) people to maintain the equipment. And these support costs may be underrepresented since they are based on peacetime operating conditions and tempos. This helps explain why our force structure has declined in both number and readiness since the 1960s.[27] Rapidly rising costs of purchasing and maintaining ever more complex equipment within an overall budget picture that does not grow means the overall capability of the force will decline.

But the problem is further amplified by our present emphasis on purchasing new equipment rather than adequately funding maintenance and readiness. Within an overall constant budget, this has pushed the support accounts to decline further in their ability to sustain the force. There are many advocates for weapon procurement, but, as an air force general once lamented to Congress, "There is no constituency for readiness."[28]

As a consequence of all this we are left with two conditions. First, we do not have a balanced and ready air and land force today. Second, since the cost of purchasing equipment is underestimated (a program is initially underfunded only to reveal its real cost once the program is under way), and since the equipment purchased will place greater and accelerating demands on the readiness accounts, and further, since we emphasize new equipment over readiness, the overall effectiveness picture will grow worse for tomorrow.[29] We will experience further and accelerating force structure decline, a reduction in the pace of modernization, and a further and rapid drop in readiness.

This suggests that the planning process is dominated by a pervasive budgetary optimism, a belief that the budget will expand to fund existing procurement desires. Based on that optimism, our plans tend to be rigid, inflexible, and unadaptable to the possibility that the budget myth will not come true. And because our budget outlook is dominated by the desire to buy hardware (revealing a dominance of the physical dimension) we heighten the risk of falling short of overall force effectiveness. In short our plans are rigid, and that rigidity imposes an inability to adapt to changes in the budgetary environment.[30] Clearly we do not see budget planning in an organic framework, nor does our planning permit variety, rapidity, harmony, or initiative related to combat effectiveness.

With this backdrop an evaluation of Tac Air's physical condition is possible. The first criterion in the physical evaluation is the readiness of Tac Air to help win a war today, should one occur. And the most important element of readiness is the human factor. How ready our people are to fight will depend on how often and how well they practice for war in peacetime. And the major constraint on the opportunity to practice will be the cost of training.

In the readiness area it is clear that we have placed ourselves in a serious dilemma. As our equipment becomes more complex it would seem to require greater training for our people, individually and as a team, to master its diverse and many-sided capabilities and weaknesses.

However, as our equipment becomes more complex we see, for financial reasons, a corresponding drop in the opportunity to train.[31] Our Tac Air flies far less than the Israeli air force, which has a sense of the immediate need for readiness. Indeed American pilots fly fewer hours today than they did in preparation for the air war in Vietnam (a war where the air environment was much less demanding than what we would encounter if fighting a major power). The reason for the reduction in flying hours is clear. The operating cost of the equipment with which pilots must train has risen dramatically. The per-hour cost of flying the F-15 is twice as high as the F-4, and it is also more labor intensive.[32]

There is another side of the readiness question, and that is the quality of training. Flying itself does not develop combat skills; it merely provides the opportunity to develop those skills. Again, given the complexity of American equipment, it would seem that a very intense and varied program of training would be required to develop the ability to cope with that system and expose, before combat, its vulnerabilities. Within the constraint of fewer flying hours Tac Air has tried to enhance the realism of training with the Red Flag program. However, it is open to doubt whether any program, however worthwhile, can keep pace with the growing tasks imposed on pilots while the opportunity to train grows slightly or declines.

Developing human readiness for war also requires weapon practice. As with the planes themselves, American weapons are complex and require more practice to understand their properties and vulnerabilities. But complex weapons are more costly to buy as well as more difficult to employ. As a consequence they are fired less than the simpler and less costly ones. The average Tac Air pilot will be fortunate to fire one radar-guided missile a year. And only about 200 air-to-ground Mavericks will be fired by all of Tac Air in one year. Once again we are caught in the predicament of paying more for the promise of greater capability and diversity while being unable to sustain a readiness program that allows our pilots to train in order to understand that diversity or to test the promise of increased capability in realistic mock combat. Pilots will not fully appreciate the advantages and disadvantages of their weapons until confronted by an enemy.

Another readiness factor is the orientation we give our pilots. Air-to-air and air-to-ground missions are extremely different. The navy has traditionally appreciated the difference and trained its pilots as specialists in one or the other mission. Combining these missions in the same person degrades the skill level he can achieve in each specialty. In the past Tac Air has produced a generalist with the ability to perform both missions. The Vietnam War highlighted the cost in doing this, especially in the CAS mission. Since then the situation has changed somewhat. The development of the A-10, a plane dedicated to CAS, ensures that these pilots will focus their thinking on the air-to-ground mission. And since the F-15 as yet does not have an air-to-ground capability, these pilots will specialize in the air-to-air mission. However, the F-16, and F-4, our most numerous modern fighters, can perform both missions, and these pilots are trained to do both.

While we have tended to focus on pilot readiness, Tac Air also includes people on the ground who make sure the planes can fly and fight. The desire to buy more complex equipment imposes the need for more and better trained maintenance people. This magnifies the need to attract and retain highly qualified people, which costs more money. It also raises the cost and time required to train them adequately. Demographic trends suggest that the available pool of such people will shrink. And the growing costs of the equipment will crowd out the funds necessary to produce the necessary skill levels. In short we need more and better trained people to keep fewer planes flying less often while the probability that we will get those people and be able to train them adequately will decline.

The other side of readiness is the equipment picture. Based on a survey of readiness data from Tac Air, it appears that there is a direct and inverse relationship between the complexity of the equipment and its readiness.[33] It should be remembered that this is the condition in peacetime, without the activity of an enemy with which to cope. Complex equipment can be made ready to fight. Surge exercises for selected squadrons and wings of the Tac Air force have been done. But this is different from making the entire force ready to fight a war. Low aircraft readiness can be attributed to the tremendous cost of keeping the equipment in fighting condition. And since the institutional bias is for equipment investment over readiness, the overall picture of material readiness is likely to worsen.

Another problem is the way readiness is estimated. In 1980 only sixty-two of 161 Tac Air squadrons were without major deficiencies.[34] However, the criteria for establishing whether or not a squadron is ready is not necessarily related to what would constitute readiness for war. Given that we are willing to tolerate fewer flying hours, constrained practice, and limited weapon practice, how "ready" is our estimate of readiness? It is highly likely that our official estimates of readiness overstate our actual condition.[35] And even within the official definition our forces are not prepared for action today.

The next major question is whether we can sustain an air war. Since we do not know what the duration of the war would be, nor do we know what the intensity of the war would be, how well are we prepared to adapt to that ambiguity to make sure we are not exhausted before we can win? It is a convenient assumption that a major war will be brief, but wars are rarely convenient.

Air missions are grueling on man and machine. But the machine can be readied for renewed action before the pilot can recuperate his strength. Therefore multiple manning of a plane allows pilots to rotate, thus keeping the plane in action against the enemy. Fewer pilots means fewer sorties, which means lowered ability to sustain even the short air war anticipated.

Another deficiency is that our war reserve stocks are low. In 1980 we had only 15 percent of the estimated requirement of spare parts.[36] This figure is low since it is based on high reliability expectations from our equipment, the effectiveness of our weapons, and the anticipation of a short war. Once again it should be mentioned that the high cost of spare parts and munitions comes from the drive for more complex equipment.

The combination of complex equipment and costly spare parts has driven responses that increase the vulnerability of our logistics net, another drain on our sustainability. Because our equipment is more difficult to maintain, maintenance has become more centralized. This produces greater vulnerability by reducing the number of targets an enemy needs to hit and guarantees that the value of a destroyed target will be high. Related to this is the dependence American planes have on operating out of these concentrated bases. Dispersing our Tac Air forces in a theater of operations is made more difficult by the specialized maintenance demands complex equipment places on us. We are caught in a circular problem: sustainability requires dispersion of operations and logistics, yet the complexity of our equipment impedes dispersion because the logistics net needed to sustain the equipment must be concentrated.

Another element of sustainability is battle-damage repair to slow the effect of attrition. In war more planes are damaged than shot down. This suggests that sustainability requires planes that can be repaired quickly in war conditions. But our complex equipment makes battle-damage repair extremely difficult. In addition, battle-damage repair funds for the A-10, our least complex modern combat plane, exceeded by seven-to-one the collective battle-damage repair funds for all other aircraft, which are more complex and vulnerable.[37]

Finally sustainability requires high aircraft production in wartime and the ability to increase or decrease production coherently and efficiently in peacetime as the budget fluctuates in the short term. Because of our concentration on complex planes we are now unable to increase production to meet war needs. Today it would take eighteen months before an additional (over the number requested before the crisis) F-15 or F-16 could be delivered.[38] Low production because of high unit costs restricts the number of producers and limits the size of their productive capacity. This reduces competition in production, which contributes to inefficiency and cost growth. Because there are fewer producers there are fewer subcontractors, which causes further surge capacity shrinkage and less competition. And because the overall productive capacity is so small there is little slack to absorb short-run reductions in procurement funding or increases in production when the budget temporarily rises.[39]

The third element in Tac Air's ability to win a war is its force structure. As was mentioned earlier, the low emphasis placed on the CAS mission and the high number of fighter and interdiction aircraft suggest that Tac Air will not pit its strength against an enemy's weakness nor will it most productively feed the prosecution of the ground war. In this sense we are not ready to use air power where it is most needed because of our procurement preferences.

How can we reverse these trends? To break the past pattern of decay three major changes must be made. First, we must remove the fixed force structure requirement. This inhibition on expanding the force has shifted our energy toward making a few systems supercapable. The result is both less capable equipment and a smaller force. Second, we must freeze the tactical air budget at its average thirty-year level. This would be an amount that would be sustainable for the foreseeable future. Third, we must stipulate, demand, and audit high readiness levels for equipment and personnel. This would require much greater opportunities to fly and shoot. More than any other single factor, this condition would greatly increase the attractiveness of the air reserves by giving pilots the chance to do what they most want to do: fly, train, and shoot. Finally, we must require a demonstrated ability to surge for war. This would ensure that there would be no gaps between equipment and personnel on hand, their war reserve stocks, and the ability of industry and mobilized soldiers to rapidly reenforce our force.

Even with an emphasis on reserves, the present equipment picture would hobble our attempt to make the transition from where we are to where we can and must be. Therefore a premium must be placed on developing equipment with very low maintenance requirements, to include base and depot. Equipment should be suitable for support and operation from austere bases. This would permit greater ease and lower cost of operation at home and make possible deployment to areas overseas that do not have a well-developed logistics infrastructure waiting for us to become dependent on. Such equipment would reduce the demand for specialized skills, lower training costs and permit retention of the skills we are able to attract into the reserves. Another bonus would be to make the force more attractive by offering more and varied opportunities to fly and shoot. Finally, in light of the doctrinal revisions mentioned previously, equipment should be designed to meet the need for more appropriate support of land force elements. Emphasis should be placed on developing a fighter and CAS aircraft and weapons.

Weapons development should follow several specific guidelines. First, competitive prototyping and production should be pursued to ensure design improvements, innovation, and lower production cost. Second, operational testing of prototypes before making a production decision is necessary. In addition, the prototype should be tested side by side with the weapon it is intended to replace. Further, the number of weapons included in the test should be related to a common cost, for example $25 million for one new weapon plus its support and spares competing with $25 million worth of competing weapons and spares. Third, as a general guide weapons should be quick to kill, small and hard to detect, agile and reliable in combat, and affordable in mass.

At this point we should turn to an evaluation of the army. People are the most important element in combat effectiveness, and land war is the most labor-intensive form of combat. It would seem that the quality and training of the people in the army would be decisive for its combat effectiveness. That is why this assessment begins with the readiness of the army's people for war.

Army personnel skill levels are at unacceptably low levels. In 1979, in the army's own test of the performance level of critical skills, it was discovered that 98 percent of the tank repairmen, 91 percent of the aviation repairmen, 86 percent of the artillery crewmen, and 45 percent of the field artillerymen performed below the minimum level set by the army.[40] Since then the situation has improved somewhat as better educated people have enlisted. Whether this represents a long-term trend or is the result of economic hard times is uncertain. And what places the issue further in doubt is that the growing complexity of army equipment will intensify the demand for more and better technically educated people in the army.

Turbulence is still a problem. Because people shift about, training and unit skill development is degraded. The chief of staff's efforts to curb this problem with the COHORT program are laudable. But as of 1982 only 3 percent of the army was affected by the program.[41]

The overall coherence of personnel training is in doubt. Because army combat ideas are in flux, the army will be in a state of internal disorder as it tries to integrate these ideas. This problem is to be expected in any large institution when organizational ideas shift. However, given that the ideas are themselves not coherent, one can wonder whether the confusion will be worth the price, or indeed if it will ever abate.

On the issue of the opportunity to train, it must be remembered that ground force training is inherently very expensive. But we should ask whether we make it more expensive still by concentrating on buying ever more complex equipment, which imposes higher operating costs, and therefore whether the investment cost of the higher priced equipment crowds out the money for training. For example, our tank gunners fire fewer rounds in training than their Israeli counterparts. And antitank missilemen in Europe fire fewer than one TOW (antitank guided missile) per year. As with Tac Air, higher complexity equipment demands more training, not less, yet the high cost of the equipment and its operation frustrates such training.

Higher level training is inadequate. Combined forces, free-play exercises are extremely rare. While the idea behind Fort Irwin is praiseworthy, it will in practice be a rare opportunity to hone critical combat skills for most of the army. And again, the growing expense of modernization with complex equipment and its attendant maintenance costs will crowd out badly needed funds for this and other training programs.

A material readiness assessment must be approached warily. First, the data on the equipment evaluated are not as accurate as they ought to be.[42] And the standards for measuring readiness are highly dependent on how one defines readiness. Given this, one would expect that readiness reports probably overstate the actual levels of readiness. Nonetheless, in 1980 only six of sixteen active army divisions were without major deficiencies.[43]

With that readiness picture in mind we should look at our ability to sustain a war. Right now the army can muster twenty-four divisions (one-third of which are army national guard). As constituted this is too small a force for a major war. And while a U.S. Army division is larger than a Soviet division by about 50 percent it is only 25 percent stronger in combat forces.[44]

Within that force we are short of reserves. As of 1980 there was a 22 percent shortage of tanks and a 60,000 shortfall of trucks.[45] The army national guard is short about $3 billion worth of equipment.[46] Similar, if less drastic shortages appear in other categories. While this is a serious problem in itself, it probably understates the magnitude of the problem. These shortages are based on estimates of expected performance from our equipment that are overly optimistic. We expect to do more damage to the enemy than we are likely to achieve, and our own equipment will not perform as well as expected.

Our defense industrial base is not sufficiently responsive to sustain a war. The drawdown of supplies from the army that were sent to Israel during and after the 1973 war was not made up as of 1980.[47] Munition production is concentrated in a very few firms. Contracts are awarded sole-source for privately owned firms or given to government-owned facilities. There is little price competition and very little tolerance for innovation. Because there is no market competition or efficiency, our resupply base is small, less efficient and modern, and more expensive. To take the example of the tank, where once we had two facilities, in 1978, that could in one year produce 1,240 tanks for $1.24 billion, we now have one plant that in one year will produce 720 tanks for $2.16 billion.

It is doubtful that we can logistically sustain a war in a theater of operations. We have a serious problem with logistic support in peacetime where we have to cope with our own internal problems. War will magnify those problems and impose new ones. Some sense of our logistic problems is suggested by our inability to keep the M-60a2, a 1960s version of a high-complexity tank, operational. This tank was withdrawn from the fleet because it was a severe maintenance drain. Highly complex equipment places higher and more exacting demands on our logistic capability for several reasons. First, complex equipment is more susceptible to damage, and when damaged more difficult to repair. Second, diagnosis of damage to complex equipment requires testing equipment that is itself highly complex, sensitive, scarce, and cumbersome. Worse, to work the diagnostic equipment requires that the electrical wiring of the tested vehicle be intact, a highly improbable situation. Third, the new, complex equipment requires more fuel, aggravating an always severe problem for logistic support. The M-1 requires 62 percent more fuel than the tank it replaces, the M-2/3 fighting vehicle system will need 200 percent more than the M-113 it replaces.[48] Finally the new equipment will require more maintenance personnel. Even if the M-1 tank works as well as the army expects, it will take two times the people (87,650 versus 45,650) to operate and maintain eighty-five M-1 battalions than eighty-five M-60 battalions. These trends indicate that we are moving from a bad logistic-sustainability position to one that is worse.

Battle-damage repair is another factor in sustainability. We should ask whether we are making it easier or harder to turn around battle-damaged equipment. To take one major combat item as an example, the M-1 will take much longer to return to combat because its armor requires specialized equipment to repair battle damage and return it to its original level of protection. Expedient and effective repair of conventional armor can be achieved more rapidly, and it can with less difficulty be returned to its previous level of protection. A similar picture emerges when engines are compared. The M-1 turbine engine is more susceptible to damage and requires higher level repair than the less expensive, more damage resistant, and easier to repair diesel of the M-60. It is hoped that a damaged M-1 engine module will be replaced if damaged, but the high cost of the replacement modules suggest that there will be few available when and where they are needed.

The third measure of the army's physical ability to win a war is its force structure. Given the rapidly rising cost of equipment and the higher rise in their support costs, even if the army budget departs from its thirty-year budget trend and sustains a constantly rising income curve, force structure will decline rather than rise. If the budget deviates from this budgetary best-case scenario, decline is guaranteed. In the period from fiscal year 1976 to fiscal year 1985 the army expects its authorized income for producing weapons, ammunition, spare parts, and so on to rise by a factor of five, while it expects an increase in this same period in its authorized manpower of less than 2 percent.[49] Since the equipment requires more (perhaps much more in combat) money to buy, operate, and maintain, and more people to perform these tasks, we can expect to get less force per division as the "teeth-to-tail" ratio shrinks.

How can this situation be reversed for the army? The immediate benefit of withdrawing overseas based forces and deactivating them and directing those resources to the army national guard and reserves would be a tremendous increase in force size. However, force expansion must go hand in hand with force effectiveness. Unless a significant reorientation is realized in the equipment emphasis of the army, even the newly liberated funds will not lead to more and better forces. We cannot tolerate a situation where we now buy only 11 percent of the tanks we bought in 1950 for the same money. And these few tanks cost us dearly in scarce operations and readiness funds.

Our dual goal should be force effectiveness and force expansion. Force effectiveness can only be achieved if our equipment permits higher levels of training and proficiency. Given the current equipment picture, levels of training adequate to combat demands are beyond realistic and sustainable budget levels. And expecting operator proficiency given the growing complexity of the equipment, is an even greater question. A large and sustainable force size that fits the needs of a reserve-based force structure can realistically come about only if combat-derived criteria that take into account the whole picture of combat effectiveness are applied to equipment design. And this will not occur as long as independent operational testing is not done (or done badly).

Force expansion will take longer but trends can be established to help it come about. By removing the fixed-force structure and setting the total land forces budget on a flat line from this point onward, incentives can be created to increase the force. Greater flexibility and range of options for new equipment can be realized through prototype competition and competitive production. This will not only improve the quality of equipment, but also reduce the unit cost and reverse the disastrous trend toward a shrinking defense industrial base. Further, through rigorous independent operational testing, to include testing of maintenance and support requirements, we can begin to reverse the trend toward fewer combat units and expanding support requirements.

The army equipment picture is very detailed and too elaborate to go into here. However, the reader is urged to read a report by the army and air national guard entitled *Vista 1999.*[50] In it details are laid out and explained.

Conclusion

Let's pull together the preceding analysis by introducing the concept of friction. Friction is that which slows an organism's ability to shape and adapt to change in a coherent way. We have seen how friction can arise in a moral, mental, and physical sense to undermine our forces' ability to confront an enemy in a coherent way in order to build up his friction and deny him the ability to function as a coherent whole.

Friction is the enemy of variety (it makes one more predictable), rapidity (it slows down one's action and reactions), harmony (it forces one to emphasize the explicit over the implicit), and initiative (it forces one to react). This chapter has noted the sources of friction in our own system and made recommendations to reduce that friction. If we reduce it we will be better able to increase friction in an enemy, and bring about his defeat. And since these recommendations flow from an appreciation for the values of a free society, we will get effective tactical air and land forces that affirm our values in peace and war.

Notes

1. Ludwig Von Mises, *Socialism* (Indianapolis, Ind.: Liberty Fund, 1981). The scope of centralized control is illustrated in the Soviet military by Andrew Cockburn, who notes that the Soviets do not even give their enlisted men maps for fear they will use them to defect. See Andrew Cockburn, *The Threat: Inside the Soviet Military Machine* (New York: Random House, 1983).

2. John Boyd, "Patterns of Conflict," Unpublished briefing, U.S. Department of Defense, Washington, D.C., January 1983.

3. Ibid.

4. Air Force Office of Scientific Research, *Pilot Opinion Survey,* quoted in *Air Force Times,* November 1980.

5. Bruce Ingersoll, *Chicago Sun-Times,* October 1, 1981, p. 15; David Griffiths, *Aviation Week and Space Technology,* October 12, 1981.

6. Richard Gabriel and Paul Savage, *Crisis in Command* (New York: Hill and Wang, 1978).

7. *Armed Forces Journal,* October 1982, p. 44.

8. John Boyd, "Organic Design," Unpublished briefing, U.S. Department of Defense, Washington, D.C., May 1983.

9. Charles Moskos, "Saving the All-Volunteer Force," *Public Interest* 61 (Fall 1980).

10. Robert McNamara, quoted in James Fallows, *National Defense* (New York: Random House, 1981), p. 10.

11. Boyd, "Patterns of Conflict." See also Thomas J. Peters and Robert H. Waterman, Jr., *In Search of Excellence* (New York: Harper & Row, 1983).

12. Second Marine Division Maneuver Warfare Board, "Maneuver Warfare," 1981.

13. U.S. Army Operational Concepts, "The Airland Battle and Corps 86," Training and Doctrine Command Pamphlet 525-5, March 25, 1981.

14. U.S. Army, *Operations FM-100-5,* Final Draft, January 15, 1982.

15. Ibid., pp. 2-1–2-25.

16. Ibid., p. 2-5.

17. Boyd, "Patterns of Conflict."

18. Jeffrey Barlow, "Close Air Support and the Soviet Threat," in *Backgrounder* (Washington, D.C.: The Heritage Foundation, August 11, 1982) p. 2.

19. Ibid., p. 4.

20. U.S., Department of War, *Overall Report, European War,* U.S. Strategic Bombing Survey, September 30, 1945.

21. Philip Supina, "To Withstand the Firestorm," *Proceedings of the U.S. Naval Institute* (November 1980):42–46.

22. Harry G. Summers, Jr., *On Strategy: The Vietnam War in Context* (Carlisle Barracks, Pa.: 1981), p. 1.

23. National Guard Bureau, Department of Defense, *Vista 1999: A Long-Range Look at the Future of the Army and Air National Guard* (Washington, D.C.: March 1982).

24. The material from Roger Folsom is taken from an earlier, longer version of his chapter that appears in this book.

25. James Fallows, "Endless Deficits," *Atlantic Monthly,* May 1982.

26. Franklin C. Spinney, "Defense Facts of Life," Unpublished

briefing for Office of the Secretary of Defense, Program Analysis and Evaluation, Washington, D.C.: U.S. Department of Defense, December 5, 1980.

27. "Implications of Highly Sophisticated Weapon Systems on Military Capabilities," (Washington, D.C.: U.S. General Accounting Office, June 30, 1980); Spinney, "Defense Facts of Life."

28. Gordon Adams, *The Iron Triangle* (New York: Council on Economic Priorities, 1981).

29. Franklin C. Spinney, "Plans Reality Mismatch," Unpublished paper, December 1982. See also, U.S. Air Force Systems Command, "Affordable Acquisition Approach," Unpublished draft briefing, Washington, D.C.: U.S. Department of Defense, 1983).

30. J. Stockfisch, "Incentives and Information Quality in Defense Management," prepared for Defense Advanced Research Projects Agency (Washington, D.C.: U.S. Department of Defense, August 1976). See also Peter Drucker, *Management: Tasks, Practices, and Responsibilities* (New York: Harper & Row, 1979).

31. Spinney, "Defense Facts of Life."

32. Ibid.

33. George Kuhn, "Ending Defense Stagnation," in *A Mandate for Leadership: Agenda '83,* ed. Richard Holwill (Washington, D.C.: The Heritage Foundation, 1983).

34. Melvin R. Laird with Lawrence J. Korb, "The Problem of Military Readiness" (Washington, D.C.: American Enterprise Institute, 1980), p. 25.

35. Ibid., p. 21.

36. Laird and Korb, "The Problem of Military Readiness," p. 14.

37. Spinney, "Defense Facts of Life."

38. Jacques S. Gansler, "Can the Defense Industry Respond to the Reagan Initiatives," *International Security* (Spring 1982): 103.

39. Jacques S. Gansler (Text of testimony given before U.S. House of Representatives Committee on Appropriations, Defense Subcommittee, July 21, 1981).

40. Laird and Korb, "The Problem of Military Readiness," p. 25.

41. Deborah Shapley, "The Army's New Fighting Doctrine," *New York Times Sunday Magazine,* November 28, 1982.

42. Laird and Korb, "The Problem of Military Readiness," pp. 20–23.

43. Ibid., p. 23.

44. Steven Canby, "The Alliance and Europe: Part IV—Military Doctrine and Technology," *Adelphi Paper 109* (London: International Institute for Strategic Studies).

45. Laird and Korb, "The Problem of Military Readiness," p. 40.

46. U.S., Department of Defense, Reserve Force Policy Board, *Fiscal Year 1981 Readiness Assessment of the Reserve Components.*

47. Laird and Korb, "The Problem of Military Readiness," p. 13.

48. U.S. General Accounting Office, "Budgetary Pressures Created by the Army's Plans to Procure New Major Weapon Systems Are Just Begun," October 20, 1981.

49. *Armed Forces Journal,* October 1982, p. 44.

50. National Guard Bureau, *Vista 1999.*

8

Military Personnel without Conscription

Roger Nils Folsom
with the assistance of
Ann Arlene Marquiss Folsom

Fundamentally there are only two ways to obtain military personnel: governmental coercion or individual choice. Chapter 1 showed that conscription, which is a feature of almost all totalitarian societies, requires so much coercion that it is clearly inconsistent with the principles and moral values of a free society. The present chapter addresses the practicality of entrusting a free society's defense to all-volunteer forces. Is it feasible for all-volunteer forces to be adequately effective? By avoiding conscription, how much do we hurt our defense—or do we improve it?

In other chapters this book calls for major changes in U.S. foreign policy and military force structure: sharply reducing U.S. commitments to "engangling foreign alliances"; greatly decreasing the number of U.S. troops stationed abroad; and replacing our large standing military forces by a mix of small standing forces and large, well-trained and well-equipped reserve forces. The recruiting problem that so worries many people today—how to get enough high-quality recruits, given the passing of the postwar baby boom—could disappear with such changes. But such changes will not likely be made soon. Therefore this chapter discusses military personnel issues in general and recommends policies appropriate for our present large standing forces, as well as for the strong reserve-force structure recommended elsewhere in the book.

The last draft call was issued in December 1972, and the last conscripted military service ended in 1974. Since then, for the first substantial period of time since before World War II, the United States has had all-volunteer military forces. Throughout this period the all-volunteer force has been continually on the defensive. Many influential persons in the military, Congress, in the press, and elsewhere have argued that all-volunteer forces have failed to provide adequate defense and that the nation should revive the draft.[1] Many Americans, sometimes a majority, have agreed.[2]

Critics of the all-volunteer force argue that recruiting difficulties inevitably make it too small in number, too low in quality, and socioeconomically too unrepresentative of middle-class America. Unfortunately, data supporting such criticisms are plentiful. And over the next ten years, a declining youth population may make recruiting even more difficult. Could involuntary military servitude conceivably be an evil necessary for the defense of a free society?

In a short-term World War II–type mobilization, conscription might be seen as not too inequitable, particularly if virtually all young people fit for military duty were required to serve. Inequities still arise, of course, if young women (or else half the young men and half the young women) are exempt. And full-mobilization conscription inevitably is inequitable to those who happen to be draft age when war breaks out, relative to those who happen to be draft age in more peaceful times. A subtler point is that wartime conscription, even if everyone were called to serve, must be inequitable (in the sense of imposing unequal real sacrifice) to those for whom military service is especially repugnant, whether for religious or humanitarian reasons.

Nevertheless in "complete" mobilizations such as for World Wars I and II, even democratic societies abandoned the market and instead used coercion (alias "planning") to allocate all types of resources, materiel as well as personnel. A possible justification for resorting to coercion is the belief that major wars cause such massive shifts in the demands and supplies of various commodities that a free wartime economy would see tremendous changes in relative prices, causing grossly inequitable and socially disruptive windfall changes in the distribution of income and wealth. "War profiteer" is an epithet, not a compliment, even if the recipient has made a major contribution to the nation's war effort. Thus it is argued that a command system of resource allocation, using direct controls and quotas on the quantities of goods produced and inputs used, is preferable to free market resource allocation in wartime.[3]

On the other hand command resource allocation systems are notorious for their inherent and inevitable inefficiencies, compared with free markets. Abba Lerner argued during World War II that the need to win the war made it imperative that the market mechanism's efficiencies be fully exploited, not only in allocating resources among competing alternative civilian uses, but also within the military, for example between the European and Asian wars.[4] Using a command system could be a good way to lose the war. Shortly after World War II ended, Walter Eucken of the University of Freiburg described and analyzed Nazi Germany's centrally planned and administered economy, and the resulting inefficiencies that contributed to the Third Reich's downfall: excessive product standardization; excessive firm and plant size; decision delays caused by arguments among planning agencies; shifting priorities; planning inconsistencies; and especially the misallocations caused by valuing goods—and making decisions—in large mass quantities. These problems were compounded by the use of fixed prices determined by prewar price controls decreed in 1936.[5]

As a practical matter, markets may thus be more efficient than command systems, even in wartime. If markets were used to allocate war materiel, they could reasonably be used to allocate people as well, even in a World War II–type massive mobilization. From a moral standpoint the freedom of choice associated with market allocations of resources and an all-volunteer force clearly is preferable to the coercion associated with command resource allocation systems and conscription.

In any case in this chapter we deal with the more tractable and more immediately relevant question of how to select people for military service during a very long-term "cold war" confrontation. In this context, we will show not only that all-volunteer forces are feasible, but also that they are preferable to conscription from a national security standpoint—aside from any moral objections to the coercion inherent in conscription. Military conscription is not in any sense necessary or even helpful to military security.

Volunteers Versus Conscripts

For each year from 1940 through 2000, figure 8–1 graphs historical data and forecast projections giving the number of active duty military personnel and the number of new recruits (volunteers and conscripts) entering the active duty enlisted ranks (excluding entrants from the reserves), compared with the nineteen-year-old male population. The purpose is to illustrate trends in the demand for, and supply of, military personnel.[6]

The figure illustrates three points. First, it is not surprising that during World War II the United States used conscription and that conscription was widely regarded as "fair," since the vast majority of young men were called to serve. Second, it is not surprising that conscription became so controversial during the Vietnam War, since only a minority of men were called to serve; relative to the nineteen-year-old male population, military personnel demands were higher in peacetime 1955 than in any Vietnamese War year. Third, unless future military personnel demands increase greatly, they can be met without overwhelming difficulty from the available supply of young men, and of course with even less difficulty the more that women are recruited. The youth population did peak in 1980 and is projected to fall until the mid-1990s, after which it is expected to rise again as the post-World War II baby boom's children come of age. But even at its lowest, the youth population will remain *above* its level prior to 1966. Indeed, throughout the 1980s and 1990s there will be more nineteen-year-olds than we had all through the 1950s and on into 1966. Yet during that time, force levels were generally higher than are projected through the end of the century.

Moreover, demographic trends over the next ten years may be less adverse for recruiting than figure 8–1 suggests. While the population younger than twenty-five will decrease, the population older than twenty-five will increase—and this increase in the supply of the economy's most productive workers may decrease the civilian economy's demand for inexperienced youth, increasing the relative attractiveness of military service.[7] Then too, the military might find it useful to recruit older persons, particularly skilled technicians who could enter the military at advanced grades.

Thus although the youth population will decline until well into the 1990s, it appears to be more than sufficient to sustain our present military forces, and even to permit some growth. It certainly will be much more than sufficient to sustain the far smaller active duty military forces that would be required if the United States withdrew from most or all of its alliances and reduced or eliminated its ground forces in Europe and Korea.

Nevertheless, although a substantial youth population clearly facilitates recruiting, it is no guarantee: poor compensation and other personnel policies can make recruiting adequate numbers of high-quality volunteers very difficult, as happened during the 1970s when the youth population was larger than ever before.

The Effect of Conscription on Quality

The all-volunteer force, particularly the army, has been short of high-quality recruits. But conscription would not necessarily improve recruit quality. A draft does conscript high-quality youth (unless it exempts them), but it also conscripts low-quality youth. And when a military service is drafting, "it cannot turn away minimally qualified volunteers to draft higher qualified non-volunteers."[8] Draft standards must be set low enough to make it impractical for most people to deliberately avoid conscription by feigning failure to qualify. Furthermore, from a practical political standpoint, draft standards must be set low enough that conscription is perceived as "fair": drafting only those in the upper 50 percent of the population according to mental ability probably would

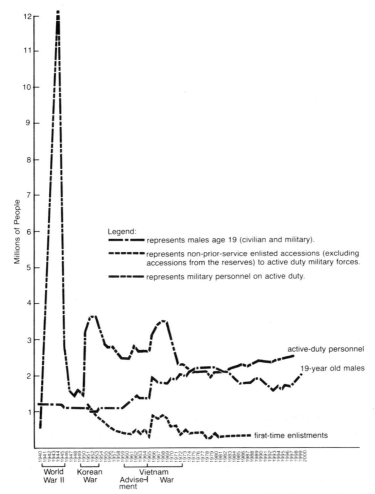

Notes: Population data for years after 1976, and military data for years after 1982, are forecasts or projections.

For military data, some early years are missing because data are either not reliable or not available; some projections are missing because data are not available, at least not to the general public.

Active duty military personnel are as of the end of the fiscal year: June 30 through 1976; September 30 thereafter. Non-prior-service enlisted accessions of 119,000 for the transition quarter (July-September 1976) are omitted.

Source: U.S. Department of Commerce, Bureau of the Census, *Current Population Reports: Population Estimates and Projections,* Series P-25. No. 311 (July 2, 1965); No. 519 (April 1974), Table 1; No. 721 (April 1978), Table 1; No. 704 (July 1977), Table 8, Series II.

U.S. Department of Commerce, Bureau of the Census, *Statistical Abstract of the United States,* 1966, p. 262, Table 366; 1971, p. 254, Table 405; 1981, pp. 362, 366, Tables 597, 610.

Unpublished military personnel projections are courtesy of the Department of Defense.

Figure 8–1. Civilian Youth, New Recruits, and Active Duty Military Personnel

be viewed as highly unfair by conscripts who tested slightly above average, compared with nonconscripts who tested slightly below average. Such perceptions of unfairness, if widespread, would rob conscription of the social legitimacy necessary for a draft to be enforced. Therefore, when a military service is drafting, minimum standards for its conscripts and volunteers alike tend to be set as low as possible. Since World War II, U.S. draft law has excused from military service only the bottom 9 percent of the male population in mental ability.

Thus conscription conceivably could either raise or lower the average level of recruit mental abilities, compared with an all-volunteer force. But by drafting not only high- but also low-ability youth, and by forcing a reduction in the minimum standards for volunteer enlistments, conscription clearly would expand the range or variance of abilities. Whether these results are good or bad for military effectiveness is not known: conscription may provide smarter and presumably better leaders, but it also provides more inept followers.

With an all-volunteer force, recruit quality could be as high as desired. "You get what you pay for." If military compensation were raised, for example, to the levels paid by large city police and fire departments, then military recruiting standards could be much higher than they are now in terms of mental and physical abilities and educational achievements. And unlike a draft, there would be no requirement that minimally qualified persons be recruited along with highly qualified persons. Even the issue of socioeconomic representativeness could disappear—or at least turn upside down. (Observe that in many police and fire departments the issue is not that blacks and other minorities are overrepresented, but rather that they are underrepresented.)

The all-volunteer force has suffered not only from shortages of qualified recruits but also from even more serious shortages of senior enlisted personnel, whose skills and maintenance experience are crucial for military forces that rely on modern technology. Conscripting recruits cannot solve shortages of senior personnel. In fact conscription makes shortages of senior personnel even worse, because high enlisted turnover requires many scarce senior noncommissioned officers to be used in recruit training (and in training support missions) instead of in operations. And recruit training does not add nearly as much to the combat effectiveness of these senior personnel as would equal time spent obtaining experience in military operations.

We will see that shortages of qualified recruits and of experienced senior personnel have arisen not because the all-volunteer concept is impractical, but because of policies adopted by Congress and the military forces themselves. Fairly simple reforms in the structure of military compensation and in other personnel policies can make an all-volunteer force even more feasible, while improving its quality and effectiveness. Fortunately, these changes need *not* increase the total *real* costs of obtaining adequate numbers of qualified men and women for military service.

Equity and the Free Rider Problem

Sometimes it is argued that volunteer military forces generate a "free rider" problem, in that those who do not volunteer get a free ride from those who do volunteer for military service. But the free rider problem cannot validly be used to criticize volunteer armed forces financed by compulsory taxes levied on the whole society. If military compensation is enough to persuade adequate numbers to volunteer, then those who choose not to serve are not getting a free ride, because they must pay the taxes. Conscription, on the other hand, does generate a kind of free rider problem, because those who are not conscripted (whether because of sex, age, mental or physical condition, or the luck of a lottery) avoid military service and also avoid paying in taxes their share of the full real costs borne by the conscripts defending the nation.

Note that military service is not the only dangerous job society needs done.[9] In the public sector there are police work and fire fighting; the private sector offers a coal mining; construction work on skyscrapers, bridges, dams, and offshore oil rigs; crop dusting; and driving of gasoline or propane-filled tanker trucks. Because the volunteers who take these dangerous jobs are compensated by the rest of us, either by taxes or in the prices we pay for goods and services, we get no free ride.

Social Representativeness

Since well before the beginning of the all-volunteer force, there has been concern that a force of volunteers would not be representative of middle-class American society. Volunteers, it was feared, would be "mercenaries" drawn primarily from among the poor, and from blacks and other racial minorities. Such a situation would be worrisome for two reasons. First, it would be unfair: "What kind of society excuses its privileged from serving in the military?"[10] Second, it could impair the quality of national defense. Military forces drawn primarily from among the poor and racial minorities might perceive the inequity of "black men dying for a white man's war"[11] and fight poorly because of low morale, or because they would resent their officers (assumed to be largely white and middle class), or simply because their mental abilities were too low to provide effective leadership "within the ranks" or to deal with the technology of modern warfare.

A major conflict would greatly expand the military, inevitably increasing white middle-class participation in the fighting and in the casualties.[12] Nevertheless fears that the military forces do not include an adequate cross-section of American society have grown, along with increases in the nonwhite proportion of military personnel.[13]

Conscription. On the other hand note that a draft need not be socially representative. During a major mobilization such as World War II, if virtually everyone is drafted, the resulting force of conscripts is likely to be broadly representative of society. (The same conclusion would tend to hold for an equally large force of volunteers.) But if not everyone is drafted, the draft will be selective, and political realism suggests that a selective draft is not nearly as likely to select the rich and privileged as the socially disadvantaged. During the pre-Vietnam draft years of 1958–1963, more than 80 percent of the black prime manpower pool *eligible* to serve in the military actually did serve; only 43 percent of the nonblack prime manpower pool served. Admittedly, during these years the percentage of *all* male youth serving in the military was *lower* for blacks than for whites. But black participation in the military was held down by ineligibility (for physical disabilities and for low test scores), not by the draft being representative. It was not representative.[14] During the Vietnam War, blacks served disproportionately, particularly in the combat forces, and incurred disproportionate casualties until black civilian leaders objected.[15]

In any case blacks could not possibly benefit from a return to conscription. Those kept out of the military (to make room for draftees) would have to rely on their relatively less attractive civilian alternatives. Those drafted against their will probably would be forced to serve at wages lower than the wages received by their civilian counterparts.

Universal Military Training and National Service. Some see universal military training as a cure for inadequate middle-class participation in the military forces and other volunteer force problems. Universal military training would require virtually all young men (or perhaps young men and women) to undergo perhaps a year of basic military training, and then to remain subject to call-up for military service in case of national emergency.

National service adds to military training various nonmilitary alternatives such as work in hospitals, convalescent homes, day care centers, retirement homes, conservation projects in national parks and forests, civil defense construction, and so forth. William R. King describes a "minimally coercive" national service, which would simply require youths to spend a week or so at some sort of camp learning about voluntary national service alternatives, including military service. A more compulsory program would require some sort of service.[16]

Universal military training and national service both assume that every young man (or woman) owes the state as much as a year (more in wartime) of his life, and that the state is entitled to use force to collect that obligation. Even King's "minimally coercive" national service requires a youth to spend time being tested and counseled, and one suspects that the psychological pressures to serve (based on "You owe it to society" guilt) would be enormous. Actually the *minimally* coercive national service is noncoercive: a free-choice national service, which is what we have now.

One could argue that universal military training or national service is no more coercive than taxes. But surely a requirement to spend time working at specific tasks is inherently *much* more onerous than a requirement to give money earned however one wishes.

As suggested earlier, some argue that military conscription (whether or not universal) could perhaps be justified as an evil necessary for the survival of a free society in extreme circumstances. But national service's nonmilitary options cannot be described as necessities under any stretch of the imagination. A national service program would be involuntary servitude without any pretense of national necessity. Thus it would be unworthy of a free society and suitable only for a totalitarian state.

A more practical problem with both universal military training and national service is that they would be incredibly expensive. The military now recruits much less than 500,000 people annually. Recall that throughout the rest of this century, three to four million men and women will reach age nineteen every year. Processing, feeding, housing, training, and using this horde of young people would be very costly not merely in dollars, but in output lost from the civilian economy.[17] (After all, only a minority of young people are unemployed; most are employed or in school.) Universal military training or national service that withdrew substantially "all" youth from the civilian economy would have an even higher economic cost (in terms of decreased production) in wartime than in peacetime, because labor and other economic resources are even scarcer in wartime than they are in peacetime.

Even King's "minimally coercive" national service would be expensive (and would duplicate testing and counseling activities that already occur in the public schools). Setting up, operating, and enforcing attendance—by three to four million youths per year—at some sort of "orientation camp" to propagandize the merits of government employment (alias national service) would consume vast resources.

To avoid displacing (or threatening to displace) civilian workers, nonmilitary national service tasks would need to be ones not now being done. Yet these tasks also should be worth doing and more important than whatever the inductees would have done had they not been inducted. Finally, in a viable national service, tasks must be *perceived* as worthwhile by the inductees themselves. The set of nonmilitary tasks satisfying all these conditions is probably null. Thus, in addition to being enormously expensive, national service would generate the resentment that pointless compulsion always causes and would be socially very disruptive. National service could not possibly be a cost-effective way to obtain military personnel, particularly if compared with using these funds for improved military compensation.

Patriotism

Some senior military officers and members of Congress fear that if military service is made financially rewarding enough to attract quality recruits and to retain experienced senior personnel, then the military's patriotism will be damaged and perhaps destroyed. Senator Sam Nunn approvingly quotes Air Force General David C. Jones, until recently chairman of the Joint Chiefs of Staff, on this theme; "The All-Volunteer Force . . . approach in recruiting of personnel for the services (means) moving away from the normative values of calling or profession embodied in the words, 'duty, honor, and country,' toward an appeal based on monetary compensation and the values of the marketplace."[18] Sociologists such as Charles Moskos and Morris Janowitz have also been concerned, particularly if the military becomes unrepresentative of and isolated from the civilian community.

Recall that the only alternative to volunteers is coercion. Does a society not demean military service if it pays so little to the minority who defend that they must be forced to do so? Especially if only a minority of youth are conscripted, could the draft's blatant inequities— with or without a lottery—fail to damage moral and fighting effectiveness? What evidence is there that involuntary servitude or financial hardship, governmentally imposed, strengthens patriotism or love of country?

Volunteer Forces as a Threat to Liberty

The fear that a large standing army will oppress individual civilians or will overthrow the civil government is long-standing in American political life. Conscription precludes neither military mistreatment of civilians nor military coups d'état, as Latin American history frequently demonstrates, but perhaps the high turnover generated by conscription would help infuse civilian values into the military culture; perhaps conscripts' attitudes would be sufficiently nonmilitary to make them unwilling to follow orders during an attempted overthrow of government. On the other hand, perhaps conscripts would be so resentful of their involuntary servitude (especially if only a minority of youth were conscripted) that they would inflict their bitterness on civilians at any opportunity and would be eager for a chance to help overthrow the government. History at least as far back as the Roman Empire contains many occasions in which military forces mistreated civilians and overthrew governments; some of these misbehaving forces were volunteers and some were conscripts. Fear of large standing military forces is far from irrational, but there is no clear historical evidence that all-volunteer forces are more dangerous than forces containing conscripts.

Of course, if this book's call for substantial reductions in U.S. treaty commitments and troop placements abroad were heeded, so that active duty forces could be sharply cut in size and replaced by greatly strengthened "citizen soldier" reserve forces, the potential military threat to civilian society would be much less. With or without such changes, however, it does seem plausible that the more isolated the military from the civilian community, the more dangerous the military might be, and that military personnel turnover and the resulting movement of people between the military and civilian community might reduce the danger. But personnel turnover does not require conscription. And note that conscripting recruits for two years does little to prevent the isolation of senior enlisted and officer personnel from the civilian community. Isolation of the officer corps would appear to be a serious potential problem that conscription does little to solve.

Rather than the "two years and out" type of turnover caused by conscription, a more useful turnover pattern might be one in which some people stayed in the active duty military for only two years, some stayed for three or four, some stayed for five or six, and so forth, with only a few staying for a full career of twenty or thirty years. This pattern occurs today, of course (less than 8 percent of enlisted recruits stay for twenty years or more), but it could be encouraged by minimizing the relative importance of retirement (which takes twenty years to vest) relative to current pay, or else by vesting retirement benefits in only five or ten instead of twenty years.

Isolation of the military from the civilian community could be reduced further by strengthening the reserve forces, requiring substantial numbers or regular personnel to spend time with the reserves, and by encouraging many reservists to take an occasional sabbatical from civilian life to spend a few months or even a year or two on active duty. Such measures, which would expose all ages and ranks to civilian influence, could be much more effective than conscription in reducing the isolation not only of active duty enlisted personnel but also of officers.

Even without such measures, military enlisted and officer personnel have extensive civilian contacts.

> There is now significant interaction between the military and the rest of society. The military is not isolated from the mass media which permeate all walks of life. Also, the forces contain a wide variety of specialists, not only in air, sea, and ground combat, but also in all branches of engineering and science, in computer applications, medicine and dentistry, law, aviation, personnel management, ship building, and others. These men are often in daily contact with their fellow professionals in the civilian sector. Much specialist and officer training takes place in the civilian sector. The Defense Department employs more than one million civilians, and many officers serve tours of duty which require daily contact with the business community, academic institutions, and other civilian organizations.[19]

These points were made by the Gates Commission on an All-Volunteer Armed Force more than a decade ago, but they remain equally true today.

The Economic Advantage of Volunteer Forces

Individual capacities and aptitudes differ for military as well as for civilian occupations. Military forces can be most effective and the civilian economy most productive when individuals choose for themselves among competing military and civilian alternatives. With all-volunteer forces, persons with the highest civilian productivities and salaries (or who would find military life particularly distasteful) remain civilians, while only those persons with lower civilian productivities and salaries (or who find military life particularly pleasant) volunteer. Thus an all-volunteer force is less costly, requiring less sacrifice of value for the economy as a whole, than if a mixture of persons with high and low civilian (or military) productivities were drafted. Additional savings result because a draft would create uncertainties that make it very difficult for young people to plan their careers efficiently.

Compared with all-volunteer forces, a draft shifts much of society's defense burden from the general taxpayer to the youth subject to conscription. For the general taxpayer, conscription may actually decrease the perceived cost of military defense. Moreover, with conscription much of the real economic cost of defense is hidden, excluded from the budget, and easily overlooked by the military and by Congress. Inefficient use of "cheap" military conscripts will be almost inevitable. Of course, the costs of defense and the inefficiency of conscription are not hidden from the youth subject to induction, but they typically are

> apolitical nonvoters who, as a group, lack political influence. . . . [However, if] the draft is replaced with an all-volunteer force, the entire cost of personnel acquisition is internalized into the budgeting process, and politicians can no longer ignore it. The hope of economists favoring the all-volunteer approach is that by internalizing this cost, the all-volunteer system will provide political and military decisionmakers with both the information and motivation necessary to make rational decisions on the acquisition and deployment of military personnel. In contrast to the situation under a draft, incentives will exist to match abilities and job requirements in personnel assignments, and not to expand manpower demands beyond the point justified by considerations of social costs and benefits.[20]

Political Pressures

The foregoing summary of the all-volunteer force's economic cost and decision-making advantages is by Dwight R. Lee. But he goes on to suggest that the realities of the political process may frustrate the volunteer force's advantages, making conscription a viable alternative. Because military personnel are widely dispersed geographically, are transient and without roots in their communities, and typically inactive politically, Lee fears that there will be only weak political pressure favoring high-quality military personnel, so that the defense budget will spend too little on people relative to hardware. When a politician secures a defense contract for his district, the benefits concentrate among his own constituents. But if he secures increased salaries for military personnel, the benefits disperse over all the districts throughout the nation that have military bases.[21] Lee's analysis may help explain why military compensation fell so far behind inflation during most of the all-volunteer force period. But it is hard to see how conscription could correct an imbalance between personnel and hardware. As discussed before, conscription could lower recruit quality, and it tends to worsen shortages of experienced senior personnel. Perhaps the military's most serious personnel problem has been an inability to retain experienced maintenance personnel, especially in high-technology specialties. And maintenance is one area where inexperienced junior conscripts, no matter how intellectually gifted, are not likely to be satisfactory substitutes for experienced personnel.

Admittedly, conscription might provide budgetary savings that could be used to raise pay and benefits for senior personnel. But given Lee's analysis of the political process, any such budgetary savings would most likely be used for hardware instead.

In any case conscription's budgetary savings would be small. Even if everyone with less than two years' service were a conscript, all other military personnel still would be volunteers who must be paid enough to persuade them to stay. Furthermore, even conscripts should be paid something. The less conscripts are paid, the larger the implicit tax they bear, the more they will attempt to avoid service, and the more the government will have to spend to enforce the draft.[22] And equity and social harmony would require that conscripts be paid something, especially if only a minority will be called to serve. Thus if conscripts received draft-era levels of compensation, restoring the draft could save "only a few hundred million dollars a year."[23] Relative to the defense budget, $105 billion in fiscal 1978 and $189 billion in fiscal 1982 ($129 billion in 1978 dollars), these budgetary "savings" are trivial. And the more that draftees are compensated for conscription's inequities, the smaller these budgetary savings become, disappearing long before compensation could be complete.

Policies for Successful All-Volunteer Forces

The recent history of the all-volunteer armed force both confirms and contradicts the volunteer force's critics. Recruit quality did deteriorate from 1977 through 1980, but this deterioration can be explained. During this period Armed Forces Qualification Test scores were severely miscalibrated statistically, which led recruiters to classify many far-below-average recruits as average test-score recruits, and reduced recruiters' incentives to find true average test-score recruits to fill their quotas. Furthermore recruit pay, adjusted for inflation using the Consumer Price Index, fell by more than 25 percent from the beginning of the all-volunteer force in 1973 to 1980; real pay and allowances for senior personnel fell by more than 15 percent; and various benefits for service personnel and their dependents were cut or eliminated. Moreover military pay was far outpaced by civilian wage increases, particularly in manufacturing. At the same time veterans' educational benefits were cut sharply and federally subsidized loans and grants for civilian college students expanded exponentially.

However, beginning in fiscal 1981, the combined effects of properly normed test scores, substantial pay raises in October 1980 and 1981 and a smaller raise in October 1982 (which still leave real military compensation adjusted for inflation well below its levels in 1973 and well below the 1973–1982 increase in manufacturing wages), and higher educational benefits (for army service only), together with higher civilian unemployment, caused substantial improvement in recruit quality and senior personnel retention, and presumably in morale.

In fiscal 1981 recruits' Armed Forces Qualification Test Scores were a good cross-section of the scores achieved by a representative sample of American youth in 1980. A substantially higher proportion of recruits than of the 1980 youth population had graduated from high school. And racially, recruits were reasonably representative of American youth: 17 percent of the recruits and 14 percent of the youth population were black, 4 percent of the recruits and 6 percent of the youth population were Hispanic, and 79 percent of the recruits and 80 percent of the youth population were white (including small numbers of other minorities such as Oriental or Native American).

Balancing Recruit Quality and Racial Mix across Services

The fiscal 1981 improvement in recruit quality and representativeness occurred in all the services, but substantial differences among the services remain. Unlike the other services (including the marines), army recruits' average test scores are below those of the representative sample of American youth. One reason for the lower quality of the army's recruits simply is that it needs more recruits than the other services, because it is both larger and has higher enlisted turnover; it draws almost all of its "extra" recruits from the below-average test-score category.

Again unlike the other services, army recruits, both men and especially women, are disproportionately black: in fiscal 1981, 24 percent black overall and 32 percent black among women recruits. Only partially does this result from the army's heavy recruitment of low-test-score recruits, among whom blacks (and to a lesser extent Hispanics) are relatively plentiful. Even among army recruits with low test scores, blacks are greatly overrepresented (and whites underrepresented) relative to their proportions among low-scoring youth. Thus even if the army reduced its recruitment of below-average test-score recruits down to the same level as the other services, it still would be disproportionately black.

The army always has used relatively more blacks than have the other services. Historically, blacks played a much stronger combat role in the army than in, for example, the navy or the marines.[24] And now blacks may be choosing the army not merely because of tradition or the army's generally better "equal opportunity" reputation, but also because the army has "unit of choice" and "station of choice" recruiting options that allow blacks to join units that already have many blacks or that at least have reputations for good race relations.[25]

Even without such recruiting options, that some military units are more heavily black (or Hispanic) than other units should not be surprising. Blacks (and Hispanics, to a lesser extent) generally score lower than whites do on the Armed Forces Qualification Test and on other military placement tests (although this comparison is less true among military recruits than in the youth population). If high-test-score recruits are used primarily in high technology specialties, then other specialties (such as the army's combat arms) inevitably must draw on the remaining recruits with lower test scores, where blacks and Hispanics are very plentiful, especially in the army.

Because the military's recruit quality and social representativeness problems show up primarily in the army, two questions arise. What is the optimal distribution of recruit quality across services? And given the distribution of recruit quality (as measured by test scores) in each service, what (if anything) can or should be done to decrease the proportion of blacks and increase the proportion of whites in the army, particularly among low-test-score recruits, while doing the opposite in other services, especially the air force?

Quality. Although we cannot hope to analyze the first question here, some comments are in order. First, the army uses more sophisticated technology and hence needs a higher quality force than would be suggested by vague recollections of World War II movies of simply equipped infantrymen slogging through Burmese jungles, trudging across North African deserts, or dashing from hedgerows to farm buildings in France. The army, after all, has a sophisticated tactical air arm, which, incidentally, relies entirely on helicopters with heavy maintenance requirements. The army also makes extensive use of ground-to-ground and ground-to-air missiles, some with nuclear warheads, and also uses highly sophisticated tanks and related equipment. Table 8–1 shows that although the army still requires relatively fewer technically skilled workers than do the navy and air force, it is much closer to these other services than it was in World War II.

A second comment is that the army's need for recruits, and hence its need for recruits from below average test-score categories, would be markedly lower if its turnover were lower, as would occur if the army moved toward an older and more experienced force. Admittedly, infantry forces full of old men probably would not be too effective, but less than 30 percent of the army is in the infantry. The importance of "youthful vigor" can be exaggerated. Even in the infantry, adding a year or two to the average age of the force would not harm its effectiveness, and conceivably could even increase its effectiveness because skill as well as strength and stamina are important in the combat arms as well as elsewhere. Numerous analysts have argued that although older and more experienced forces in the army (and also in the other services) would be more expensive per person, the total cost of fielding equally effective military forces would be less if the forces were older and more experienced.[26] We return to this point later.

A third comment is that if pay, allowances, and bonuses are equal in all the services, the resulting distribution of high-test-score and low-test-score recruits across the services is *not* likely to be optimal. For example, a young person interested in aviation mechanics naturally

Table 8–1
Enlisted Personnel Occupational Groups
(Percentages)

	Army		Marines		Navy		Air Force	
Major Occupational Category	*1945*	*1977*	*1945*	*1977*	*1945*	*1977*	*1945*	*1977*
White collar								
Clerical	15	17	15	17	11	12	20	23
Technical	10	24	12	17	19	36	16	32
Blue collar								
Craftsmen	16	18	24	21	60	40	41	30
Service and supply	19	12	15	15	11	7	14	14
Infantry, gun crews, and seamanship	39	29	34	30	n.a.	5	10	2
Skilled (technical and craftsmen)	26	42	36	38	79	76	57	64

Source: As reported by Martin Binkin and Irene Kyriakopoulous, *Youth or Experience? Manning the Modern Military.* Studies in Defense Policy (Washington, D.C.: The Brookings Institution, 1979), p. 20, table 3–2.

Note: The last row is not reported in the source document.

thinks first of joining the air force, or perhaps the navy, but not the marine corps or army. Consequently the air force and perhaps the navy will have a relatively plentiful supply of recruits interested in and with aptitudes for aircraft maintenance, while the marine corps and army will be trying to turn sow's ears into aircraft mechanics. But if pay, allowances, or bonuses are allowed to rise for specialties with personnel shortages, no matter what the service, then an optimal distribution of high- and low-quality personnel across the services is at least possible.

Currently basic pay and allowances are the same in all the services, but bonuses and special pays do differ among the services. Sailors get sea pay; soldiers do not. Issues of "equity" among the services prevent differentials from being as large as they should be. A bigger problem is that the compensation structure of pay, allowances, special pays, and bonuses is so complex that it is difficult for any recruit (or anyone else, for that matter) even to estimate the financial rewards from serving in different branches and specialties of the military.

Race. With regard to the question of how to balance the racial mix of each military service (much less each specialty within each service), finding good recommendations is difficult. Of course, if recruit quality as measured by test scores were more evenly distributed among the services, then the races would be somewhat more evenly distributed, although apparently not completely. The army could eliminate its "unit of choice" and "station of choice" recruiting options, although doing so would persuade some prospective recruits (white and Hispanic as well as black) to remain civilians rather than merely to choose another service. Alternatively other services could adopt such recruiting options also, although these options add constraints that could make personnel management more difficult, particularly in the navy with its ship-to-shore rotation problem. Perhaps the best idea is to adopt military compensation and other personnel management policies that strive to maximize effectiveness for a given cost while achieving a reasonably representative military overall, and let the racial distribution of each service take care of itself.

The Structure of Military Compensation

Although properly normed test scores, higher military pay and allowances and educational benefits, and higher civilian unemployment substantially alleviated the military's recruiting and retention problems in fiscal 1981, these problems have not been solved for the long run. Recruiting tests presumably will stay properly normed, and one may hope that future military pay and benefits will keep up with inflation, particularly given recently heightened awareness of the Soviet threat and recent experience with the effects of inadequate compensation on military recruitment and retention quantity and quality. But one also would hope for (and expect) lower civilian unemployment rates, and in any case the youth population is projected to decline, as discussed previously. In fact, assuming the civilian economy does improve, the military may face very serious retention problems in four to five years if whatever number of current recruits who enlisted solely because of civilian unemployment fail to reenlist at the usual rates.[27] Thus if active duty military forces are to remain at their current levels, or even if they are cut back to a smaller, but very high-quality, cadre, more substantial changes in military compensation and other personnel policies are needed.

One long-run solution would be simply to raise the current structure of military compensation to whatever level was necessary to attract and retain the desired quantity and quality of personnel. But such an approach would be inefficient. Military compensation now includes not only basic pay, but also an incredibly complex structure of allowances, special pays, and bonuses for enlistment, reenlistment, subsistence, quarters, uniforms, sea duty, family separation, hazardous or other special duty (flight, submarine, parachute jumping, underwater diving, demolition, combat, and hostile fire), and in-service education, as well as retirement, and veterans' benefits.[28] Some of these are taxable, others are nontaxable. This mess inevitably is extremely ineffective in attracting and retaining qualified personnel, because it lacks visibility and is not nearly flexible enough to cope even with long-run shortages and surpluses in various military occupations.[29]

More than twelve years ago, the Gates Commission on an All-Volunteer Armed Force recommended replacing the current mix of taxable basic pay, taxable enlistment and reenlistment bonuses, and nontaxable allowances for subsistence and quarters with a simple, visible, fully taxable "salary" (including proficiency pay differentials for those working in critically scarce occupations) that could be compared easily with civilian wages.[30] The commission also wanted military pensions to vest (at least partially) after five instead of twenty years, so pensions would attract first reenlistments. It also suggested that enlisted personnel should have the same limited "right to resign" that officers have: discharged on request, after a term long enough to pay back the government's cost of training, unless that request is to avoid foreign or sea duty or is during a national emergency.[31] Finally the commission urged less reliance on noncash compensation:

> Compensation in cash has an inherent advantage . . . it allows each individual to decide how he or she will use whatever he earns. He can thus get the full value of whatever costs are incurred by the government in paying him. When he is compensated in noncash form, however, the value of what he receives is often less to him than its cost to the government. Meanwhile, he is encouraged to consume more of particular goods or services than he otherwise would. Noncash pay also tends to result in inefficient patterns of compensation by favoring some individuals (heavy users of these items) over others, independent of performance.[32]

Visibility. Congress has ignored almost all of these recommendations. Military pay remains a conglomeration of payments and benefits, lacking visibility, controversial, inequitable, and inefficient.[33] People in military service never actually see their total pay, not even on a paystub or W-2 form.[34] When asked, they substantially underestimate their total pay, including the cash benefit of their tax-free allowances; these underestimates are more severe for junior personnel.[35] Thus military pay is perceived to be even less competitive with private sector pay than it really is.

The difference between basic pay and total military compensation is substantial. As shown in table 8–2, in 1978 for all military personnel taken together, basic pay constituted only 42 percent of total personnel compensation *excluding* in-service educational benefits and veterans' benefits. The situation for 1983 was not markedly different.

The complexity of the military pay structure can hardly be overemphasized. Even a brief perusal of publications such as *Army, Navy,* and *Air Force Times,* particularly from August through November when Congress is considering pay changes for the following fiscal year, illustrates the structure's complexity. Articles try to explain not merely proposed changes, but also the existing rules regarding basic pay, special pays, allowances, bonuses, and other benefits, and how these rules interact. In fact, these private publications appear to be the major compensation information source for military personnel; even recruiters appear to rely almost exclusively on tables copied from these private publications to obtain information about pay and benefits.

Time-in-Service Pay. Another problem is that the present military compensation structure is remarkably insensitive to the speed with which promotions occur. Even if less productive career personnel are pro-

Table 8–2
Components of Total Military Compensation, Fiscal 1978

	Percentage of Category	Percentage of Total Compensation
Regular military compensation		63
Basic pay	67	42
Quarters and subsistence		
Allowances (cash and in-kind)	27	17
Tax advantage (estimated)	6	4
Special pay		3
Enlistment and reenlistment		
bonuses	21	1
Medical officers' extra pay	12	*
Hazardous duty	25	1
Miscellaneous	14	*
Separation (from military		
service)	28	1
Supplemental benefits		33
Retirement pay	69	23
Medical care	21	7
Government contribution to		
Social Security	7	2
Commissary, exchange, and		
other	3	1
Other Allowances		1

Source: Based on Martin Binkin and Irene Kyriakopoulos, *Paying the Modern Military* (Washington, D.C.: The Brookings Institution, 1981), p. 14, table 2–1.

Primary Source: Zwick, *Report of the President's Commission on Military Compensation* (Washington, D.C.: U.S. Government Printing Office, April 1978), p. 9.

Notes: *indicates less than 0.5%.

Retirement pay is that paid to current retirees. It underestimates the present value of the future retirement benefits that will be paid to military personnel now on active duty who remain for twenty or more years.

moted slowly, they earn almost as much as more productive personnel who are promoted more rapidly. One reason is fringe benefits, many of which (such as subsistence allowances, medical care, and commissary and exchange privileges) are largely independent of paygrade. But even the basic pay structure tends to be insensitive to promotions, because basic "pay is more a function of years of service than of pay grade."[36] Consequently military compensation probably is too generous for marginal people and not attractive enough for exceptional people. Replacing the present grade and time-in-service pay table with a time-in-grade pay table would be a simple but very desirable reform.[37]

Family Bias. The current military compensation structure is substantially less generous for single than for married personnel. For example, quarters allowances are as much as 56 percent higher for married personnel. The quality of on-post housing—usually worth even more than the alternative cash allowances—again favors married personnel. Most serious is that married personnel assigned abroad without their dependents, or to sea duty, keep all of their housing allowances, while singles lose most of theirs.

Not surprisingly the military's recruiting and retention efforts emphasize the importance of family-oriented noncash benefits (subsidized housing, medical and dental care, exchange and commissary privileges) relative to cash pay. Military compensation appears designed to be particularly attractive to persons with large sickly families. Most important, however, is the pay structure's lack of appeal to single individuals unencumbered with dependents.

Bonuses. Enlistment and reenlistment lump-sum bonuses now constitute the military's primary means of adjusting supply and demand imbalances in various occupational specialties. When shortages appear in a particular specialty, for example in the army's combat arms or the navy's nuclear power plant technician ratings, enlistment and reenlistment bonuses are raised; if the shortages become surpluses, bonuses are reduced or canceled.

To deal with personnel imbalances, the military prefers bonuses over differentials in regular pay because bonuses preserve the tradition that regular pay is the same in all occupational specialties in all the services.[38] But casual empiricism suggests that this bonus approach is not very successful because the shortages do not seem to go away: the army has had trouble manning its combat arms ever since the end of the draft, and the navy has had trouble manning its nuclear submarines ever since the first one sailed. Apparently the bonuses are too small (as suggested by their small size relative to other compensation, shown in table 8–2).

Even if bonuses were adequately large, they would have disadvantages. First and foremost, their visibility may be temporary: they may be received, enjoyed, and then forgotten.[39] Another problem is that if the bonus recipient fails to fulfill his contract (for example, if a recruit later is discharged or even deserts), retrieving the bonus may be difficult or impossible.

Bonuses often are based on occupational specialty, rank at time of reenlistment, and length of reenlistment. Thus the career service member faces a complex mathematical problem in order to figure out his best reenlistment schedule. Compensation should be based on the individual's military usefulness and productivity, not on his ability to calculate or intuitively guess the answer to such a problem. Bonuses should be eliminated and replaced by some system of regular pay differentials.

Retirement. Military personnel who remain on active duty for less than twenty years receive no retirement benefits (although involuntarily separated officers may receive up to $15,000 severance pay). But as soon as they leave the active forces, military personnel who remained on active duty for twenty years receive retirement pay equal to half their basic pay in their last year of active duty, gradually rising to three-quarters of basic pay for those who remained for thirty or more years. Thus on the twentieth anniversary of entry into the active duty military, the service member's net worth suddenly increases by as much as several hundred thousand dollars.[40]

This system was adopted in 1948 to encourage the retirement of a "hump"of officers from World War II who were blocking promotion of more junior personnel. The same system (although allowing fifteen-year army retirement) had been adopted in 1935 (and suspended during World War II) to deal with an officer hump left over from World War I. Similar systems had been used for the hump problem after the Civil War.

Now, however, deferring so much compensation as retirement pay that takes twenty years to vest, coupled with relatively small financial rewards for remaining in the service past twenty years, creates a military in which "careers are both too long and too short."[41] Talented individuals unwilling to put in twenty years quit too early; others, who contribute little, "hang on" for twenty years; and the best performers are discouraged financially from staying more than twenty years. These perverse incentives are very serious problems. Moreover retirement benefits have little effect on initial enlistments or first reenlistments, because few of these people expect to reenlist for the required twenty years.[42]

In governmental circles, however, concern focuses on a different aspect of military retirement: its rapid growth (fivefold from 1968 to 1978) relative to other components of military pay, largely because of rapid growth in the number of military retirees (doubled from 1968 to 1978) and also because nominal basic pay rose and retirement pay cost-of-living adjustments outpaced actual inflation.[43] (In recent years some retirees received higher benefits than they would have received if they had retired later at the same rank and years of service.) Hence proposals for reform usually have been designed primarily to cut costs, typically by making the plan at least partially contributory or by postponing or at least reducing retirement benefits until age fifty-five or sixty, on the grounds that most military retirees take on a second job. Such proposals, which would move military retirement closer to civil service retirement, generate adamant opposition from the military and have not come close to congressional passage.[44]

A related problem is that because retirement is driven by basic pay excluding allowances, special pays, and supplemental benefits, there is a great incentive to reduce future retirement costs by shifting pay increases out of basic pay into other types of compensation, thus exacerbating the visibility problem.[45]

Compensation Reform: Obstacles and Benefits

We have seen that the present structure of military compensation discourages recruitment and retention in many ways. First, complexity-caused "lack of visibility" makes military service appear financially worse than it really is. Second, heavy reliance on benefits largely independent of pay grade, and use of a grade- and time-in-service instead of a time-in-grade basic pay table, overcompensates mere longevity and undercompensates real productivity. Third, payment in family-oriented benefits instead of cash discriminates against the single unattached individual who might be most receptive to military service—and who might make the best soldier, at least in the junior ranks. Fourth, lump-sum bonuses that are too small—and too complex for their worth to be readily obvious to the service member—perpetuate serious personnel shortages in critical occupational specialties. Fifth, deferring so much compensation to retirement, together with twenty-year vesting, encourages too many mediocre people to stay for twenty years and encourages too many others to get out after only twenty years.

Martin Binkin notes that "a significant portion of total military pay is based on factors other than work performed; indeed, close to 40 percent of total earnings depends on other things: (1) marital and dependency status, (2) availability of government facilities, and (3) whether a member of the armed forces serves until retirement."[46] The inevitable consequence is, as he puts it, "unequal pay for equal work," and severe constraints on pay structure adjustments to attract and retain qualified personnel in critically short specialties. Instead the services have tried to use lump-sum bonuses that are plagued with inevitable difficulties and hence are inadequate to do the job.

Compensation by Occupational Specialty

Binkin (and his more recent collaborator, Irene Kyriakopoulos), in addition to recommending drastic simplification of the military compensation structure and reform of the retirement system, also wants military compensation to vary by occupational specialty.[47]

Critical occupations could receive "specialty pay" on top of a basic salary paid to everyone, or else each military specialty could have its own pay scale. A different approach would be to establish a single payscale (so that everyone in pay grade E-4 earned the same amount), but to pay different occupational specialties using different portions of the common pay scale: computer technicians, for example, might start at pay grade E-5 and rise to E-9, while cooks might start at pay grade E-1 and rise to E-5. This latter approach is used in the federal civil service. In the military, it would require that rank in the sense of military hierarchical title (corporal, sergeant, chief petty officer) be severed from pay grade, so that each occupational specialty could have full use of all ranks (from private to sergeant major) even though it used only a portion of the pay scale. In a sense pay grades would attach to jobs, while ranks would attach to people.

A military in which rank is independent of pay grade is so revolutionary that imagining how it would work is difficult. But it could facilitate movement toward older forces in those occupational specialties (such as equipment maintenance) where experience is an enormous advantage, while retaining younger forces in specialties (such as the army's combat arms) where "youth and vigor" remain especially important. Most long-term military careers now available are primarily for supervisors. The number of reenlistments desired by each service is driven by the need for supervisors. People without supervisory promise typically are not permitted to reenlist after their first or second tour of duty. Severing rank and pay grade would encourage career patterns in which skilled personnel could have long *non*supervisory careers, thus raising experience levels and decreasing the number of supervisors needed in experience-critical occupational specialties.[48]

Simplification and Flexibility

Successful and cost-effective recruitment, retention, and personnel management clearly require a simple, visible, fully taxable salary that does not discriminate against single persons, that rewards productivity more than mere longevity, that incorporates adequate differentials for persons with critical skills in shortage-prone occupational specialties as well as adjustments for assignment to high-living-cost areas, and that does not defer excessive amounts of compensation (vesting in one huge jump at twenty years) to retirement.

These recommendations are not new. Specific proposals along these lines have been made by numerous analysts, study groups, and commissions going back at least to World War II. But Congress has done nothing to simplify and strengthen the pay structure.[49]

Congress has spent some time worrying about retirement. But the retirement pay problem should be solved as part of a complete overhaul of the military compensation structure. The goal should be to increase greatly the relative importance of current compensation, not only by raising current cash pay relative to retirement pay, but also by vesting any retirement plan at no more than five years of military service, with retirement benefits gradually rising with pay grade and time in pay grade. Benefits should be based on total compensation rather than on some portion such as basic pay. To avoid "unequal pay for equal work," and also for actuarial soundness, benefits should be based on pay during the entire career rather than on pay during the last year before retirement. Even better would be to maximize compensation visibility, by fully financing all retirements with actuarially determined post-vesting salary deductions (e.g., deductions from salaries earned after five years of service), after first raising salaries enough to finance the expected retirement costs.[50] In any case each year's defense budget should include an estimate of the pension costs earned by persons currently on active duty. If "retirement" benefits are paid prior to age sixty or sixty-five (for example if they continue to be paid immediately after twenty years of service), they should be paid regardless whether the individual has remained on active duty, to avoid penalizing those who do remain. Finally retirement benefits should be as simple and easily understood as possible.

Compensation reform could raise military effectiveness while saving taxpayers' money by increasing retention rates and reducing training costs. One estimate, by Richard V. L. Cooper, is that revising the military compensation structure to reduce its inefficiency could have saved more than $3 billion annually during the 1970s. An additional $2 to $6 billion yearly might have been saved by decreasing the proportion of inexperienced first-term personnel, reforming training programs, and substituting relatively cheap capital equipment for relatively expensive labor particularly in support activities.[51]

Many components of the nation's reserve forces have been judged seriously understaffed. Such shortages should not be surprising. Inactive reservists who are merely subject to call-up in case of a presidential or congressional declared emergency, but who need not train or maintain their skills or physical fitness, typically receive no compensation whatever. Active reservists receive only one day's basic pay for each drill session attended (although admittedly they are paid for four drills per monthly weekend training session). They receive no quarters or subsistence allowances (except while on active duty for training), or any significant medical, exchange, or commissary privileges; their retirement plan, which does not begin payment until age sixty, is much less generous (even on a per-day-worked basis) than the retirement for active duty careerists. Thus their hourly compensation, especially after allowing for commuting costs to monthly training sessions, is much lower than that received by active duty personnel—even though service in the reserves must compete with opportunities for civilian overtime, and though many reservists must use their only two-week vacation from civilian employment for annual reserve training.

If inactive reservists really could be useful, then they should be paid something for being subject to call-up (and for keeping their whereabouts known), rather than (as at present) merely subjecting them to this obligation as an "add on" to their regular military or active reserve service.[52] Perhaps additional compensation would encourage them to undergo a few weeks of refresher training every few years.

For active reservists, the compensation reforms needed are similar to those needed for active duty personnel: simple, visible, fully taxable pay based on time in grade rather than time in service, with adequate differentials for persons with critical skills in shortage-prone occupational specialties. For reservists, if current pay were adequate, there would seem to be no need for retirement pay or other deferred compensation. The temptation to solve reserve-recruiting problems by using bonuses, fringe benefits, or other gimmicks should be resisted for the same reasons of visibility and simplicity that apply to regular active duty forces.

The Age Distribution of Military Forces

Moving to more experienced forces in the occupational specialities, where experience is worth more than youth and vigor, would be a rational, albeit long-delayed, response to the relative costs and productivities of first-term (less than four years' service) versus experienced career personnel. First termers are less expensive than careerists, but they are much less productive because of the large amount of time they spend in training and because they are so inexperienced.[53]

In 1977 Cooper estimated that decreasing the proportion of first termers from roughly 60 to 50 percent would permit an estimated 200,000 man decrease in the armed forces, without decreasing effectiveness, for an annual saving of at least $1.6 billion. Alternatively, decreasing first termers from 60 to 50 percent while holding force size constant (increasing military capability by about 8 percent) would decrease the number of non-prior-service male recruits needed annually during the middle- and late-1980s by about 18 percent, would decrease recruiting costs, and would permit training reforms that could decrease costs by more than $1 billion per year. More experienced forces would need less rotation not only of first-term but also of more senior personnel, further decreasing costs and increasing the attractiveness of military service.[54]

Nonsupervisory Careers. As noted earlier, most long-term military careers now available are primarily for supervisors. In a successful military career, either officer or enlisted, promotions through the ranks typically change one's primary activity from doing something oneself to supervising or managing the activities of others. In contrast with civilian life, long-term nonsupervisory careers are hard to find in the military. On one hand the services need many supervisors because so many military personnel are young and inexperienced. On the other hand the services have many supervisors because they often cannot figure out what else to do with senior personnel other than create supervisory positions for them. Demand and supply work in the same direction: virtually to eliminate nonsupervisory military careers.

Military services excessively rich in supervisors are unnecessarily costly. Moreover supervisory careers often fail to attract and retain people who prefer and may be very skilled at doing things themselves rather than supervising others. And when enough supervisory positions are not available to accommodate all of those who do want to remain on active duty, the excess people are passed over for promotion and eventually discharged, even if they might have served with distinction in nonsupervisory duties.

Raising the experience level of the military forces could markedly reduce the need for supervisors. Establishing military career patterns in which successful people move horizontally among specialties rather than vertically to supervisory positions could greatly decrease the supply of supervisors. Military forces less dependent on supervisors not only would be less costly and able to retain skilled people who see themselves as doers rather than supervisors, but also might be much more capable of fighting in relatively small independent units whenever necessary, because broadly experienced individuals with knowledge and initiative would be readily available in the lower ranks.

Many of these points are illustrated by military aviation. Most pilots join the military because they love to fly. Yet as they rise in rank, their duties typically involve less and less flying and more and more supervising. Combat flying, particularly in fighter aircraft, tends to be a young person's game because it requires very quick reflexes and tremendous stamina. The only thing the military thinks it can do with an aging fighter pilot is to promote him into less flying and more supervisory work. If this changing job description does not appeal, or if there is no promotion into a supervisory position, the pilot often leaves the service for civilian aviation—as a highly paid commercial airline pilot if that is available, but often as a commuter or corporate business pilot, where financial rewards may be substantially less than in military service but where the day is spent flying an airplane rather than a desk. Training his military replacement is a very expensive proposition.

Actually the military has many flying jobs that require much experience and skill but that—like civilian aviation—do not need a fighter pilot's reflexes and stamina. A long-term nonsupervisory flying career could start out in fighters, move to heavy bombers, and end in antisubmarine patrols or air transports. But this virtually never occurs, because the flying jobs suitable for older pilots are already filled with young pilots. Right after flight school, young pilots enter a "community" (navy carrier-based fighters, air force land-based fighters, strategic bombers, navy carrier-based antisubmarine warfare, navy land-based antisubmarine warfare, air transport) where they typically spend their entire "flying" career, which gradually becomes more and more supervisory. Movements across these narrowly defined communities, even within a service, almost never occur.[55]

For many pilots a nonsupervisory career spanning several flying communities or even a mix of flying and nonflying specialties such as air traffic control or maintenance or supply could make much more sense. And if such careers were the norm, pilots might not need to be officers with baccalaureate degrees. At least some of those four years instead could be spent as a fighter pilot, no younger than many of those who saved the Battle of Britain in 1940, or who flew in U.S. forces. Nonsupervisory flying careers could, of course, involve several services (e.g., both the navy and air force), but changing uniforms generally should not be necessary because each service (except perhaps for the army and marines) has many types of flying.

A Regimental Personnel System. Typical U.S. military careers have long consisted of a series of short (three years or less) tours in many places. As Janowitz and Moskos note, " 'permanent change of station' is still the dominant motif of military life."[56] This pattern of course inflates the government's moving-expense budget. For the service member it may create financial problems by making a civilian career difficult or impossible for his spouse; it disrupts family life generally; and it may damage morale. Perhaps most serious, these frequent moves make it much more difficult for the service member to identify with his unit, to become skilled in his assignment, and to be responsible for the results.[57] Thus it has been alleged that Canadian antisubmarine warfare air crews typically do much better at finding submarines than their American counterparts do because Canadian crews stay together and work as a team for many years, while American crews undergo personnel changes every few months.[58]

As a partial solution, Janowitz and Moskos want to move away from present "worldwide" service personnel systems, in which people are frequently assigned as individuals to new units. They favor more decentralized and less impersonal recruitment, training, and personnel administration: a "British regimental system," in which people remain attached to particular units for long periods of time, and in which each unit is responsible for much of the training of its own personnel. This suggestion appears to be well worth considering, to reduce costs and increase the capabilities of our military forces.

The army now is installing a highly modified version of such a regimental personnel system, for persons in its combat arms. By late 1984, all combat forces should be assigned to an administrative regiment (for example, an armored regiment or a field artillery regiment) that will be assigned to a permanent U.S. base, and a permanent overseas base. The goal is for each soldier always to return to the same U.S. home base, and always to have the same overseas assignment.[59] As individuals move between U.S. and overseas bases, they will join units with at least some familiar faces, which should enhance group cohesion, thus enabling most combat personnel to develop long-term roots to a U.S. base and in its civilian community.

But implementation of this system will not be easy. Retention will tend to be higher in regiments based in desirable locations. If retention differences turn out to be large, the resulting need for interregimental transfers will impair or even destroy the system. Pairing desirable U.S. bases with undesirable foreign bases and undesirable U.S. bases with desirable foreign bases would help. But it may become necessary to assign each regiment to two foreign locations, one desirable and one undesirable, so that career soldiers in every regiment will get both good and bad duty assignments.

Simultaneously the army may be moving toward a "new manning system," in which companies stay together for three years and rotate their U.S. and overseas bases as units rather than as individuals, and in which at least some of a unit's noncommissioned officers form the cadre for the next three-year company.[60] Two years ago, the plan was to experiment with only 10 percent of the army's combat arms components, but the experimental new system now involves much more than 10 percent of the combat arms, and some observers expect to see it throughout the combat arms before the experiment's scheduled end in 1986. By then the army should know whether rotating company-sized units is feasible, whether new promotion and other personnel policies are needed, whether companies that stay together really are significantly more cohesive with higher morale and greater "operational readiness," and whether these gains, if any, are offset by any tendency for more cohesive companies to get into disciplinary trouble. A more thoroughgoing reform, which allowed rotation of units larger than a company, which included officers, and which extended beyond the combat arms, might have even more substantial benefits, but the present changes seem to be a major achievement for an organization as large as the army.

Social Representativeness. Janowitz and Moskos are less concerned with cost-effectiveness than with increasing the short-term participation of middle-class college-bound youth in the military forces. They and others, such as Jerald Bachman, John Blair, and David Segal think that the military ought to include more middle-class youth, not only in the interest of equity among social classes, but also to leaven the military with more "citizen soldiers" who would impede development of a dangerously separate "military ethos" because they would be less likely than careerists to be excessively "gung ho" militarists or zealous patriots. Thus some of these observers favor making the military more attractive to middle-class youth by making it less rigid, for example by (1) using "more participative management practices, (2) reducing the amount and effects of bureaucracy, and (3) increasing opportunities for independence in personal lives."[61] The feasibility and usefulness of these suggestions is difficult to determine: for example, the marines are relatively more successful than is the army in recruiting middle-class youth (as measured by test scores, high school graduation status, and race), and yet the marines have relatively more discipline problems, presumably because they are more rigid.

Educational Benefits. All of these observers favor increased use of educational benefits to recruit middle-class youth. Moskos, for example, wants to restrict federal government aid for college educations to students who previously participated in some sort of national (or private charitable) service, including military service. Then he wants to reestablish generous World War II-type "GI Bill" educational benefits for "citizen-soldier" veterans with two years of low-paid military service in the low-skill occupational specialities mentioned previously. Careerists would receive three times as much pay as the citizen-soldier (even during their initial enlistments), and would be eligible for in-service educational benefits in lieu of the citizen-soldier's "GI Bill."[62] He does not explain how a citizen-soldier who later decided to stay aboard for a full military career would recoup his financial losses from time spent as a low paid "citizen-soldier," but perhaps this problem is a minor detail.

One alleged recruiting advantage of educational benefits over cash pay is that "youth surveys show that pay motivates less qualified youth (for example, high school dropouts and graduates with poor grades) to join the armed services more than it does college-bound youth."[63] Such data are not surprising. Small or even moderate raises in military enlisted pay make it competitive with civilian job opportunities available to less qualified youth, but do not make it competitive with the job opportunities anticipated by most college youth. (And college-bound youth may realize that cash pay typically is taxable, while educational benefits usually are tax free: the alternatives compared may not be financial equals.) In any case there is no logical reason why educational benefits would be more attractive to anyone than an equal amount of cash pay net of taxes, which the recipient would be free to spend as he chose, either on education or on other things.

Furthermore the military's *primary* personnel problem will not be solved by recruiting college-bound youth who stay for only two years. The primary problems are to recruit and retain adequately high-quality skilled forces, useful in small conflicts and capable of serving as a cadre around which any military expansion for a major war must be built.

Educational benefits are an inherently inefficient way to recruit such a skilled military force. They appeal only to people planning on higher education and civilian careers; they discourage military careers because to be a full-time student and obtain the maximum monthly benefit, one usually must leave military service. They do not appeal to potentially fine service members who have little interest in higher education. They do not appeal to those who distrust complex deferred-compensation schemes from a government that frequently changes or "clarifies" its promises, ex post facto.

Moreover, the morality of using education benefits (or other discriminatory fringe benefits) to attract a particular social class into military service is at best doubtful. Such benefits make military compensation dependent on *who* a service member is (college bound or not college bound), rather than on *what* he does in the military, and how well he does it. To the extent that military compensation includes extensive educational or other discriminatory fringe benefits, then the middle- or upper-class soldier who later goes to college receives more compensation for military service than does the lower-class soldier who chooses not to go to college, even though they both may have had the same military job and made equally valuable contributions to the nation's defense. Indeed the purpose of such discriminatory benefits, according to many of their advocates, is to raise military compensation for middle- and upper-class youth who otherwise would not enlist, without unnecessarily raising compensation for lower-class youth willing to enlist at current payscales. Such discrimination (in both the common everyday and technical economic meanings of the word) is unworthy of a free society and in any case frustrates the egalitarian goals of many other governmental policies.

If more recruits from middle and upper classes are really needed, the right solution is to raise cash pay for everyone. Giving higher cash pay to middle- or upper- than to lower-class youth, or to whites than to blacks, would be obviously discriminatory. Educational benefits can be equally discriminatory in a subtler way.

Thus the military's existing veterans' educational benefits should not be expanded and restored to earlier "GI Bill" levels; instead they should be canceled (along with other discriminatory fringe benefits) and replaced by a real increase in cash pay adequate to recruit *and retain* however many college-capable (rather than college-bound) military people are needed.

There are better ways of keeping the professional military familiar and comfortable with civilian viewpoints and attitudes than to provide expensive educational benefits. For example, as mentioned in a previous section, reservists and regular military personnel could be intermixed together frequently. Doing so would not only introduce civilian viewpoints and attitudes to the professional military, but it also should provide important opportunities to strengthen the military competence of the reserve forces, as well as the technical competence of the active duty forces.

Liberty, Equity, Efficiency, and Effectiveness

Conscription is coercion. It is involuntary servitude. It is totalitarian. Advocates of conscription take strong offense at such statements and prefer to speak of "duty to country." Yet even that phrase is totalitarian if considered carefully. To say that a government may legitimately require any of its citizens—regardless of their religious or humanitarian beliefs—to kill others is the ultimate totalitarian rejection of the free society. With or without lottery, and with or without possible "conscientious objector" status (granted by some draft board or other government agency upon showing that one's beliefs validly qualify and are sufficiently sincere), conscription is a massive—and inevitably inequitable—violation of individual liberty.

But the all-volunteer military force concept itself raises a host of serious concerns: the adequacy of force quantity, quality, and effectiveness; its social representativeness; whether it will be too "mercenary" and not sufficiently patriotic; whether it will be so isolated from civilian society that it will threaten civilian institutions and individual liberty; and whether its budgetary cost will be so high that a democratic political system will be unable to finance it adequately. Of course we have seen that conscription could generate equally serious concerns, particularly with regard to force quality and effectiveness; social representativeness; patriotism and possible threats to civilian institutions and individual liberties from embittered conscripts.

Fortunately such concerns can be dealt with more readily with volunteer than with conscript forces. "You get what you pay for" is a cliché, but it is largely true. Increased compensation for volunteer forces certainly can improve quality of military personnel, as well as enlarge middle-class participation in the armed forces. And if the compensation structure were less chaotically complex, more visible, based more on performance and less on mere longevity, less discriminatory against single individuals unencumbered with dependents, more responsive to shortages in critical skills and occupational specialties, and less deferred to retirement, the military forces' quality and social representativeness could improve markedly.

However, compensation reform is not enough. The efficiencies that volunteer forces permit should be exploited: nonsupervisory careers, longer tours in each assignment, and possibly a regimental personnel system, would do much to lower the cost and improve the capabilities of our armed forces. And as argued in chapter 7, strong reserve forces, adequately integrated with the regular forces, not only could cut the cost of defense and bolster the regular forces by keeping them in close contact with civilian knowledge and skills, but also could prevent the military from becoming isolated from civilian viewpoints and attitudes, and thus could discourage the development of a dangerous "separate military ethos" hostile to the society it is supposed to defend.

Even if the military compensation structure were reformed, the all-volunteer force might seem to be too expensive. But conscription saves little or nothing in budgetary outlays. And in any case major government policies should be determined not by mere budgetary outlays, but by real costs. Whether volunteers or conscripts, military personnel are removed from the production of nonmilitary goods and services. The civilian output lost to society is basically the same in either case. The primary difference is who bears the defense burden: society in general via taxes, or those who happen to be draft age in years when the youth population happens to be small or military activity happens to be extensive.

Actually the foregoing oversimplifies. With conscription the output lost to society is greater than with all-volunteer forces simply because all warm bodies are not identical interchangeable parts. Conscription into the military makes no more sense than conscription into a civilian career. If you would not want your appendix removed by a plumber conscripted into medicine, then you do not really want your society protected by a romantic poet conscripted into a tank crew. Our economy cannot afford the draft, much less the chimera called "universal" military or national service, because economic efficiency improves when free markets are allowed to allocate labor (as well as other resources) into their most productive uses.

There is no need for a free society to mimic its totalitarian enemies in order to survive. Some analysts have suggested that the United States probably did not need the draft even during World War II. We certainly do not need it now. In a hostile world a country whose economy is barely growing cannot afford conscription's inefficiencies. It had better adopt efficient and adequate military compensation and other personnel policies, and it had better structure its reserve and regular forces so that they work together, and work well.

Acknowledgments

This chapter was drawn from an underlying and more detailed research paper, "Effective Military Forces—without Conscription," by the same author. Many helpful suggestions came from the editor and associate editor, and from the other contributors to this book. Thanks go to them—and to Richard S. Elster, W. J. Haga, and George W. Thomas at the Naval Postgraduate School; to Major William J. Gregor; to Captain Patrick Kane of the U.S. Military Academy; to Joseph P. Martino of the University of Dayton's Applied Systems Analysis Research Institute; to Charles C. Moskos of Northwestern University; to Neil M. Singer of the Congressional Budget Office; and to Rodolfo A. Gonzales, Stephen L. Mehay, and Geoffrey Nunn of San Jose State University—for help, comments, and suggestions. Thanks also to Velma Burrs, Education Coordinator for the San Francisco District of the U.S. Army's recruiting command, for help in understanding army educational benefits; and to Ronald Humke, Assistant Director of the Student

Financial Aids Office at San Jose State University, for extensive explanations of governmental educational benefits for civilians. Barbara J. Mountrey, Media Relation Chief, Public Affairs Office, U.S. Army Seventh Infantry Division Headquarters, Fort Ord, California, provided information on the army's new national personnel system. Mr. Parnell, of the *Army, Navy,* and *Air Force Times* research library, provided the references in note 24.

Statistical data and other information to update published sources came from many very helpful (but mostly anonymous) people in the federal government. Among these, thanks can be given to William Hagen, Donna Volland, Gene Ebner, and Tom Lewis of the Office of Management and Budget; Lars Johanson of the Census Bureau; Lieutenant Commander Haggart of the Department of the Navy; and Leonard Campbell of the Office of the Assistant Secretary of Defense (Comptroller). Special thanks go to Colonel Thomas R. Cuthbert, Lieutenant Colonel Robert Baker, Lieutenant Terryl L. Wisener, and Ronald Moore, Office of the Deputy Assistant Secretary of Defense for Military Personnel and Force Management, and to Robert Brandewie, of the same office's Defense Manpower Data Center (Monterey, California), for unpublished data tabulations.

None of these people are responsible in any way for the accuracy or completeness of the data and information as presented and interpreted here, and none of them should be assumed to agree with the opinions given here.

Notes

1. For a sample of the influential criticisms of the all-volunteer force, see Sam Nunn, "Those Who Do Not Serve in the All Volunteer Armed Forces," *Journal of the Institute for Socioeconomic Studies* 4 (Autumn 1979):10–21. For a rebuttal, see Roger Nils Folsom, "Can Conscription Work?" *Cato Institute Policy Analysis,* May 15, 1981. For a more philosophical discussion, see the debate between Doug Bandow, "The Case against Conscription," and "Rejoinder," and MacKubin T. Owens, Jr., "Reply: Libertarian Follies," *Journal of Contemporary Studies* 5 (Fall 1982):43–57, 67–71, and 59–66, respectively.

2. For example, a Louis Harris poll in fall 1981 found that 60 percent of the Americans polled favored reviving the draft. *Army Times,* October 19, 1981, p. 17.

3. For expositions of this view, see Gardner Ackley, *Macroeco-*

nomic Theory (New York: Macmillan, 1961), pp. 428–429, and John Kenneth Galbraith, *A Theory of Price Control* (Cambridge, Mass.: Harvard University Press, 1952).

4. Abba Lerner, "Design for a Streamlined War Economy," Unpublished paper, 1942.

5. See Walter Eucken, "On the Theory of the Centrally Administered Economy: An Analysis of the German Experiment," trans. T.W. Hutchison, *Economica* 15 (May and August 1948):79–100; 173–193.

6. Total non-prior-service active duty accessions (male and female, enlisted and officer, from the reserves as well as from civilan life) would make a much better comparison with the nineteen-year-old population, but reliable data and forecasts are unavailable for most of these years. We use the population of nineteen-year-olds, rather than a broader and more realistic recruiting age span, simply in order to dramatize rather than smooth the effects of changing birthrates. What counts here are trends and relative magnitudes, not absolute magnitudes.

7. This argument, together with other implications for military recruiting, is presented by Paul Hogan and Lee Mairs in "Some Implications of U.S. Demographic Trends: 1980–1990," in U.S., Department of Defense, Office of the Assistant Secretary of Defense for Manpower, Reserve Affairs, and Logistics, *America's Volunteers* (December 1978), pp. 289–296, app. G. If current military compensation is kept comparable to civilian compensation, the Defense Department expects to be able to satisfy its future recruiting goals in every service except the army, where "relatively modest" shortfalls may occur due to inability to satisfy congressionally mandated recruit quality standards. Small increases in army compensation could solve the problem. (But see note 27). U.S. President, Executive Office, *Military Manpower Task Force: A Report to the President on the Status and Prospects of the All-Volunteer Force* (Washington, D.C.: October 1982), pp. III9–III12, A4. Hereafter referred to as the *Military Manpower Task Force Report.*

8. U.S., Department of Defense, Office of the Assistant Secretary of Defense for Manpower, Reserve Affairs, and Logistics, *America's Volunteers: A Report on the All-Volunteer Armed Forces* (Washington, D.C.: December 1978), p. 166. See also, *Military Manpower Task Force Report,* pp. A8–A10.

9. Or even the most dangerous, unless one focuses on particular wartime military activities that make a highly visible target. Admittedly, every military person potentially faces a dangerous assignment—but

every highway patrol officer faces similar danger every time he stops an unknown car with unknown occupants.

10. Charles Moskos, "Making the All-Volunteer Force Work," *Foreign Affairs* 60 (Fall 1981):17–34.

11. John Thompson and Richard Hunter, "Subjective Criticism in Perspective," in *America's Volunteers,* p. 246.

12. Ibid., p. 246.

13. As of September 1981, U.S. military forces were 28 percent nonwhite overall, only somewhat more than the 20 percent nonwhite proportion of the U.S. population. But the army's enlisted ranks were 42 percent nonwhite and some units were more than 50 percent nonwhite. See Martin Binkin and Mark Eitelberg, with Alvin Schexnider and Marvin Smith, *Blacks and the Military* (Washington, D.C.: The Brookings Institution, 1982), pp. 78–79, and also pp. 160–183. For data suggesting that U.S. military forces' socioeconomic (racial) backgrounds broadly reflect U.S. society as a whole, see *Military Manpower Task Force Report,* pp. II14–II17.

14. In later years, black performance on physical examinations and written tests improved markedly and there was some growth in the black proportion of the youth population. See Richard Cooper, *Military Manpower and the All-Volunteer Force,* prepared for the Defense Advanced Research Projects Agency by the Rand Corporation, September 1977, pp. 201–221. Also see *Military Manpower Task Force Report,* p. II15.

15. Although they constituted only 11 percent of the youth population, blacks suffered more than 20 percent of the Vietnam casualties from 1961 through 1966—a rate roughly proportional to their presence in army combat exposure units. See Binkin and Eitelberg, *Blacks and the Military,* pp. 76–77.

16. See William King, "National Service: An Alternative to the All-Volunteer Military," in *Defense Manpower Planning: Issues for the 1980s,* eds. William Taylor, Jr., Eric Olson, and Richard Schrader (New York: Pergamon Press, 1981), pp. 217–227. See also Nunn, "Another Look at the All-Volunteer Force," *The Washington Post,* March 28, 1977.

17. In 1977 Richard Cooper estimated the federal budget cost of a males-only national service program at $15 to $25 billion. More recently the annual costs for males-only universal military training and for a broad national service program for both men and women were estimated at $11 and $40 billion, respectively, plus the costs of facilities and career force expansion. See Cooper, "AVF vs. Draft: Where Do

We Go from Here?" in *Defense Manpower Planning,* p. 98, ed. Taylor et al. For the second set of figures, see *Military Manpower Task Force Report,* p. 16, A18.

18. Nunn, "Another Look at the All-Volunteer Force," pp. 17–18.

19. Thomas Gates et al., *The Report of the President's Commission on an All-Volunteer Armed Force* (New York: Macmillan 1970), p. 135. Hereafter, this will be referred to as the *Gates Commission Report.* For other references, see Martin Binkin and Irene Kyriakopoulos, *Youth or Experience? Manning the Modern Military* (Washington, D.C.: The Brookings Institution, 1979), pp. 45–47. For survey evidence that a "separate military ethos" could develop, see Gerald Bachman, John Blair, and David Segal, *The All-Volunteer Force: A Study of Ideology in the Military* (Ann Arbor: University of Michigan Press, 1977).

20. Dwight R. Lee, "The All-Volunteer Army and Its Troubles: Where Economists Went Wrong," *Journal of Contemporary Studies* 5 (Spring 1981):22–32. Reprinted with permission of the author and the *Journal of Contemporary Studies.* Copyright 1982 Institute for Contemporary Studies.

21. Ibid., pp. 25–26. Detailed support for Lee's proposition that the military budget spends relatively too much on hardware and too little on personnel *and training* is given by Bruce Arlinghaus in " 'Dumb' Soldiers and 'Smart' Bombs: Precision-Guided Munitions and the All-Volunteer Force," in *Defense Manpower Planning,* ed. Taylor et al., pp. 80–87.

22. Cooper, *Military Manpower and the All-Volunteer Force,* pp. 83–86, estimated that in 1964 when the implicit tax paid by conscripts was between $2.1 and $4.4 billion, the costs-of-collection (including the potential draftees' cost of avoiding and attempting to avoid the draft) were between $2.6 and $3.6 billion.

23. Ibid., ch. 11. In *America's Volunteers,* the "few hundred million" were estimated more precisely at $250 million in fiscal 1977. For further discussion, and a historical comparison of draft and volunteer force costs, see Mike Kelly, "The Case against a Peacetime Draft," *Strategic Review* 10 (Fall 1982):64–75.

24. See Neil A. Wynn, *The Afro-American and the Second World War* (New York: Holmes & Meier, 1975), chs. 1 and 2; U.S., Dept. of Defense, Office of the Deputy Assistant Secretary of Defense for Equal Opportunity, *Black Americans in Defense of Our Nation;* (Afro-American History Role Model for Youth, publication for Black History Month), February 1981; and in *Navy Times,* May 3, 1982.

25. Sar Levitan and Karen Cleary Alderman, *Warriors at Work: The Volunteer Armed Forces* (Beverly Hills, Calif.: Sage Publications, 1977), p. 175.

26. For example, Cooper, *Military Manpower;* and Binkin and Kyriakopoulos, *Youth or Experience?*—particularly ch. 5.

27. The author is indebted to George W. Thomas of the Naval Postgraduate School for this point. Defense Department plans, however, expect continued high reenlistment rates. See, *Military Manpower Task Force Report,* p. III17. Mike Kelly notes that the military's real pre-1981 personnel problem was retention of noncommissioned officers, not recruiting. In 1979 the services taken together were *over* strength in the lower enlisted ranks. But recruiting goals were increased in an attempt to inflate the strength of the lower ranks so that there would be enough reenlistments despite low reenlistment percentages. Kelly, "The Case against a Peacetime Draft," p. 66.

28. For an incomplete list of pays, bonuses, and allowances, see Charles J. Zwick, *Report of the President's Commission on Military Compensation* (Washington, D.C.: U.S. Government Printing Office. April 1978), pp. 9–10, 18–20, hereafter referred to as the *Zwick Report.* Also see Martin Binkin, *The Military Pay Muddle* (Washington D.C.: The Brookings Institution, 1975); Levitan and Alderman, *Warriors at Work,* ch. 2; and Martin Binkin and Irene Kyriakopoulos, *Paying the Modern Military* (Washington, D.C.: The Brookings Institution, 1981), ch. 2.

29. This point is made by Cooper, *Military Manpower,* pp. 361–364; and in the *Zwick Report,* pp. 123–132.

30. Ibid., pp. 57, 60. The military salary should be large enough to compare favorably. *Gates Commission Report,* p. 201, app. B.

31. *Gates Commission Report,* pp. 61–64.

32. Ibid., p. 62.

33. Ibid., p. 60.

34. Beginning in 1983, as an experiment the services began distributing to each member a document detailing his total direct cash compensation, and a multipage worksheet on which he can estimate the cash value of *some* of his other benefits.

35. Cooper, *Military Manpower,* pp. 365–366; *Zwick Report,* pp. 102–103. In the author's experience when on the Naval Postgraduate School faculty in the late 1960s and early 1970s, officers typically underestimated their Regular Military Compensation (which, as noted in table 8–2, is substantially less than total compensation) by more than 20 percent.

36. This statement is less true in the very highest enlisted ranks and in the highest officer ranks. Cooper, *Military Manpower,* p. 367,

n. 17, and pp. 370–371, 379. For fascinating diagrams illustrating the present "no method to the madness" basic pay structure, and comparing it with a more systematic alternative, see Ludvik Pfeifer, "The Military Compensation Mess," *U.S. Naval Institute Proceedings* 7, (February 1981), pp. 24–32.

37. *Zwick Report,* p. 139. A time-in-grade pay table would eliminate other "unequal pay for equal work" anomalies. For example, under present practices, someone who enters active duty in a "delayed entry" program or after spending time in the reserves (even if he was inactive with no attendance at training sessions) now is paid more—throughout his military career—than someone else of the same rank and time on active duty who entered the service directly from civilian life.

38. Military manpower analysts also often prefer bonuses, on grounds that individuals face higher interest (or discount) rates than government does, so that cash "up front" is worth more to individual service members than it costs the government. But this argument does not hold up. Government funds come from a mixture of taxes and borrowing. To pay a lump-sum cash bonus the government may levy taxes on some civilian to whom cash is at least as valuable as it is to the service member. More generally the government's cost of financial capital will be a weighted average of the cost of funds raised by taxes and borrowing, where the cost of taxes is the taxpayer's opportunity cost of capital. Thus there is no general reason why the government's discount rate should be lower than the average or typical discount rate among private individuals whom it taxes and from whom it borrows.

39. John T. Warner, *Issues in Navy Manpower Research and Policy: An Economist's Perspective,* Professional Paper 322, (Alexandria, Va.: Center for Naval Analyses, Naval Studies Group, December 1981), p. 40. For a generally favorable discussion of bonuses, see pp. 39–44.

40. See Binkin and Kyriakopoulos, *Paying the Modern Military,* p. 63.

41. Cooper, *Military Manpower,* pp. 376, 349–351; also see *Zwick Report,* pp. 26–27, 41–57.

42. *Zwick Report,* pp. 27, 49–51, presents survey data confirming this intuitively unsurprising fact.

43. Binkin and Kyriakopoulos, *Paying the Modern Military,* p. 67, especially n. 11.

44. For discussion of such proposals, see Binkin and Kyriakopoulos, *Paying the Modern Military,* pp. 65–67. See also *Zwick Report* recommendations for retirement reform and a deferred compensation plan, pp. 62–73.

45. Sometimes this shift occurs in the pay proposals presented by

the administration to Congress, and sometimes it occurs within Congress. Also under current laws, the president can reallocate as much as 25 percent of any congressionally passed basic pay increase into subsistence and quarters allowances.

46. Binkin, *The Military Pay Muddle,* p. 37.

47. Binkin and Kyriakopoulos, *Paying the Modern Military,* pp. 48–61.

48. Richard Cooper discusses the advantages of more experienced forces, but he does not mention severing rank and paygrade. Cooper, *Military Manpower,* pp. 318–319, 351–352.

49. In 1980 Congress did enact a geographically variable housing allowance based on regional housing costs. This innovation has been particularly helpful to naval personnel living in expensive seacoast areas such as Norfolk, San Diego, or San Francisco.

50. Such proposals would require a transition from the present system. Current service members could receive two pensions if they retire after more than twenty years of service; one based on the present system, prorated by their years of service to date, and a second based on future salary deductions.

51. Cooper, *Military Manpower,* pp. 380, 319, n. 57, 394, and also pp. 188–193, 277–303, 311–319, 343–355. He estimated also (pp. 291–303, particularly p. 301, and p. 319, n. 57) that because the total costs of civil service and military labor were approximately equal, nothing could be gained by substituting one for the other, assuming them to be equally productive. However, additional cost savings of $1 billion could have resulted from "contracting out" to private firms various tasks done by 250,000 civil servants. Also see Martin Binkin, with Herschel Kanter and Rolf H. Clark, *Shaping the Defense Civilian Work Force: Economics, Politics, and National Security* (Washington, D.C.: The Brookings Institution, 1978).

52. Michael Hinz, "What's Good for America Is Good for the Army," *Reason,* December 1981, pp. 34–46. Hinz suggests paying inactive reservists a lump-sum payment at the beginning of their service, but a monthly payment would give the reservist an incentive to keep his address current. The administration may propose a bonus to those who extend their individual ready reserve membership. See *Military Manpower Task Force Report,* p. VI11.

53. In 1977, 14 percent of military personnel filled nonproductive "pipeline" positions, mostly as students and trainees. Binkin and Kyriakopoulos, *Youth or Experience?,* p. 53.

54. Cooper, *Military Manpower,* pp. 169–193, 311–312, 343–349,

353–355. Work by Binkin and Kyriakopoulos supports the conclusion that youth are overrepresented in the military. See *Youth or Experience?*

55. A rare exception to the tradition of separate pilot communities occurred in the air force during the Vietnam War. Under the pressure of an "everyone goes once before anyone goes twice" policy, strategic air command heavy bomber pilots found themselves in Vietnam flying transports, or even gunships in close air support of grounded combat troops. Systems command weapons systems engineers, many of whom also were qualified pilots or navigators, found themselves flying similar tactical missions. And after an engineer had completed his Vietnam flying tour, tactical air command often opposed his return to systems command, because TAC judged these people to be unusually high quality.

This bit of history comes from private correspondence with retired air force Colonel Joseph P. Martino, now with the University of Dayton's Applied Systems Analysis Research Institute. He concludes: "Thus under severe pressure, the tradition does break down. But only under severe pressure."

56. Morris Janowitz and Charles Moskos, "Five Years of the All-Volunteer Force: 1973–1978," *Armed Forces and Society* 5 (February 1979), pp. 171–218, particularly pp. 210–211, and n. 40 on p. 217.

57. For further discussion, see David Evans, "The AVF—Making it Work," *U.S. Naval Institute Proceedings* 6 (December 1980):47–53.

58. Students gave this assessment to the author while he was on the Naval Postgraduate School faculty in the late 1960s and early 1970s.

59. See "Nine More Regiments near Activation," *Army Times,* April 13, 1983. Also see "U.S. Army may use British System to Boost Morale," *Christian Science Monitor,* November 13, 1980, p. 1.

60. An army company, the next to smallest unit commanded by a commissioned officer, typically contains four platoons of forty-five men each. For further discussion, see Thomas Edmund Kelly, "Towards Excellence: The Army Develops a New Personnel System." Unpublished MA thesis, Massachusetts Institute of Technology, Cambridge, Mass.: May 1982.

61. Bachman, Blair, and Segal, *The All Volunteer Force,* p. 144.

62. Charles Moskos, "Making the All-Volunteer Force Work," *Foreign Affairs* 60 (Fall 1981):17–34, and Moskos, "Making the All-Volunteer Force Work," in *Defense Manpower Planning,* ed. Taylor et al., pp. 232–235.

63. Moskos, "Making the All-Volunteer Force Work," *Foreign*

Affairs 60 (Fall 1981):23. For excellent discussions of the difficulties facing econometric attempts to measure the effects of pay, bonuses, benefits, recruiting efforts, and other variables on the supply of recruits, see John A. Cirie et al., *Department of Defense and Navy Personnel Supply Models,* Proceedings of a workshop held in Arlington, Va., January 22–23, 1981, prepared under Navy Manpower Research and Development Program of the Office of Naval Research, May 1981. Also see Warner, *Issues in Navy Manpower Research and Policy,* pp. 6–13.

9

Intelligence in Defense of a Free Society

Joseph B. Ford

Strategic planning and tactical planning both hinge upon the adequacy of *knowledge and evaluated information* regarding military threats. In this sense intelligence constitutes a key—perhaps *the* key—to successful defense. Yet intelligence in a free society brings into clear focus the paradox of means and ends, legitimate needs to achieve and to preserve freedom amid external and internal threats to the rights of individuals.

Intelligence gathering can be one of the capital menaces to the freedoms of the individual citizens in any society. In an unfree society there may be few if any real freedoms to shield, but intelligence in a free society ineluctably involves the need to know about all enemies while preserving and protecting the freedoms of its own citizens, and hence the paradox of achieving necessary ends without resort to means that unfree societies may exploit to the hilt.

George Bush, former director of the Central Intelligence Agency (CIA), stated just after his return from Brezhnev's funeral that as far as his impressions of the new Soviet leadership were concerned, it was not particularly relevant that the former KGB (Soviet intelligence) director had risen to topmost power and, further, that there is "very little similarity between the KGB and our CIA." Yet it has been highlighted by a number of writers that the description of the KGB by Allen Dulles, another former CIA director, would apply just as aptly to the historic record of the CIA: "It is a multi-purpose, clandestine arm of power . . . more than an intelligence or counter-intelligence organization. It is an instrument for subversion, manipulation, and violence, for the secret intervention in the affairs of other countries."[1]

While Bush, as a potential (and past) candidate for president, exaggerated the differences between the CIA and KGB, nonetheless it is significant that there have been numerous exposés of the CIA in the United States, despite efforts to suppress some of these, while only the underground press can dare to criticize the KGB in the Soviet Union.

Intelligence agencies should provide the best intelligence and judgments of capabilities and intentions of societies that pose a direct threat to the United States. However, intelligence should be sharply distinguished from "subversion, manipulation, and violence" abroad. In addition, foreign intelligence should be distinguished from surveillance of our own citizenry. Yet the United States must shield itself from internal enemies, especially those in the employ of real or potential foreign enemies or acting in common cause with those enemies.

How can the United States acquire information about internal threats without threatening the freedoms that we try to defend? We may work out the best program for gathering intelligence against threats to our survival, but still we must be equally concerned with the preservation of freedom.

Intelligence must involve evaluation, not just information. In treating the limits of intelligence, we shall focus both on the inherent limits, the uncertainties that always prevail, and the limitations that a free society must place on its intelligence operations so that we may have the best defense while still protecting individual liberty.

Background: History of Intelligence

The history of intelligence is replete with tall tales that have misled even responsible historians, along with a valid residue that should prove illuminating. Out of the capsule history that may be compressed into this section, two central truths emerge regarding the role, value, limits, and perils of intelligence for defense of a free society.

First, the value of intelligence shines through all the tales that saturate early recorded histories as well as in authenticated facts of recent conflicts. The second truth is that the limits, unreliability, and *perils* of intelligence, especially when concentrated or centralized in powerful and power-seeking groups, stand out as clearly, if less shiningly, as the successes. This leads to the related problems of controlling intelligence and especially its "guardians." If intelligence can mislead nearly as often as lead us correctly—some even hold the historical balance to be about even—then how much of our freedom can we risk to afford intelligence gatherers enough backing and wherewithal to accomplish legitimate objectives? No one would gainsay that the immense proportion of intelligence that is garnered from public and other than "secret" sources must continue even in the most utopian society. However, we may seek to keep a rein on the "secret" activities, especially in counterintelligence.

Most of the earliest recorded chronicles highlight intelligence in victories. A quote from the oldest Chinese source confirms the antiquity of intelligence. Sun Tzu set out the principles and methods in his *Ping Fa (Principles of War)* around 510 B.C.: "Hostile armies may face each other for years, striving for the victory which is decided in a single day.

This being so, to remain in ignorance of the enemy's condition simply because one grudges the outlay of a hundred ounces of silver in honors and emoluments is the height of inhumanity."[2]

Much of the case on the need, limits, and perils of intelligence rests on the historical data and parallels from the times of Sun Tzu until today; but the complexity and diversity of history defy summary even of the highlights. The full history of intelligence in the United States from revolutionary beginnings to the labyrinthine bureaucracies of the 1980s would be beyond the present compass. The heritage of our participation in World War I left the elements of what today is known as the "intelligence community" with both its positive role in establishing the continuous means of gathering information on threats to the United States from abroad and examples of the great potential for restricting and even eliminating freedom in the name of "patriotism" and defense.

The positive side of the heritage of World War I lay largely in the work of Herbert Yardley and Ralph Van Deman. One tremendous spin-off of Van Deman's heritage was the famous American Black Chamber, better known through Yardley's book of that name.[3] This predecessor of the contemporary National Security Agency (NSA) was developed by Yardley, an obscure State Department code clerk whom Van Deman placed in charge of MI-8, the branch of military intelligence devoted to intercepting and decoding messages. Yardley oversaw the growth of this source of intelligence to a sophisticated bureau.[4] It was abolished in 1929 at the hands of Secretary of War Stimson, but was later resumed and amplified, leading to great successes in World War II. There was no threat to our individual liberties in having U.S. policymakers know what the Japanese and later the Germans were doing in preparing for world conquest in World War II. Indeed, prior to establishing permanent intelligence activity, its absence may have threatened American freedom. Without a permanent intelligence establishment, "the country was an easy target for spies and terrorists; . . . German agents had a field day here in the years leading up to both world wars, and the Soviets were suspected of doing the same during the 1930s."[5]

There is one aspect of Van Deman's work that foreshadowed the perils of modern intelligence. American intelligence, once organized on a multilevel national scale in the interests of "making the world safe for democracy," harbored a practice and an organization that could menace that democracy: the American Protective League (APL). A group of self-acknowledged vigilantes, the APL was composed of "volunteers" aiming to help uncover "enemies" and was justified in Van Deman's eyes by the need to be on the alert against German subversion in the armed forces. But, once begun, such an organization is hard to harness, much less stop, when its activities turn to civilian "enemies" rather than just serving as an aid to the legitimate efforts of the Military Intelligence Division (MID) to guard against espionage, sabotage, and "infiltration."

The APL, with the support of officials of the Justice Department as well as MID, extended its attacks against organizations supposedly and falsely reported to be funded by German agents (like the Industrial Workers of the World) to labor organizations in general, especially when organizing efforts resulted in activities that the vigilantes deemed hostile to the interests of the country (which they uniformly identified with those of industry in any dispute with labor). The writings and statements of APL leaders themselves are enough to illustrate the perils of trying to blend vigilantism with the need to have adequate counter-intelligence, especially in wartime.

Some historians have emphasized the role of the individual as paramount in the saga of American intelligence from the revolution to the present. Van Deman was one of those individuals, but one who failed to appreciate fully the need to safeguard the freedoms of citizens. The eternal problem of balance enters. Vigilantism *per se* tips the scales, as does abuse of power. Unfortunately, vigilantism outlasted the war itself and compounded the errors in the infamous "Palmer Raids" after World War I. These were named after Attorney General A. Mitchell Palmer, who convinced committees of Congress of the need for special appropriations to fund a drive against aliens and "reds" in order to deport the former and prevent the latter from planned riots and uprisings in favor of communism. Before the "red scare" ran its course and receded, Palmer even persuaded Congress to make supplementary appropriations of $1 million in December 1919 (when a million dollars was more than a drop in the governmental bucket) on the assurance "that the money would be expended largely in prosecution of the red element in this country. . . ."[6] Even after the exposé of the excesses and crudity of these antisubversive "raids" led to their reduction and suspenson, still a new phase emerged in the American "political intelligence system" under J. Edgar Hoover, later to become famous in his own right as head of the Federal Bureau of Investigation (FBI).

Thus World War I and its aftermath left two major trends in the relatively "free" society of the United States: the one, the emergence of a form of surveillance with great inherent potentialities for restriction and even elimination of freedom; the other on the positive side, the emergence of elemental continuous means for the collection of intelligence on possible enemies: the heritage of the Yardley "Black Chamber," the so-called intelligence subculture. This is the term applied by many to the professional specialists who came to comprise a "select band of brothers," responsible for the foundation of later successes, during the approach and reality of World War II and its succeeding crises of cold and some "hot" wars. Unfortunately this band of brothers has also aided and abetted the multiplication by intelligence agencies of extralegal and illegal activities that have generally rendered any investigation of these activities onerous if not—as some hold—"futile." In this context the historic case of Albert Dreyfus becomes particularly relevant and instructive. In a unique way it epitomizes the problems of intelligence in a free society: both the need for guardians and the eternal question, especially as to the *guardians of secrets,* of "who is to guard the guardians?"

In August 1894 a French officer, Major Ferdinand Esterhazy, de-livered a promise or offer of information to the Germans regarding new French artillery and other matters. The message, known as the *bordereau,* was supposedly delivered, according to Esterhazy's belated confession, as part of an elaborate disinformation policy devised by French counterespionage chief, Jean Sandherr. Eventually this infa-mous *bordereau* came into the hands of the French General Staff, who were unaware of Sandherr's disinformation plans. A maze of events led to the suspicion that Captain Alfred Dreyfus had written and de-livered the *bordereau* to the Germans.

Dreyfus, a Jew born in Alsace, had previously distinguished himself as a model officer in the French army despite continuing anti-Jewish bias among the French officer corps of his day. He had been among the top ten graduates of the Ecole de Guerre, becoming eligible for the General Staff as a probationer. This notable success for a Jewish officer came even though Jean Sandherr had reported that Dreyfus was a security risk.

Once the original decision to prosecute Dreyfus had been made, zealots in the army and General Staff contrived to prove their case through fabrications and forgeries. Even where evidence of judicial error in the case had accumulated in abundance, the opponents of Dreyfus persisted, regarding any correction of the errors as a threat to the integrity of the army.

After several trials and appeals, Dreyfus eventually achieved full annulment of an earlier guilty verdict and his rank and honors were restored. Georges Picquart, who had made the first revelations to his superiors that Esterhazy, not Dreyfus, had written the *bordereau,* was vindicated and promoted to general and later minister of war in the first cabinet of Georges Clemenceau.

Meaning of the Dreyfus Affair

The Dreyfus affair reveals both the positive and negative aspects of secret agencies. Above all the affair illustrates "what a tangled web we weave when first we practice to deceive." Thoughtful analysis of the meaning of the whole affair must center on several prime issues. First, it involved real and significant espionage. New developments in artillery and other matters that Esterhazy either delivered or promised to supply to the Germans were all significant. Second, the concentration of intelligence authority in the military made possible the elaborate cover-up. There is irrefutable proof of a cover-up, once the decision was made to make Dreyfus the culprit, and especially once the first court-martial was convened. From that point, the affair offers renewed and strengthened proof of the dangers in allowing a secret agency such leeway as to forge and fabricate new "secrets" to shield exposure of past errors, in the thought that national unity and strength require this.

Third, part and parcel of the same issue but worth separate stress is, again, the proof that intelligence is inherently imperfect. The French General Staff became involved in the defense of the mistakes of its own intelligence arm.

Fourth, the affair highlights the role of the individual in intelligence. Picquart, who participated in the arrest of Dreyfus, became head of intelligence the next year as the youngest lieutenant-colonel in the French army. A careful scholar as well as a brilliant and honest officer, he came to realize the judicial error as well as intelligence fiasco in the affair. Documents came to his attention proving that the real spy, Esterhazy, was continuing his activities. The General Staff preferred to protect its own cover-up, even though evidence mounted against the real culprit. Picquart's persistence against the opposition of his superior officers makes him a true hero in the history of intelligence, and without it the later journalistic exposés would have been difficult, if not impossible. Thus one honest individual may play a highly significant role.

Finally, abuse of power at the *highest military level* should serve as a signal warning. The powers of those *over and above* the intelligence agencies must be limited in a free society. How to "guard the guardians" remains a key problem.

The Dreyfus affair is often remembered and recited more in connection with the exploitation of anti-Jewish prejudice. However, in historical perspective it offers a unique illustration of both the need for sound intelligence (and counterintelligence) and the dangers to individual liberty inherent in its abuse.

Limits of Intelligence

Turning now to modern intelligence activity, be forewarned that any attempt to embrace the vast apparatus of U.S. intelligence, grown to gargantuan proportions, would be far beyond the scope of one chapter.

Eleven major components constitute the current intelligence community (see figure 9–1). Despite an appearance of decentralizaton, American intelligence, in contrast to its European counterparts, is highly centralized. "The American structure, headed by the director of central intelligence (DCI), has lumped a veritable array of responsibilities— for paramilitary operations, technological collection, military order-of-battle estimates, and political and economic analysis—into one institutional framework."[7] Reforms resulting from President Carter's Executive Order of January 24, 1978, accentuated rather than loosened this centralized structure. Thus the director of central intelligence acts as chief of the CIA itself; has complete authority for approving the CIA's budget, as well as those of intelligence agencies in the departments of Defense, State, Treasury, and Energy, and the FBI and Drug Enforcement Administration; and oversees all intelligence appraisals.[8]

Even U.S. military inteligence is centralized, providing a largely unified analysis to policymakers. Though the army, navy, and air force have separate intelligence operations, the Defense Intelligence Agency, established by Secretary of Defense Robert McNamara to provide unified military positions on intelligence matters, has "'tended to produce brokered intelligence compromises" that distill any competitive analysis that might otherwise have surfaced.[9]

Estimates for the cost of this intelligence structure ranged from $4 billion to $10 billion in 1980. More precise figures are impossible to obtain because overall intelligence expenditures are not disclosed by the federal government.[10]

As we do have in the United States a relatively free society, there has been already a vast literature published on the developments of intelligence from their humble beginnings in World War I and the modest preparations for World War II. This literature has reported the notable successes of intelligence that highlight its utility, indeed its necessity, in mounting an adequate defense. But it has also unveiled numerous failures that reveal limits of intelligence, as well as the particular flaws of the American intelligence establishment.

David Kahn has given us a thorough and scholarly report on the intelligence of the greatest totalitarian power prior to postwar Soviet Union: that of Nazi Germany.[11] The glaring weaknesses were at the highest levels. Many battles were won, but the war was lost, especially on the code-breaking front. Unbeknownst to the Nazis, the British had obtained the secret Enigma machines (with help from Polish and French intelligence agents) which the Germans had adopted as their standard vehicle for encodement before and during World War II. British experts were able to construct why they called the Bomb, a solving machine that promptly translated the German cipher into what is known by its

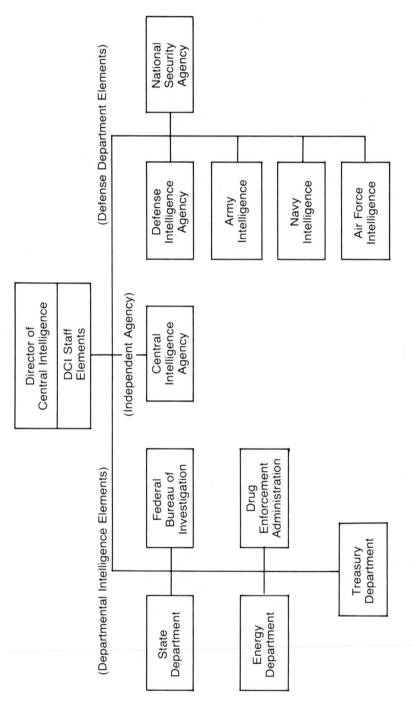

Figure 9–1. U.S. Intelligence Community

literal meaning as *plaintext.* The product was Ultra. This invaluable advantage was shared by the British with Allies during the early years of losses that it did not succeed in stopping as well as in the middle and later years of general success.

In November 1978, at a remarkable conference in Germany, the cryptographers of both sides, together with historians, reviewed this eventful history both in general and in some of the most dramatic details. It proved too much for one German, who had assured the grand admiral of the *Kriegsmarine* Doenitz that the naval Enigma was not being deciphered. He blurted out: "If the Allies could read it all, why didn't they win the war sooner?" The answer from an historian was "They did." No one dissented. Ultra was, as one veteran put it, "the most important sustained intelligence success in the history of human conflict."[12] While Ultra illustrates the fundamental importance of intelligence in wartime, the discovery of Soviet missiles in Cuba that resulted in the Cuban missile crisis in 1962 underlines the necessity of peacetime intelligence. Without the intelligence effort that gathered and evaluated the information about Soviet activity in Cuba, however flawed it may have been, the United States would probably have been faced with an irreversible presence of Soviet strategic missiles barely 90 miles from U.S. shores.

This need for intelligence during peacetime is particularly acute given current trends in weapons development. Robert Ellswater and Kenneth Adelman, both formerly with the Department of Defense, argue that "the United States desperately needs to know not just what the Soviets have done or are doing, but what they wil be doing years from now. Most weapons systems take somewhere between two and twelve years to research and develop and have a lifespan of five to twenty years. Thus today's defense planning must be based on estimates of . . . tomorrow's adversary capabilities."[13] Clearly such intelligence calls for a continuous and sophisticated effort.

Though Ultra and the Cuban missile crisis stress the importance of intelligence in both peacetime and wartime, they also expose some inherent limits of intelligence as well as defects in America's intelligence operations. However successful Ultra ultimately was, its warnings were sometimes neglected. Furthermore, when Rommel and later Hitler ordered radio silence during the former's defeat of the Americans at Kasarine Pass in North Africa and the latter's final counteroffensive in December 1944, overreliance proved the fatal flaw of the Allied commanders, who by then had been so attuned to warnings by Ultra that they neglected other indications of enemy intentions and capabilities— all very elementary in intelligence.

Intelligence operations leading up to the Cuban missile crisis demonstrate particularly well the shortcomings of American intelligence. Nearly one month before the U.S. flight that confirmed the presence of Soviet installations in Cuba, the intelligence "system" contained numerous pieces of information that could have alerted analysts to Soviet activity. These included refugee reports of missile sightings, U-2 photos showing the construction of SAM (surface-to-air missile) sites and other defensive missiles, a CIA sighting of the rear profile of a strategic missile in Cuba, and shipping intelligence from which it might have been inferred that the Soviets were shipping "space-consuming" cargo.[14]

Two key problems prevented this information from being promptly utilized. First, these facts were contained among a vast number of other intelligence reports. This deluge of information had to be checked, compared, and analyzed to determine which items were correct, as well as significant, a processing that required at least two weeks before any of it reached policymakers in Washington. Furthermore, until all the puzzle pieces were in one place, many of the isolated pieces of information carried no special significance. This time delay between acquiring information, evaluating its importance, and transmitting it to policymakers is an almost inevitable consequence of information overload and limited resources. A second problem compounded the delays. Standard operating procedures designed to mitigate risk entailed delays such that the transmission time from the CIA "agent sighting to arrival in Washington typically took nine to twelve days. Shortening this time would impose severe costs in terms of danger to subagents, agents, and communication networks."[15]

Bureaucratic rivalry further delayed confirmation that the Soviet Union had begun installing missiles in Cuba. The air force squabbled with the CIA over who should assume responsibility for U-2 flights over Cuba required to verify Soviet activity there. The rivalry resulted in a ten-day delay before a successful U-2 overflight occurred. Of this delay, Graham Allison writes that "though this delay was in one sense a 'failure,' it was also a nearly inevitable consequence of two facts: many jobs do not fall neatly into precisely defined organizational jurisdictions; and vigorous organizations are imperialistic."[16]

In the interaction of the intelligence network with policymakers during the Cuban missile crisis, two other tendencies are evident: that of wishful thinking on the part of policymakers; and that of acquiescence to their superior's viewpoint by lower level analysts. Thus Kennedy dismissed CIA director John McCone's assertion that the Soviets were about to introduce offensive missiles into Cuba as the suspicions of a hawk. "Knowing that McCone had informed the President of his suspicions . . . others were reluctant to confirm his suspicions."[17]

Nor have these kinds of flaws been isolated occurrences in U.S. intelligence operations. A breakthrough comparable to Ultra was achieved by U.S. Naval Intelligence in breaking the Japanese code prior to the Japanese attack on Pearl Harbor. It was known by the equally dramatic title of Magic. But the limits of its value were clearly, up to Pearl Harbor at least, in the realm of evaluation. The distribution of intercepts was limited. Top officials in Washington sent to commanders in the Pacific what they deemed relevant. The "Basic Navy War Plan" of the United States, dated May 26, 1941, envisioned explicitly the potential damage of an opening attack on Pearl Harbor, where, contrary to the wishes of the top commander dismissed earlier that year, the bulk of the U.S. Pacific fleet was still concentrated. By fall the U.S. political and military leaders had come to believe, on the basis of their evaluation of the decoded intercepts and other evidence, that Japan was planning a major movement into Southeast Asia. The army and navy commanders at Pearl Harbor were warned in a general way, but were not given sufficient information to be on full war-alert by December 7, 1941.

The patterns of history may be more reliable than even good intelligence, such as was being furnished in many ways before Pearl Harbor but most notably in the interception and decoding of military, naval, and diplomatic messages. Junior officers, especially those acquainted with Japanese language and culture, had only parts of the jigsaw puzzle, yet put the pieces together as to the time of probable (or nearly certain) attack at 7:30 AM, December 7 in Hawaii. As Pearl Harbor was the major American base in the Pacific, one would expect that at least the decoded message to the Japanese consul at Honolulu requesting the location of ships at Pearl Harbor would have been relayed to the Pacific commanders, as well as the probable time of a war begun by the Japanese. Both the majority and minority reports of the postwar Joint Committee on the Investigation of the Pearl Harbor Attack give immense praise to the communications and intelligence services that gave valuable and valid secret information on Japanese plans and espionage operations, as well as a large body of intelligence that the Japanese were resolved to begin the war by December 7.[18] But the higher authorities in Washington did not view the possibility of a Pearl Harbor attack seriously enough.

There were enough warnings that the Pacific commanders themselves might well have been disposed to order full alert, dispense with weekend leaves, have better air reconnaissance, utilize the radar facilities to the full, and have their reports sent to headquarters. Even on the morning itself, the hunting and destruction of a midget submarine was disregarded when it alone should, in retrospect, clearly have led to a full alert at least a couple of hours before the attack. Also, the radar unit being operated for training purposes at the northern end of Oahu showed the approaching carrier planes. The two operators reported the two trackings—first of a float-plane preceding the main group for reconnaissance, then the major attacking vanguard itself—to their young lieutenant. Knowing some B-17s were expected, he simply dismissed the reports and did not bother to pass them on. It was not simply historical ignorance that led to what Admiral Ernest King was later to call an "unwarranted feeling of immunity from attack" in all ranks at Pearl Harbor. Even the telltale indications of the early morning of December 7, 1941, were ignored. Whether this was self-deception or overreliance on horseback judgments, the ignorance and errors in evaluation may be charged equally to all levels in Washington as well.

The recent history of U.S. intelligence has demonstrated that these weaknesses persist. U.S. policy in Vietnam suffered acutely from a tendency toward wishful thinking, acquiescence, and even a near-fatal stifling of dissent among intelligence analysts. These tendencies are largely a product of the "encrustation of leadership" that has characterized U.S. intelligence. "American intelligence has long been stultified by the domination of a clique. . . . Its directors over virtually all of its history have been linked—by shared experience, psychological inclination, and profession—to the CIA's Operations Directorate (which is responsible for covert activities)."[19]

Several problems have accompanied this homogeneity in leadership. First, intelligence analysis lacks competing perspectives with the result that policymakers, faced with a consensus of advice, perceive no real policy alternatives. Second, the domination of intelligence by covert action experts has resulted in a downplaying of the need for regional and "country" specialists. Third, this homogeneity has led to a shocking "failure of imagination" in which rigid "preconceptions have screened out data that, if properly quested and digested, should have prevented strategic intelligence failures."[20]

This "groupthink" in part explains President Kennedy's poor record in the Bay of Pigs fiasco, in which intelligence reports provided him with a narrow range of choices. Vietnam too illustrates the monumental dangers of relying on a homogeneous source of intelligence that excludes real "country" experts and discourages dissent.

More recently the stunning inadequacy of American intelligence in Iran reflects this same narrowness of vision and the neglect of local expertise characteristic of a homogeneous intelligence operation that has favored covert action and fact-gathering to expert evaluation.

At the close of 1978, a congressional intelligence committee requested a full briefing on the situation in Iran. The CIA responded by sending its Operations—not its Analysis—people who, of course, testified from their own limited perspective. They lacked the imagination to see that a massive, popular counterrevolution had been launched against the shah's modernization revolution. These covert officers had treasures within Iran (including) the now-famous listening posts on the Soviet border. These men swayed the entire intelligence community to report that the shah's opponents were numerically insignificant and politically impotent.[21]

These cases indicate that the limits of intelligence break down into at least two main headings: facts (or data) and evaluation. Even though advances in science and technology have made it possible to accumulate volumes of information, evaluation is still a critical factor. Today our technical means of interception are beyond even the dreams of the junior officers who tried to pass on their interpretations as well as data to their superiors prior to Pearl Harbor; yet evaluation remains the major stumbling block to adequate use of whatever information is available.

The evaluation of facts and even the determination of what is a fact is not easy. Frequently the evidence conflicts, and all the information must be jelled into a pattern upon which a judgment can be based.

Personal traits of the assayer of information, including ignorance and stubbornness, have warped many a judgment. But the most frequently recurring errors in appraisal spring from overconfidence, complacency, and clinging to preconceptions. Ignorance, especially neglect of historical parallels and patterns, almost always plays a role.

Before the Yom Kippur War, the Israeli intelligence service was rated by many the best in the world, and yet the Egyptian-Syrian attack caught Israel by surprise on October 6, 1973. After the war, the Israeli Agranat Inquiry Commission found that its army intelligence possessed ample information indicating an attack.[22] The commission determined that the failure to call up the reserves was negligent and placed the blame on the chief of staff, the chief of intelligence, and others.

The commission ascribed two main reasons for the failure: (1) the belief of army intelligence that Syria would not go to war without Egypt, which would not start a war until the Egyptians were able to stage deep air strikes against Israel's major military airfields to neutralize the Israeli air force; and (2) the judgment by army intelligence that the Syrian military buildup was defensive and the Egyptian forces were conducting their maneuvers. Both mistakes in *evaluation* resulted from stubbornly held preconceptions. Overconfidence also contributed to the mistaken appraisal. The belief was prevalent in Israel that because the Arabs had been so inept in 1967, they would remain inept. Furthermore Anwar Sadat of Egypt had been clever. He frequently talked about attacking and then did not, which lulled his adversary into complacency.

In addition to the unreliability of secret information and mistaken assays of it, intelligence in our time has another serious problem. This is the problem of *volume*. Modern high technology, especially in the realm of computers, has made possible a tremendous, unprecedented explosion in communication in general and a corresponding (and even exaggerated) problem of choosing which data to evaluate and accumulate—or, as it turns out, accumulate even if evauation is not possible.

This problem reaches its peak in the National Security Agency (NSA) which has the prime responsibility not only for intercepted intelligence data, but also the photographs of satellites, all the public and secret communications that come to the CIA, the State Department, and numerous others in the alphabetical list that may be found in various compendia on the subject.[23] The result is "noise," overload of information and raw data, and difficulties in evaluating and producing "finished intelligence" that decisionmakers can absorb. What is true for the NSA is equally applicable to military intelligence. One analyst has suggested that as much as 90 percent of the military intelligence budget goes toward the collection of information, while only 10 percent is for actual analysis. Thus, he writes, "a fortune in U.S. tax dollars is spent on collecting intelligence that is never analyzed."[24]

The volume of this information can be understood from the number of persons employed to handle it by only two of the agencies of the U.S. intelligence community. In 1956 NSA's director told a Senate committee that the code-breaking agency employed 9,000 civilians; David Kahn calculated that by 1973 the number had increased to 14,000; in 1974 Victor Marchetti and John D. Marks stated that the number was 24,000. By 1978 the estimates were over 68,000![25]

The CIA does not make public the number of its employees, but in 1973, 10,000 in Washington alone was considered a fair estimate by intelligence writers. As all this is hidden in the budget, one can only speculate how much greater these figures may be today.

The sheer volume of raw intelligence data means that it simply cannot all be minutely analyzed. Moreover, even the material that is analyzed must be summarized for presentation to policymakers. During the administration of President Dwight Eisenhower, the CIA printed and delivered to him every morning a short intelligence newspaper for his eyes alone. The editor of the newspaper summarized items from the preceding twenty-four hours that seemed important. It was his selection and his editing that determined what the president read. The form of the presentation may change from time to time, but the immense volume of the information dictates that the method will remain essentially the same. No intelligence chief, much less the president, can find time to read all intelligence information, let alone to understand it well enough to use it in timely decisions. And computers are only as good as the data fed into them.

However, there is a grave danger in having just one evaluation and interpretation presented to the final decisionmakers. A middle way between brevity and completeness of alternative interpretations (and when applicable, determination of what are the "facts") should be available to policymakers. Yet national intelligence estimates are furnished to the president in papers that reflect a "consensus of the views of the intelligence community. Although agencies may register a formal dissent on particular points, a high value is placed on consensus. Even under the best of circumstances this emphasis results in an enshrinement of the lowest common denominator of intelligence opinion, and all too often leads to 'party-lining' or anticipating the views of policymakers."[26] Regarding Soviet military buildup, that party-line has reflected an essentially optimistic world view in which the United States and the Soviet Union have been perceived as moving increasingly toward cooperation. This in turn has led the CIA continually to avoid worst-case assumptions about Soviet military intentions and to screen out data that conflicted with their optimistic world view.

A prime example of this optimism is furnished by the public data reviewed by Albert Wohlstetter of the University of Chicago, who used the Defense Department's own reports on projected and actual verified deployment of Soviet nuclear missiles.[27] Results were startling. Wohlstetter's amply substantiated conclusions may be summarized: the Department of Defense made predictions of expected Soviet nuclear deployment each year from 1962 through 1969 and *systematically underestimated* the number of nuclear weapons and vehicles the Soviets would deploy. Moreover, they did not learn from hindsight; as reality overtook their predictions, the Defense Department continued to underestimate.

The underestimation was substantial. From 1965 through 1972 the ratio of our prediction to actual deployment for bombers was: low range 70 percent, median range 79 percent, high range 89 percent. For ICBMs even the highest range of our prediction was 80 percent of actual deployment, while in the high range for submarine-launched ballistic missiles (SLBMs), the prediction was only 84 percent. As the Soviets expanded, we explained away their expansion. When they finally exceeded the United States in numbers, U.S. analysts said equality was all they had in mind.

In constant dollars (dollars adjusted for inflation) the U.S. nuclear budget was nearly three times as high at the end of the Eisenhower administration as it was in 1974. From that fact Wohlstetter concluded that the "arms race" was run in different directions. The Soviets were racing forward; the United States was running backward. This decline in our nuclear budget may at least be partly attributed to the failure of the U.S. intelligence process.

Underestimates have not been confined to future Soviet nuclear deployment, but also to Soviet total current military spending, which counts heavily in gauging Soviet nuclear capacity. In 1976 the Defense Department admitted that it had uncovered an enormous error in its estimates of Soviet military spending and doubled its former estimates from 1969 to that time. How many such misses can the United States afford?

Two officers who have unique qualifications say that the United States is still appraising far too low. In January 1976 Lieutenant General Daniel Graham resigned in protest against Gerald Ford's dismissal of James Schlesinger as Secretary of Defense. Graham had been director of the Defense Intelligence Agency and had served since 1959 in numerous intelligence assignments (including Deputy to the Director of Central Intelligence) for the intelligence community. Graham thinks that doubling the estimates of Soviet military spending was not enough; they should have been tripled. Major General George Keegan retired from the air force in January 1977. He had been chief of Air Force Intelligence since March 1972, a post that capped his long career in intelligence. Keegan says that the doubling is still a gross understatement and that for the period 1969 and beyond the doubling will have to redoubled. It is unnecessary to agree with Graham or Keegan; underestimating by half for a period of eight years is error enough!

In addition to the failure of U.S. intelligence attributable to the absence of competing evaluations, the intelligence community has relied too heavily on scientific surveillance in building their analysis. Yet this so-called national technical means (NTMs) of surveillance has many shortcomings. NTMs cannot, of course, provide any guide to intent regarding the utilization of military capabilities. Nor can NTMs acquire complete information regarding Soviet (or other enemy) military capabilities.

Our own numbers about nuclear strength are supposedly public. The illuminating questions are what we can and cannot know about corresponding Soviet numbers and quality from the technical means of verification available to the United States.

A leading authority on treaties summarizes the situation with precision:

> Until 1972 we refused to make arms control treaties that did not provide for on-site inspections to verify performance. This long-held American position succumbed in the 1972 SALT treaties to "national technical means of verification," the words used in the pacts as a euphemism for scientific surveillance. The technical means are prin-

cipally our eyes in the sky—satellites and aircraft overflying enemy land and photographing it—aided by various electronic and other detection instruments. But our supposedly all-seeing eyes in the sky, supported by every technical device we have, do not and cannot give us the information we need about Soviet nuclear strength.

We can count deployed bombers, other aircraft, surface ships, submarines, and the number of tubes they have for launching. We cannot determine, however, whether Soviet submarines contain additional submarine-launched ballistic missiles (SLBMs). We have tailored both the SALT I interim agreement and the SALT II agreement to our ability to count rather than to our need to know. Neither pact limits the number of nuclear *missiles;* each limits the number of nuclear *launchers,* and it is with the number of launchers that Defense Department reports deal. Nonetheless, these reports are generally treated as a comparison of Soviet and American nuclear strength in *missiles.*[28]

The Soviet launchers can use a cold launch technique that enables them to be refired. In 1977 Keegan related how the Soviet Union acquired the technique, the failure of U.S. intelligence to take it into account, and the resultant large Soviet superiority that the United States does not calculate.[29]

Our national technical means of verification cannot detect dormant warheads on the surface of the earth, especially if there is a great deal of electromagnetic radiation. Our eyes in the sky cannot look into caves, mines, or structures (e.g., warehouses or camouflaged silos) in which missiles can be hidden. Men now can go underground in huge buildings beneath the surface of the earth. One of our own installations at Pearl Harbor is mostly underground. In short, there are endless ways of concealing nuclear offensive missiles and the same is true of some elements of antiballistic missile installations.

In answer to questions put by Senator William Proxmire, the Joint Chiefs of Staff replied in February 1977: "The United States has a substantial lead over the Soviet Union in . . . number of warheads.[30] The chiefs may or may not have guessed correctly, but they did not and cannot know. The number of warheads the Soviet Union has depends on how many of its missiles have multiple independent reentry vehicles (MIRVs) attached and the number of MIRVs. The report of the 1976 Senate Select Committee to investigate U.S. military intelligence stated that detecting "MIRV missiles which are concealed in silos or submarines" would be highly difficult.[31] In fact, the United States cannot count the number of MIRVs by technical means; so the United States does not know how many warheads the enemy has.

Once it is realized that the United States can count neither enemy missiles nor warheads, the very basis of a technical means of verification collapses. The future of verification is even gloomier. Since Hiroshima, nuclear weapons have improved not only in size, destructiveness, and range, but also in quality. The trend to seek quality is the present one, and it seems likely to continue. Quality is impossible to verify by technical means. And of course the United States cannot know how far Soviet research has progressed.

National technical means of verification are necessary and we cannot abandon them. However, they do not give us reliable estimates of Soviet nuclear strength. The expected refinement in quality of nuclear weapons augurs a decrease in our ability to measure their potentialities, as well as numbers.

U.S. intelligence operations are thus plagued with problems inherent to any effort to collect and analyze data about enemy capabilities. In addition our intelligence establishment has suffered from structural flaws that have engendered misperceptions, institutional biases, waste, and a shortage of actual evaluation. These shortcomings reduce the ability of the intelligence community to provide the kind of information and analysis that is essential in forging an adequate defense policy.

Perils of Intelligence in a Free Society

We turn now more specifically to the *perils* that intelligence activities pose to people's liberty. There is no necessary order in listing of the salient threats to freedom that *may* be involved in domestic intelligence, but it should be foremost in our minds that dissent is inherent in a society where individual freedoms are fundamental. The United States arose from a breakdown in the security of the regime that was held guilty in the Declaration of Independence of a series of wrongs and injustices that the Bill of Rights was designed to interdict. Some founding fathers, especially Thomas Jefferson, warned against many of the threats that excessive concern with internal security could bring to freedom. Jefferson helped defeat the federalist supporters of the Alien and Sedition Acts, again demonstrating the important role of individuals in battling against abuses of power in the name of "internal security." This highlights the point that it must be freedoms of individuals as well as groups that are to be shielded from the perils of unrestrained collections of data under the aegis—or the guise—of intelligence.

Threats to individual freedoms already exist in American intelligence practices. First, the gargantuan data banks of intelligence agencies, including those whose mandates have been directed to foreign intelligence or even more specifically to military intelligence, have come to include juicy bits of information and misinformation on an uncounted number of individuals. To all this must be added even more mountainous data gathered by agencies like the FBI, charged with certain domestic inquiries. No one could calculate how much of all this "intelligence" has been gathered by illegal means, or how much of it—a small proportion at best—has actually protected the freedoms of U.S. society. One study by the General Accounting Office showed that barely 3 percent of the FBI's domestic intelligence investigations led to federal prosecutions.[32]

If one goes on to electronic and other advances in surveillance, the perils to individual freedoms and even privacy that George Orwell's *1984* highlighted as one of the most total sacrifices on the altar of Big Brother are too glaring to leave any doubts. Any or all of these means may be proper in gathering information on enemies abroad, and, within severe legal limits, on citizens who might constitute genuine threats to a free society; but it is frightening to learn that many of our own topmost leaders and most thoroughly loyal citizens have been unwitting victims of the same kind of surveillance and "snooping" that leaders of totalitarian societies have used not only on their population but on one another.[33]

Second, there is the matter of the enormous expense and waste in the intelligence bureaucracies. Neither of these can be precisely calculated since restrictions protect most of the former, and the latter can be assessed only in retrospect from public documents and revelations as they occur, as did David Kahn with the Nazis. But enough has surfaced to evidence the perils of excess bureaucratic spending and waste in intelligence agencies as well as other governmental and corporate bureaucracies in general. Billions of dollars per year of possibly excess expenditures cannot be ignored. In the effort to improve efficiency—the goal of bureaucratic planning and development—the perils of waste, especially domestic waste, in garnering largely useless and unused "intelligence" should not be ignored. This waste has been amply documented by various analysts of our intelligence system. A study authorized by CIA Director Richard Helms concluded that the U.S. intelligence community collects too much information that includes extensive duplication and much useless data.[34] A 1971 House Appropriations Committee report attacked military intelligence, in particular, as redundant.[35]

The total peril to the national well-being of the United States must include the excess and inflated expenditures abroad as well, especially when careful studies have shown that the growth of the element of surprise in twentieth-century conflicts has paralleled the rise in the enormous expenditures on intelligence. The irony may have been both *despite* the advances in intelligence technologies and *because* of them, as all major powers have shared in most of the scientific and technical knowledge.

Nor can the perils of too much bureaucratic power be overlooked. A future national emergency or war might heighten the threats from concentration of intelligence powers. Surely it should be an added consideration in placing adequate safeguards, wherever and whenever possible, against fiscal excesses and outright waste, as well as against the high costs of unrestrained illegal means in domestic snooping.

Third, vigilantism has been mentioned in this capsule history, but if the term is extended to include all private snooping (and such police snooping as is directed at dissidents that constitute no immediate or present danger), then the measure of "spook-hunting" and its threat to privacy of individuals may vie in quantity with that of federal governmental activities. When we recall that there has been, even in relatively free societies like the United States, official condonation and even outright support of such excesses, then the myriad snoopers, informers, denouncers, baiters, and organized groups (with strong support at the high official levels in some cases), cannot be viewed as an idle threat.

Fourth, spying by agencies such as the NSA on confidential business communications clearly exceeds the mandate of counterintelligence. A report by the House Select Committee on Intelligence cited examples of electronic eavesdropping on business and inquired whether such spying threatens the privacy of Americans.[36] A vacuum cleaner approach to gathering data in which large numbers of communications are indiscriminately monitored in order to intercept relevant intelligence clearly violates any notion of due process and a right to privacy fundamental to preserving individual liberty.

Fifth, secrecy orders imposed ostensibly to promote "national security" seriously threaten free speech and individual privacy. The NSA has been especially zealous in trying to keep a tight rein on communications security. Consequently it has imposed "patent secrecy orders and similar tools to limit the availability of communications security devices."[37] Ostensibly these impositions are designed to prevent communications security devices from falling into the hands of Third World governments who might then be able to prevent their communications from being decoded. This reasoning is dubious, however, because most such countries already have relatively secure systems and "the major powers have had extremely secure systems for years."[38] A less public reason for restricting patents on communications devices is to prevent

U.S. citizens from securing their own privacy against government eavesdropping.

Finally, the overuse of secrecy classifications has a disquieting effect on American freedom. It not only unnecessarily shackles much of the scientific community, but it encourages public ignorance on matters such as defense policy.

The historical references ranging from the Alien and Sedition Acts (that had at least the color of legality) to the manifestly illegal actions that rose in later crises, like the Civil War and the two world wars, even in times of supposed peace or at least undeclared war as in the case of Attorney General Palmer and Attorney General Mitchell, prove that, in present and future crises, we can hardly rest at ease about the potential abuses to freedom posed by intelligence operations.

One cannot say "My free society, right or wrong" because, if it becomes unfree, a key element in its *rightness* is lost. The preservation of freedom—and freedom for all individuals who do not threaten the freedom of others—is the heart of the matter. Intelligence for the defense of freedom must never be allowed to destroy freedom. Even in this brief survey, the perils of this becoming *real* are only too evident.

Peacetime espionage and counterespionage have been evaluated by many specialists and general historians. A large number of these hold that the limits of intelligence are so inherent and omnipresent that a serious case could be made that the flaws outweigh the advantages. However, the previous discussion suggests that many of the failures and abuses of U.S. intelligence have resulted more from institutional problems than from the inherent dictates of intelligence gathering and evaluation. Thus changing the institutional structure and scope of the intelligence network could improve its performance.

Guidelines

Given that intelligence is an essential element of the defense of a free society, what can be done to minimize both its shortcomings and its dangers? While no blueprint can be spelled out in the space of a few pages, some guidelines can be offered, based both on history and on current understanding of the nature of bureaucracies.

Provide For Competing Agencies and Assessments

Since the creation of the Central Intelligence Agency in 1947, the operative principle of U.S. intelligence has been centralization. The director of the CIA not only heads that specific agency but also serves as the Director of Central Intelligence—that is, as at least the de facto supervisor of all eleven agencies that constitute the intelligence community. In that role he is responsible for the preparation of the basic intelligence summaries presented to the president—the National Intelligence Estimates. The NIEs are drafted by the CIA's National Intelligence Officers, based on inputs from the various intelligence community agencies—NSA, the Defense Intelligence Agency (DIA), the individual military intelligence agencies, State Department intelligence, and so on. The basic idea is to present the president with a *consensus* viewpoint, with dissent at best relegated to footnotes.

Thus until 1978 NIEs predicted that the Shah of Iran would remain in power throughout the 1980s. (U.S. policy was based on having the shah as a strong regional ally.) Until 1979 NIEs stated that the Soviets would not place offensive weapons in Cuba, and evidence to the contrary was assessed as nonsignificant. (U.S. policy was premised on continued Cuban adherence to the 1962 Kennedy-Khrushchev agreement.) Even though various intelligence sources provided a number of warnings of a possible Soviet invasion of Afghanistan, NIEs contended that the Soviets would stick to proxy wars, thus leaving President Carter genuinely surprised when the invasion occurred.

The one major recent exception to intelligence-by-consensus occurred at the end of President Gerald Ford's term. Responding to reports of repeated CIA underestimates of Soviet strategic advances, the President's Foreign Intelligence Advisory Board urged Ford to appoint a team of outside experts to make competing assessments of Soviet strategic progress. The resulting "B Team" accurately assessed the Soviet arms buildup as striving for superiority, not parity, and predicted the rapid increases in Soviet missile accuracy and addition of MIRVed missiles that have subsequently occurred. But despite the success of this one venture, no moves to institutionalize the principle of competing intelligence assessments have been made.

What is needed is abandonment of the principle of consensus and of "central" intelligence. The world is complex and ambiguous, and we must expect the president and his cabinet to cope with that fact. There is no reason why the president could not be presented, routinely, with multiple, independent assessments of key intelligence issues. There should be no centralized director through whom these assessments must be passed. Rather, several independent information pathways must lead directly to the president.

To an extent, some competition exists today between the CIA, on the one hand, and the military intelligence agencies (DIA plus the three services agencies) on the other. Although the military agencies formally report to the Director of Central Intelligence (who does have budgetary review authority over them), they are organizationally a part of the Defense Department and therefore report to the Secretary of Defense and the Joint Chiefs of Staff. Some observers, such as John Prados, see the military intelligence agencies as more influential today than the CIA, thanks to high-level changes made by Henry Kissinger during the Nixon administration.[39]

But there are problems with this particular form of competition. To begin with, the DIA itself tends to produce consensus estimates, based on compromises among the vested interests of army, navy, and air force intelligence. The objectivity of the individual service intelligence agencies has long been suspect, given that the size of the army, navy, and air force budgets can be dramatically affected by the definition of the threat each must face. Centralizing their inputs via DIA encourages the same kind of log-rolling trade-offs that congressmen make in supporting each others' pork-barrel projects.

Although it would be rash to suggest abolition of the service-connected agencies—since there are, after all, specific departmental intelligence concerns in which each is legitimately a specialist—it would be naive to rely on the present DIA/service agency structure as an adequate source of competing assessments, even if DIA reported directly to the president. Military agency parochialism is simply a fact of life that must be taken into account in assessing the intelligence products of those agencies.

Besides abolishing the position of DCI and allowing individual agencies to report to the president, another source of competing assessments is the private sector. Over the past decade, in particular, the political risk analysis business has become quite sophisticated. Although staffed in part by former CIA, DIA, and other intelligence community people, such firms operate in a distinctly different environment from government bureaucracies. Because they seek to attract and retain paying clients (such as multinational corporations), these firms have strong profit-and-loss incentives to make accurate, reliable assessments of social, political, and (sometimes) military trends in other countries. To the extent that such a firm develops a reputation for accuracy, it will gain and keep clients; if it forecasts poorly, it will lose clients and go out of business. Comparable incentives for performance simply do not exist within government bureaucracies.

The competition among risk analysis firms leads to experimentation with new methods of making assessments; some rely largely on the judgment and contacts of former intelligence operative while others may utilize computer models, social indicators, newspaper content analysis, and various unconventional techniques.[40] Most significantly, risk analysis firms have no reason to distort the outcome of a study to "tell the client what he wants to hear." With perhaps hundreds of millions of dollars in investment decisions depending on the *correctness* of the firm's analysis, the premium is on being correct, not on justifying a preconceived notion or existing policy.

There is no reason, in principle, why the government could not contract with political risk analysis firms in order to obtain alternative assessments. Firms could be selected by competitive bidding, depending on their expertise and track record as well as price. By contracting out a portion of the intelligence function, the government would gain access to alternative world views and methodologies—and might find the results to be significantly more cost-effective as well.

Slash Agency Budgets

One refrain runs through study after study of our intelligence problems: there is far too much information and far too many people unproductively manipulating the information. Victor Marchetti contends that the revolutionary technological developments in reconnaissance and electronics during the 1960s created a vicious circle: the more data that *could* be collected, the more that was alleged to be needed, leading in turn to further requirements for data collection. He also reveals that a series of special commissions from 1967 through 1970 all concluded that the U.S. intelligence system collects far too much information. There is tremendous duplication (especially by the military intelligence agencies), a glut of raw data (especially within NSA), and even too many *finished* intelligence reports for policymakers to cope with.[41] Predictably, two of these three studies—Hugh Cunningham's and Frederick Eaton's—led to no changes, while the third—the Fitzhugh report—led only to further centralization.

The only effective way to solve this problem of bureaucratic proliferation is to slash the agencies' budgets. Congress should not presume to tell the NSA which of its myriad programs are or are not essential. But by cutting its budget drastically, Congress can force the agency's experts to make hard choices about what data they really need. Similarly, if the budgets of army, navy, and air force intelligence were cut drastically, those agencies' costly overlaps and redundancies might at last be done away with, as they struggled to maintain those operations that were truly essential.

Some will contend that this amounts to taking a meat cleaver to vital government programs. The same argument is raised whenever *any* overgrown bureaucracy is under attack. The crucial point to remember in this context is that the intelligence agencies are bureaucracies, too, subject to the same bureaucratic pathologies so well described by political scientists Anthony Downs and William Niskanen in a largely civilian context.[42] Bureaucracies develop strong self-perpetuating tendencies, reinforced by their monopoly status, taxpayer funding, interest-group support, and civil service mentality. All of those attributes, and their consequences, apply in full measure to U.S. intelligence bureaucracies. Given the strong evidence that they are overgrown, duplicative, and self-protective—like civilian bureaucracies generally—it would seem only appropriate to apply the same budget-cutting remedy to the intelligence agencies as has been applied to civilian bureaucracies at the state and national level. After all their protests have been vented, we can be quite confident that they will, indeed, know where the fat is and be able to cut it out. But they will never do so unless the money is cut off.

Reform Personnel Policies

Large-scale reductions in budget mean large-scale reductions in staff. And that raises the question of the system used to attract and motivate intelligence personnel. Unfortunately, the present civil service and military personnel policies work against developing and retaining highly competent intelligence *analysts*. In both personnel systems the path to advancement lies in getting *out* of intelligence analysis and moving "upward" into management (or to higher officer ranks). Supergrade (GS 16–18) ranks do not exist in intelligence agencies. Although the CIA tends to have more higher-ranking positions than the other agencies, even the CIA has relatively few GS 13–15 analysts.

Along with the lack of upward career paths, there is no regular quality review of the intelligence assessments made by individual analysts. Yet, according to a top-level report prepared for President Reagan, "quality review is the best method of weeding out those incapable or deliberately prone toward drawing incorrect assessments."[43] Even if there were such a system, normal civil service regulations make it extremely difficult to fire incompetent employees. But at least a quality-tracking system would permit less competent analysts to be transferred to less critical work. Better still would be exemption of intelligence agencies from the civil service system, in view of the critical nature of their function. Relying more on outside contractors *instead* of large in-house staff is another way around the problem of less competent bureaucrats.

Congressional Oversight

Intelligence operations are presently reviewed by several committees of Congress. There has been much debate in recent years over whether the reforms of the 1970s may have exposed intelligence operations to greater public scrutiny than is wise. The more committees that have access to classified information, the greater the likelihood of leaks. To the extent that such information is genuinely essential to national security, the concern is valid. But much of the controversy in recent years has concerned various CIA "covert activities" overseas, operations that chapter 1 has held to be inconsistent with the proper role of a free society's government. Given that such operations are not at issue, and that classification regulations cover only essential military secrets, then the concern over leaky committees is valid.

Nevertheless, given the perils inherent in intelligence agencies, it seems prudent to have at least *two* types of congressional oversight committees. One would be the obvious one, whose role is to deal with the substance of defense-related intelligence and the management of the agencies, their budgets and personnel, and so on. The other type of committee should have as its sole purpose the protection of the rights of the citizenry vis-à-vis the intelligence community, especially as regards counterintelligence operations within the United States. Such a committee would have a broad charter to inquire into excesses of classification (as might impede, for example, scientific research), the operation of data banks, electronic surveillance, and similar matters.

Separate Intelligence from Counterintelligence

Counterintelligence amounts to a particular type of police work. It has little in common with intelligence, per se—the collection and analysis of information on actual and potential enemy governments. Thus there is no a priori case for both functions to be performed by the same agency. And in fact, because of the perils to liberty involved in efforts to seek out spies within our midst, it seems prudent to vest these duties in a specialized domestic agency, under the close supervision of congressional authorities.

The present arrangement, under which the FBI has the principal responsibility for counterintelligence activities (spending 80 percent of all "budgeted" counterintelligence funds), seems basically appropriate, however one might view the excesses of that agency over the years. Some degree of liaison and cooperation with the intelligence agencies will, of course, always be necessary, since in the course of their work those agencies will acquire knowledge of the organizations sending spies to our shores (e.g., the KGB). Such knowledge helps establish the context in which those agents work, and can probably aid in their apprehension. But the temptation to give domestic spy-chasing duties to the intelligence agencies themselves must be resisted. It is neither their area of expertise (provided they are shorn of "covert action" operations and stick to information gathering) nor will they be operating under the intensive scrutiny applied to the counterintelligence agency.

Limit the Extent of Classification

The creation of "secrets" by the stroke of a classification officer's pen has grown to completely unreasonable dimensions. Every such addition to the volume of classified material creates the need for additional enforcement and further impedes the flow of knowledge. All too often classification serves principally to conceal information from taxpaying citizens, who are prevented thereby from being able to make informed judgments about defense-related issues. Nuclear physicist Edward Teller, a man greatly knowledgeable about classified defense research and a stalwart advocate of strong defense efforts, has for many years argued for a drastic reduction in the extent of classification.[44] With mounting evidence that seldom if ever can there be long-term secrets in the field of scientific ideas and research, a free society may have offsetting advantages in the new discoveries that, it may be hoped, will help keep free scientific research ahead of that in a closed society, no matter how obvious may be the advantages to the closed society in the protection of its own "secrets." Freedom of research and publication is a vital component of total freedom. To be sure, in time of war and in cases of extreme threat of war, there will inevitably be restrictions, but this is again an issue where trust will have to be put somewhere, and the cross-checking by a select committee can play a critical role both in shielding freedoms and in trying to prevent abuses of the power of secrecy.

Publicize the Intelligence Budget

Expenditures on intelligence are currently budgeted in the United States under various guises. Though this may be justified to some degree, it is clearly an invitation to waste, limitless expansion of bureaucracies, and all the other perils of "Big Government" and (in the field of intelligence and counterintelligence) "Big Brother." It is doubtful that such budget secrecy really disguises U.S. intelligence activity from our enemies who have extensive and sophisticated means for assessing U.S. intelligence activity. However, such budget secrecy does obscure the extent of intelligence activities from the public, making agency accountability and responsibility to the public more elusive.

Conclusion

Accusations against American intelligence have focused on two separate issues: its effectiveness and its excesses. The preceding guidelines attempt to address both problems, suggesting how intelligence operations might provide more accurate analysis without undermining the principles of individual freedom.

Two caveats must accompany those guidelines. First, whatever changes are made in the bureaucratic structure and procedures of the intelligence community, it will remain susceptible to the problems that accompany all government bureaucracies, which do not have to meet the test of the marketplace to survive. It is for this reason that competing sources of intelligence analysis are especially critical. Second, the guidelines must be placed into the broader context of the role for intelligence that is considered compatible with the foundations of a free society. In chapter 1 that role was delimited to include only operations designed to gather and analyze information about individuals and nations that pose a direct threat to American security. Thus the intelligence community should operate under a detailed charter that prohibits certain activities (such as covert military operations) and defines areas of jurisdiction as clearly as possible without altogether undermining discretion. Because we can never foresee all hypothetical situations, constant oversight and routine reexamination of the ground rules for intelligence activity are essential.[45]

We should try to achieve, cross-check, validate or discard (or modify) all intelligence that can be attained without means that wreak harm to the freedoms that we are trying to shield. The temptation to adopt the devil's methods to defeat the devil will always be there. In "hot wars," one suspects it will tend to prevail in the future as in the past, with each side always defending its own devils and its enemies or those it deems disloyal among its citizens. Ideally, a free society would eschew such devilish means even in wartime, but recorded history will have to be refuted by powerful future idealists for such a principle to prevail *in toto*.

Thus eternal vigilance must be a keynote for those who would protect a free society—vigilance against vigilanteeism as well as official governmental interference with the freedoms that the legitimate weapons of intelligence and counterintelligence have a vital mission to shield. In the end a free society can never compete in thoroughness of internal spying with an unfree one. That may be an inherent weakness, but it is also part of its essence as a free society.

Notes

1. V. Marchetti and J. D. Marks, *The C.I.A. and The Cult of Intelligence* (New York: Knopf, 1974), p. 370.

2. Sun Tzu, *The Principles of War,* quoted in Richard Deacon, *The Chinese Secret Service* (New York: Taplinger, 1974), p. 1.

3. Herbert Yardley, *America's Black Chamber* (London: Faber and Faber, 1952).

4. For more details on the NSA, see James Bamford, *The Puzzle Palace: A Report on N.S.A., America's Most Secret Agency* (Boston: Houghton-Miflin, 1982).

5. Sanford J. Ungar, "The Intelligence Tangle," in *At Issue: Politics in the World Arena,* ed. Steven L. Spiegel (New York: St. Martin's Press, 1977), p. 367.

6. F. J. Donner, *The Age of Surveillance* (New York: Knopf, 1980), especially pp. 290–293, 412, 417–418.

7. Robert F. Ellsworth and Kenneth L. Adelman, "Foolish Intelligence." Reprinted with permission from *Foreign Policy* 36 (Fall 1979):158. Copyright by the Carnegie Endowment for International Peace.

8. Ibid.

9. Taylor Branch, "On Political Books," *The Washington Monthly* (April 1982):58.

10. These figures appeared in Morton Halperin's statement in, "Disclosures of Funds for Intelligence Activities," in U.S., Congress, House, Permanent Select Committee on Intelligence, *Hearings,* 95th Cong., 2d sess., January 24–25, 1978.

11. David Kahn, *The Code Breakers* (New York: Macmillan, 1967).

12. Kahn, "Cryptology Goes Public," *Foreign Affairs* 58 (Fall 1979):541.

13. Ellsworth and Adelman, "Foolish Intelligence," p. 155.

14. Graham Allison, "Conceptual Models and the Cuban Missile Crisis," *The American Political Science Review* 63 (September 1969):704. Reprinted with permission from American Political Science Association.

15. Ibid., p. 705.

16. Ibid.

17. Ibid., p. 712.

18. Among countless references now available, one of the briefest is *Senate Document No. 244,* 79th Cong., 2d sess., 1946. This is a minority report in accord with the much longer majority report on key points, which are largely lost in the greater volume of the latter.

19. Ellsworth and Adelman, "Foolish Intelligence," p. 151.

20. Ibid., p. 155.

21. Ibid., p. 154.

22. Laurence W. Beilenson, *Survival and Peace in the Nuclear Age* (Chicago: Regnery-Gateway, 1980), p. 84. Pages 79–87 comprise a cogent summation of "limits."

23. See the glossary in W. R. Corson, *The Armies of Ignorance* (New York: Dial, 1977).

24. Peter N. James, *The Air Force Mafia* (New Rochelle, NY: Arlington House, 1975), p. 32.

25. Bamford, *The Puzzle Palace.*

26. William C. Green, "Reforming Intelligence Analysis," *National Security Record* 36 (August 1981):1.

27. The figures cited here and in the following paragraphs are from A. Wohlstetter, *Legends of the U.S. Strategic Arms Race* (Washington, D.C.: U.S. Strategic Institute, Report 75-1, 1975).

28. Beilenson, *Survival and Peace in the Nuclear Age,* p. 82.

29. G. Keegan, address to newsmen in Washington, March 11, 1977, published in *Washington Report WR 77-4* (Washington, D.C.: American Security Council, April 1977).

30. *U.S. News and World Report,* February 14, 1977, p. 61.

31. U.S., Congress, *Foreign and Military Intelligence, Report No. 94-755, 94th Cong., 2d sess., 1976.*

32. Sanford Ungar, "The Intelligence Tangle," p. 372.

33. Marchetti and Marks, *The C.I.A. and the Cult of Intelligence,* p. 370.

34. Ibid., p. 95.

35. Ibid., p. 100.

36. U.S., Cong., House, Report by the Permanent Select Committee on Intelligence, *Implementation of the Foreign Intelligence Surveillance Act; Report No. 97–974,* 97th Cong., 2d sess., Dec. 17, 1982.

37. Sylvia Sanders, "Data Privacy: What Washington Doesn't Want You to Know," Reprinted, with permission, from *Reason,* January 1981, 26. Copyright 1980 by the Reason Foundation.

38. Ibid., p. 29.

39. John Prados, *The Soviet Estimate: U.S. Intelligence Analysis and Russian Military Strength* (New York: Dial Press, 1982).

40. See C. Byron and others, "In Search of Stable Markets," *Time,*

May 25, 1981; M. Reese, "The Risk Analysts," *Newsweek,* June 7, 1982; M. Tuthile, "Cloak-and-Dagger Men Aid Executives," *Nation's Business,* August 1982; and P. H. Stone, "High Times in the Political Risk Business," *Nation,* December 25, 1982.

41. Marchetti and Marks, *The C.I.A. and the Cult of Intelligence,* pp. 95–100.

42. Anthony Downs, *Inside Bureaucracy* (Boston: Little, Brown, 1966) and William A. Niskanen, Jr., *Bureaucracy and Representative Government* (Chicago: Aldine-Atherton, 1971).

43. Quoted in Jack Anderson, "Why Presidents Stumble," *Parade,* March 13, 1983.

44. Edward Teller, "The Secrecy Charade," *Reason,* November 1982.

45. Ungar, "The Intelligence Tangle," p. 376.

10 Aid to Freedom Fighters

Laurence W. Beilenson

Long before an atomic weapon was a gleam in its father's eye, Karl von Clausewitz wrote:

> The Russian Empire is no country which can be really conquered, that is to say, which can be held in occupation, at least not by the forces of the present states of Europe, nor by the 500,000 men with which Bonaparte invaded the country. Such a country can only be subdued by its own weaknesses, and by the effects of internal dissension.[1]

Clausewitz referred only to war. In our time nuclear war against the Soviet Union has become suicidal, and we have no desire "to subdue" the country; our enemy is its government. Only one other tool in the statesman's chest is capable of striking the enemy decisively. Our use of it would promote internal overthrow of all communist governments, primarily that of the Soviet Union, by stepped-up truthful propaganda to the people of all communist-ruled states and by our giving their dissidents money, and when propitious, supplies and arms. Such actions by the United States truly would be aid to freedom fighters, but by whatever phrase we characterize our assistance, it also would be subversion.[2]

The Ethics of Subversion

Internal subversion is carried on by dissidents against their government; external subversion by helping the dissidents without resorting to war. In our popular lexicon subversion customarily is coupled with "communist" to denote its noxious odor. But as our Declaration of Independence proclaims: "When a long train of abuses and usurpations . . . evinces a design to reduce [the people] under absolute Despotism, it is their right, it is their duty, to throw off such government." The abuses and usurpations the American colonists suffered were mild compared to those long endured by the communist-ruled people. The revolt of the colonies against their lawful sovereign George III would have been defeated save for the money, supplies, and arms furnished to our rebels by France and Spain (1776–77). External subversion to aid freedom fighters is a good deed, and as American as the Fourth of July.

With apt propaganda sense, communists call their external subversion "aid to wars of liberation," which would be noble except for the catch: if the war of liberation succeeds, the communists replace the overthrown government with a more repressive totalitarian regime.

An assumed good end justifying foul means is the other moral flaw in communist subversion. False propaganda to aid revolution is right according to the communist mentor V.I. Lenin.[3] The facts about communist rulers need no embellishment; for the United States, therefore, efficacy joins ethics in counseling adherence to truth. For both reasons Americans can also cheerfully forgo bribery, another blade of the subversive tool. Usually bribery is wasted.

Still another blade the United States should not use is terror, of which there are two varieties: defensive, through which a government attempts to cow the populace by imprisonment, torture, and murder; offensive, a blade of subversion which kills people and sabotages property not as part of the final blow by force to topple the government, but to prepare for overthrow by intimidating either the people or the rulers. Lenin copied and praised the extensive defensive terror employed by the Jacobins in the French Revolution.[4] In abjuring assassination as a method of offensive terror, because ineffective, he took pains to say: "Of course we rejected individual terror only out of considerations of expediency."[5] Defensive terror always has been a basic part of communist rule; Lenin's heirs now embrace offensive terror.

Its efficacy has been tested by experience since Lenin's day. Terror has contributed to the success of modern revolts, notably against the French in Algeria and against the British in Palestine and Cyprus. Terror, however, is a two-edged blade that often has cut the wielder by alienating supporters at home and abroad.

Regardless of effectiveness, American subversion must renounce terror by refraining from it and by refusing to tolerate terror by the freedom fighters we help. Unlike tyranicide, which may be morally justified, terror, which indiscriminately kills the innocent, is ethically repugnant.

Shunning chicanery is the last step in cleansing American subversion. While the means of delivery will be secret, the intention of the United States to aid freedom fighters against communist governments should be proclaimed for all to hear. The American people have the right to be informed in advance, not of a particular operation, but of the course of conduct their government will pursue, thereby at the outset affording Congress the opportunity to say "Yea" or "Nay" to the executive branch. We should be equally frank and fair to the dissidents. Our public announcement should warn them that money, with supplies and arms when propitious, is as far as we will go; we will not go to war or even break diplomatic relations with communist governments to bring about the triumph of the freedom fighters. Finally, although Lenin believed that even failed revolutions, such as the 1905 Russian revolt, promoted the desired end, we should not burden our conscience by urging the European satellites to rebel prematurely and be crushed by tanks against which we will not protect them.

Our actions should conform to our public declarations. Under these conditions, as chapter 1 points out, the morality of American subversion would be beyond question. Its wisdom turns on whether aid to freedom fighters against communist governments is likely to advance or retard our supreme aim: survival as a free people.

The Situation and Its Origins

We cannot determine the answer without reference to our situation and tracing how it came about. Lenin declared a state of permanent hostility against all noncommunist governments, to be pursued by all the instruments of statecraft, especially the two striking tools: war and subversion. Unlike previous conquerors, however, Lenin chose subversion as his chief tool. Defensive wars, he said, were of course necessary. Offensive wars also would be waged, but only if not "adventurous," that is, if they did not risk losing the national base already won in Russia for subversion throughout the world. He believed wars between the communist and capitalist camps were nonetheless inevitable.

Two periods with which Lenin was especially conversant demonstrated the need that always has existed for a strong national base from which to conduct external subversion. The secret revolutionary societies, formed or existing in practically all European countries soon after 1815, incited the waves of European revolts that broke out in the 1820s, the 1830s, and that crested in 1848. But though the societies kept in touch with each other, none of them could offer their fellow revolutionists in other countries the substantial money required in the preparatory stage of overthrow or the money, arms, and supplies in quantity needed for the blow by force and the civil war that might follow. The 1848 revolution that won in France might have provided a base, but the new republican government in France gave no help elsewhere. The small assistance of the communist First International to the Paris Commune revolt (1871) was utterly ineffective against the French troops that suppressed the rebellion.

Lenin began his worldwide subversive campaign as soon as he captured power in Russia, but when he died in 1924, he had won no countries except Outer Mongolia, which fell by a combination of war and subversion. The advent of Adolf Hitler preoccupied the United States in the period between the two wars; besides, the United States was largely inactive on the world scene during this interlude.

Thrust into the international maelstrom by World War II, the United States resolved in 1947 to contain Soviet communist expansion by a system of military alliances, troops overseas, and subsidies. As recounted in chapter 3, the United States has lost the superiority in nuclear weapons it once enjoyed, and the American people, soured by the Vietnam War, are unwilling for their government to fight conventional wars to contain communism. As related in chapter 5, the unfairness of American allies in failing to share the common burden to the extent of their abilities and the devastating effects of nuclear weapons comprise other salient elements of our situation.

The Soviet Union has not changed its intentions; Lenin's heirs, strong in armed might, continue the struggle he began against the noncommunist world. Observing their outward push, aided by new bases, such as Cuba, the United States ought to consider aid to freedom fighters in the communist-ruled countries as an alternative to wars of containment.

The rewards of success would be great. If the government of the Soviet Union were brought down and replaced by a non-Leninist government, nuclear peace would become far more likely. It makes no difference to a Soviet citizen whether Argentina or Zaire or Pakistan is communist or capitalist. Possessing one-sixth of the earth's land surface and ample natural resources, the Soviet Union needs no more territory. The Leninist ideology that commands the Soviet Union to communize the world is the power that drives the Soviet machine; without it the contest between the Soviet Union and the United States would in all likelihood disappear.

An overthrow in any other communist-ruled country would not lead to such a dramatic result, but would shatter the illusion that rule by a communist party is irreversible. And such an overthrow would hearten freedom fighters throughout the communist world.

Popular revolt against an experienced modern dictatorship, according to George F. Kennan, "is simply not a possibility."[6] With more wisdom Niccolo Machiavelli wrote:

Another . . . powerful motive that makes men conspire against their

princes . . . is the desire to liberate their country from the tyranny
to which it has been subjected by the prince . . . No tyrant can secure
himself against such attacks except by voluntarily giving up his usur-
pation. But as none of them ever take this course, there are few who
do not come to a bad end.[7]

If despots had been invulnerable to overthrow, the long history of their
depositions would not have been written. As the 1979 fall of Iran's
Shah Mohammed Reza Pahlavi proved, it is always possible to oust
tyrants.

The latent causes for rebellion in the communist-ruled countries
are numerous. The long-standing nationalities problem in the Soviet
Union has been exacerbated by rates of ethnic growth; soon less than
half the people will be Russian, but Russians dominate the bureaucracy.
Members of the communist party receive the plums; a tiny percentage
of the people are members. With no means to ensure peaceful succession to power, a time of trouble ever hovers over the communist scene.
Struggles for power occurred at the deaths of Lenin and Josef Stalin;
Nikita Khrushchev was deposed. From Rome through the military dic-
tatorships of our day, a standing army, though the shield of the rulers,
frequently has been the agent of their downfall. "A standing force,"
James Madison wrote, "is a dangerous, at the same time that it may
be a necessary, provision. . . ."[8] The armed forces may turn their swords
against the regime in any society; the danger is aggravated when, as is
true in communist-ruled states, power is concentrated at the center
waiting to be seized. Modern weapons are more deadly than ancient
ones, but as Mao Tse-tung (Zedong) noted, men fire them and can
turn them against their rulers. In the downfall of the Shah of Iran, his
strong army melted away.

Educating their people in order to compete in our technological
age, the Soviet rulers have endeavored to indoctrinate them, but the
educated learn to think for themselves. Despite the governmental control of information, the Soviet people know that their economic condition lags far behind the West. While the people of the Soviet Union
and China may seem to accept the lies and changes of line so often
perpetrated by their masters, they must see through them; the people
are not fools.

The desire to own land has been universal among peasants; it was
no different in the Soviet Union and China. Leaders in both countries
tricked the tillers and took away their ownership. The small plots each
country has allowed to remain in individual hands far outproduce the
collective farms. The tillers witness this every day. Count them among
the potential recruits for revolt.

It may be granted that there is an authoritarian tradition in both

Russia and China, but there were strong strains of liberty in both the March 1917 Russian Revolution and the 1911 Chinese Revolution led by Sun Yat-Sen. In the 1917 election campaign before the Bolsheviks seized power, Lenin for the Bolsheviks found it necessary to promise the Russian people every democratic reform, including recall of judges. The French Revolution occurred in a country with as strong an authoritarian tradition as Russia or China, against a king whose legitimacy did not rest on a dubious succession, and where monarchy had been accepted for centuries. The Soviet and Chinese rulers have preached the virtue of revolution. It would be astounding if the Russian and Chinese people did not see that what is sauce for the goose is sauce for the gander.

Among the underlying causes for revolt in the communist world, above all is the repression of liberty. Pessimists in the Western world—unconsciously under the sway of a materialist philosophy—doubt that people care enough about liberty to rise in its favor. The rebellious American colonists were as well off economically as any people on earth, and their burden of taxation was lighter than in the mother country. They revolted for freedom, of which there was little in the 1775 world. The years preceding the French Revolution were among the most prosperous France had ever enjoyed. The Irish did not revolt from 1691 to 1778 despite their miserable economic lot, which greatly improved from 1778 to 1796 and 1798, when the Irish did rebel. The Greeks were prosperous before their 1821 revolution against the sultan; Greeks with high standards of living were among the most active revolutionists. People do revolt for political liberty.

The Historical Patterns of Subversion

If there exists, then, in all communist-ruled states what Lenin without his Marxist blinkers would have called a revolutionary situation, why have not the people thrown off their governments without outside help? As Lenin pointed out, a revolutionary situation does not necessarily engender revolution.[9] A broader answer to the question that goes to the root emerges from exploring the historical patterns of subversion.

Dissidents always have been present everywhere because of, as, Madison wrote, the many causes of faction which "are sown in the nature of man." "The Gauls," Julius Caesar said, "always want to change the existing regime." "One always finds malcontents and such as desire a change," Machiavelli observed. *The Federalist* summed up: "Our own experience has corroborated the lessons taught by the examples of other nations . . . Seditions and insurrections are, unhappily, maladies as inseparable from the body politic as tumors and eruptions from the natural body."[10] Our least worry will be in discovering dissidents against the misrule practiced in the communist world.

Royal birthright, election, or appointment pursuant to the laws have been the lawful methods of succession to state power.[11] Subversive overthrow by coup or revolution has been just as normal. It was pervasive in the ancient and medieval worlds; of twenty-six Roman emperors from Augustus to Maximimus (27 B.C.–238 A.D.), sixteen were assassinated; in the eastern Roman Empire forty-one out of 118 emperors were deposed (364–1453 A.D.). Nine out of seventeen English rulers (1087–1452) seized power by force. The sultanate in Turkey was hardly a model of stability; fourteen of twenty-nine sultans were forcibly toppled (1500–1911). After eight religious civil wars (1562–1629), France settled down, but from 1792 through 1870 eight more French governments were overturned. Despite an abortive coup at the death of Tsar Alexander I in 1825 and the assassination of Alexander II by revolutionists, the Russian succession passed legitimately until Nicholas II was deposed by the March 1917 revolution, but Russia has not always been so comparatively placid. Ivan III fomented sedition in and conquered the Russian republics. From his death in 1505 through 1801 there were thirteen overthrows, not counting a series of overthrows during a period of anarchy (1610–1613).

Our own government, born by revolution and rescued from disunion in the Civil War, has never been overturned, but south of the Rio Grande, the chronicle has been the reverse. The countries of Europe, Asia, and Africa have undergone many changes of government by force or its threats. Most of the present governments on earth owe their existence to a subversive overthrow of a preceding government, and in many the overturn has been recent. When we weigh the chance of ultimately deposing governments in the communist world, history gives cause for good cheer; the basic pattern has been the vulnerability of governments to overthrow.[12]

One reason for this pattern affords additional grounds for optimism because of a warranted pessimism concerning the future. Whatever has been the form of government, rulers have tended to abuse their power, many grossly, in consequence of which the governed have sought to redress their grievances by force. The other reason for the vulnerability of governments to overthrow, while not praiseworthy, has been equally potent: the Outs have coveted the power the Ins have held. Both causes underlie the fundamental pattern of subversive history: a government has been a sometime thing.

The other basic historical subversive pattern warns us against expectation of quick success in subverting the communist world; the time, place, and outcome of attempted overthrow all have been unpredictable. The enemies of Julius Caesar believed they had finally eliminated him in the elections of 50 B.C. Hence most of the influential senators with inside knowledge backed Gnaeus Pompey in his civil war against Caesar. No prognosticator in 50 B.C. could have foretold that Augustus would seize and hold the scepter as the final act of two civil wars. The outbreak of the French Revolution surprised the contemporary monarchs of Europe. France was a peasant country in 1789. The economic condition of the peasants in most countries of the Continent where there was no revolution was far worse than in France, and before the event the English throne seemed more unstable than the French. If instead of Louis XVI, Henry IV had sat on the French throne, or if an able advisor, such as William Pitt, had been at the helm in France, the king would have retained his head and his throne.

Lenin himself made one good guess leading to his successful overthrow of the Provisional Government in November 1917, but he had sadly told a Zurich audience on the eve of the March 1917 Russian Revolution: "We of the older generation may not live to see the decisive battles of this coming revolution."[13] After the July 1917 Bolshevik uprising against the Provisional Government had failed, Lenin said to Leon Trotsky: "Now [the Provisional Government] will overthrow us." Lenin was ready to start the retreat.[14] Writers about revolution speak confidently of inevitability—after the event. For uncertainty of time, place, and outcome, many reasons can be adduced, all correct, but they reduce themselves to the only real inevitable—the human variables.[15]

Though the when, where, and who wins are uncertain, a third historical pattern points to the wisdom of American aid to freedom fighters: the expectance of foreign help and its giving have strongly stimulated revolution and also have been significant in coups. A review of the five greatest revolutions in the last 300 years—the "glorious" English Revolution of 1688, the American Revolution, the French Revolution, the 1917 Bolshevik Revolution, and Mao's communist overthrow of Chaing Kai-Shek—shows that external subversion was a potent factor in all except the French Revolution, and in it a considerable French literature argues that English gold played a large part in the downfall of Louis XVI.[16]

The long history of subversion, discerningly read, offers further encouragement. It falls into two parts: before and after Lenin.

Traditional External Subversion

External subversion is a tool of statecraft almost as old as war. Routinely in the ancient world, one response to an invasion was to aid malcontents in the invader's country in order to give the would-be conqueror something to worry about in his own backyard.

The internal subversive game always has two principal players, the dissidents and their target government. The players can widen—and usually have—to include foreign governments helping either side of the internal game. Unless, however, the assisting player supporting the Outs changes tools by going to war, as France did in 1778 against England, the external subverter cannot overthrow the target government; only the internal Outs can. Hence the chief blade of external subversion has been furnishing money, arms, supplies, or other aid to the internal Outs to promote their becoming the Ins. The process may start in the preparatory stage to finance propaganda-agitation or sometimes terror against the government, with bribery also sometimes employed, all aimed at weakening the government to pave the way for the final blow by force. That may be delivered at the top, a coup, or by a wider application of force, a rebellion in all or part of the territory belonging to the sovereign.

Subversion before Lenin, traditional external subversion, had been an often used tool. Its lineaments have been distinct since ancient times. The Corinthian delegate at Sparta on the eve of the Peloponnesian War said, "There are other ways open to us for carrying on the war. We can foster revolts among the [Athenian] allies."[17]

Fostering revolts was not confined to wars in progress. Because all statesmen understood that peace was—in Lenin's phrase—only a respite between wars, the subversion anticipated. Expecting Philip II of Spain to make an attack on England sooner or later, Elizabeth I, at peace with Philip, gave money and arms to the Dutch revolting against Spanish rule in the Netherlands. For her purpose it was unnecessary for the internal subversion to be crowned with success; it was enough that it kept Philip busy in his own domain. French subversive help to the American Revolution was to weaken England in a future war with France.

Traditional external subversion cut across ideological lines. Typically imperial Japan helped to finance the 1905 Russian revolt.

Because, however, the chief characteristic of traditional external subversion was its function as an auxiliary to war in progress or expected to come, the subversion was never global; global subversion was too remote from the immediate objective. External subversion before Lenin was also sporadic—turned on and off like a spigot. Belgian insurgents revolted against their Austrian ruler in 1789. With arms furnished by British Prime Minister William Pitt through his allies Holland and Prussia, the Belgians drove the Austrians out of the country. The purpose of the subversion was to divert Austria from a Russo-Austrian war being waged against Turkey. As a result of the subversion, Austria agreed to quit the war. Thereupon England, Prussia, and Holland abandoned the Belgians and joined in guaranteeing renewed Austrian rule over Belgium.

This dirty trick was not an aberration; it was in accord with the customary manner of playing the international game. After the recipients of the subversive help have accomplished their purpose, they have been no less unfaithful to the subverter. During the first of eight French religious wars, the Prince de Condé received potent aid from Elizabeth I of England in his Protestant rebellion against the regency of Catherine de' Medici. Condé then patched up a peace with Catherine, whom he joined in recapturing Havre, which as part of his bargain with Elizabeth he had turned over to England. Lest we feel too righteous, the infant United States is a prime example that Outs lack gratitude after they become Ins. Our fledgling country would have perished in infancy except for France. Successively the United States repaid by making a separate peace behind the back of France in breach of our alliance treaty; then after France forgave us, lent us money, and the breach was patched up, we again broke our alliance treaty when France and England went to war in 1793. To make our thanks complete, we shattered our treaties with France by Jay's Treaty with England (1795), which favored England in its war with France.

Expressed in affairs of moment, there has been no gratitude among nations. His throne wobbling from the victorious assault of the rebelling Hungarians in 1849, the young Austrian Emperor Franz Josef sought aid from the tsar, who sent 150,000 Russian soldiers across the Carpathians to defeat the rebels and the new Hungarian republic. Five years later in the Crimean War, Franz Josef sided with England and France against the tsar. On the eve of World War I, the same Franz Josef, then very old, was fomenting revolt in Russia.

The Lenin Adaptation

When Lenin began to practice subversion as a youth (he was born in 1870) the techniques of the final blow by force and all the blades of the subversive tool long had been perfected. Though Lenin wrote tirelessly and somewhat tediously about all the facets of his beloved art, he contributed nothing new except for a simple but momentous change in the whole traditional tool.

Lenin cared nothing about ennobling subversion: "For us," he said, "morality is subordinated to the interests of the class struggle of the proletariat."[18] He adopted traditional subversion just as it had been used by his power precursors but adapted it to his purpose as the preferred tool to place communist parties in control of all the governments of the earth. The Lenin Adaptation is traditional subversion, internal and external, as modified by Lenin.

War had been the major tool of conquest with subversion only as an auxiliary. Lenin changed the relation. Though he expected war between the communist and capitalist camps, as he called them, and approved aggressive war to advance communism if it was safe and did not endanger the base won for worldwide subversion, he made subversion his chief tool for world conquest.

Lenin's subversion was global. He took steps to organize communist parties in all countries as the nuclei of revolution, supported and orchestrated from the central base in the Soviet Union.

In the country to be subverted, the traditional external subverter took internal conditions as it found them without a protracted sustained attempt to reshape them by preparatory work in order to make the government ripe for overthrow. The protracted sustained effort distinguishes the Lenin Adaptation from the traditional sporadic brand. Internally the difference is in degree; externally in kind.

Traditional subversion always had been secret, though in practice an open one. A government would have to be singularly dull not to know about sizable delivery of arms to insurgents or even large injections of money in the preparatory stage. Still the cloak of secrecy was attempted. Lenin went public.

The key words to distinguish Leninist subversion from that of its predecessors and from that of the West since Lenin and into the 1980s are *preferred, global, protracted, sustained, public.*

The Lenin Adaptation rests firmly on subversive historical patterns. Governments have varied from bad to tolerable; hence the chronicle of governments relates a history of overthrows, ejecting the Ins and bringing in the Outs by a coup or a revolution. Times of trouble have occurred in all countreis from social and economic internal conditions, or from struggles for personal power, or from the dislocation of wars, whose recurrence has been a fact of life among states as long as states have existed. The foundation of the Lenin Adaptation is the justified expectance of times of trouble and overthrows sooner or later in most of the world.

By the protracted length of the struggle and its geographic universality, the Lenin Adaptation compensates for uncertainty of time, place, and outcome of a particular revolt. Despite the Marxian theory of inevitability, Lenin characterized predicting the where and when of revolution as "absurd efforts to ascertain what cannot be ascertained."[19]

Lenin scattered throughout his works advice to foreign comrades and to his heirs on how to carry out their subversive mission, but his most comprehensive directions are in *"Left Wing" Communism, An*

Infantile Disorder (1920).[20] Its neglected aspect is Lenin's acceptance of uncertainty in time, place, and outcome of revolts as a guide for practicing subversion. The Dreyfus case in France, Lenin said, was enough to serve as the "unexpected" and "petty" cause that brought the people "to the verge of civil war!" In regard to England, he wrote, "We cannot say, and no one is in a position to say beforehand, how soon the real proletarian revolution will flare up there, and *what* will most of all serve as the *cause* to rouse it, to kindle it." Accordingly, he exhorted his followers "to carry on our preparatory work," and in so doing to "stir up . . . all spheres."[21]

"To forecast when the revolution will break out . . . would be deceiving you," Lenin said. "The progress of the revolution cannot be foretold and . . . revolution cannot be called forth. We can only work for the revolution."[22]

The Lenin Adaptation adopts the insurance principle of spreading the risk—the risk that revolution will not break out—by global coverage and the protracted struggle. Sooner or later a revolutionary situation will arise, but nobody can foretell when or where or the outcome of an attempt. But if a communist party as a nucleus is in place everywhere and is assisted by the main base, sooner or later the communists will win somewhere, and with additional bases finally triumph by attrition.

Going public was a tactic well designed to promote the desired end. There was no chance to conceal such extensive subversion, and constant exhortation and propaganda were necessary to win and hold followers. Lenin and his heirs, while working as secretly as possible on the particular means, have nonetheless proclaimed their intentions from the housetops.

The Lenin Adaptation has been a great success. In 1913 there was no socialist—let alone communist—government on this earth. Today communists rule more than one-third of mankind. To be sure, the Lenin Adaptation cannot be credited with all the captures; some were by war.[23] Even in such cases the Lenin Adaptation assisted, and in the most important captures it rates the entire credit. Nor is there an end; the communists are pressing hard against the doors of many governments.

The weaknesses of the Lenin Adaptation at its Soviet heart and in the rest of the communist-ruled countries are defensive and internal. Without denying some of the real accomplishments of communist rule, which together with police tactics have enabled the party to obtain acquiescence, the communist yoke has borne heavily on the people. The basic failure of communist rule is evident from the fact that nowhere have the masters permitted the people a choice. This is still true in the Soviet Union after two-thirds of a century under communist rulers.

Why, then, have not the people thrown off their communist governments? To which another question should be added: What have been the mistakes of the West? In answering, it would not be a sin for us to learn from Lenin. Although a moral monster, he understood subversion.

Mistakes of the West

The quality of the leadership on the opposing sides ranks high among the variables that determine success of a revolt or a coup. The Bolsheviks boasted about their mastery of the art of insurrection.[24] Tactically, however, the communists have blundered frequently. They have made up by their mastery of the fundamentals. Despite the revolutionary situation created by the Russian reverses in and mismanagement of World War I, the Bolshevik Revolution, which was really a coup, might have failed save for poor judgment by the Provisional Government and excellent leadership by Trotsky and Lenin. Luck, another important variable, probably accounts for the fact that no inspired Russian leader against the communist tyrants has come forth; nobody knows when one will. There would have been and still would be, however, better chances for such internal leaders in every communist country, if the rulers in the West, including the United States, had not failed in their response to the Lenin Adaptation.

We have been prisoners of our illusions. The hope that the communist rulers will mellow and forsake their ideology has plagued western statesmen from David Lloyd George in the 1920s to the West Germans today. Hostility to the noncommunist world is the rationale of the communist dictatorship at home; the Kremlin will mellow when shrimps learn to whistle. Compromise in the Leninist dictionary means a temporary pause or retreat to lull the enemy while the communists gain strength.

The leaders in the West since 1947 never have exhibited a full grasp of the capabilities or limitations of the statesman's tools. Generally they have regarded the contest as a classic coalition struggle. As noted in chapter 5, the usual outcome of such coalition struggles has been war, and a nuclear war could threaten our survival as a free people.

Western leaders still consider ending the hostility by diplomacy and the treaties which are its fruits. But treaties have been habitually broken. We attempt to induce communist good conduct by loans and trade; in part, we say, to help the people of the communist world. This is a mistake. While the time of a revolt's outbreak is impossible to foretell, nonetheless internal discontent is the basic nourishment of overthrow.

True, the discontent has sprung from varied causes. Rebellion broke out in Ireland (1796 and 1798) and in Greece (1821) while the economic lot of the people was improving, because of resentment of alien rule. The American Revolution was for liberty. The miserable economic conditions that prevailed in Russia during and after World War I and in China after over three decades of chaos were among the underlying causes of the Russian and Maoist revolutions. Whatever be the causes, however, discontent is the key. Hence for people ruled by communist governments, for us, and for peace, the worse conditions, including economics, become in any communist country the better; for such worsening conditions will make the people eager to remove their chains.

Forgetting that we were born by revolution, we prate about stability and attempt to impose it on an inherently unstable world. The pattern of overthrow teaches that the world always has been unstable. Since the American and French revolutions, the world has been churning. With pauses on the surface, but not underneath, the ferment has continued. Add the misery occasioned by two world wars and numerous smaller ones, the liquidation of colonialism, resurgent ethnic consciousness, and growing expectations among the poor of the world fed by easy communications made possible by new inventions. The sum translates not into stability, but into the upheavals that are grist for the Leninist mill.

Good government in most of the world never has been anything but a pious hope; governments always have varied from tolerable to execrable. Most of the present governments of the world are bad—corrupt, inefficient, unfair to the poor, and repressive; they richly deserve to be overthrown. The "free world" is a justified object of derision by communists; in most of the free world there is little freedom. It may be granted that a distinction between totalitarian and authoritarian governments is valid, and that communist governments are much worse and much more oppressive than most authoritarian governments. Using that distinction to justify subsidies to prop up authoritarian repressive governments, however, disregards the character of the struggle in which we are engaged. Such allies will do the United States no good in a war against the Soviet Union, which in all probability will become nuclear.[25] Our support of such allies weakens our moral position, and morality does count in the battle for the hearts and minds of mankind. It is small comfort to a citizen of a country that has suffered misrule to tell him he would be worse off under the communists, whose oppression he has never experienced; it is for his own good that we subsidize the government that he would like to see overthrown. If he laughs sardonically, who can blame him? We do not have to be perfect, but so as not to alienate supporters at home and abroad, we should stop trying to prop up such governments.

A good deal of the so-called covert action of the Central Intelligence Agency (CIA) has been directed to that end. This has not been the fault of the agency, but of the presidents who directed the efforts and the Congresses that either knew about it or did not know about it because they chose not to know. Much of our covert action has not been subversion at all, but secret subsidy to friendly governments, many of them repressive. Some of the rest of the CIA money has been spent to sway governments rather than to overthrow them. Where the United States and the West have tried subversion, it has been traditional rather than the Lenin Adaptation type.

Geographically, not only has the United States not covered the whole communist world, it has barely touched it. True, the United States has made some sporadic efforts in communist domains, but it has never mounted a protracted sustained campaign to overthrow a single communist government. Instead, pursuant to containment, the United States has been extremely busy in the noncommunist world, precisely the wrong place and using the wrong kind of subversion.

Nor has the United States gone public. The sinister-sounding covert action, the name the CIA—with its foot in its mouth—applies to its subversion and the rest of its dirty tricks, reveals an appalling lack of sensitivity. The agency defines covert action as "clandestine activity designed to influence governments, events, organizations, or persons in support of U.S. foreign policy in such a way that the involvement of the U.S. government is not apparent."[26] In the latter effort the CIA has obviously failed. "The knowledge regarding such operations has become so widespread that our country has been accused of being responsible for practically every internal difficulty that has occurred in every country of the world."[27] Our own definition includes deceit. In the CIA definition "influencing governments" includes trying to overthrow them, as the actions of the agency have demonstrated. The agency also has been a conspicuous failure in that effort. As noted in chapter 5, the CIA has overthrown not a single communist government, but the communists have captured many countries during the CIA's period of operation, which has been coterminous with the Truman Doctrine and containment. The agency boasts of two successful overthrows: J. Arbenz in Guatemala (1954) to give us the present repressive government of that unhappy country and N. Mossadegh (1953) in Iran eventually to present us with the Ayatollah Ruhollah Khomeini.

This is not to condemn the brave and able agents who have risked their lives for their country in carrying out missions all over the world. Nor, although the past Directors of the agency have failed to comprehend the Lenin Adaptation, are they primarily at fault. The blame lies squarely on our whole national government.

Not going public is symptomatic of our failure to understand propaganda. The whole CIA attitude of portraying itself as the great machine whereby the United States carries on its undercover machinations all over the world further exemplifies our failure. Even the literature, factual and fictional, which the CIA seems to like, depicts it as the big bold agency that secretly saves the United States in a totally amoral way. The code of ethics of the agency parallels the communist code: a supposed good end justifies any foul means.

Our chance of success coincides with good ethics. The bag of dirty tricks, which the CIA learned from their use by the Office of Strategic Services (OSS) during World War II, and which the OSS had learned from the British Secret Service during that war, has small efficacy for aid to freedom fighters in peacetime. To be sure, the communists also use dirty tricks, which would hurt them too if the United States were not imitating them. The harm done at home and abroad by amoral tactics outweighs their benefits.

An American Adaptation

It would be presumptuous to prescribe the form of the state paper or public address by which the United States should announce a change of policy, but the following pages suggest its major content. Leaving no doubt that we are departing from our past conduct of the contest with the communist-ruled states, that contest will be sharply defined and the United States will express regret that continued communist hostility forces the United States to continue the contest.

We would go on to say: Each country should be free to choose the political and economic system it desires without outside interference, and be content, as the founding fathers were, to leave the rest of the world alone, relying only on example to convert other countries. But because the communist-ruled states by their adherence to Leninism assert that they will attempt to undermine all noncommunist governments, and because we have observed totalitarianism in action, the United States intends to continue to resist, and unlike the past, to counterattack.

Not by war. Any war between the United States and the Soviet Union is likely to become nuclear, and the cure is worse than the disease. The United States maintains its armed might only as a surety of peace.

We should reiterate that sentiment constantly. Peace is the high ground in the propaganda contest. Who wants to be killed by nuclear war?

Our announcement should state that the United States will continue to maintain diplomatic relations with communist-ruled states, as they do with us, but we are changing the rules of the game. Heretofore, despite formal diplomatic relations, all communist-ruled countries have tried to subvert all noncommunist governments; we intend to do the same to communist governments by propaganda and aid to freedom fighters.

One reason is not only to make the game a fair one; we want peace, which is endangered by the state of hostility Leninism engenders. But we will not use false propaganda, bribery, or terror. We will merely reserve our right to offer money, and when propitious, supplies and arms, to dissidents against oppressive communist rule. We do not urge any people to revolt; the where and when they will determine for themselves. And we will leave no doubt in any minds about how far we will go.

There will be marginal cases. Countries in flux present a question of judgment in applying the general principle. For example, reasonable people may reasonably differ about whether Nicaragua was communist-ruled in 1983. By then, however, the telltale signs became sufficient to warrant aid to freedom fighters there. Angola poses no problem; the United States should help the rebellion. We should support the insurgents in Afghanistan, though historically its governments have been repressive, and if the insurgents should win, in all likelihood the government they set up scarcely will be a model of freedom. We should not whitewash this obvious fact, but always tell the truth. The justification for American aid is Soviet intervention. The Afghans have the right to prefer their native rulers over rulers imposed by foreigners. The Heng Samrin government of Cambodia, the puppet of Vietnam, is so egregiously bad that it is tempting for the United States to help any resistance fighters, but Pol Pot's Khmer Rouge, with its record of murderous terror, is beyond the pale. Under no circumstances should the United States associate itself with such villains. In contrast the resistance led by Prince Norodom Sihanouk and his prime minister, Son Sann, deserves our help because their adherents are trying to expel the Vietnamese. We should have begun external subversion against Vietnam long ago. But as Lenin would say in reverse, subversion against the Soviet Union is the main objective.

We will aid fredom fighters against communist rulers, but not against other dictatorial regimes. We recognize that there may be governments as bad as those of the communist-ruled states, and we hope they will improve. Our different course against the communist masters is because they openly proclaim a continuing attempt to destroy all we hold dear, and because they threaten the peace. Were that not true, we would mind our own business.

To what does this amount? First, steady truthful propaganda to the people of the communist-ruled states about their governments. We should not pussyfoot, as much of our present propaganda does. Neither should we exaggerate; we do not need to. Guard always against lying both because it is unethical and because in a long contest the truth will overtake the big lie or the twisted truth, which is no less a fraud. Second, follow the example of the American Revolution by supplying freedom fighters against oppressive communist governments primarily with money, and possibly later with supplies and arms.

We are now justifying our amoral means by a supposed good end, just as communists do. We should rid ourselves of the dirty tricks commonly associated with our covert action. True, we shall expect internal violence ultimately in the communist-ruled countries, but their rulers deserve the violence, as our Declaration of Independence proclaims. At home, we shall bring the subversive tool out of its dark closet; not dark in real secrecy, but dark in seeking such secrecy and by the means we have tolerated. Abroad, we shall for once get on the right side. That side is not the status quo of bad governments or of an illusive stability. By ceasing to prop up such governments by subsidy, we remove our taint as the accomplice of the oppressors. The sum of all these changes may be called the American Adaptation.

Why not, then, assist freedom fighters everywhere? Because we have not the resources, or the wisdom, or the inclination to meddle all over the world. Our aid to freedom fighters is an exception to our general rule of minding our own business. Nor will the United States lose the gratitude of Outs in the noncommunist world after they become Ins if we fail to support them as Outs and the Soviet Union does. There has been no gratitude by the Outs when they have become Ins.

We shall leave no doubt in the minds of the American people that the struggle may be protracted. Nobody knows when, but the success of the American Adaptation has a good chance, maybe later, maybe sooner. Lenin's own case illustrates. In March 1917 he was an obscure expatriate revolutionist, living in Switzerland, with a minuscule following and little hope. When he first heard of the overthrow of the tsar, he refused to believe it. In November 1917 he became the ruler of the largest country on earth in extent of territory. Who could have predicted before the event? We can only work for the revolution in the communist-ruled states. And work for it we should because it is right and forwards our survival as a free people.

Aid to freedom fighters will not cost much money. Subversion is far cheaper than subsidy.

To the communist rulers, our announcement will seem no great change. It is a tenet of Leninism that the capitalist countries will try to overthrow communism. The Soviet Union is not going to make a nuclear strike against the United States because we play by the same rules as it does. If that fear deters us from subversion in the communist world, we have already lost, and to bolster our confidence we ought to strengthen our nuclear arsenal.

The American Adaptation, before it succeeds, far from making war more likely, will make it less likely. Once Americans realize that a communist capture is not irreversible, the United States will not be tempted to wage war to prevent one, as it did in Korea and Vietnam. Even where communist governments are not overthrown, our help to dissidents will keep the rulers busy in their own territories. We shall be encouraged to withdraw our far-flung military forces because we have another tool in our chest besides war.

Our announced help to freedom fighters will color them with a foreign tinge. This is a valid objection to the American Adaptation. But the communist rulers so claim now, and the advantages outweigh the detriment. The other plausible objection is that we ought to mind our own business, and let the internal dissidents do their own job. History teaches, however, that aid from abroad helps revolution.

The communists will not be deterred from making mischief by our diplomacy, treaties, trade, loans, or any other soothing syrup. War against the Soviet Union is not a feasible tool. Even if we had a perfect defense against nuclear weapons and the Soviets did not, it would shock the conscience to kill countless millions of Soviet citizens because their rulers transgress. The only tool in our chest with a chance to end the contest favorably for us, for the world, and for peace, is subversion, cleansed as has been indicated. Our selection is among three choices: our present posture, total isolation, and the American Adaptation— our best choice.

There is no inconsistency between aid for freedom fighters and chapter 5; the two complement each other. Isolationism and fortress America are pejorative words coined by proponents of deploying our forces worldwide to cast contumely on opponents of such disposition.

Chapter 5 does not champion isolating ourselves; it advocates only the withdrawal of our far-flung forces and the termination of our present system of alliances to prevent war. The American Adaptation continues to strike at communist governments, not by war, but by subversion. We turn Lenin's preferred tool against his heirs.

An American Adaptation could be pursued without abandoning our present propping up of noncommunist authoritarian governments. They are not as repressive and do not add to our menace, as they would if they became communist (totalitarian). Nor would an American Adaptation perforce rule out a traditional defensive coup such as the one staged by the CIA in Guatamela (1954).(In *Power through Subversion* (1972), I was willing to tolerate an occasional exception.[28] Further observation and reflection have changed my mind.)

At first blush it seems logical to prevent communist takeovers by supporting existing noncommunist governments rather than trying to overthrow communist governments or to do both for the same end. Why not add the American Adaptation (subversion) to our present policy of propping up by subsidy? Subsidy is expensive, external subversion, comparatively cheap. And as chapter 5 showed the money available is not unlimited. In practice, heavy expenditures on subsidy will lessen our outlays for armed might and subversion. In addition, support of the status quo puts us in the position of opposing all rebellions because some may become communist, though whether they will so become is impossible to foresee and in a world of bad governments, oligarchies, and ferment, in the long run the attempt to prop up is bound to fail.

The deeper objection is strategic. The contest between the communist and free camps will not be decided by this or that tactical victory at the outposts.The strategic struggle is ideological, and if we are to win, we must mind our ethics. Our tactic of subsidizing authoritarian governments puts us on the side of the oppressors against the oppressed and alienates our natural advocates abroad. Even worse is the damage of such a posture to our home front. Many Americans, including their moral leaders among the clergy, will be driven to oppose their government if it pursues such a subordination of means to end. In our long contest with communist governments, which are willing to do any foul deed, it will pay for the United States to cling to good morals.

It is tempting to assert that an American Adaptation must succeed in the foreseeable future, but while the patterns of history predict a triumph sooner or later, nobody can forecast with certitude. Meanwhile the very existence of this American subversion openly announced will yield beneficial dividends. It will offer a substitute offensive tool to those itching to fight wars of containment. It can serve as a surrogate for the illusory tool of treaties. It will encourage us to flood communist-ruled countries with a steady flow of truthful propaganda. It will probably bring down a communist government, and though overthrow is not contagious, victory in one country encourages freedom fighters in others. It will keep our enemies so busy in their own backyards that they will have less time to make mischief in ours. It will encourage us to forgo subsidies to prop up bad governments with consequent advantage both to our ethical position and to our purse. It will enable us to tell our own people, the rest of the world, our enemies, and their dissidents the same truth. No longer will we be required to support our agency of dirty tricks and thus weaken our home front. Not the least of the benefits will be the puncture of the stability balloon: the notion that it is either possible or good to impose stability on a world ruled by bad governments. And an American Adaptation will improve our moral stance without, however, feeding our present insufferable self-righteousness.

The goal of an American Adaptation is overthrow. A coup acquiesced in by the Soviet people could have the same effect as a revolution. Even if the successor government is not to our liking, the deposition of the present masters probably will begin a process that has a good chance of leading to democracy.

In all likelihood, if we knew the Soviet government from the inside, we would be confident of success. Faint hearts win no victories in love, in war, or for peace. In the tradition of the Fourth of July, it is high time for the United States government openly to proclaim and give aid to freedom fighters against all communist rulers.

Notes

1. Karl von Clausewitz, *On War,* bk. 8, ch. 9.
2. Elsewhere I have classified all subversion as "influencing," which attempts to sway a government without overthrowing it, or "decisive," which attempts to overthrow a government in all or part of its territory. See *Power through Subversion* (Washington, D.C.: Public Affairs Press, 1972). In this chapter "subversion" means decisive subversion.
3. V.I. Lenin, *Collected Works,* vol. 25 (London: Lawrence and Wishart, 1960–1967), pp. 287–289; vol. 28, pp. 210–211; *Selected Works,* vol. 10 (New York: International Publishers, 1943), p. 97; vol. 7, pp. 19, 377–378. Manifested also by his deeds contrasted to his promises shortly before.

4. Lenin, *Collected Works,* vol. 13, p. 472. See also Leon Trotsky, *The Defense of Terrorism* (London: Allen and Unwin, 1935).

5. Lenin, *Selected Works,* vol. 10, p. 72.

6. George Kennan, *On Dealing with the Communist World* (New York: Harper, 1964), p. 11.

7. Niccolo Machiavelli, *Discourses,* bk. 3, ch. 6.

8. James Madison, *The Federalist,* no. 41.

9. Lenin, *Selected Works,* vol. 5, p. 174. See also Lenin, *Collected Works,* vol. 23, p. 330; vol. 9, p. 368.

10. James Madison, *The Federalist,* no. 10; Alexander Hamilton, *The Federalist,* no. 28; G.J. Caesar, *War Commentaries; The Gallic Wars,* bk. 4, ch. 1; Machiavelli, *The Prince,* ch. 4.

11. Frequently circumvented by fraud.

12. For further examples, see L.W. Beilenson, *Power through Subversion* (Washington, D.C.: Public Affairs Press, 1972), ch. 2 and passim.

13. Lenin, *Selected Works,* vol. 3, p. 19.

14. Leon Trotsky, *Lenin* (New York: Blue Ribbon Books, 1925), p. 77.

15. For further examples, see Beilenson, *Power through Subversion,* chs. 3–5.

16. For a collection of French writings on the subject, see Beilenson, *Power through Subversion,* ch. 3, p. 259, n. 18, ch. 9, pp. 264–265, n. 15.

17. Thucydides, *History of the Peloponnesian War,* bk. 1, ch. 9.

18. Lenin, *Selected Works,* vol. 9, p. 426.

19. Lenin, *Selected Works,* vol. 7, p. 353. *Power through Subversion,* ch. 5, collects Lenin's statements about uncertainty.

20. Lenin, *Selected Works,* vol. 10, p. 55. It shows also that Lenin did not regard economics as the sole cause of revolution.

21. Ibid., pp. 140–143.

22. Ibid., vol. 7, pp. 414–415.

23. East Germany, Rumania, Hungary, Bulgaria, Poland, and fairly, South Vietnam. North Korea is a special situation. See Beilenson, *Power through Subversion,* pp. 180–182, North Korea, The Case of the Nucleus in Exile.

24. Leon Trotsky, *The History of the Russian Revolution,* vol. 3, (New York: Simon and Schuster, 1936), ch. 6, pp. 167–199.

25. See chapter 5. Where we need bases, mostly for tracking, pay for them. The price of an alliance is in practically all cases too high.

26. U.S., Congress, Senate, *Foreign and Military Intelligence,* bk. 1, 94th Cong., 2d sess., 1976, pp. 131, 141.

27. Ibid., p. 141.

28. Beilenson, *Power through Subversion,* p. 242.

11 A Grand Moral Strategy

Jack D. Douglas

The moral is to the physical as three to one.   —Napoleon Bonaparte

The soundest strategy in war is to postpone operations until the moral disintegration of the enemy renders the delivery of the mortal blow both possible and easy.   —V.I. Lenin

Force can always crush force, given sufficient superiority in strenth or skill. It cannot crush ideas. Being intangible they are invulnerable, save to psychological penetration, and their resilience has baffled innumerable believers in force.   —B.H. Liddell Hart

In classical military strategy, "moral factors" comprise all non-material factors. Material (physical force) strategy is aimed at the bodies and territories of foes. *Moral* (psychological) strategy is aimed at the inner, subjective persons. (*Grand strategy* includes both grand force strategy and grand moral strategy.) The moral component includes morality, but it also includes emotions and thinking. It includes such factors as feelings and ideas of good and evil, the will to fight, self-confidence, political values, myths, uncertainty, anxiety, hope, morale, panic, despair, deception, and lies.

As Michael Burns has pointed out (see chapter 7), most of the great military strategists have recognized that moral factors are by far the most important in successfully waging peace, and in resisting and defeating a foe. This fact is most obvious in the extreme instances in which an entire nation is remoralized—that is, converted—so that it joins its former foes, as happens frequently in our time of fluid international relations. But this ancient truth is also seen in the obvious but rarely remembered fact that almost all of the great empires throughout history have been built by nations that were dwarfed in population and territory by the many peoples they conquered and ruled, but that towered over their subjects in some combination of will-power, persistence, intelligence, creativity in building and using new weapons, and political acumen. Those who assert that power flows from the barrel of a gun forget that a gun or a hydrogen bomb in the hand of a pacifist is useless—or

317

even a dangerous provocation to aggressors aware of the value of surprise, preemptive strikes. Those who assert that superior weapons are the ultimate determinant of victory in modern war forget that those superior instruments of force and their more effective use come only from greater clarity in perceiving the real threats, intelligence, creativity, consensus of moral purpose, conviction that victory is possible, and the will to resist or conquer.

Europe today trembles before the massed might of the Soviet empire, certainly not because the impoverished and smaller population of the Soviet Union is inherently more powerful, but because the ruling class of this empire retains a more powerful will to conquer and rule. As Alexander Solzhenitsyn and other tortured Soviet escapees have warned prophetically, the greater population, wealth, and technological creativity of the Western world will surely fall victim to the Soviet empire if we do not rediscover and assert our once vast moral strength. It is not the physical strength of the Soviet dwarf that threatens our civilization and all our basic freedoms, but our own moral crisis.

The superiority of the moral is easily forgotten in our age of science and technology. It is especially tempting to Americans to believe in technological panaceas of force, both because we are the world's center of science and technology and because, like most free societies, we are dedicated to values and pursuits destroyed by war. We are tempted by myths of technological panaceas for everything from recessions, which the "scientific" wizardry of John Maynard Keynes was supposed to end forever but greatly exacerbated, to guerrilla tactics. It was this fatal temptation to believe in the myths of technological panaceas that led our "best and brightest" to forget the moral factor and stake our fate in Vietnam on phony "body counts" and ludicrous computer simulations, rather than on hard-headed estimates of the situational moral strength of the foe and of ourselves, and on "free fire zones," village pacification programs, and corrupt officials that gravely undermined American legitimacy among the Vietnamese people. When the United States had vast superiority in nuclear weapons, it was most tempting to believe they were the technological fix. As this superiority waned, and American nuclear forces were seen as an "uncertain trumpet," as Maxwell Taylor put it, it became clear that in the nuclear age the moral factor was going to be increasingly important both in waging peace to prevent Armageddon and in winning the Cold War. Liddell Hart summarized this growing ascendency of the moral factor most prophetically as early as 1954:

> The common assumption that atomic power has cancelled out moral strategy is ill-founded and misleading. By carrying destructiveness to

a "suicidal" extreme, atomic power is stimulating and accelerating a reversion to the indirect methods that are the essence of strategy— since they endow warfare with intelligent properties that raise it above the brute application of force.

The trust which the statesmen place in such a weapon as a deterrent to aggression would seem to rest on illusion. The threat to use it might likely be taken less seriously in the Kremlin than in countries on the near side of the Iron Curtain whose people are perilously close to Russia and *her* strategic bombing forces. The atomic threat, if exploited for their protection, may only suffice to weaken their resolution in resistance. Its 'back-blast' has already been very damaging.[1]

In the nuclear age, general wars, if not local and guerrilla wars, must be dreaded last resorts growing out of a failure of moral strategy.

Grand Moral Strategy is the *flexible* (changeable and partially situated) general plan (1) to deal with *both* friends and foes to achieve one's general (real) interests and values peacefully; (2) to complement force strategy in winning war *if* waging peace fails; and (3) to win the peace after the war is over. Grand Moral Strategy today involves an entire world (and even space) of vastly different societies. Executing an effective Grand Moral Strategy is immensely more difficult than constructing and executing a Grand Force Strategy, all the more so because they are highly interdependent. In the end we must never forget Henry Kissinger's evocation of the inherent and frightening uncertainty facing any geopolitical strategist: "No President-elect or his advisers can possibly know upon what shore they may finally be washed by that storm of deadlines, ambiguous information, complex choices, and manifold pressures which descends upon all leaders of great nations."[2] Rigid pursuit of oversimplified "foreign policy doctrines" is usually disastrous when executed. Given our rapidly changing and inherently uncertain world, a Grand Moral Strategy must always be seen and used as a highly *heuristic plan:* it must be constantly reviewed, updated, flexible, open to the situation, and obviously overridden by situational exigencies.

The Failure of Foreign Aid

The Marshall Plan was one of the most successful grand moral strategies ever waged for peace. In its heady afterglow in the 1950s and 1960s, the best Grand Moral Strategy for the United States seemed obvious: the Marshall Plan worked "wonders," so a similar plan would work around the world. "Foreign aid" became the heart of America's Grand Moral Strategy and this consisted overwhelmingly of giving money to governments and their supporters in poor nations. It seemed so simple, but, with few exceptions, it did not work. Some of the biggest recipients, such as India, have become more pro-Russian in their foreign policies and have gained much more economically from new strains of rice than from foreign aid. In general foreign aid fails overwhelmingly—and indeed often does the exact opposite from that intended—because it is politicized and bureaucratized at both ends.[3] If America's domestic welfare politics and bureaucracies breed widespread dependency at monstrous cost, as they obviously do, how could we possibly hope to end poverty around the world by having the same kind of politicians and bureaucrats interact across cultural and linguistic barriers with even more ineffective bureaucrats and politicians—most of them oppressing the people they were supposed to make efficient? It was like the U.S. Department of Health, Education and Welfare (HEW) not squared, but taken to the fourth power. This is why, as Melvyn Krauss has shown in detail, nations like Taiwan and South Korea developed economically in *inverse* proportion to the degree of foreign "aid" the United States gave them.[4]

Why did we believe in these technological and collectivist panaceas? The statist "expert" economists of development told us foreign aid would work. It mainly subsidized collectivism and political oppression, which in turn subsidized economic inefficiency—and thus, poverty. It also bred envy and resentment (for reasons to be given). In Europe and Japan we were simply lending capital to already highly efficient, successful, modern businessmen who became even more efficient and successful after the war, given their greater freedom. Their governments were barred from oppressing the people by our military occupation and were forbidden to use any money on military forces. (Germany was admitted to NATO only in 1955 after extensive debate.) Their situation bore not the slightest resemblance to Uganda—or even India where we subsequently poured our "aid." Just as the best way to further ruin a profligate is to subsidize his profligacy, so the best way to stop economic freedom and the increased productivity and wealth it allows is to subsidize governments that oppress freedom.

During this period of Cold War "massive retaliation terror" for declared foes and foreign aid for potential friends, our only other major thrust of Grand Moral Strategy was the United Nations. The United Nations was never intended, at least not overtly, to be a world government. It was to be a forum for deliberation and negotiation. It immediately became a highly visible, concentrated arena of moral warfare. As such, it too was enmeshed in American foreign aid strategy and, as such, failed. But, aside from the shifting moral tactics of each crisis debated in this "grand morality play," we really have had only one other Grand Moral Strategem—universal friendliness and tactfulness. Trying to be a friend to everyone—being likeable to all—is a fatal moral flaw guaranteed to prevent or destroy any true friendship.

Friendliness and good manners with actual and potential friends in international relations is certainly valuable; and the greater friendliness and decency of Americans gives us a real moral advantage over the "ugly Russians"—the small-minded, dull, totalitarian, and prejudiced apparatchiki (never to be confused with the great mass of Soviet citizens) trusted enough by their fellow party apparatchiki to go abroad and to entertain visitors at home. But friendliness to all in the arena of moral warfare downgrades true friendship (as Helmut Schmidt was reminded after his infamous claim to be the "middleman" between the Soviet Union and the United States) and is an incentive for others to take one's friendliness, for what little it's worth, for granted. It also precludes effective moral counterstrategy. There has been so much forbearance and outright defensiveness by Americans that even slightly stern "stares" by former President Richard Nixon (in Moscow) and words by ambassadors Patrick Moynihan and Jeanne Kirkpatrick on the great moral stage of the United Nations have elicited shock (and applause from true friends). Thomas Schelling long ago argued that a presentation of self as irrational, such as Hitler's "carpet-chewing" outburst for Neville Chamberlain and Nikita Khrushchev's "shoe-pounding" outburst for President John Kennedy, can create a great moral advantage by giving the appearance of far greater emotional commitment (fury) and resolution, hence a greater willingness to take risks.[5] The bigger bully may not be loved, but he will be unopposed by most and toadied to by those of a sycophantish bent. Since many lesser politicians who become powerful move up in the world by practicing precisely that bent, it is not surprising to find that Mr. Nice-Guy-to-All often is abandoned in the crunch with the shoe-pounding bully.

The friendliness campaign reached a pitch of hysteria with the photogenic, smiling Kennedyites and the too trusting Jimmy Carter. Most international analysts suspect President Kennedy's seeming lack of confident counterassertion following the shoe-pounding incident led to a miscalculation of his moral strength that led to the dangerous Cuban missile crisis. John Kennedy then responded with a sense of outrage, as if the Kremlin despots had betrayed him, when in fact he had deceived himself into believing all of Khrushchev's avowals that he would "bury" us and all of his actions had no meaning. It is almost unbelievable that little more than fifteen years later Jimmy Carter was to repeat this same campaign of friendliness and trusting, only to have his eyes "opened" by the too shocking reality of Soviet actions in Afghanistan. The friendliness-and-trusting campaigns signaled a tempting weakness of will to the Soviets. Soviet will, intentions, words, and expansionist actions hardly swerved from their historical trend during this entire period. But Americans and other Westerners were fatally tempted repeatedly to deceive themselves into believing the despots had changed drastically. So immense was this bent to self-deception that even Richard Nixon`and Henry Kissinger, the team of "red baiter" and "real politician," set the most fatal self-trap of all—unilateral détente, which inspired unilateral disarmament masquerading as arms limitation.

The Failure of Détente and Treaties in General

The failure of conventional containment in Vietnam and the likelihood Congress would continue to defeat military appropriations sufficient to match the Soviet pace of armament, combined with the growing recognition of the failure of the earlier Grand Moral Strategy, convinced Nixon and Kissinger of the need for a new "geopolitical strategy" in which the moral component of treaties would become far more important as the component of massive-retaliation terror would wane. There were two major thrusts of this new Grand Moral Strategy.[6] One thrust, the rapprochement (entente pseudocordiale) with China, was intended to be close enough significantly to raise the Soviet perception of risk of a two-front war if they should attack the West, but not so close as to make us hostage to Chinese policy (unable to act independently) or to threaten Soviet policymakers so much as to tempt them to make a preemptive strike. This, of course, was a classic balance-of-power ploy. It continues today to help tie down one-fourth or more of the Soviet forces on the Chinese border and should remain a key thrust in any Grand Moral Strategy. (But it must not be pursued in a manner implying that the United States condones the communist tyranny of the Chinese government, for that would taint America's entire moral strategy.)

The second and more important thrust of the Nixon-Kissinger Grand Moral Strategy was progressive détente through treaties with the Soviet Union, especially treaties on strategic arms limitation. Kissinger argues in *White House Years* that they always knew this strategy was risky, both because of the tendency of adversaries not to live up to such treaties and because an open and democratic society would be very tempted by such treaties to relax its physical and moral efforts in the prolonged struggle. Few careful observers in recent years would doubt that this is precisely what happened. We did, indeed, fall into the "treaty trap" (see chapter 5).[7] The most powerful jaws of this trap have proven to be our own misconceptions of Soviet feelings, beliefs, and strategies, which formed vital planks in the foundation of our détente strategy.

The most important assumption of U.S. détente strategy was that the Soviet Union could be progressively weaned from its policies of massive armament and aggression around the world by a combination of steady containment with sufficient defensive armament coupled with reciprocal restraints on the most destructive weapons through treaties and foreign aid to the Soviet empire in the form of Western loans and technology imports. The generally *implicit* assumption underlying these overt assumptions was that Soviet leaders are economic rationalists who will act to optimize their own safety and prosperity the way any economic rationalist will: if we offer them carrots (in the form of foreign aid, more physical safety, and kind words) for less aggressive policies and *implied* sticks for more aggressive policies, then surely they will move toward the carrots by being less aggressive. They did take all the carrots the United States offered, and will no doubt continue to do so as long as American misconceptions persist, but the carrots, especially the nearly $80 billion in Western loans to Warsaw Pact nations, were used to subsidize aggressive totalitarian policies at home and around the world. Why? Partly because Soviet leaders are indeed economically rational enough to take something for nothing. We gave them carrots; they were aggressive; we *implied* sticks but gave more carrots; and so on right up to the Reagan administration's decision to pay some of the interest on loans to the military dictatorship in Poland rather than force them to suffer for their repression of Solidarity.

But, suppose we actually rewarded détente behavior and punished aggressive behavior. Would this make détente work? Yes and no. A strictly observed policy of reciprocally altruistic behavior across-the-board and over the long run works when we are dealing with rational people. That is, a policy of rewarding nonaggression and punishing aggression toward us *of all kinds* (physical and moral) over the long run will produce less aggressive behavior toward us—progressive détente from a mutually aggressive stance and, possibly some day, even entente. But the policy of détente through treaties with the Soviet Union and other treaties and "entangling alliances," which the United States has now pursued for thirty years, will not work (see chapter 5).

Real American Interests

A Grand Moral Strategy can succeed only to the degree it is based on a general understanding of our real interests and those of our adversaries and allies. Our real interests are radically different from those of our adversaries. The Soviet Union is a classic empire dominated by an imperial state bureaucracy. It is also one of the most cruelly totalitarian empires in history, one of the few states in the same league as that of the Assyrians, Shih Huang-Ti, and Ivan the Terrible.

All empires quickly stifle economic and technological freedom, thereby eroding their economies in direct proportion to their degree of centralized power. They survive only by threatening and subjugating other people and extracting tribute from them. Thus the more centralized and totalitarian an empire is, the more it must expand to extract tribute. Moreover, the bureaucracy—in the case of the Soviet Union, the Communist party and the military—attracts precisely those people with the greatest lust for power.[8] This lust combines with the necessity of tribute to produce powerful expansionist drives.

Because this is both their own policy and the general tendency of empires, Soviet rulers seem convinced this is what the United States is trying to do. Indeed, given the lure of power of our own government, some American politicians have acted in precisely that way. (Lyndon Johnson and Richard Nixon were obviously power hungry.) But the majority of Americans recognize, though generally in a nonverbal way, that real American interests are *not* served by an imperial expansion of the U.S. government. Whenever a Western democracy suddenly gets involved in a war, its stock market plummets because investors know war impoverishes us. The believer in free enterprise knows that free trade among free and independent peoples, operating on the principle of comparative advantage, will produce far more wealth for all involved than any form of imperial tribute could. Imperial tribute may make the victor rich for a while, but in the long run the domestic imperial controls and the cost of the military erode the economy.

Real U.S. interests are best served by the expansion of freedom around the world with as little direct involvement (and thus as little cost) on our part as possible (see chapter 2). How much direct involvement is necessary must vary with the situation, but it clearly stops short of military treaties, and it stops short of using force to protect the property interests of American business in other nations (see chapters 1 and 5). Any government that seizes productive businesses will learn soon enough that this is suicidal; and businesses can and do protect themselves against these dangers by avoiding such governments and buying political hazard insurance. These are vitally important truths which most Americans vaguely take for granted, but they are rarely articulated. They should be made crystal clear in word and deed for the entire world. Perhaps some day even Soviet leaders will understand that American vital interests really differ from what the Soviets now perceive them to be.

Building and Presenting Moral Strength

Will and confidence born of experience are the twin pillars of *moral strength*—of "morale." Military strategists have always recognized these two as the vital components of the moral factor in battles and thus the most important determinants of the outcomes of battles. The will to fight is the crucial motive in the "moral strength"—"morale"—of troops (see chapter 7). Steady self-confidence born of successful experience in training and battle is the other crucial component of the moral strength of troops. It both inspires the will to fight and "unnerves" the enemy. As military historian James Dunnigan has said of British and Argentine troops in the Falklands:

> Good infantry is worth three or more times as much as inferior infantry. Courage and fanaticism are not enough. British troops attacked larger Argentine forces and won because they had the initiative, planned carefully, trained hard and were well led. Superior morale and reputation, moreover, can be decisive weapons. The British have a long reputation for winning. The Argentines have not fought a war in this century. All things being equal, the side with the superior reputation will inevitably win.[9]

This does not mean that appearances ("self-presentations") are generally the most important determinants of the outcomes of waging peace and war, as some sociologists argue about society in general. Over the long run the realities behind the appearances will *almost* always prevail. (After all, Napoleon's appearance may not initially have inspired gasps of awe, but his lightning marches and hinge-crushing cannonades did.) But in the short run appearances of moral strength can be highly significant. In nuclear wars, which might have trouble (in worst-case scenarios) lasting an hour, these appearances could be fatal. And even in the long run of conventional conflicts, they remain important.

Democracies in general suffer badly in this *war of morale appearances*. As Albert Speer makes clear, a crucial reason Hitler took the risk of invading Poland was his complete mistake in estimating the will of the British and French to fight.[10] Not long after, the Japanese warlords calculated that Japanese will-power was so much greater than the American version that they could overcome our great long-run advantages of military force.

Totalitarians do not generally understand free peoples any more than the latter understand the totalitarian mind. Totalitarians are commonly more ambivalent, indecisive, unconfident, and lacking in will-power than they appear. (In fact, their lust for power and their bluster commonly spring from profound personality insecurities that are counteracted by power, arrogance, and bluster. Napoleonic arrogance as a counteraction against the dreaded insecurities of the "little man complex" is legendary, but Napoleon was almost a rock of personal security compared to the picture of Hitlerian self-justification and bluster painted of the "little corporal" even by his former friend, Albert Speer.[11] Yet Hitler too seems less extreme in his personal insecurity than the murderous paranoid who named himself "Stalin"—meaning *steel* in Russian—probably to dispel by defiance his early dread of his drunken father's brutal beatings. These insecurities easily make totalitarians paranoid, trigger-happy, and suicidal when backed into a corner.) Their oppressed peoples are especially apt to appear homogeneously submissive and ready to do as commanded—until they escape or revolt. And free peoples are commonly more in agreement on basics, more secure, decisive, and confident than their eternal peacetime bickering makes them appear to contemptuous totalitarians, who prefer only submissive homogeneity.

It will, of course, do us no good to argue that Americans and other Western peoples should try to look more harmonious and tough to the Soviets. That would be to oppress freedom and is unlikely to happen unless the Soviets precipitate a military crisis, at which time they will learn of the vast synergistic moral strength in our diverse free peoples. Our freedom dooms us to appear more and more disintegrated, frightened, and weak-willed as Soviet power and threats increase—right up to the point at which they make the fatal mistake of believing we are ready for the *coup de grace* of totalitarian order. This is what happened in the 1930s. As the Nazi menace grew, our peace movements ("America Firsters," Oxford Peace Movement, etc.) mushroomed.

This is exactly what happened in our streets and on our television screens in the summer of 1982. As the full extent of the Soviet menace grows and as their armies and proxy armies strike around the world, the more ignorant, frightened, wishful, and ambivalent among us are frantically performing peace dances for the television cameras, as if ritualized expressions of wishes for peace will sway the war gods in the Kremlin. If they are swayed, they will be swayed to estimate American moral strength as tattered and quickly fading, thus making a fatal miscalculation and war far more likely. The likelihood of this fatal miscalculation has been heightened by the appearance of moral weakness we have been giving by our "promiscuously friendly stance" and, above all, by paying tribute rather than building our strength. As Liddell Hart said prophetically so many years ago:

It is folly to imagine that the aggressive types, whether individuals or nations, can be bought off—or, in modern language, "appeased"— since the payment of danegeld stimulates a demand for more danegeld. But they can be curbed. Their very belief in force makes them more susceptible to the deterrent effect of a formidable opposing force. This forms an adequate check except against pure fanaticism that is unmixed with acquisitiveness.[12]

But there are at least four major things that can be done to try to prevent these fatal miscalculations. The first two are easy; the last two are more important. First, in their major addresses our leaders can remind our people and the Soviet rulers of those facts of life, especially of those earlier miscalculations. The Soviets know Hitler toted up a fatal miscalculation when he underestimated their own will to resist. The Soviets, as well as ourselves, need constant reminders that television ratings for peace dances are not the important realities. Second, our leaders must avoid the appearance of feeling guilty, indecisive, and weak-kneed. They should always make it clear that we will pursue a policy of military nonintervention (see below) except when our security is clearly threatened, in which case we are ready to strike. Certainly it is important not to look like a "warmonger," but recent leaders have had a tendency to overdo understatement.

Third, we should immediately begin systematically to develop civil defense. A really effective system of civil defense is vital to our national defense efforts in the nuclear age (see chapter 4). The more frightened people are by the specter of nuclear Armageddon and by the uncertainty of what they *might* suffer, the more they will turn to peace dances.

Finally, we must avoid all direct military involvement in foreign conflicts that do not clearly threaten our security. Vietnam should by now have reminded every would-be American leader that the American people are ambivalent about any involvement in foreign lands. It feels good to have prestige and easy victories, but we know deep down that any foreign conflicts that are not real threats to our survival as a free people are not worth the costs. Fortunately some of us are magnificent warriors; but equally fortunately, most of us are magnificent peacemongers except when threatened. At home we see ourselves as friendly people. But when attacked we want to strike fiercely—then become magnanimous. We loathe military bureaucracy and subordination, as anyone can see from the vastly popular *Catch-22* or "M*A*S*H," but the same soldiers who trip out on "R and R" are fierce fighters with the "Kill-A-Tank" spirit. No soldiers have ever been more dedicated, courageous, and willing to sacrifice than ours *in all of those causes which were theirs*. Because of their training, the high calibre of their

officers, and their generally intense morale, they even fought extremely
well in Vietnam. But as the realities of that war—above all its irrele-
vance to our security or survival—sank in, more and more Americans
fought not to go or to get out. Vietnam was a disastrous mistake of
Grand Moral Strategy. The use of American forces to protect OPEC
sheiks in the Persian Gulf would be an even more cataclysmic mistake
and probably would have more cataclysmic consequences.[13] Even threats
to intervene in places like Angola or Central America undermine support for our leaders, encourage miscalculations by totalitarian foes when
Americans resist, and discourage local resistance. Nonintervention except where we are clearly, gravely threatened, coupled with a fierce
will and confidence to fight when we are, is by far our most potentially
successful Grand Moral Strategy.

Managing Envy and Ambivalence

Benevolent nonintervention coupled with cooperative encouragement
by the example of action is clearly the best Grand Moral Strategy the
American government can use in pursuit of all our real interests around
the world. By a Grand Moral Strategy of nonintervention I mean both
military nonintervention and economic nonintervention. By cooperative encouragement I mean *sincere* programs of action to our mutual
(reciprocal) benefit, not exhortations and "aid" that imply subordination and produce dependency.

The power of envy to distort the judgments and channel the actions
of even the best-disposed and most rational human beings is obvious
to children, but too often forgotten or repressed by rationalistic analysis
of international affairs. In *The Federalist* (no. 5) John Jay warned that
any nation that rises much above others will elicit both envy and fear
and that these passions will lead inferior nations to "countenance, if
not to promote, whatever might promise to diminish her importance."
He warned also that these "invidious jealousies and uncandid impu-
tations, by instilling distrust in the inferior, would in turn instill distrust
in the dominant, because distrust naturally creates distrust." Though
Americans today are the most tolerant and pacific great power ever to
have existed, there is a grave danger that we will be embittered by the
many outrageous and arrogant charges prosecuted against us by those
whom we have helped most of all, including our European allies, for
whom we have put our very existence at grave risk. Such embitterment
and the malice and spite it would trigger could lead Americans to
become imperialists in fact. We must guard against this by recognizing
the power of envy.

The United States is still perceived around the world as the richest and most powerful nation of all time. Great success always arouses both a desire to be like the success, on the part of those who identify with the success, and envy, which produces resentment, on the part of those who do not identify with the success. Often it inspires both in the same individual and then the ambivalent individual can easily swing from one extreme to the opposite with even slight changes in situations or interpretations of them. American wealth and power commonly arouse both, probably making most people around the world ambivalent toward us. Even normally pro-American people easily become defensive and hostile when they believe the United States is "slighting" (shaming) or, worse, threatening them or someone with whom they identify. And it often takes very little to trigger that shift from friendliness to outrage.

This ambivalence is most obvious in our near neighbors, Canadians and Latin Americans. The anti-American rhetoric and policy of so many Canadians, including the government of Pierre Trudeau, seems on the surface bizarre, since it is justified by such obvious distortions, including the self-deception that Anglo-Canadians are notably different from Anglo-Americans. (Why? Because they pronounce their short "a's" differently?) But it makes sense when we recognize the real reason— envy of their far more powerful, if not much richer, "brothers." The "anti-gringo" feeling of our Latin neighbors, especially strong in next-door Mexicans, is much easier to understand because it stems from a greater envy, produced by less identification with us and far greater gaps of both wealth and power, and is inflamed by still strong resentment of earlier American imperialism—and suspicions that we might be imperialist again.

Because Americans have been at the very center of world progress, power, and wealth for so long, we seldom experience envy for any other nation. Certainly we sometimes feel hatred toward some who threaten us, such as the Soviet Union or even the Ayatollah Khomeini's Iran, but it would be totally absurd for us to envy Soviets, Iranians, or any other people. This lack of envy makes it easy for us to be friendly and helpful to those who wish to cooperate with us; and this attitude is a great plus in exercising any moral strategy face to face. But our lack of envy also has the disadvantage of encouraging our blindness to the envy of others and the results of that envy.

Americans are often enraged by the seeming incomprehensibility— the absurdity!—and the injustice of the way so many people judge us, contrasted with their reactions to others, including Soviets. For example, Jean François Revel recently pointed out that the Western press, especially the European and Latin American press, had already condemned the United States over its opposition to the rebels in El Salvador and the Sandinista government in Nicaragua—almost from the very beginning—with almost no objective weighing of the evidence. Why? Many Americans thought it was due to the leftist bias of the press. Certainly such a bias exists, but a crucial reason for this bias is envy. To fail to understand that is to fail to understand our international situation and deal realistically with it.

Rebels, especially poor peasant rebels, are extreme underdogs. Almost everyone champions the underdog because almost everyone can identify with him. The underdog effect is the other side of the "topdog" effect: the normal tendency is to identify with and sympathize with the underdog, while envying and resenting the topdog. Since most people around the world cannot really decide objectively what is occurring in faraway Central America, their feelings about underdogs and topdogs dominate their judgments of what is happening. When they see the Soviets saying "Hurrah for the underdogs!" and, possibly, doing nothing militarily, while *the* superdog is overtly shipping arms and *threatening* these poor people every day on the world's airwaves and in its headlines, the underdog-topdog effects go into full force and the United States winds up looking like the villain.

Until the last few years the Soviets have been very much underdogs compared to Americans. They remain poor and backward by American standards. Very important, they are so backward that even their small amount of economic trade does not compete with other nations, whereas American competition, especially in vital technological segments, is fierce and overwhelming. When the Soviet Union trades with Europe, it mainly sends basic commodities Europeans do not have, so the Soviets are not threatening European jobs but, rather, creating jobs. When Americans trade with Europe we send cars, computers, airplanes, and other high-technology items that threaten European jobs in these segments. Americans today deeply resent the fierce competition of the Japanese. So do the Europeans, but they also feel even more threatened by the "American challenge" in high technology.[14] This strongly reinforces the envy and resentment of the topdog.

The Soviet Union poses as the great champion of the underdog everywhere in extremely histrionic ways. This pose has appealed strongly to the ignorant and "idealistic" identifiers with the underdog everywhere. As soon as they started using their very real military power to oppress real underdogs in Hungary and Czechoslovakia, more and more people began to see their pose for what it is—a lie used to enslave people everywhere they are gullible enough to believe it. In Eastern Europe, including the oppressed nations within the Soviet Union itself, the truth has been obvious almost from the beginning. Most Eastern Europeans would love American power *if only* we would use it against the Soviet Union. They resent only our weakness. Solzhenitsyn pleads on their behalf for the United States to use its force and condemns the United States for not using its power to stop this vile monster. But elsewhere people have learned only through direct contact with the "ugly Russians," as Egyptians did and, I suspect, as Cubans now have. But with the invasion and brutal murder of impoverished Afghan peasants and the proxy oppression of Solidarity, the mask of the poser has been further rent. If the Soviet Union finally invades Poland, or if some hideous and criminal use of biochemical warfare against the Afghan peasants is ever filmed and presented on international television, the mask will be further torn aside and international relations may be transformed.

Even then, but especially before the final exposé, the best Grand Moral Strategy with which the United States can confront these powerful underdog-topdog effects is benign nonintervention coupled with cooperative encouragement through reciprocal action. By *not* intervening except where we are clearly threatened strategically, we avoid all those local instances in which we emerge looking like "imperialistic aggressors." In most cases we can simply announce our view of the situation and lament the suffering to the people, but note that we do not see any direct threat and therefore see no basis for intervening.

At the same time that it avoids triggering the powerful ambivalent swings of the underdog-topdog effects, benign nonintervention also encourages self-help, which makes other friendly people stronger and richer and, thus, helps us in the long run. Consider, first, how it encourages self-help militarily. Just as our present dominant—"leading"—role in NATO encourages our allies to leave it up to us and to lapse into self-indulgent "cheating," so it does everywhere else. As long as the Soviet Union or other strategic threats to us are not involved, nothing that happens in Central America is a military threat to us. We can and should deplore all oppressions of freedom, whether it be by Somocistas or Sandinistas. But their immorality and suicidal behavior is a local problem, not ours. If they do build up their military forces and export arms, they do not threaten us. But they do threaten others— those nearby. In Central America all the nearby nations are threatened to some degree. Mexico is certainly threatened by any exportation of peasant revolution.

Though our officials and journalists seem as taken in by Mexican rhetoric here as much as anywhere else, the fact is that Mexican leaders only *talk* sympathetically about Marxism and similar leftist, utopian ideologies. Mexico is a plutocratic corporate state, an oligarchy in Aristotelian terms, run very much the way Richard Daley ran Chicago. Its officials talk like underdogs in the same guise and for the same reasons Daley did and the Soviets do—to mislead underdogs, the in-experienced young, and intellectuals (including journalists). But the last thing in the world they want is a revolution by poor peasants. It suits Mexican leaders' purposes to have the United States do their "dirty work" of opposing the peasant leftists. In fact the more the United States does it, the more they can pose as supporters of the underdogs, play up to anti-gringo envies and resentments by attacking the United States, and thus gain local support from the poor peasants for their plutocracy. As soon as we do not "play the heavy," the Mexicans, Venezuelans, and other local people will deal with their local problems far more effectively and at no cost to us in money or, more importantly, moral image. It is absurd to think local people cannot or will not do what we think we can do from afar with little contact with the local situation and all the moral disadvantages of the topdog.

Collectivism Fails

It is equally absurd to believe that every new leftist government, or even "leftist tilt," is a victory for the Soviet Union and a defeat for the United States. Even when these takeovers and political shifts lead in the short run to alliances with the Soviet Union they almost always lead in the long run to disaffection from the Soviets, either overtly or covertly, and to mass-mediated demonstrations of the failures of communism and socialism. Our political leaders have failed worst of all in this realm of Grand Moral Strategy because they have not understood or had enough confidence in the powers of freedom. "Popular revolt against a ruthless, experienced modern dictatorship, which enjoys a monopoly over weapons and communications, which has its own armed forces under tight control, and which retains its unity and its will to power, is simply not a possibility in the modern age."[15] Here George Kennan has unknowingly presented us with an avowal of the myth of the inherent superiority in strength of despotism over democracy and, far more ominously, an example of the grave moral crisis that today afflicts so much of the Western world. Where the founders of our democracy avowed an inherent and fatal flaw in all forms of despotism because they violate the passion for freedom of the human spirit, one of our foremost diplomats now avows the inherent stability of modern dictatorship, in spite of all the massive evidence of history to which Laurence Beilenson points (see chapter 10).

The obverse of our own slogan of truth for freedom—"Freedom

Works"—is our slogan of truth for communism, socialism, welfare-statism, fascism, corporate statism, and all other brands of collectivist oppression: "Collectivism Fails!" Not only do nations like Egypt and Cuba learn that playing slaves and cannon fodder to communist apparatchiki is demeaning and dangerous, they also learn that collectivist economics is a sham that ultimately immiserates the masses. Expropriation (theft), massive foreign borrowing, inflation, and eating of seed-corn can produce a carnival spirit for a few years, but in their wake come the long, excruciating years of poverty and despair.

People are getting that message around the world *precisely because many nations tried collectivism and learned the hard way.* The Chinese are trumpeting the message around the world as they go tin cup in hand to the Japanese, Europeans, and Americans. The moans of collectivist agony are rising like a dirge to socialism from the once prosperous nations of Africa who made the lunge for socialist utopia. The Soviet and East European ship-jumpers, plane-jumpers and barbed-wire-fence-burrowers risk their lives every day, and, thereby, expose the lies of the "workers' paradises." The Vietnamese and Cuban boat people have pled frantically to be let in *anywhere* in the free world. Knowing all of this, the Soviets pay from $1 to $3 billion a year to maintain the vastly rich (in potential resources) island of Cuba at the Marxist margin of subsistence and many more hundreds of millions to maintain a massive Soviet-Cuban army of oppression.

Because of the underdog-topdog blindness of our intellectual journalists, and their ignorance and gullibility for totalitarian lies, these facts rarely get into the media; and still the truth has escaped the guns and death camps to fly to all the corners of the world. In spite of all their censorship and statistical lies, Eastern Europe and the Soviet Union are now the best advertisements for economic freedom Madison Avenue could ever dream up. The Jaruzelski regime in Poland could not be cast better by the Central Intelligence Agency. In spite of the often oppressive plutocracies of Latin America, and in spite of the self-defeating firebrands launched like boomerangs by American politicians, Castroism, Allendeism, and other forms of communism are dying in Latin America. Certainly the illiterate peasants and the envy-blinded intellectuals still often see communism as a savior (presumably heavily disguised), but more and more of the literate workers see the realities of communism and see that it does not work: now they know that communism is a form of economic suicide bought at the price of monstrous oppression. When American politicians and officials stay off the international television screens long enough for Latin Americans to see through their anti-Gringo lenses what is really happening, that message gets across to more and more of them.

The Adventages of Free Trade

It is equally important that we encourage self-help through benign nonintervention economically. It is one thing to be generous, but quite another to give "free gifts." The rich and powerful should always be generous and magnanimous. We must not be hagglers. Nothing is more resented than a topdog haggling over every penny, or every trade advantage. We should be as generous in cooperative trade as we are magnanimous in military victory.

But we must not try to be the godlike bearers of manna. Only gods can give manna, and any mortal who plays at being a god dispensing manna will be deeply envied, resented, and hated for that fact (even if loved ambivalently). People may not say it directly, for they may want to continue getting the gifts. (Generally, it is their oppressive rulers who want and get the gifts, which they use to support their oppression.) But an unreciprocated gift necessarily implies the inferiority of the receiver. The rule of reciprocity among equals (not among parents and children, superiors and inferiors) is a universal human rule. Violating it breeds resentment on both sides and contempt from the givers and shame and countercontempt from the receivers. Remarkably enough, it does this at the very time it breeds dependency, thus discouraging self-help while destroying self-confidence and building secret self-contempt. Highly dependent adults eventually become "demoralized," largely unable to do anything much, hating themselves and those they depend on at the same time they moralistically demand ever more from the hated upperdog. This is exactly what we see in "spoiled" children, in "welfare families," and in whole nations spoiled by aid.

Aid-dependency is especially demoralizing for postcolonial people because colonial submission is merely replaced by a new dependency just at the time of independence, when they hoped to end dependency and gain self-respect. The Indians may never forgive all the foreign aid we gave them in their postcolonial era. Our so-called aid rubbed their noses in their hated submission to Westerners. Little wonder they like the Soviets so much more today. (In a brilliantly revealing and honest statement, G.K. Reddy, political columnist for *The Hindu* newspaper, notes the Indian ambivalence: "We have a sneaking admiration for the Americans, but it won't be translated into foreign policy."[16] The admiration is a repressed secret. The Nehru contempt for us is shown for all the world to see.) After all, the Soviets never gave them anything (except words against China, and cheap arms the Soviets hope they will use against Pakistan) and get tit-for-every-tat.

Private free trade *in action* is by far the most effective form of cooperative encouragement. In the immediate postwar era, up to roughly the 1960s, American multinationals were so dominant in some foreign markets that there was not enough competition to "make" a very efficient free market price. This, combined with the ancient dread of monopoly which has been inherited by "Big Business," led to a great deal of envy and resentment in some nations, though generally far more among professional intellectual supporters of the underdogs than the underdogs themselves, since the underdogs *knew* they were getting richer from it. These markets are becoming increasingly competitive and the poorer nations, including communist China, are courting foreign manufacturers and traders. They now often hire American or other Western experts to advise them on making the best deals possible in the world markets. Moreover Big Business is rapidly being outcompeted by more efficient small businesses. In spite of the recent turn to protectionism in some markets, the reciprocal advantages of private free trade are so vast, and American tariff protection now so low, that we are within reach of a truly free worldwide market that will enrich everyone. (In the last thirty-eight years U.S. tariffs have fallen from an average of over 50 percent in the 1930s to about 10 percent, and this has been an era of greatly increased wealth for almost all involved in world trade in a major way.)

We must communicate the basic ideas of the "system of natural liberty," including the reciprocal comparative advantages, to people around the world through speech and print; but example through action in the worldwide marketplace will always be the best teacher. President Ronald Reagan's *announced* Caribbean Basin Initiative is an excellent plan for trade, but so far has been gravely marred by being coupled with dependency-breeding "aid" and by congressional haggling over scores of protectionist demands. We should recognize that areas like the Caribbean have immense development problems, some of which go back to the dependency bred by slavery and the "latifundia" (giant estates run with slaves and, later, paternalism). But benign noninterventionism and the reciprocal encouragement of private free trade *by abolishing all tariffs* will do more than anything else can to help them and us—reciprocally, in a self-reinforcing way.

It is, of course, asserted by leftist critics of trade that we need and support such trade as a way of exploiting the poor in other nations by keeping them in low-skill mining or factory jobs. Nothing could be more contrary to fact. It is the poor of the world who have by far the most to gain from trade, as is obvious from their protests when any mine or factory owned by the multinationals is closed. And during years when world commodity prices are down sharply, the pleas by nations heavily dependent on extractive sectors of their economies make it obvious who benefits most from this trade. It is a misfortune for them that the world's supply of copper, iron, nickel, and many other minerals and substitutes, is growing so rapidly. It is vitally important to them to free up their own markets to allow the development of domestic industries and services. Given their unskilled work forces, they will have to begin with the less technical businesses, but the steady "march up-market" of whole nations like Japan and Taiwan of once poorly skilled workers illustrates clearly that starting with the first steps—the A, B, C's of industrialism—not only does not prevent reaching the end, but is actually a necessity. Moreover multinational firms now commonly accept contracts that involve the progressive movement of local people upward in the organization. In seemingly stable nations with low wage scales, it is now often even worthwhile for multinationals to grant part ownership to locals. There are highly varied adaptations being created that benefit both sides.

Political instability and government intervention are overwhelmingly the greatest obstacles to development from within and from without.[17] They are the overriding uncertainties that make investment so risky. The development of smaller, more mobile and flexible firms with lower capital requirements (which can be lost through war or expropriation) will help to mitigate problems associated with these risks. But nothing else will do as much to promote development as a recognition by people, especially leaders, around the world that political instability and government intervention are the major blocks. Revolution and government intervention are the problem, not the solution.

The Morality of America's Moral Strategy

The "system of natural liberty" which formed the fundamental ideas of the American Constitution was built on one idea above all others: *"Freedom works!"* Freedom works for all human beings by allowing them creatively to adapt all of their own strengths and weaknesses to the evolving situations of their lives, to produce and consume to fit all of their vastly complex abilities and changing desires, to forge an optimum of justice through their inherently problematic moral decisions, and fully to adapt all of their own strivings to the complementary strivings of their citizens through the institutions of the free market, law, and representative democracy. The great system of natural liberty—political freedom, economic freedom, and cultural freedom exercised through the rules of moral consensus and law—works by allowing all individuals to be more creative, productive, just, caring, equal, peaceful, satisfied, and yet aspiring than any other possible arrangements of human life.[18]

The great majority of Americans has always shared this faith in freedom. However inconsistent some of our lesser values and, worse, some of our actions have been with it, our faith in freedom has eventually inspired us to strive to overcome these failures. But there have always been small minorities of us who secretly revile the faith in freedom and far more of us who are deceived into violating the implications of our own faith. The mythical deceits of would-be collectivist rulers of all types have been mightily aided by the self-deceits of many who are lured by utopian hopes of easy wealth and arrogant pride or driven by great anxieties in times of crises. Thus collectivism—government power—in one form or another, by any name and under any pseudoconstitutional guise that appealed to the ignorant and deceived, has often become the fiery faith of the counterrevolution against liberty.

For over a hundred years now all civilized societies have been progressively swept up by this counterrevolution of collectivism. The names, the institutional forms, the sacred symbols, the pseudo-scientific theories, and the degrees of government repression have varied greatly. Socialism, Marxism, communism, fascism, social-democratism, liberal-unionism, welfare-statism, corporate-statism, state-capitalism, Maoism, progressive-laborism, liberalism, state-planned industrialism, Japan-Inc., American-Inc.—on and on roll the sonorous tones of collectivism. But all of them share one basic idea, the core-enabling idea of modernist collectivism: government power to scientifically plan society is necessary to make individuals safe, rich, happy, and free.

"Collectivism Works!" That is the collectivist faith. Since all collectivists strive mightily to wrap themselves in the sacred mantle of the system of natural liberty, none proclaim "Freedom Fails!" Instead they all proclaim, to the strains of their various marching tunes, "Only collectivism is real fredom." In short, if you would be free from power, you must support massive increases in state power. So it was that Lenin lured the Russian peasants and workers into the dictatorship of the party by proclaiming the dictatorship of the proletariat; and welfare-statists lured the American "masses" into collectivism by proclaiming the Square Deal, the New Deal, the Fair Deal, and many other statist programs to "save" free enterprise. State slavery becomes the necessary foundation for political freedom, and government economic rule becomes the necessary foundation for economic freedom. Such are the absurdities of political double-think in our age of modernist collectivism.

The greatest tragedy, the most fatal flaw of collectivism, is that it feeds upon itself. The truth is precisely as the founders of the American system of natural liberty proclaimed: freedom works and, conversely, collectivism fails. Freedom works because it allows the fullest *possible* expressions and satisfaction of human nature and because free markets and free forms of politics produce the optimal degree of information feedback on failures and successes, thus producing optimal adaptation to our ever-changing world and a system of creative efficiency in all spheres. Conversely collectivist decision making (by any name and any form) fails in direct proportion to its degree because it suffocates human nature and produces misinformation (and disinformation) on failures and successes, thus preventing successful adaptation to our ever-changing world and promoting inefficiency. As the drift toward inefficiency reaches higher levels, the rulers always begin to use ad hoc measures of arbitrary rule—dictates, ukasi, etc.—to try to correct for the growing misinformation. These measures drift toward maximum uncertainty—secrecy and arbitrariness—to uncover the truth the people are hiding from them. This is the very nature of terrorism. Collectivism, then, always drifts toward terrorist methods to try to overcome its own flaws.

Every ratchet-up in collectivism intended to solve some problem not yet solved by free men, may do so in the short run but eventually produces greater unintended problems than the problems it ever solves; and these new problems then become the enabling crises legitimizing the next ratchet-up in collectivist powers. Any abridgement of individual liberty intended to produce greater collective welfare (the "common welfare") inevitably winds up producing less. That is the one great message American libertarians and others created and announced to the world. Individual liberty and constitutional democracy, the institutional expression and guarantee of individual liberty, are held sacred by the majority of people throughout the world today. Individual liberty and representative democracy are the founts of all political legitimacy today.

In our free Western societies, in which ideals of liberty and representative democracy were given rebirth, they have now dominated for so long that they are taken for granted by almost everyone, and thus only rarely do we consciously consider what a treasure they are. We too easily take the delights of liberty and democracy for granted and focus our attention on our inevitable failures to live up to these ideals completely. And in this way we blind ourselves both to the threats to our ideals and to our greatest potential source of strength in defeating those threats.

The revolution of liberty and representative democracy was launched by the American sons of liberty in 1776. The success of the great American experiment in liberty inspired hope everywhere and ignited the "Age of the Democratic Revolution" as R.R. Palmer has called it.[19] In the succeeding twenty-five years democratic revolutions erupted across Europe. Some succeeded; more were put down by aristocratic reactions. A few, most notably the explosion against the corrupt, repressive collectivism of the French monarchy, were quickly seduced by even more repressive forms of collectivism. After his defeat Napoleon revealed his own total cynicism about liberty and the French Revolution when he said, "Vanity made the revolution, liberty was merely a pretext." During his reign, however, he used the powerful rhetoric of liberty to inspire democrats throughout Europe to embrace what they only later discovered to be a new tyranny complete with a new and generally more repressive monarchy and aristocracy.

But the seeds of hope for a new and better world of individual liberty had been set loose upon the world. These hopes have since been increasingly enflamed by the unprecedented growth of science, technology, and wealth created by the individual enterprise and creativity unleashed by individual liberty. These values of liberty and democracy and the hopes they inspire have now spread to the entire world and become more powerful than ever. So powerful is the lure of the torch of freedom in the modern world that all of the counterrevolutions against individual freedom are inspired by the promises of greater freedoms.

It is a tragedy of our age that almost all of these revolutions inspired by the hope for liberty and its fruits are now either launched by cynical Bonapartists manipulating symbols of liberty to win totalitarian power or soon fall victims to totalitarians out of self-deception. All of the most formidable totalitarians of our age are completely aware of the power of the sacred symbols of liberty and constitutional democracy. Even today, when so many of our own misguided and deceived people have begun to despair of the values of liberty, the most terrible slave states in memory wrap themselves tightly in the mantle of the names of democratic freedoms and hide their brutal oppressors behind the eternal forms of republican constitutionalism. As Friedrich Hayek noted forty years ago, "wherever liberty as we understand it has been destroyed, this has almost always been done in the name of some new freedom promised to the people."[20]

In the nations where most of the people are ignorant of the ancient meanings of our Western ideas of liberty and representative democracy, the totalitarians merely superimpose these symbols on their brand of collectivism and then use massive censorship and propaganda to try to prevent the people from ever learning the difference. But the more knowledgeable the people are about these ideals, the more deceit the totalitarians must use in their desperate efforts to maintain some shreds of legitimacy to cover their use of police terror to build their power. They do this by using all the forms of Hitler's Big Lie and all the powers of modern mass education and the mass media. Above all, they must fabricate plausible rationalizations to present the foundations of their totalitarian collectivism—government planning, regulation, and control of everything from money to literature and science—as the one and only true "new freedom." As Peter Drucker has said, "the less freedom there is, the more there is talk of the 'new freedom.' Yet this new freedom is a mere word which covers the exact contradiction of all that Europe ever understood by freedom."[21] This "new think" and "new talk" about liberty and democracy have obviously been most necessary in the West itself, especially among our intellectuals, to seduce people into abandoning the foundations of all they have held sacred. But everywhere that educated people have been important these new forms of double-talk have been vital in legitimizing the new and ancient forms of totalitarianism. Most totalitarians today have come to power where the majority of people were largely ignorant of Western civilization, but where the educated people have known the rudiments of our liberty and democracy and have been too important to neglect. Thus the totalitarians have retained the traditional names and outer forms of liberty and democracy for the masses, while directing "new freedoms" rhetoric at intellectuals.

Though Western leaders today rarely even mention liberty or democracy, and almost as rarely call the new forms of totalitarian slavery what they really are, all totalitarians freely brandish these symbols as the shibboleths of their regimes and *never* name themselves what they are. Every dictator is a self-proclaimed "president" or "premier" of the "People's Republic;" every modern Ghenghis Khan flies bright banners of "wars of liberation" and denounces true liberators as "imperialists;" every imperialistic Soviet totalitarian who has murdered other Soviets and socialists proudly declares himself the humble servant of the "Union of Soviet Socialist Republics."

The deceit of tyrants and totalitarians has always had great seductive powers. That is a basic reason why liberty and democracy have been so rare. But seldom have tyrants been as successful as our modern totalitarians in carrying out their counterrevolutions in the very name of liberty and democracy. It is absolutely vital that all free people— and aspirants of freedom—today understand how these totalitarians have deceived people, why they have so often succeeded, what their moral weaknesses are, and how this tide of reactionary rhetoric can be turned back on its propagators.

The first crucial thing that must be done about this drift into the absurdities of totalitarian newspeak is for people everywhere candidly to speak the truth: the Soviet rulers, the Chinese rulers, the Castros, and all totalitarian collectivists are the tyrants of terrorist slave states. This is a precise, technical historical usage of the terms. The slaves of the Soviet Union, Cuba, China, and many other nations have fewer freedoms than the slaves of ancient Rome or the antebellum South. Ancient slaves were often freed within the state and by law. Only desperately dangerous flight can free the slaves of the Soviet Union, China, Cuba, and the other tortured lands of communism. The Romans sometimes crucified slaves who revolted, but Soviet communists have murdered tens of millions, routinely brutalize many thousands in the living-crucifixion of the Gulags, and systematically terrorize the entire nation for merely saying (or potentially saying) things against the regime.

Our leaders must speak the obvious about these terrorist slave states. Even more important, intellectuals, especially journalists, must end their great betrayal and proclaim the truth. Out of blindness and their own envious lust for power, the intellectuals of the Soviet Union, China, Eastern Europe, Cuba, and all the other totalitarian lands led their deceived people into slavery. Some do so knowingly. Far more do so because they refuse to look into the glare of truth streaming from every nation that has followed this Marxist path. Many more "go along" with, or merely remain silent when their colleagues preach the Marxist faith from our campus pulpits, our church pulpits, and our media pulpits. They know the lies, misinformation, and agitprop when they see it, but prefer ease and repose rather than face the wrath of the activists. They are terrorized by the mere thought of being branded "right-wing extremists"—or even "conservative." It is almost unseen by those outside, but there is a continuing Marxist revolution going on in our humanities, social sciences, churches, and news media throughout the Western world. The intellectuals are building the "road to serfdom."

No freedom-loving person can ever invoke official controls or censorship against these lies and this far more ominous silence. We can only assert our own freedom of speech. But that is all we need. Freedom and truth work. They need only to be exercised—strenuously, consistently, courageously.

This truth and freedom of speech against the terrorist slave states is needed even more in entertainment and the daily news media than in our college classrooms and intellectual forums. One gripping movie like "Missing" can insinuate more doubts about American businessmen and political leaders than dozens of intellectual journals or hundreds of lectures can undo by the most meticulous analysis of facts. Our news media are awash with the best intended, most extreme ignorance about simple economic matters. This ignorant economic moralism of the journalists is a powerful wedge which opens the way for the more openly Marxist phalanx.

We do not need—and must sternly oppose—any forms of censorship or agitprop. Nor do we need any form of government interference in behalf of truth and freedom. Our government obviously has enough problems trying to be truthful about itself and conveying that truth. What is needed is a recognition of the threats by our intellectuals and other influential people. Here I believe William Simon's proposals in *A Time for Truth* are the most effective.[22] What we need is *privately* financed organizations for ferreting out and spreading the truth. CIA-type clandestine purveyors of the supposed truth will always be suspected—of political self-seeking even by us. Even openly government-financed institutions are not very effective or needed. American businesses, foundations, and individuals committed to the system of national liberty give billions every year to colleges and groups which gladly, if generally unknowingly, disburse much of that money to collectivist sympathizers. They would do much better for their own cause by financing gripping movies about the heroes who fight against slavery in Siberian Gulags, broadcasts to Cuba from Miami's Cuban exiles, free market newspapers, and magazines that expose the effects of massive government powers. Detailed tactics are not my concern here, but just consider what an impact war films from the peasants of Afghanistan could have in exposing the Soviet pose. Since most American journalists find the task too daunting (and it certainly would not be like living at the Saigon Hilton and sallying forth for a few rice paddy shots before cocktails), why not finance the training of a few dozen bright Afghan correspondents and arm them with super-8 cameras? That is precisely the sort of thing real believers in freedom can do far more effectively than any government. Self-reliance—individual initiative—in truth-seeking and truth-broadcasting is the most effective weapon in all moral strategy.

Our Future

We have much to be pessimistic about today. We are faced with two growing crises that American and other Western voters and their elected leaders unknowingly chose over the last several decades. First, they chose the newly camouflaged but ancient path to imperial state bureaucracies that have, as always before, progressively inflated, regulated, and stagnated our economies and embittered and demoralized our societies with internal conflicts. Our worldwide economy is now threatened by the spectre of another Great Depression because of our fifty-year romance with the short-run delights of inflation and government meddling. If we fall into that deflationary abyss, some Western governments will likely try the equally ancient "solution" of totalitarian command in the modern guise of Marxism. It is imperative that we try to avoid that by rapidly cutting back the deadening hand of government regulation and taxation; and by deflating slowly. It is grim prospect, but we have a good chance of avoiding the abyss if we act now.

At the same time, we are faced with the menace of the vast Soviet buildup that has continued over the last two decades while we were diverting our taxes into creating welfare dependency and massive bureaucracies. We must rearm and build a civil defense system to forestall a preemptive strike, but this strains our economy. That strain can be greatly reduced by curtailing our military commitments, by adopting military noninterventionism as a crucial part of our grand strategy. In the nuclear age the dangers of any direct military confrontation with the Soviet Union are grave indeed, for, as Laurence Beilenson argues in chapter 5, any direct war will probably escalate. For both reasons we stress a strategic force withdrawal to positions of maximum strength and minimum cost and risk, coupled with a material defense and moral offensive that plays to our strengths and against Soviet weaknesses.

The greatest flaw of free individuals in facing a serious threat to their survival is the short-run incentive to destroy the very foundations of freedom from within, thereby destroying their greatest strength and the fundamental purpose for fighting in the first place. As the perceived threat grows, and especially as it gets extreme, a growing proportion of the people come to see the dictates of collectivism—actually the dictates of their own fears—as *the* only effective solution. Soon the basic trust and rules of tolerance and compromise that are vital to free societies are discarded, as those who still cherish freedom are more and more oppressed by the growing number and stridency of collectivists. The social entropy of collectivism grows rapidly and the war becomes one of a new (if lesser) collectivism fighting an old collectivism. At that stage the experienced collectivists normally win and enslave the once free individuals. As Thucydides said of the Athenians, "In the end it was only because they had destroyed themselves by their own internal strife that finally they were forced to surrender." Edward Gibbon laid the blame for this growing internal strife more squarely on the growth of the spirit of the Athenian welfare state (collectivism): "In the end, more than they wanted freedom, they wanted security. They wanted a comfortable life and they lost it all—security, comfort, and freedom. When the Athenians wanted not to give to society, but society to give to them, when the freedom they wished for most was freedom from responsibility, then Athens ceased to be free."

We must deal with our own increasing path toward collectivism and the menace of the vast Soviet military buildup on a higher priority than we do our longer run Grand Moral Strategy for foreign policy. While some moral tactics and strategies can be initiated quickly and at little or no cost, a Grand Moral Strategy is very much a long-run strategy. Rapid military buildups are *not* in general good moral strategy. Rapid buildups are economically wasteful, always run some danger of panicking foes into preemptive strikes (so our strategic forces must be in a high state of alert to discourage that), and cloud our longer run grand moral image. We must rearm (though in ways different from those proposed by the Reagan administration), but this is all the more reason to pronounce our new Grand Moral Strategy and begin enacting it. A Grand Moral Strategy is potentially our most powerful weapon in winning both peace and security. In the long run it is not the material strength of the terroristic Soviet dwarf that most threatens our civilization, all of our basic freedoms, and our very existence, but our own moral weakness. We must recognize how grave the threat is, summon our will, rekindle our faith in freedom, and act with creative intelligence to surmount the Soviet threat. If we play to our own strengths and against their weaknesses, we shall prevail and the spirit of freedom will burn brightly for all mankind.

Notes

1. B.H. Liddell Hart, *Strategy* (New York: Praeger 1954), p. 235.

2. Henry Kissinger, *White House Years* (Boston: Little, Brown, 1979) p. 16.

3. See Melvyn Krauss, *Development without Aid* (New York: McGraw-Hill, 1982); and Peter Bauer, *Dissent on Development* (Cambridge, Mass.: Harvard University Press, 1976).

4. See Krauss's *Development Without Aid;* and "Foreign Aid and the Gang of Four", *The Wall Street Journal,* December 20, 1982.

5. Thomas C. Schelling, *The Strategy of Conflict* (Cambridge, Mass.: Harvard University Press, 1960).

6. See Kissinger, *White House Years.*

7. Laurence W. Beilenson, *The Treaty Trap* (Washington, D.C.: Public Affairs Press, 1969).

8. Friedrich A. Hayek, *The Road to Serfdom* (Chicago: University of Chicago Press, 1972).

9. James F. Dunnigan, "New Weapons, Old Truths," *Forbes,* June 21, 1982. Reprinted with permission from the author.

10. Albert Speer, *Inside the Third Reich* (New York: Avon Books, 1971).

11. Ibid.

12. Hart, *Strategy,* p. 372.

13. See Laurence W. Beilenson and Kevin Lynch, "Should We Spill Blood over Oil?" *Reason,* February 1982, pp. 25–26.

14. Jean-Jacques Servan-Shreiber, *The American Challenge* (New York: Atheneum, 1968).

15. See George F. Kennan, *On Dealing with the Communist World* (New York: Harper, 1969).

16. Quoted by June Kranhop, "Is India's Romance with Russia Losing Its Thrill?" *The Wall Street Journal,* June 14, 1982.

17. Bauer, *Dissent on Development.*

18. I have dealt with all of the major topics of the successes and failures of freedom and collectivism in my forthcoming book, *The Myth of the Welfare State.* The most important sources for this work are the many works by Friedrich Hayek, Ludwig von Mises, and their many successors. See, especially, the recent elaboration and exposition of Hayek's theory of information exchange, economic behavior, and bureaucracy by Thomas Sowell, *Knowledge and Decisions* (New York: Basic Books, 1980).

19. R.R. Palmer, *The Age of the Democratic Revolution* (Princeton, N.J.: Princeton University Press, 1959).

20. Hayek, *The Road to Serfdom,* p. 117.

21. Peter Drucker, *The End of Economic Man* (New York: John Day, 1939), p. 74.

22. William Simon, *A Time for Truth* (New York: Reader's Digest Press, 1978).

Glossary

AAW	Antiaircraft weapon system
ABM	Antiballistic missile
ALCM	Air-launched cruise missile
ASM	Antishipping missile
ASUW	Antisurface vessel warfare
ASW	Antisubmarine warfare
AWACS	Airborne warning and control system
BB	Gun battleship
BVN	Nuclear battleship
C³	Command, control, and communications
CAS	Close air support
CBG	Carrier battle group
CGN	Cruiser
COHORT	Cohesion, operational training and readiness
counterforce	Targeting military forces
countervalue	Targeting the enemy's cities and industries or the enemy regime's civilian control facilities
CSA	Combat support aircraft
CVN	Aircraft carrier
DIA	Defense Intelligence Agency
ELF	Extremely low frequency
EMP	Electromagnetic pulse
EMT	Equivalent megatons $= n\ Y^{2/3}$, where Y is the yield of a weapon and n is the number of such weapons
FFG	Guided missile frigate
first strike	A nuclear attack initiating nuclear war launched against offensive strategic forces of the other side

LHD	Assault landing ship
LSA	Logistic support aircraft
ICBM	Intercontinental ballistic missile
IRBM	Intermediate-range ballistic missile
kilotons	An explosive equivalent to 1,000 tons of TNT
KT (or **Kt**)	See *Kilotons*.
MAD	Mutual Assured Destruction. Technically, as originally formulated by Secretary of Defense Robert McNamara, this is a strategic policy that assumes (1) a strategic balance in which both the United States and Soviet Union can mutually and assuredly destroy each other with their second strike *and* (2) that achieving and maintaining this balance is a mutual policy. Popularly this has come to have various meanings, including the policy of nuclear deterrence (deterring war through the threat to destroy the Soviet Union if they attack the United States), or that of a "balance of terror" in which each side's second strike could destroy the other
megatons	An explosive equivalent to 1 million tons of TNT
MIRV	Multiple interdependently targetable reentry vehicle
MRBM	Medium-range ballistic missile
MT	See *Megatons*.
MX	An ICBM capable of carrying 12 MIRVs each 350 kilotons, with a circular error probability (CEP) of 300–400 feet
NIE	National intelligence estimates
NSA	National Security Agency
NTM	National Technical Means of Verification
OSS	Office of Strategic Services
RPV	Remotely piloted vehicle
SALT	Strategic arms limitation talks
SAM	Surface-to-air missile

second strike   A countervalue or counterforce nuclear attack launched against the other side after having absorbed its first strike

SLBM   Submarine-launched ballistic missile

SSBN   Ballistic missile submarine, nuclear-powered

SSM   Surface-to-surface missile

SSN   Nuclear attack submarine

Tac Air   Tactical air forces

third strike   A countervalue or counterforce attack with reserve nuclear forces by the side launching the first strike and after absorbing the other side's second strike

throw weight   The useful weight that is placed on trajectory toward the target by the boost stages of the missile

Trident   An SSBN that will carry 24 SLBM (the Trident C-4) each with a range of 4,000 nautical miles and carrying 8 × 100 KT MIRVs

V/STOL   Vertical/short take-off and landing (capabilities)

Index

About the Contributors

Laurence W. Beilenson is a graduate of Harvard Law School and a veteran of both world wars. Since his retirement from law, he has studied political and military history, producing three books, *The Treaty Trap, Power through Subversion,* and *Survival and Peace in the Nuclear Age.*

Michael R. Burns is on the staff of the U.S. Global Strategy Council. He received the M.A. in political philosophy from St. Johns University and has done Ph.D. work in political philosophy and Russian studies at Georgetown University. Formerly he was a Heritage Foundation congressional fellow and defense assistant to Representative Newt Gingrich.

Samuel T. Cohen is a member of the technical staff at R&D Associates. A graduate in physics from the University of California at Los Angeles, Cohen took part in the Manhattan Project during World War II and developed the original neutron bomb concept while on the staff of The Rand Corporation. He is the author of numerous books and articles on weapons systems, most recently *The Truth about the Neutron Bomb.*

Jack D. Douglas is professor of sociology at the University of California at San Diego. He received the Ph.D. from Princeton University. He is the author or editor of numerous books and articles, including the forthcoming volume, *The Myth of the Welfare State.*

Michael J. Dunn is a weapons system engineer and analyst for the Boeing Aerospace Company. He holds three degrees in aeronautics and astronautics from the University of Washington, is a member of the U.S. Naval Institute and the American Defense Preparedness Association, and is editor of *American Defense* newsletter.

Roger Nils Folsom is professor of economics at San Jose State University. He received the Ph.D. in economics from Claremont Graduate School. Before moving to San Jose, he spent seven years teaching economics and systems analysis at the Naval Postgraduate School in Monterey, California. His articles on economic theory and public finance have appeared in a variety of professional journals.

Joseph Brandon Ford is professor of sociology at California State University at Northridge and first vice-president of the Institute International de Sociologie. He has been visiting professor at the Universities of Madrid, Rome, and Vienna, National University of Mexico, American University of Beirut, and the University of Gratz. He served ten years in U.S. Naval Intelligence during and after World War II.

Eric Mack is associate professor of philosophy at Tulane University. He received the Ph.D. from the University of Rochester. His writings have appeared in journals including *Ethics, Philosophy and Public Affairs,* and *Philosophical Studies.*

R.J. Rummel is professor of political science at the University of Hawaii. He received the Ph.D. from Northwestern University. He was the director and principal investigator of the 1963–1975 Dimensionality of Nations project, which led to his five-volume work *Understanding Conflict and War.*

About the Editor

Robert W. Poole, Jr., is president of the Reason Foundation and editor-in-chief of *Reason* magazine. He holds two engineering degrees from the Massachusetts Institute of Technology, and has worked for both an aerospace firm and a defense-oriented think tank. The author of numerous articles and syndicated radio and newspaper commentaries, he is also the author of *Cutting Back City Hall* and the editor of *Instead of Regulation* (Lexington Books, 1982).